FROMMER'S
EasyGuide
TO
SAN FRANCISCO

By
Diane Susan Petty

EasyGuides are ✦ Quick To Read ✦ Light To Carry
✦ For Expert Advice ✦ In All Price Ranges

FrommerMedia LLC

ISBN 978-1-62887-008-4 (paper), 978-1-62887-038-1 (e-book)

Editorial Director: Pauline Frommer
Editor: Pauline Frommer
Production Editor: Jana M. Stefanciosa
Additional Reporting by: Jason Cochran
Cartographer: Tim Lohnes
Cover Design: Howard Grossman

For information on our other products or services, see www.frommers.com.

FrommerMedia LLC also publishes its books in a variety of electronic formats. Some content that appears in print may not be available in electronic formats.

Manufactured in the United States of America

5 4 3 2 1

CONTENTS

ABOUT THE AUTHOR

Diane Susan Petty was born in Toronto, Canada where she made the grave mistake of getting a useless law degree, instead of going to journalism school. She moved to the Bay Area in 1995, and, after wreaking havoc on the U.S. economy for years as a mortgage banker, decided she wanted a more meaningful life. Naturally, she became a travel writer. She has written a number of stories for the *San Francisco Chronicle* and other outlets since then, and works part time for United Airlines. She spends as much time as possible traveling the world on a very modest budget with her wonderful husband and two children.

ABOUT THE FROMMER TRAVEL GUIDES

For most of the past 50 years, Frommer's has been the leading series of travel guides in North America, accounting for as many as 24% of all guidebooks sold. I think I know why.

Though we hope our books are entertaining, we nevertheless deal with travel in a serious fashion. Our guidebooks have never looked on such journeys as a mere recreation, but as a far more important human function, a time of learning and introspection, an essential part of a civilized life. We stress the culture, lifestyle, history and beliefs of the destinations we cover, and urge our readers to seek out people and new ideas as the chief rewards of travel.

We have never shied from controversy. We have, from the beginning, encouraged our authors to be intensely judgmental, critical—both pro and con—in their comments, and wholly independent. Our only clients are our readers, and we have triggered the ire of countless prominent sorts, from a tourist newspaper we called "practically worthless" (it unsuccessfully sued us) to the many rip-offs we've condemned.

And because we believe that travel should be available to everyone regardless of their incomes, we have always been cost-conscious at every level of expenditure. Though we have broadened our recommendations beyond the budget category, we insist that every lodging we include be sensibly priced. We use every form of media to assist our readers, and are particularly proud of our feisty daily website, the award-winning Frommers.com.

I have high hopes for the future of Frommer's. May these guidebooks, in all the years ahead, continue to reflect the joy of travel and the freedom that travel represents. May they always pursue a cost-conscious path, so that people of all incomes can enjoy the rewards of travel. And may they create, for both the traveler and the persons among whom we travel, a community of friends, where all human beings live in harmony and peace.

Arthur Frommer

THE BEST OF SAN FRANCISCO

San Francisco's reputation as a rollicking city where almost anything goes dates back to the boom-or-bust days of the California gold rush. It's always been this way: This city is so beautiful, exciting, diverse, and cosmopolitan that you can always find something new to see and do no matter if it's your 1st or 50th visit. Oh, and bring a warm jacket: Bob Hope once remarked that San Francisco is the city of four seasons—every day.

THE best ONLY-IN-SAN FRANCISCO EXPERIENCES

- **A Powell–Hyde Cable Car Ride:** Skip the less-scenic California line and take the Powell–Hyde cable car down to Fisherman's Wharf—the ride is worth the wait. When you reach the top of Nob Hill, grab the rail with one hand and hold your camera with the other, because you're about to see a view of the bay that'll make you weepy. See p. 100.
- **An Adventure at Alcatraz:** Even if you loathe tourist attractions, you'll dig Alcatraz. Just looking at the Rock from across the bay is enough to give you the heebie-jeebies—and the park rangers have put together an excellent audio tour with narration by former inmates and guards. Heck, even the boat ride across the bay is worth the price. See p. 104.
- **Visit the Painted Ladies of Alamo Square:** We may be a liberal city, but we don't mean that kind of painted ladies; this is, after all, a family-oriented guidebook. These Painted Ladies are that row of Victorian houses you've no doubt seen on postcards with the modern Financial District buildings off in the background. See p. 119.
- **A Sourdough Bread Bowl Filled with Clam Chowder:** There is no better way to take the chill off a freezing July day in San Francisco than a loaf of Boudin bread, brilliantly hollowed out to form a primitive chowder vessel, filled with hot steamy clam and potato soup.
- **A Walk Across the Golden Gate Bridge:** Don your windbreaker and walking shoes and prepare for a wind-blasted, exhilarating journey across San Francisco's most famous landmark. It's simply one of those things you have to do at least once in your life. See p. 130.
- **A Stroll Through Chinatown:** Chinatown is a trip—about as close to experiencing Asia as you can get without a passport. Skip the ersatz camera and luggage stores and head straight for the food markets, where a cornucopia of critters that you'll never see at Safeway sit in boxes waiting for the wok. (Is that an armadillo?) Better yet, take one of Shirley Fong-Torres's Wok Wiz tours of Chinatown. See p. 117.

- **A Night of Comedy at Beach Blanket Babylon:** Giant hats, over-the-top costumes, and wicked humor are what it's all about at this North Beach classic, the longest running musical review in the country. See p. 180.
- **A Wander Down Lombard Street:** Zig and zag your way down eight tight hairpin turns in 1 Russian Hill city block on the "crookedest street in the world." Look for the house where the first season of MTV's "The Real World" was filmed. See p. 122.
- **Visit the California Sea Lions:** These giant, blubbery beasts are probably the most famous residents of the City by the Bay. Though they left en masse for greener pastures—or bluer seas—back in 2009, they are now back in full force, barking, belching, and playing king of the mountain for space on the docks at Pier 39. See p. 109.

THE best HOTEL EXPERIENCES

- **Best Value:** Imagine a room in one of the most expensive cities in the world for under $100 per night, including free breakfast and parking. Crazy? I think not! The **Fort Mason Hostel** offers private rooms (bathrooms are shared—but that hardly seems like a big deal) in a historic building, just a few minutes' walk from Fisherman's Wharf. If you are willing to bunk with some new friends in the dorms, the price drops to as low as $30 per night. See p. 68.
- **Best Water View:** Again, this goes to the **Fort Mason Hostel.** Wake up to a panoramic view of Alcatraz and the bay if you get one of the bayside private or dorm rooms in this National Park treasure perched high on a hill. See p. 68.
- **Best Service:** The **Ritz-Carlton** is the sine qua non of luxury hotels, offering near-perfect service and every possible amenity. Even if you can't afford a guest room, come for the mind-blowing Sunday brunch—they still treat you like royalty. See p. 60.
- **Best Beat Generation Hotel:** The **Hotel Bohème** is the perfect mixture of art, funky style, and location—just steps from the sidewalk cafes and shops of North Beach. If Jack Kerouac were alive today, this is where he'd stay—an easy stagger home from his favorite bar and bookstore. See p. 66.
- **Best Old Luxury:** Hands down, the **Palace Hotel.** Built in 1875, and quickly rebuilt after the 1906 earthquake, the regal lobby and stunning Garden Court atrium—complete with Italian marble columns, and elegant chandeliers—will take you back 100 years to far more simple times. See p. 82.
- **Best Hotel in the Woods:** Surrounded by trees in a national park just south of the Golden Gate Bridge, the **Inn at the Presidio** is the perfect place for nature lovers. With a golf course close by, hiking trails out the back door, and a fire pit on the back patio, you may never get to Fisherman's Wharf. See p. 67.
- **Best with Children:** The **Argonaut Hotel** is set in the heart of Fisherman's Wharf, with sea lions, ice cream sundaes at Ghirardelli's, the beach at Aquatic Park, and the Musee Mechanique, all only a few minutes away. With its cool nautical theme throughout, and a toy-filled treasure box they can pick from in the lobby, the little ones will never want to leave. See p. 65.
- **Coolest Doormen:** Nothing can possibly compete with the **Sir Frances Drake Hotel** in this category. The jovial doormen greet guests wearing their signature red Beefeater costumes—complete with white frilly collar, top hat, and tights. The most

famous doorman in the city, Tom Sweeney, has been blowing his whistle and handling bags at the Sir Francis Drake for over 35 years. Heavy bags are nothing for him; he used to play football with Joe Montana and Dwight Clark. See p. 58.

THE best DINING EXPERIENCES

- **The Best of the City's Fine Dining: La Folie** (p. 84) has been the place to go for cuisine at its finest since 1988. Celebrity chef Roland Passot never fails to offer his guests a delightfully long, lavish meal. And then there's **Restaurant Gary Danko** (p. 88), always a sure bet for a perfect contemporary French meal complete with polished service, an amazing cheese cart, and flambéed finales.

- **Best Value:** For less than $6, you can buy a plate of handmade, succulent potstickers—each one the size of your fist; add a plate of noodles, and a couple of drinks, and you can feed a couple of people for under $20. Where, you ask, can such a bargain be found? On Nob Hill, no less, at **U-Lee Restaurant.** See p. 85.

- **Best Authentic San Francisco Dining Experience:** The lovable loudmouths working behind the narrow counter of **Swan Oyster Depot** have been satisfying patrons with fresh crab, shrimp, oysters, and clam chowder since 1912. See p. 85.

- **Best Dim Sum Feast:** At **Ton Kiang** (p. 99), you'll be wowed by the variety of dumplings and mysterious dishes. Don't worry about the language barrier; just point at what looks good and dig in.

- **Best Kept Secret:** Far, far away from Fisherman's Wharf, hidden on a residential street a few blocks from the heart of the Castro, step through the heavy curtain at the front door and enter **L'Ardoise.** Zee food is magnifique, as is zee friendly owner from zee French Alps, chef Thierry Clement. See p. 97.

- **Best View:** That's an easy one: **The Cliff House** (p. 98). Perched high on a cliff (duh), the views—of the crashing Pacific Ocean, the sunsets, and the sea lions out front on the rocks—are simply stunning.

- **Best Dive Restaurant:** Hands down, **Mission Chinese Food.** Who would have guessed that rock-star-foodie-darling-chef, Danny Bowien, hides out in a non-descript hovel on the gritty streets of the Mission District? The windows are cracked, and the bathroom is filthy—no matter, the food is mouth-watering amazing, and I can't wait to go back. See p. 96.

- **Best Out-of-this-World Decor:** This has to be the undersea adventure that is **Farallon.** Chances are, no matter where you hail from, you have never seen a place like this. With giant handblown jellyfish lamps, glass clamshells, kelp columns, and a sea-life mosaic underfoot, you'll feel like you're on the bottom of a beautiful ocean floor while you munch on scallops and slurp down oysters. See p. 81.

- **Best Splurge:** Poetry instead of a menu. Food served on rocks and tree branches and slabs of bark. A waiting list for reservations that usually tops 2 months. The poetic culinaria at **Atelier Crenn** will set you back a pretty penny, and then some, but it is an experience you will never forget. See p. 89.

- **Best in the Country:** According to the recent James Beard Foodie Awards—and judging by the throngs waiting hours just to stand at the bar to eat, this one goes to **State Bird Provisions.** With dim sum-style service—and no Chinese food in sight—this is the perfect place to try just a few bites of all sorts of fab food. See p. 92.

THE best THINGS TO DO FOR FREE (OR ALMOST FREE)

○ **Meander Along the Marina's Golden Gate Promenade and Crissy Field:** There's something about strolling the promenade that just feels right. The combination of beach, bay, boats, Golden Gate views, and clean, cool breezes is good for the soul. Don't miss snacks at the Warming Hut. See p. 133.

○ **Take a Free Guided Walking Tour:** With over 90 tours to choose from, including Murals and the Multi-Ethnic Mission, Castro: Tales of the Village, and Gold Rush City, **San Francisco City Guides** has to be one of the best deals in town. See p. 136.

○ **Pretend You're a Guest of the Palace or Fairmont Hotels:** You may not be staying the night, but you can certainly feel like a million bucks in the public spaces at the **Palace Hotel** (p. 61). The extravagant creation of banker "Bonanza King" Will Ralston in 1875, the Palace Hotel has one of the grandest rooms in the city: the **Garden Court,** where you can have high tea under a stained-glass dome. Running a close second is the magnificent lobby at Nob Hill's **Fairmont San Francisco** (p. 59).

○ **Tour City Hall:** Come see where, in 2004, Mayor Gavin Newsom made his bold statement to the country about the future of same-sex marriage in this beautiful Beaux Arts building. Free tours are offered to the public. See p. 121.

○ **Cocktail in the Clouds:** One of the greatest ways to view the city is from a top-floor lounge in hotels such as the **Sir Francis Drake** (p. 52), or the venerable **InterContinental Mark Hopkins** (p. 58). Drinks aren't cheap, but considering you're not paying for the view, it almost seems like a bargain.

○ **Browse the Ferry Building Farmers' Market:** Stroll booth to booth sampling organic food. Buy fresh produce alongside some of the big name chefs of the Bay Area. People watch. It is always a party and always free. Held rain or shine every Tuesday, Thursday, and Saturday, this is one of the most pleasurable ways to spend time the city. See p. 114.

○ **Wells Fargo Museum:** Have a look at pistols, mining equipment, an original Wells Fargo stagecoach, old photographs, other gold rush-era relics at the bank's original location. See p. 114.

○ **Free Culture Days:** Most every museum in San Francisco opens its doors to the public for free on certain days of the week. We have a complete list on p. 121.

THE best OUTDOOR ACTIVITIES

○ **A Day in Golden Gate Park:** Exploring Golden Gate Park is an essential part of the San Francisco experience. Its arboreal paths stretch from the Haight all the way to Ocean Beach, offering dozens of fun things to do along the way. Top sights are the **Conservatory of Flowers** (p. 125), the **Japanese Tea Garden** (p. 127), the fabulous **de Young Museum** (p. 126), and its eco-fabulous cross-concourse neighbor, the **California Academy of Sciences** (p. 126). The best time to go is Sunday, when main roads in the park are closed to traffic. Toward the end of the day, head west to the beach and watch the sunset. See p. 124.

○ **A Walk Along the Coastal Trail:** Stroll the forested **Coastal Trail** from Cliff House to the Golden Gate Bridge, and you'll see why San Franciscans put up with living on a fault line. Start at the parking lot just above Cliff House and head north. On a clear day, you'll have incredible views of the Marin Headlands, but even on foggy days, it's worth the trek to scamper over old bunkers and relish the cool, salty air. Make sure to dress warmly. See p. 143.

o **A Wine Country Excursion:** It'll take you about an hour to get there, but once you arrive you'll want to hopscotch from one winery to the next, perhaps picnic in the vineyards. And consider this: When the city is fogged in and cold, Napa and Sonoma are almost always sunny and warm. For more information about a day trip to Napa, see p. 209.

o **A Climb up or down the Filbert Street Steps:** San Francisco is a city of stairways, and the crème de la crème of scenic steps is Filbert Street between Sansome Street and the east side of Telegraph Hill, where steep Filbert Street becomes Filbert Steps, a 377-stair descent that wends its way through flower gardens and some of the city's oldest and most varied housing. It's a beautiful walk down from Coit Tower, and great exercise going up. See p. 141.

o **Bike the Golden Gate Bridge:** Go see the friendly folks over at Blazing Saddles in Fisherman's Wharf and ask them to hook you up. Rent a bike and pedal over this San Francisco icon on your own. Take a guided tour over the bridge down into Sausalito, and return to the city by ferry. Heck, they even rent electric bikes—now that is my kind of outdoor adventure. See p. 138.

THE best OFFBEAT TRAVEL EXPERIENCES

o **A Grumpy Old Man Passing Out Cookies and Insults in Chinatown:** A San Francisco institution for years, no visit to Chinatown is complete without visiting **Uncle Gee** in front of his tea shop on Grant St. He will give you a Chinese name, offer you some sound advice…and threaten to take you downstairs and beat you if you don't follow that advice. Yes, it sounds weird, but Uncle is hilarious; people line up for his abuse. See p. 154.

o **A Soul-Stirring Sunday Service at Glide Memorial Church:** Every city has churches, but only San Francisco has the Glide. An hour or so with Reverend Cecil Williams, or one of his alternates, and his exuberant gospel choir will surely shake your soul and let the glory out. No matter what your religious beliefs may be, everybody leaves this Tenderloin church spiritually uplifted and slightly misty-eyed. See p. 118.

o **A Cruise Through the Castro:** The most populated and festive street in the city is not just for gays and lesbians (though some of the best cruising in town *is* right here). This neighborhood shows there is truth in San Francisco's reputation as an open-minded, liberal city, where people are free to simply love whomever they want. If you have time, catch a flick and a live Wurlitzer organ performance at the beautiful 1930s Spanish colonial movie palace, the Castro Theatre. See "Neighborhoods in Brief," beginning on p. 22, for more info.

o **The Bushman of Fisherman's Wharf:** This famous street performer has been "bushing" people—hiding behind a couple of Eucalyptus branches, jumping out, and scaring the heck out of unsuspecting tourists—for over 30 years now. The subject of the short film "Behind the Bush," the Bushman, aka David Johnson, is a homeless gentleman who claims to earn over $60,000 in a good "bushing" year.

- **Catching Big Air in Your Car:** Relive *Bullitt* or *The Streets of San Francisco* as you careen down the center lane of Gough Street between Ellis and Eddy streets, screaming out "Wooooeee!" Feel the pull of gravity leave you momentarily, followed by the thump of the car suspension bottoming out. Wimpier folk can settle for driving down the steepest street in San Francisco: Filbert Street, between Leavenworth and Hyde streets.

- **AsiaSF:** The gender-bending waitresses—mostly Asian men dressed *very* convincingly as hot-to-trot women—will blow your mind with their performance of lip-synched show tunes, which takes place every night. Bring the parents—they'll love it. Believe it or not, even kids are welcome at some seatings. See p. 83.

- **Browse the Haight:** Though the power of the flower has wilted, the Haight is still, more or less, the Haight: a sort of resting home for aging hippies, ex-Deadheads, skate punks, and an eclectic assortment of young panhandlers. Think of it as a people zoo as you walk down the rows of used-clothing stores, hip boutiques, and leather shops. See p. 123.

- **The Sisters of Perpetual Indulgence:** A leading-edge "Order of queer nuns," these lovely "ladies" got their start in the Castro back in 1979 when a few men dressed in 14th century Belgian nun's habits "and a teensy bit of make-up so as not to be dowdy on a Friday night" to help chase away visiting church officials who regularly came to town preaching about the immorality of homosexuality. With their Adam's apples, and sometimes beards, these dames appear at most public events, and have devoted themselves to community outreach, ministry, and helping those on the fringes of society. Amen.

THE best ARCHITECTURE

- **The Transamerica Pyramid:** Without this tall, triangular spire gracing its presence, the skyline of San Francisco could be mistaken for almost any other American city. Though you can't take a tour to the top, on the Plaza Level—off Clay Street—there is a Visitor Center with videos and facts, a historical display, and a live feed from the "pyramid-cam" located on the top. Did you know this icon appears white because its façade is covered in crushed quartz? Located at 600 Montgomery St.

- **The Palace of Fine Arts:** This Maybeck-designed stunner of Greek columns and Roman ruins is one of the only structures remaining from the 1915 Panama-Pacific International Exhibition which was held, in part, to show that San Francisco had risen from the ashes of the 1906 earthquake destruction.

- **Mission Dolores:** Also known as Mission San Francisco de Asis, this was the sixth in a chain of missions ordered built by Father Junipero Serra. Built in 1776, it is the oldest surviving building in the city. See p. 119.

- **Sentinel Building/Columbus Tower:** Real estate is at such a premium in our city; every speck of land has to be used if at all possible. There is no better proof of this than Francis Ford Coppola's triangular-shaped flatiron building, located at the corner of Columbus and Kearny Streets. Under construction in 1906, it was one of the few structures in the city to survive the earthquake and ensuing fires. See p. 160.

- **Recycled Buildings:** Since San Francisco was the first city in North America to mandate recycling and composting; it only follows we would be good at recycling our old buildings as well. The **Asian Art Museum** (p. 120) was once the city library. The **Contemporary Jewish Museum** (p. 111) was created from an old power substation designed by Willis Polk. Built in 1874 to hold the "diggings" from the gold rush, the old US Mint (at 5th and Missions Sts.) is currently being recycled and will house the **San Francisco Museum at the Mint** when it's completed in the next 3 to 5 years. The **Ferry Building Marketplace** (p. 114) was—surprise—the old ferry building. Built between 1895 and 1903, 170 ferries were docked here daily.

o **The Painted Ladies of Alamo Square:** Also known as the Six Sisters, these famous Victorian homes on Steiner Street (p. 119) are among the most photographed sights in the city. The characters from the sitcom "Full House" lived here in TV land.

THE best MUSEUMS

o **Palace of the Legion of Honor:** Located in a memorial to soldiers lost in World War I, this fine arts museum features Renaissance and pre-Renaissance works—many from Europe—spanning a 4000-year history. See p. 134.

o **The de Young:** Appropriately housed in a new modern building in Golden Gate Park, the Legion of Honor's modern fine arts sister, the de Young, features works from more recent times. Both can be entered on the same day with one admission ticket. See p. 126.

o **California Historical Society:** Established in 1871, this little-known gem invites visitors to explore a rich collection of Californiana, including manuscripts, books and photographs pertaining to the Golden State's fascinating past. See p. 111.

o **Contemporary Jewish Museum:** Even if you have absolutely no interest in Jewish culture, history, art, and ideas, go to visit the old-meets-new building, created when New York architect, Daniel Libeskind, "dropped" shiny steel cubes onto the roof of the 1907 Willis Polk-designed Beaux Arts brick power substation. See p. 111.

o **Asian Art Museum:** Located in the big showy Civic Center space, across the way from City Hall, this is my favorite museum in the city. I never tire of looking at the variety of treasures from countries I had no idea were in fact a part of "Asia." See p. 120.

THE best THINGS TO DO WITH CHILDREN

o **The Exploratorium:** Imagine a hands-on science museum where kids can play for hours, doing cool things like using a microscope to search for miniscule sea creatures, and then watch them attack each other with teeny, tiny claws. Throw in a drinking fountain in a real toilet and you've got the sweetest science museum on the planet. See p. 113.

o **Pier 39 and the California Sea Lions:** Featuring ice cream and candy stores, bungee jumping, a puppet theater, and lots of cool shops, Pier 39 is every kids' dream come true. To top it all off, this pier is home to the famous barking sea lions. See p. 109.

o **Musee Mechanique:** Filled with old fashioned penny arcade games, kids love to pop in quarters and experience what their great, great grandparents did for fun 100+ years ago. See p. 107.

o **Aquarium of the Bay:** Stand on a conveyor belt. Move through a tube in an aquarium while all sorts to sea creatures swim over and around you. Repeat. What's not to love? See p. 106.

o **Ghirardelli:** In the 1850s, I imagine the Gold Rush-era kids must have stood at the corner of Beach and Larkin Streets, crying for ice cream the way yours will if you don't take them into Ghirardelli for an Earthquake Sundae or a Golden Gate Banana Split. See p. 96.

o **Cable Car Museum:** Kids love to learn what makes things happen and move. They'll be fascinated when they enter this cool working museum, especially if they've just hopped off a cable car. On the main level you can see giant wheels turning the very cables that pull the cars around the city. Below, you might catch a gripper actually grabbing a cable. See p. 115.

o **California Academy of Sciences:** At this 150-year old institution located in the middle of Golden Gate Park, kids' favorite activities include watching Claude, the cool albino alligator, and learning about the planets while laying back in their chairs at the Morrison Planetarium. See p. 125.

SAN FRANCISCO NEIGHBORHOODS & SUGGESTED ITINERARIES

How fast the time flies on a visit to San Francisco! With so many sightseeing and entertainment options, the job of organizing a day of touring can be a daunting task. That's why I've inserted this chapter at an early point in your reading. In it, I've suggested several workable ways to organize your time: several different itineraries from which to choose, several different tastes and interests to satisfy. Each one hits many of the "bucket list" sights (and some of the more unique ones). And each one, I hope, will lead to an enjoyable Northern California vacation. Along the way, I'll also explain how San Francisco is laid out and what you'll find in the various neighborhoods, so that, if you decide to skip our suggested itineraries, you'll at least be able to create a logical alternative designed to satisfy your own particular wants.

BEST OF SAN FRANCISCO IN 1 DAY

If you've got only 1 day to explore the city, you have my condolences. You've got a lot of ground to cover just to get to the must-sees, but luckily, condensed geography (and hopefully weather) are in your favor. This whirlwind jaunt starts with a scenic ride on a cable car followed by a tour of Alcatraz Island. Next you'll hoof it up to two of the city's most colorful neighborhoods—Chinatown and North Beach—for lunch, shopping, browsing, cocktails, dinner, cappuccino, and a show. Get an early start, because you're about to have a long yet wonderful day in the City by the Bay. **Start:** *F-Line Streetcar to Union Square.*

1 Union Square

Union Square—which was named for a series of pro-union mass demonstrations staged here on the eve of the Civil War—isn't an attraction in itself, but it's the epicenter of the city's shopping district. Macy's, Saks, and Tiffany & Co. are located here and are surrounded by blocks of other high-end boutiques. There are very few shopping bargains, but it's fun to play lookey-loo.

Just 3 blocks down, at Powell and Market streets, is the cable car turnaround where you'll embark on a ride on the nation's only moving National Historic Landmark. See p. 115.

2 Cable Cars & Lombard Street ★★★

Don't be intimidated by the line of people at the cable car turnaround at Market and Powell streets—the ride is worth the wait. The $6 thrill ride starts with a steep climb up Nob Hill, and then passes through Chinatown and Russian Hill before plummeting down Hyde Street to Fisherman's Wharf. It's an experience you'll never forget. (*Note:* If you want to check out the famous winding stretch of Lombard Street, hop off the cable car at the intersection of Hyde and Lombard streets and, when you've seen enough, either walk the rest of the way down to Fisherman's Wharf or take the next cable car that comes along.) For maximum thrill, stand on the running boards during the ride and hold on Doris Day style. See p. 100.

3 Buena Vista Cafe 🍷

After you've completed your first Powell–Hyde cable car ride, it's a San Francisco tradition to celebrate with an Irish coffee at the Buena Vista Cafe, located across from the cable car turnaround. The first Irish coffees served in America were mixed here in 1952, and they're still the best in the Bay Area. See p. 88.

4 Alcatraz Tour ★★★

To tour "the Rock," the Bay Area's famous abandoned prison on its own island, you must first get there, and that's half the fun. The brief but beautiful ferry ride offers captivating views of the Golden Gate Bridge, the Marin Headlands, and the city. Once inside, an excellent audio tour guides you through cellblocks and offers a colorful look at the prison's historic past as well as its most infamous inmates. Book well in advance because these tours consistently sell out in the summer. Bring snacks and beverages for the ride (the ferry's pickings are slim and expensive, and nothing is available on the island). See p. 104.

Hop back on a cable car to Chinatown. There are two locations for cable cars near Fisherman's Wharf. The Powell–Hyde line (PH) and the Powell–Mason line (PM). The PH line is located at Beach and Hyde streets; the PM line is at Bay and Taylor streets. Both lines intersect each other. Best place to get off is Washington and Mason streets or Powell and California streets. Walk down a few blocks and you will be in:

5 Chinatown ★★

One block from North Beach is a whole other world: Chinatown. San Francisco has one of the largest communities of Chinese people in the United States, with more than 80,000 people condensed into the blocks around Grant Avenue and Stockton Street. Although frequented by tourists, the area caters mostly to Chinese, who crowd the vegetable and herb markets, restaurants, and shops carrying those ubiquitous pink plastic bags. It's worth a peek if only to see the Stockton Street markets hawking live frogs, armadillos, turtles, and odd sea creatures destined for tonight's dinner table. *Tip:* The dozens of knickknack shops are a great source of cheap souvenirs. See p. 117.

6 Great Eastern Restaurant 🍷

You can't visit Chinatown and not try food so terrific President Obama himself popped in back in 2012. Walk to the Great Eastern Restaurant and order salt and pepper fresh crab and sizzling chicken in a clay pot. See p. 84.

7 North Beach

One of the best ways to get the San Francisco vibe is to mingle with the locals, and one of our favorite places to do so is in San Francisco's "Little Italy." Dozens of Italian restaurants and coffeehouses continue to flourish in what is still the center of the city's Italian community. A stroll along Columbus Avenue will take you past eclectic little cafes, delis, bookstores, bakeries, and coffee shops that give North Beach its Italian-bohemian character. See p. 86.

8 Mario's Bohemian Cigar Store 🍺

Okay, so the menu's limited to coffee drinks and a few sandwiches (the meatball is our favorite), but the convivial atmosphere and large windows that are perfect for people-watching make this tiny, pie-shaped cafe a favorite even with locals. It's at 566 Columbus Ave. (🕐 415/362-0536).

9 Dinner at Original Joe's ★

The best thing about North Beach is its old-school restaurants—many owned by the same family for generations. **Original Joe's** is one of our favorites, where patrons sit in red leather booths and dine on classic Italian-American comfort food. See p. 86.

10 Caffè Greco 🍺 ★

By now you should be stuffed and exhausted. Good. Time for a cappuccino at Caffè Greco (423 Columbus Ave.; 🕐 415/397-6261). Sit at one of the sidewalk tables and reminisce on what a great day you had in San Francisco.

11 Beach Blanket Babylon at Club Fugazi ★★

You thought you were done for the night and heading home? Well fugedaboudit; it's time to wander around the corner and see the outrageous costumes and giant hats of the longest-running musical review in the country. See p. 180.

BEST OF SAN FRANCISCO IN 2 DAYS

On your second day, get familiar with other famous landmarks around the city. Start with breakfast, a science lesson, and a pleasant bayside stroll in the Marina District. Next, cross the famed Golden Gate Bridge on foot; then take a bus to Golden Gate Park. After a stroll through the city's beloved park, it's time for lunch and power shopping on Haight Street, followed by dinner and cocktails back in the Marina District. Smashing. ***Start:*** *Bus nos. 22, 28, 30, 30X, 43, or 76.*

1 Good Morning Marina District

The area that became famous for its scenes of destruction after the 1989 earthquake has long been one of the most picturesque and coveted patches of local real estate. Here, along the northern edge of the city, multimillion-dollar homes back up to the bayfront **Marina,** where flotillas of sailboats and the mighty Golden Gate Bridge make for a magnificent backdrop on a morning stroll.

Start the day with a good cup of coffee on Chestnut Street; then walk to the **Palace of Fine Arts,** built for the Panama Pacific Exhibition of 1915, and then walk over to **Crissy Field** (p. 133), where restored wetlands and a beachfront path lead to historic **Fort Point** (p. 133) and to the southern underside end of the **Golden Gate Bridge.**

2 The Grove ☕

If you can't jump-start your brain properly without a good cup of coffee, then begin your day at The Grove (2250 Chestnut St.; ☎ 415/474-4843), located in the Marina District—it's as cozy as an old leather couch.

3 The Golden Gate Bridge ★★★

It's one of those things you have to do at least once in your life—walk across the fabled Golden Gate Bridge, the most photographed man-made structure in the world (p. 130). As you would expect, the views along the span are spectacular and the wind a wee bit chilly, so bring a jacket. It takes at least an hour to walk northward to the vista point and back.

When you return to the southern end, board either Muni bus no. 28 or 29 (be sure to ask the driver if the bus is headed toward Golden Gate Park).

4 Golden Gate Park ★★★

Stretching from the middle of the city to the Pacific Ocean and comprising 1,017 acres, Golden Gate Park is one of the city's greatest attributes. Since its development in the late 1880s, it has provided San Franciscans with respite from urban life—offering dozens of well-tended gardens, museums, a buffalo paddock, a Victorian greenhouse, and great grassy expanses prime for picnicking, lounging, or tossing a Frisbee. See p. 124.

Have the bus driver drop you off near John F. Kennedy Drive. Walking eastward on JFK Drive, you'll pass four of the park's most popular attractions: Stow Lake (p. 129), the de Young Museum (p. 126), the California Academy of Sciences (p. 125), and the wonderful Conservatory of Flowers (p. 125).

5 Cha Cha Cha ☕ ★★

By now you're probably starving, so walk out of the park and into the Haight to Cha Cha Cha (1801 Haight St.; ☎ 415/386-7670). Order plenty of dishes from the tapas-style menu and dine family style. Oh, and don't forget a pitcher of sangria—you've earned it.

6 Exploring the Haight-Ashbury District ★★★

Ah, the Haight. Birthplace of the Summer of Love and Flower Power, shrine to the Grateful Dead, and the place where America's nonconformists still congregate over beers, bongos, and buds. Spend at least an hour strolling up Haight Street (p. 165), browsing the cornucopia of used-clothes stores, leather shops, head shops, and poster stores. There are some great bargains to be found here, especially for vintage clothing.

When you get to the intersection of Haight and Masonic streets, catch the Muni no. 43 bus heading north, which will take you through the Presidio and back to the Marina District.

7 Dinner & Drinks

You've had a full day, my friend, so rest your weary bones at the bar at **Zushi Puzzle** (p. 91), a fantastic place to experience the ancient Japanese art of "omakase," which basically translates into "the big chef with the big knife will feed you whatever he wants to."

BEST OF SAN FRANCISCO IN 3 DAYS

You've done lots of sightseeing, time for a change of pace. Today we're going to do one of our all-time favorite things to do on a day off—ride a bike from Fisherman's Wharf to Sam's Anchor Cafe in Tiburon (that small peninsula just north of Alcatraz Island). The beautiful and exhilarating ride takes you over the Golden Gate Bridge, through the heart of Sausalito, and along the scenic North Bay bike path, ending with a frosty beer and lunch at the best outdoor cafe in the Bay Area. And here's the best part: You don't have to bike back. After lunch, you can take the passenger ferry across the bay to Fisherman's Wharf—right to your starting point. Brilliant. *Start: Powell–Hyde cable car line. Bus nos. 19, 30, or 47.*

1 Rent a Bicycle

Walk, take a bus, or ride the Powell–Hyde cable car (which goes right by it) to one of the bike shops (p. 138) near Ghirardelli Square. Rent a single or tandem bike for a full day, and be sure to ask for: 1) a free map pointing out the route to Sam's in Tiburon, 2) ferry tickets, 3) a bicycle lock, and 4) a bottle of water. Bring your own sunscreen, a hat (for the deck at Sam's), and a light jacket—no matter how warm it is right now, the weather can change in minutes. Each bike has a small pouch hooked to the handlebars where you can stuff your stuff.

Start pedaling along the map route to Golden Gate Bridge. You'll encounter one short, steep hill right from the start at Aquatic Park, but it's okay to walk your bike (hey, you haven't had your coffee fix yet). Keep riding westward through Fort Point and the Marina Green to Crissy Field.

2 The Warming Hut ☕

At the west end of Crissy Field, alongside the bike path, is the Warming Hut (p. 133), a barnlike building where you can fuel up with a light (organic, sustainable) snack and coffee drinks. Several picnic tables nearby offer beautiful views of the bay.

3 Biking the Golden Gate

After your break, there's one more steep hill up to the bridge. Follow the bike path to the west side of the bridge (pedestrians must stay on the east side), cross the bridge, and take the road to your left heading downhill and crossing underneath Hwy. 101. Coast all the way to Sausalito.

4 Exploring Sausalito

You'll love Sausalito (p. 198). Cruising down Bridgeway is like being transported to one of those seaside towns on the French Riviera. Lock the bikes and mosey around on foot for a while.

5 Poggio Trattoria ☕

If it's sunny, ask for a table outside at Poggio Trattorio (777 Bridgeway; ☏ 415/332-7771; www.poggiotrattoria.com) and order a cocktail, but don't eat yet.

6 North Bay Tour

Back on the bike, head north again on the bike path as it winds along the bay. When you reach the Mill Valley Car Wash at the end of the bike path, turn right onto East Blithedale Avenue, which will cross Hwy. 101 and turn into Tiburon Boulevard. (This is the only sucky part of the ride where you'll encounter traffic.) About a

Best of San Francisco in 3 Days

To Alcatraz ↑

0 _____ 1 mi
0 _____ 1 km

SAN
FRANCISO
BAY

Pier 41
Ferry term. ■ Pier 39
FISHERMAN'S
WHARF Beach St.
North Point St.

Marina Blvd.
Fort
Mason
Beach St.
Francisco St.
Ghirardelli Square ■ Bay St.

MARINA
Bay St.
Chestnut St.
Lombard St.
COW HOLLOW
Filbert St.
101
RUSSIAN
HILL
Union St.
Greenwich St.
Green St.
Octavia St.
Franklin St.
Vallejo St.
Broadway
NORTH
BEACH
Coit
Tower
Exploratorium

Grant Ave.
Stockton St.
Sansome St.
Battery St.
Front St.
The Embarcadero

Columbus Ave.
Beach St.
North Point St.

PACIFIC HEIGHTS
Alta
Plaza
Sacramento St.
Buchanan St.
Laguna St.
Pacific Ave.
Washington St.
Clay St.
California St.
NOB
HILL
CHINA-
TOWN

Van Ness Ave.
Larkin St.
Hyde St.
Leavenworth St.
Taylor St.
Jones St.
Powell St.
Mason St.

Jackson St.
Transamerica
Pyramid
Ferry Building
Embarcadero

FINANCIAL
DISTRICT
Montgomery St.

Pine St.
Bush St.
Kearny St.
Market St.
Fremont St.
Main St.
Beale St.
Spear St.

Broderick St.
Divisadero St.
Scott St.
Pierce St.
Steiner St.
Sutter St.
Post St.
Geary Blvd.
Ellis St.
UNION
SQUARE
Geary St.
O'Farrell St.
Eddy St.
Powell St.
Yerba
Buena
Gardens

Lyon St.
Baker St.
Presidio Ave.
Central Ave.
Masonic Ave.

WESTERN
ADDITION
Golden Gate Ave.
McAllister St.
Fulton St.
Webster St.
Turk St.
City Hall
Civic
Center
Plaza
Civic Center/
UN Plaza
Grove St.
SOMA
80
SOUTH
BEACH

HAIGHT-
ASHBURY
Haight St.
Waller St.
Duboce Ave.
HAYES
VALLEY
Oak St.
Page St.
Fell St.
Hayes St.
Otis St.
10th St.
11th St.
12th St.
101
14th St.
Mission St.
Howard St.
Folsom St.
Harrison St.
Bryant St.
3rd St.
4th St.
Townsend St.
King St.
AT&T Park

Buena
Vista
Park
Corona
Heights
Park
States St.
CASTRO
Mission Dolores ■
16th St.
Mission
17th St.
Guerrero St.
Sanchez St.
Shotwell St.
Valencia St.
MISSION
DISTRICT

MILL
VALLEY
131
Tiburon Blvd.
Paradise Beach
County Park
Bluff Pt.
1
6
MARIN
CITY
101
TIBURON
7
Angel I.
State Park
Angel I.

GOLDEN GATE
NATIONAL
RECREATION
AREA
4
SAUSA-
LITO
5
Bridgeway
8
Alcatraz I.

Pt. Bonita
The
Presidio
101
SAN FRANCISCO

Castro St.
Noe St.
Eureka St.
Diamond St.
Douglass St.
Market St.
18th St.
Dolores
Park
19th St.
20th St.
Liberty St.
21st St.
Church St.
Fair Oaks St.
Dolores St.
S. Van Ness Ave.
Capp St.
Mission St.
Folsom St.
22nd St.
23rd St.
Elizabeth St.
NOE VALLEY
24th St.
Mission
24th St.

mile past Hwy. 101, you'll enter a small park called Blackie's Pasture. (Look for the life-size bronze statue erected in 1995 to honor Tiburon's beloved "mascot," Blackie the horse.) Now it's an easy cruise on the bike path all the way to Sam's.

7 Sam's Anchor Cafe 🍺

Ride your bike all the way to the south end of Tiburon Boulevard and lock your bike at the bike rack near the ferry dock. Walk over to the ferry loading dock and check the ferry departure schedule for "Tiburon to Pier 39/Fisherman's Wharf." Then walk over to Sam's Anchor Café (27 Main St.; ℭ 415/435-4527; www.samscafe.com), request a table on the back patio overlooking the harbor, and relax with a burger, oysters, and cool drink. Sweet.

8 Ferry Ride Back to San Francisco

When it's time to leave, board the ferry with your bike (bike riders board first, so don't stand in line) and enjoy the ride from Tiburon to San Francisco, with a short stop at Angel Island State Park. From Pier 39, it's a short ride back to the rental shop.

After all this adventuring, it's time to reenergize your body and soul with another Irish whiskey at the **Buena Vista Cafe** (p. 88), across from the cable car turnaround, a short walk from the bike rental shop. After libations, take the cable car back to your hotel for some rest and a shower; then spend the rest of the evening enjoying dinner.

If this isn't one of the best days you've had on your vacation, send us this book, and we'll eat it.

SAN FRANCISCO FOR FAMILIES

Knowing kids have different interests than their folks, we've put together a couple of kid-friendly days to make sure you and your offspring cover some of the "musts" with a bit of time to hang and relax.

BEST OF SAN FRANCISCO WITH KIDS IN 1 DAY

If you've only 1 day to explore the city, you'll have to come back; you can't possibly hit all the "musts" in 1 day. That said, let's give it our best. We are going to spend most of the day around every kid's favorite—Fisherman's Wharf—and The Embarcadero. First stop of the day is "The Rock," and when we return from Alcatraz, we'll walk a few minutes to Pier 39, see the sights, including the sea lions, grab some lunch, and then head to the aquarium. Next stop will be one of the greatest science museums in the world, and then a really cool underwater restaurant for dinner. Finish the night with a cable car ride. ***Start: F-Line Streetcar to Pier 33.***

1 Alcatraz ★★★

The boat ride over is half the fun. Once onto The Rock, my kids always like to run around the landing area for a few minutes. If you're lucky, one of the wardens, or even a former prisoner, might be there to greet your boat. Watch a quick movie about the place, and then get your audio tour. Step into a real cell and grab the bars for a photo. Check out solitary confinement. Look at the dummy masks the three guys who escaped left in their beds to fool the guards. When you feel like leaving, take the ferry back to Pier 33. See p. 104.

Walk a few minutes towards Golden Gate Bridge to Pier 39.

2 Pier 39 ★★

Yes, I know, it's touristy and packed with people. No, there is nothing really historic about the place. No matter. With a carousel, non-stop puppet shows and magicians on the stage (behind the carousel), a store with barrel after barrel of candy, cool shops, and bungee jumping, Pier 39 will probably be what they remember most about their visit. See p. 109.

3 Crepes for Lunch ☕

Why have a healthy lunch when you can have a crepe dripping with melted Nutella instead? Ok, have a ham and cheese crepe for lunch, and save the Nutella crepe for dessert. The Crepe Café is located about halfway down Pier 39. See p. 89.

Now, sneak out the back door to:

4 The California Sea Lions ★★

Watch the beasts bark, swim, sleep, and fight for space on the docks. If you're lucky, naturalists from the Aquarium of the Bay might be on hand to give a sea lion lesson. See p. 109.

5 Aquarium of the Bay ★

We're not quite done with Pier 39. At yet another "kid favorite" place, you'll be able to see all sorts of sea critters in their near-to-natural habitat (my family's favorite are the otters). Though you can touch bats and starfish, and hunt for eels, the highlight for kids is always the conveyor belt that slowly takes you through a tube under a sharks and ray infested tank. Located streetside, where Pier 39 meets the Embarcadero. See p. 106.

Now, walk 15 minutes, or take that historic F-Line streetcar, from Pier 39 to Pier 15.

6 The Exploratorium ★★★

One of the best science museums in the world, period. Frankly, a family could spend the entire day here without getting bored. If you end up staying longer than intended, know that healthy snacks are available in the cafe at the entrance if anyone's hungry. Pier 15. See p. 113.

Right next door, walk to Pier 17.

7 Tcho Chocolate Factory ★

Take a tour if you have arranged it ahead of time. If not, no worries; stop in for a few samples, and buy a treat. Pier 15. See p. 170.

Walk 15 minutes, or hop back on the F-Line streetcar, back to Pier 39.

8 Dinner at Forbes Island ☕ ★

You've had a long day exploring and it is time to take a break. Take a water taxi to the floating restaurant beside the Pier 39 sea lions we saw earlier today. Come a little early so kids can climb the lighthouse. Dinner will be served underwater, in a modified houseboat. See p. 86.

Walk 15 minutes to the corner of Hyde and Jefferson sts.

9 Cable Car Ride ★★

It's time for one last adventure before bed. Cling clang your way over the hills of San Francisco on the Powell–Hyde line. See p. 100.

Best of San Francisco with Kids

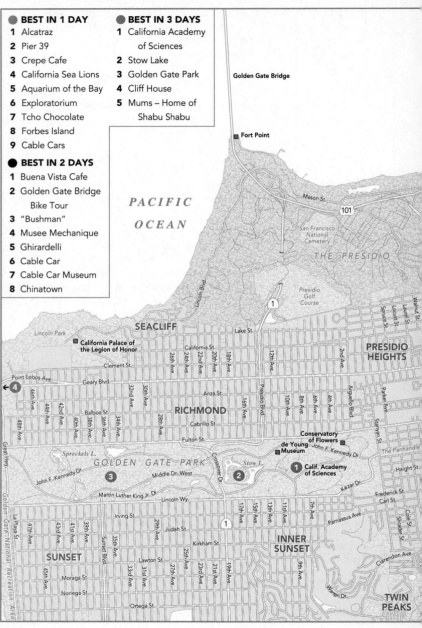

● **BEST IN 1 DAY**
1 Alcatraz
2 Pier 39
3 Crepe Cafe
4 California Sea Lions
5 Aquarium of the Bay
6 Exploratorium
7 Tcho Chocolate
8 Forbes Island
9 Cable Cars

● **BEST IN 2 DAYS**
1 Buena Vista Cafe
2 Golden Gate Bridge
    Bike Tour
3 "Bushman"
4 Musee Mechanique
5 Ghirardelli
6 Cable Car
7 Cable Car Museum
8 Chinatown

● **BEST IN 3 DAYS**
1 California Academy
    of Sciences
2 Stow Lake
3 Golden Gate Park
4 Cliff House
5 Mums – Home of
    Shabu Shabu

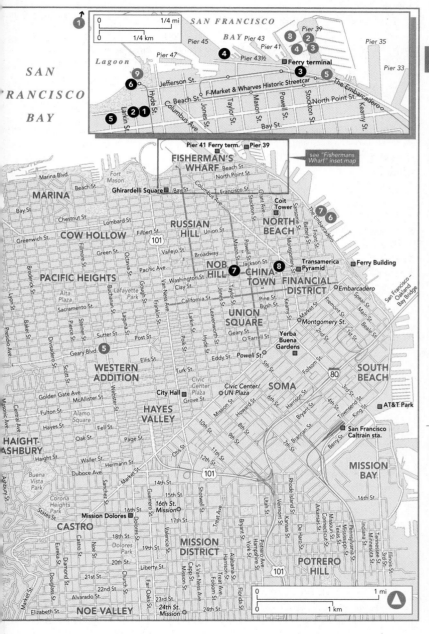

SAN FRANCISCO BAY

SAN FRANCISCO BAY

Pier 45

Pier 43

Pier 41

Pier 39

Pier 43½

Pier 35

Pier 33

Pier 47

Ferry terminal

Lagoon

Jefferson St.

F-Market & Wharves Historic Streetcar

The Embarcadero

Beach St.

North Point St.

Columbus Ave.

Taylor St.

Mason St.

Powell St.

Stockton St.

Keamy St.

Bay St.

Hyde St.

Jones St.

Larkin St.

0   1/4 mi
0   1/4 km

Pier 41 Ferry term.   Pier 39

see "Fishermans Wharf" inset map

FISHERMAN'S WHARF

Beach St.

North Point St.

Fort Mason

Marina Blvd

Beach St.

Ghirardelli Square

Bay St.

Francisco St.

Columbus Ave.

Coit Tower

MARINA

Bay St.

Chestnut St.

Lombard St.

COW HOLLOW

Filbert St.

RUSSIAN HILL

Union St.

Grant Ave.

Stockton St.

Sansome St.

Battery St.

The Embarcadero

NORTH BEACH

Greenwich St.

Green St.

101

Vallejo St.

Broadway

Front St.

Pacific Ave.

PACIFIC HEIGHTS

Octavia St.

Fillmore St.

Pacific Ave.

NOB HILL

Jackson St.

CHINA TOWN

Transamerica Pyramid

Montgomery St.

Ferry Building

Lyon St.

Broderick St.

Baker St.

Pierce St.

Buchanan St.

Laguna St.

Gough St.

Van Ness Ave.

Washington St.

Clay St.

Mason St.

Powell St.

Taylor St.

Leavenworth St.

Hyde St.

Larkin St.

FINANCIAL DISTRICT

Kearny St.

Embarcadero

San Francisco – Oakland Bay Bridge

Alta Plaza

Lafayette Park

Sacramento St.

California St.

Pine St.

Bush St.

Spear St.

Main St.

Beale St.

Presidio Ave.

Masonic Ave.

Central Ave.

Scott St.

Divisadero St.

Steiner St.

Geary Blvd.

Sutter St.

Post St.

UNION SQUARE

Geary St.

O'Farrell St.

Market St.

Montgomery St.

Fremont St.

2nd St.

1st St.

WESTERN ADDITION

Ellis St.

Yerba Buena Gardens

Golden Gate Ave.

McAllister St.

Turk St.

Eddy St.

Powell St.

3rd St.

4th St.

SOUTH BEACH

Webster St.

Alamo Square

Fulton St.

City Hall

Civic Center Plaza

SOMA

5th St.

6th St.

Harrison St.

Bryant St.

Brannan St.

80

HAIGHT-ASHBURY

Hayes St.

Fell St.

Oak St.

HAYES VALLEY

Grove St.

Civic Center/ UN Plaza

Mission St.

Howard St.

Folsom St.

7th St.

8th St.

Townsend St.

King St.

AT&T Park

Page St.

Haight St.

Waller St.

Hermann St.

Duboce Ave.

Otis St.

9th St.

10th St.

11th St.

12th St.

Berry St.

San Francisco Caltrain sta.

Buena Vista Park

101

14th St.

15th St.

Showwell St.

Treat Ave.

MISSION BAY

Corona Heights Park

States St.

Sanchez St.

Market St.

16th St.

Mission

16th St.

CASTRO

Mission Dolores

Dolores Park

17th St.

18th St.

19th St.

20th St.

Liberty St.

Dolores St.

Guerrero St.

Valencia St.

Capp St.

Folsom St.

Harrison St.

Alabama St.

Florida St.

Bryant St.

Rhode Island St.

Kansas St.

De Haro St.

Carolina St.

Wisconsin St.

Arkansas St.

Connecticut St.

Missouri St.

Texas St.

Mississippi St.

Pennsylvania Ave.

Indiana St.

Minnesota St.

Tennessee St.

3rd St.

Illinois St.

POTRERO HILL

Castro St.

Noe St.

Eureka St.

Diamond St.

Douglass St.

21st St.

22nd St.

Alvarado St.

Fair Oaks St.

Church St.

Dolores St.

San Jose Ave.

Guerrero St.

Valencia St.

Mission St.

23rd St.

24th St. Mission

24th St.

Utah St.

Vermont St.

Potrero Ave.

Hampshire St.

York St.

San Bruno Ave.

101

MISSION DISTRICT

Elizabeth St.

Market St.

NOE VALLEY

0   1 mi
0   1 km

BEST OF SAN FRANCISCO WITH KIDS IN 2 DAYS

On your second day, it's time to leave Fisherman's Wharf and get familiar with a couple of the other famous spots in the city. Start with a tour over that big orange bridge, lunch in Sausalito, and a ferry ride across the bay. Next, we must hunt for the elusive "Bushman," play a few old fashioned video games, and then off to a working museum. Finally we will hit Chinatown and meet a grumpy old man your kids will never forget. ***Start:** Historic F-Line streetcar to Fisherman's Wharf.*

1 The Buena Vista for Breakfast ☕

Load up on the carbs and proteins, it's going to be a long day and you're all going to need your strength. The Buena Vista Cafe. See p. 88.

Walk up Hyde St. about half of a block.

2 Guided Golden Gate Bridge Bike Tour

The perfect way to start your day is a pedal across one of the most recognized landmarks in the world. Don't worry, you are not alone! You'll have a wonderful guide from one of the Fisherman's Wharf area bike shops (p. 138).

Bring a jacket and meet a few minutes early for a safety briefing. Follow your guide up and over the bridge, then down into Sausalito. Say goodbye to your guide and stop for lunch or refreshments anywhere along Bridgeway (the main drag through Sausalito). Two of my favorites are the outdoor seating at **Poggio** (777 Bridgeway; ✆ **415/332-7771;** www.poggiotrattoria.com) and the beachside bocce ball and firepits at **Bar Bocce** (1250 Bridgeway; ✆ **415/331-0555;** www. barbocce.com). Explore the town, and then take the ferry from Sausalito back to the city. It is a quick ride back to Blazing Saddles to ditch the bikes. See p. 141.

Walk 3 blocks to the corner of Taylor and the Embarcadero at Pier 45. Keep your eyes peeled for the famous "Bushman" of Fisherman's Wharf. See p. 101.

3 The Musee Mechanique ★★

Give the kids a roll of quarters and let them run free at this antique penny arcade where everything works. Located at Pier 45. See p. 107.

Walk back towards the corner of Beach and Larkin sts.

4 Ghirardelli for Ice Cream ★

Kids need a treat every once in awhile. This is one of the best places to grab a sweet treat in the city. See p. 96.

Walk back to the corner of Jefferson and Hyde sts.

5 Powell–Hyde Cable Car to Nob Hill ★★★

Yes, you rode the cable car last night. No one is going to complain about a second cling clang over the hills.

Hop off at the corner of Washington and Mason sts. on Nob Hill for the:

6 Cable Car Museum ★★

After riding these moving landmarks twice in the last 2 days, kids will love this quick museum that shows how the cable cars work. The actual cables that pull all the cars through the city are right here spinning on giant wheels. See p. 115.

Walk a few blocks down Washington St. to:

7 Chinatown ★★★

The perfect way to end the day is a stroll through this very colorful neighborhood. Kids will love the shops selling everything from air guns to fireworks to live animals. For a detailed tour itinerary, see p. 150. When it's time for dinner, choose from one of the many Chinatown restaurants in the box on p. 84. Whatever you do, don't miss a visit with Uncle Gee on Grant St. See p. 154.

BEST OF SAN FRANCISCO WITH KIDS IN 3 DAYS

If you are lucky enough to have 3 full days in San Francisco with your kids, we are going to head to the other side of town today and hit Golden Gate Park. Inside we'll visit a science museum, go for a boat ride, wander through the park some more, then go relax at the beach, and have yummy shabu shabu for dinner. *Start: Bus nos. 5, 28, or 44.*

1 California Academy of Sciences

Visit a planetarium. Find Claude, the albino alligator. Climb through a tropical rainforest. Learn about earthquakes. This recently remodeled science museum in the middle of Golden Gate Park is a favorite with children. Grab a snack at the cafe if anyone is hungry. See p. 125.

Walk west for a few minutes until you reach Stow Lake.

2 Rent a Boat on Stow Lake

Whether you want a pedal boat, a row boat, or a low-speed electric boat, you can rent one at the Boathouse (p. 129).

Head over to Strawberry Hill in the middle of the lake.

3 Golden Gate Park

By now the kids are probably tired of having an agenda. It is time to explore the park. Maybe the Japanese Tea Garden? See p. 127. Perhaps the Conservatory of Flowers? See p. 125. For a list of things to do see p. 124.

Either walk or hop on a bus and head to the beach. Use www.511.org to figure out which bus to take, depending on where you are in the park.

4 Cliff House

Stop in for a drink and a bathroom break. Look at the pictures all over the walls showing what it looked like in this area 100 years ago. Once refreshed, head outside and look for wildlife on Seal Rocks. Walk to the right and climb around the ruins of the Sutro Baths. Go relax on the beach and take a nap, or dig a hole. Do not go swimming here; the currents are dangerous. The **Cliff House,** see p. 98.

Take the bus no. 38 to the corner of Geary and Fillmore sts.

5 Shabu Shabu for Dinner

Chinese last night; how about Japanese tonight? Kids will love the opportunity to cook their meal all by themselves—with a little help from the bubbling vat in front of them. See p. 91.

CITY LAYOUT

San Francisco occupies the tip of a 32-mile peninsula between San Francisco Bay and the Pacific Ocean. Its land area measures about 46 square miles, although the city is often referred to as being 7 square miles. At more than 900 feet high, towering Twin Peaks (which are, in fact, two neighboring peaks), mark the geographic center of the city and make a great place to take in a vista of San Francisco.

With lots of one-way streets, San Francisco might seem confusing at first, but it will quickly become easy to navigate. The city's downtown streets are arranged in a simple grid pattern, with the exceptions of Market Street and Columbus Avenue, which cut across the grid at right angles to each other. Hills appear to distort this pattern, however, and can disorient you. As you learn your way around, the hills will become your landmarks and reference points.

MAIN ARTERIES & STREETS   **Market Street** is San Francisco's main thoroughfare. Most of the city's buses travel this route on their way to the Financial District from the outer neighborhoods to the west and south. The tall office buildings clustered downtown are at the northeast end of Market; 1 block beyond lies the Embarcadero and the bay.

The **Embarcadero**—an excellent strolling, skating, and biking route (thanks to recent renovations)—curves along San Francisco Bay from south of the Bay Bridge to the northeast perimeter of the city. It terminates at Fisherman's Wharf, the famous tourist-oriented pier. Aquatic Park, Fort Mason, and Golden Gate National Recreation Area are on the northernmost point of the peninsula.

From the eastern perimeter of Fort Mason, **Van Ness Avenue** runs due south, back to Market Street. The area just described forms a rough triangle, with Market Street as its southeastern boundary, the waterfront as its northern boundary, and Van Ness Avenue as its western boundary. Within this triangle lies most of the city's main tourist sights.

FINDING AN ADDRESS   Because most of the city's streets are laid out in a grid pattern, finding an address is easy when you know the nearest cross street. Numbers start with 1 at the beginning of the street and proceed at the rate of 100 per block. When asking for directions, find out the nearest cross street and your destination's neighborhood, but be careful not to confuse numerical avenues with numerical streets. Numerical avenues (Third Ave. and so on) are in the Richmond and Sunset districts in the western part of the city. Numerical streets (Third St. and so on) are south of Market Street in the east and south parts of town.

Neighborhoods in Brief

See the "San Francisco Neighborhoods" map on p. 24.

UNION SQUARE

Union Square is the commercial hub of San Francisco. Most major hotels and department stores are crammed into the area surrounding the actual square, which was named for a series of violent pro-union rallies staged here on the eve of the Civil War. A plethora of upscale boutiques, restaurants, and galleries occupy the spaces tucked between the larger buildings. A few blocks west is the **Tenderloin** neighborhood, a patch of poverty and blight where you should keep your wits about you. The **Theater District** is 3 blocks west of Union Square.

FIDI—THE FINANCIAL DISTRICT

East of Union Square, this area, bordered by the Embarcadero and by Market, Third, Kearny, and Washington streets, is the city's business district and the stomping grounds

tips FOR GETTING AROUND

Here are a few strategies, both mental and practical, for making your way around the city:

1. San Francisco is really quite a small city. If you're in reasonably good shape, and you've left your Jimmy Choos at home, you can hoof it quite easily between many of the sights we are going to suggest you visit in this book, without stressing about taxis, buses, cable cars, and such.

2. If you only remember the "F-Line" historic streetcar, you will be able to get almost anywhere you want to go in the Eastern half of the city. The F-Line starts at the Castro, close to Mission Dolores in the Mission District, and runs northwest "up" Market Street to within a couple of blocks of City Hall, the Asian Arts Museum, and many of the performing arts venues in the Civic Center area. The route continues along Market Street to within a couple of blocks of Union Square and the Yerba Buena District, through the Financial District, and on to the historic Ferry Building. Now the F-Line turns left, running along the Embarcadero passing right in front of the Exploratorium, past Coit Tower in North Beach, and on to Pier 39 and the rest of Fisherman's Wharf, where the route ends. Add in the no. 5 Fulton bus, which runs east-west from downtown to the ocean, and you have most of the city covered with only two routes to remember.

3. If all else fails, use your smart phone to search www.511.org. You can input your current and desired addresses and this idiot-proof site will give you all your public transportation options and tell you when the next vehicle will be along to save you.

for many major corporations. The pointy Transamerica Pyramid, at Montgomery and Clay streets, is the district's most conspicuous architectural feature. To its east sprawls the Embarcadero Center, an 8½-acre complex housing offices, shops, and restaurants. Farther east still is the old Ferry Building, the city's prebridge transportation hub. Ferries to Sausalito and Larkspur still leave from this point. However, in 2003, the building became an attraction all its own when it was completely renovated, jampacked with outstanding restaurants and gourmet food—and wine-related shops, and surrounded by a farmers' market a few days a week, making it a favorite place of San Francisco's residents seeking to stock their kitchens.

NOB HILL & RUSSIAN HILL

Bounded by Bush, Larkin, Pacific, and Stockton streets, Nob Hill is a genteel, well-heeled district still occupied by the city's major power brokers and the neighborhood businesses they frequent. Russian Hill extends from Pacific to Bay streets and from Polk to Mason streets. It contains steep streets, lush gardens, and high-rises occupied by both the moneyed and the bohemian.

CHINATOWN

A large red-and-green gate on Grant Avenue at Bush Street marks the official entrance to Chinatown. Beyond lies a 24-block labyrinth, bordered by Broadway, Bush, Kearny, and Stockton streets, filled with restaurants, markets, temples, shops, and, of course, a substantial percentage of San Francisco's Chinese residents. Chinatown is a great place for exploration all along Grant and Stockton streets, Portsmouth Square, and the alleys that lead off them, like Ross and Waverly. This district has a maddening combination of incessant traffic and very few parking spots, so don't even think about driving around here.

San Francisco Neighborhoods

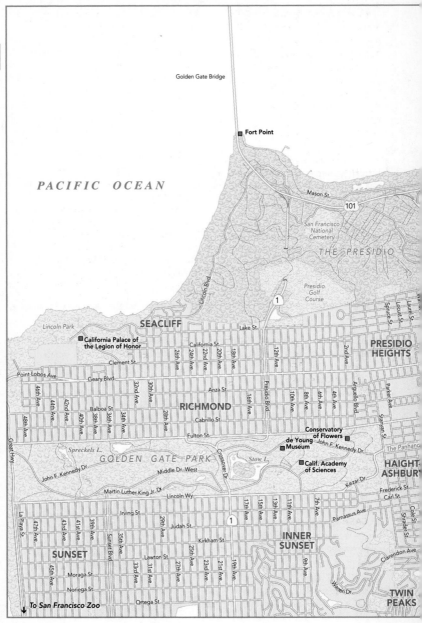

To Alcatraz ↑

0   1 mi
0   1 km

SAN

FRANCISCO

BAY

Pier 41
Ferry term.   ■Pier 39

FISHERMAN'S
WHARF

Marina Blvd   Fort   Beach St.   North Point St.
Mason
Beach St.   Francisco St.
■Ghirardelli Square ■ Bay St.

MARINA   Grant Ave.   Coit   ■Exploratorium
Bay St.   Stockton St.   Tower
Chestnut St.   Lombard St.   NORTH
Greenwich St.   RUSSIAN   BEACH
COW HOLLOW   Filbert St.   HILL   Union St.   The Embarcadero
Green St.   101   Front St.
Vallejo St.   Battery St.
Octavia St.   Broadway   Montgomery St.   Ferry Building
PACIFIC HEIGHTS   Pacific Ave.   NOB   Jackson St.   Transamerica ■
HILL   CHINA- ■Pyramid
Alta   Lafayette   Washington St.   TOWN   FINANCIAL
Plaza   Park   Clay St.   DISTRICT   ○Embarcadero
Sacramento St.   California St.   Pine St.   Market St.
Bush St.   Montgomery St.
UNION   Geary St.   SQUARE   2nd St.
Post St.   O'Farrell St.   1st St.
WESTERN   Ellis St.   Yerba   3rd St.
ADDITION   Eddy St.   Powell St.   Buena   SOUTH
Golden Gate Ave.   Turk St.   Gardens   BEACH
McAllister St.   Folsom St.
Fulton St.   Alamo   Civic   80
Square   City Hall ■   Center   SOMA   AT&T Park
HAYES   Plaza   Civic Center/   ■
VALLEY   ○UN Plaza
Hayes St.   Grove St.   Harrison St.   King St.
Oak St.   Mission St.   Brannan St.   San Francisco
Page St.   Howard St.   ■ Caltrain sta.
Waller St.   8th St.   Berry St.
Haight St.   Duboce Ave.   Hermann St.   9th St.
Buena   10th St.   MISSION
Vista   11th St.   BAY
Park   Corona   12th St.   Market St.
Heights   101
Park   14th St.   16th St.
15th St.
CASTRO   16th St. ○   16th St.
Mission Dolores ■   Mission   POTRERO
17th St.   HILL
18th St.   MISSION
Dolores   19th St.   DISTRICT
Park   20th St.
Liberty St.
21st St.
22nd St.   101
Alvarado St.   23rd St.
Elizabeth St.   NOE VALLEY   24th St. ○   24th St.
Mission

NORTH BEACH

This Italian neighborhood, which stretches from Montgomery and Jackson streets to Bay Street, is one of the best places in the city to grab a coffee, pull up a cafe chair, and do some serious people-watching. Nightlife is equally happening in North Beach; restaurants, bars, and clubs along Columbus and Grant avenues attract folks from all over the Bay Area, who fight for a parking place and romp through the festive neighborhood. Down Columbus Avenue toward the Financial District are the remains of the city's Beat Generation landmarks, including Ferlinghetti's City Lights Booksellers and Vesuvio's Bar. Broadway Street—a short strip of sex joints—cuts through the heart of the district. **Telegraph Hill** looms over the east side of North Beach, topped by Coit Tower, one of San Francisco's best vantage points.

FISHERMAN'S WHARF

North Beach runs into Fisherman's Wharf, which was once the busy heart of the city's great harbor and waterfront industries. Today it's a popular tourist area with little, if any, authentic waterfront life, except for a small fleet of fishing boats and some noisy sea lions. What it does have going for it are activities for the whole family, with honky-tonk attractions and museums, restaurants, trinket shops, and beautiful views everywhere you look.

THE MARINA DISTRICT

Created on landfill—actually rubble from the 1906 earthquake—for the Panama Pacific Exposition of 1915, the Marina District boasts some of the best views of the Golden Gate, as well as plenty of grassy fields alongside San Francisco Bay. Elegant Mediterranean-style homes and apartments, inhabited by the city's well-to-do singles and wealthy families, line the streets. Here, too, are the Palace of Fine Arts, Fort Mason, and Crissy Field. The main street is Chestnut, between Franklin and Lyon streets, which abounds with shops, cafes, and boutiques. Because of its landfill foundation, the Marina was one of the hardest-hit districts in the 1989 quake.

COW HOLLOW

Located west of Van Ness Avenue, between Russian Hill and the Presidio, this flat, grazable area supported 30 dairy farms in 1861. Today, Cow Hollow is largely residential and largely yuppie. Its two primary commercial thoroughfares are Lombard Street, known for its many relatively inexpensive motels, and Union Street, an upscale shopping sector filled with restaurants, pubs, cafes, and boutiques.

PACIFIC HEIGHTS

The ultra-elite, such as the Gettys and Danielle Steel—and those lucky enough to buy before the real-estate boom—reside in the mansions and homes in this neighborhood. When the rich meander out of their fortresses, they wander down to Fillmore or Union Street and join the pretty people who frequent the chic boutiques and lively neighborhood restaurants, cafes, and bars.

JAPANTOWN

Bounded by Octavia, Fillmore, California, and Geary streets, Japantown shelters only a small percentage of the city's Japanese population, but exploring the Japanese knickknack shops and noodle restaurants inside the Japantown Center is a whole day's cultural experience. Duck inside one of the photo booths and take home a dozen Hello Kitty stickers as a souvenir.

CIVIC CENTER

Although millions of dollars have gone toward brick sidewalks, ornate lampposts, and elaborate street plantings, the southwestern section of Market Street can still feel a little sketchy due to the large number of homeless who wander the area. The Civic Center at the "bottom" of Market Street, however, is a stunning beacon of culture and refinement. This large complex of buildings includes the domed and dapper City Hall, the Opera House, Davies Symphony Hall, the new SFJAZZ building, and the Asian Art Museum. The landscaped plaza connecting the buildings is the staging area for San Francisco's frequent demonstrations for or against just about everything.

SOMA

No part of San Francisco has been more affected by recent development than the area south of Market Street (dubbed "SoMa"), the area within the triangle of the Embarcadero, Hwy. 101 and Market Street. Until a decade ago it was a district of old warehouses and industrial spaces, with a few scattered underground nightclubs, restaurants, and shoddy residential areas. But when it became the hub of dot.commercialization and half-million-dollar-plus lofts, its fate changed forever. Today, though dot.coms don't occupy much of the commercial space, the area is jumping thanks to fancy high-rise residences, AT&T Park (the Giants' baseball stadium), a bevy of new businesses, restaurants, and nightclubs, and cultural institutions that include the Museum of Modern Art, Yerba Buena Gardens, the Jewish and African Diaspora museums, and Metreon. Though still gritty in some areas, it's growing more glittery by the year, as big-bucks hotels and residence towers dominate over what's left of the industrial zone.

MISSION DISTRICT

This is another area that was greatly affected by the city's Internet gold rush. Mexican and Latin American populations make this area home, with their cuisine, traditions, and art creating a vibrant cultural area. Some parts of the neighborhood are still poor and sprinkled with the homeless, gangs, and drug addicts, but young urbanites have also settled here, attracted by its "reasonably" (a relative term) priced rentals and endless oh-so-hot restaurants and bars that stretch from 16th and Valencia streets to 25th and Mission streets. Less adventurous tourists may just want to duck into Mission Dolores (San Francisco's oldest building), cruise past a few of the 200-plus amazing murals, and head back downtown. But anyone who's interested in hanging with the hipsters and experiencing the hottest restaurant and bar nightlife should definitely beeline it here.

THE CASTRO

One of the liveliest districts in town, the Castro is practically synonymous with San Francisco's gay community, who moved here back in the 1970s, turning this once Irish working-class neighborhood into a bustling hotbed of shops, bars, and restaurants. Located at the top of Market Street, between 17th and 18th streets, the Castro offers a thoroughly entertaining dose of street theater, and while most businesses cater to the gay community, it's more than welcoming to open-minded straight people.

HAIGHT–ASHBURY

Part trendy, part nostalgic, part funky, the Haight, as it's most commonly known, was the soul of the psychedelic free-loving 1960s and the center of the counterculture movement. Today, the gritty neighborhood straddling upper Haight Street on the eastern border of Golden Gate Park is more gentrified, but the commercial area still harbors all walks of life. Leftover aging hippies mingle with grungy, begging street kids outside Ben & Jerry's Ice Cream Store (where they might still be talking about Jerry Garcia, or was that Cherry Garcia?), nondescript marijuana dealers whisper "Buds" as shoppers pass, and many people walking down the street have Day-Glo hair. But you don't need to wear tie-dye to enjoy the Haight—the ethnic food, trendy shops, and bars cover all tastes. From Haight Street, walk south on Cole Street for a more peaceful and quaint neighborhood experience.

RICHMOND & SUNSET DISTRICTS

San Francisco's suburbs of sorts, these are the city's largest and most populous neighborhoods, consisting mainly of small homes, shops, cafes, and neighborhood restaurants. Although they border Golden Gate Park and Ocean Beach, few tourists venture into "the Avenues," as these areas are referred to locally, unless they're on their way to the Cliff House, zoo, beach, or Palace of the Legion of Honor Museum.

SAN FRANCISCO IN CONTEXT

Unlike most American cities that have evolved in a more measured fashion, San Francisco has been molded politically, socially, and physically by a variety of (literally) earthshaking events. In this chapter, we give you a rundown on the history of the City by the Bay along with some other useful background on local views and customs.

SAN FRANCISCO TODAY

Shaken but not stirred by the Loma Prieta earthquake in 1989, San Francisco has witnessed a spectacular rebound in recent years. The seaside Embarcadero, once plagued by a horrendously ugly freeway overpass, was revitalized by a multimillion-dollar face-lift, complete with palm trees, a new trolley line, and wide cobblestone walkways. SoMa, the once industrial neighborhood south of Market Street, has exploded with new development, including the beautiful Yerba Buena arts district, the sleek lofts of Mission Bay, and a slew of hip new clubs and cafes. South Beach is the new darling of young professionals living the condo-in-the-city life, and the spectacular new California Academy of Sciences and de Young Museum have given even the locals two new reasons to visit Golden Gate Park.

All that glitters is not the Golden Gate, however. At the end of World War II, San Francisco was the largest and wealthiest city on the West Coast. Since then, it has been demoted to the fourth-largest city in California, home to only 815,000 people, less than 5% of the state's total. The industrial heart of the city has been knocked out and shipped off to less costly locations such as Oakland and Los Angeles, and increasingly, San Francisco has had to fall back on tourism as a major source of revenue. The Occupy SF movement, itself part of Occupy Wall Street, brought the city's economic struggles front and center in the fall of 2011, as hundreds camped out and protested in San Francisco, Oakland, and throughout the Bay Area. (The scene that went global—the image of Lt. John Pike pepperspraying peaceful protesters—happened at University of California, Davis.) A legitimate question we heard from the encampment in Justin Herman Plaza: *Why can't everyone who works in San Francisco afford housing in or near San Francisco?* Some worry we may someday become another Las Vegas, whose only raison d'être will be pleasing its visitors like one vast Fisherman's Wharf—a frightening premonition. Then, of course, there are the typical big-city problems: Crime is up along with drug use, and despite efforts to curb the ubiquitous problem of homelessness and panhandling, it's still a thorny issue.

But the spirit of San Francisco is still alive and well. Its convention halls are fully booked and, after a brief dip caused by the subprime housing debacle, the real estate market is heating up—seeing multiple offers on million dollar "starter" homes. The Giants are riding high after two World Series wins in 2010 and 2012. Since the U.S. Supreme Court struck down "Prop 8" in June 2013, Governor Jerry Brown has instructed all county clerks to issue same-sex marriage licenses. Dot.com companies seem to be staging a comeback, this time around with an actual plan to make money. As a further sign the recession is over, San Franciscans are finding ways to have fun—lining up for hot, new restaurants and nightspots, packing theaters and film festivals, and crowding into Apple Stores to get their hands on the latest iPhone. Though it may never relive its heady days as the king of the West Coast, San Francisco will undoubtedly retain the title as everyone's favorite California city.

LOOKING BACK AT SAN FRANCISCO

In the Beginning

Born as an out-of-the-way backwater of colonial Spain and blessed with a harbor that would have been the envy of any of the great cities of Europe, San Francisco boasts a story that is as varied as the millions of people who have passed through its Golden Gate.

The Age of Discovery   After the "discovery" of the New World by Columbus in 1492, legends of the fertile land of California were discussed in the universities and taverns of Europe, even though no one really understood where the mythical land was. (Some evidence of arrivals in California by Chinese merchants hundreds of years before Columbus's landing has been unearthed, although few scholars are willing to draw definite conclusions.) The first documented visit by a European to northern California, however, was by the Portuguese explorer João Cabrilho, who circumnavigated the southern tip of South America and traveled as far north as the Russian River in 1542. Nearly 40 years later, in 1579, Sir Francis Drake landed on the northern California coast, stopping for a time to repair his ships and to claim the territory for Queen Elizabeth I of England. He was followed several years later by another Portuguese, Sebastian Cermeño, "discoverer" of Punta de los Reyes (King's Point) in the mid-1590s. Ironically, all three adventurers completely missed the narrow entrance to San Francisco Bay, either because it was enshrouded in fog or, more likely, because they simply weren't looking for it. Believe it or not, the bay's entrance is nearly impossible to see from the open ocean. It would be another 2 centuries before a European actually saw the bay that would later extend Spain's influence over much of the American West. Gaspar de Portolá, a soldier sent from Spain to meddle in a rather ugly conflict between the Jesuits and the Franciscans, accidentally stumbled upon the bay in 1769, en route to somewhere else, but then stoically plodded on to his original destination, Monterey Bay, more than 100 miles to the south. Six years later, Juan Ayala, while on a mapping expedition for the Spanish, actually sailed into San Francisco Bay and immediately realized the enormous strategic importance of his find.

Colonization quickly followed. Juan Bautista de Anza and around 30 Spanish-speaking families marched through the deserts from Sonora, Mexico, arriving after many hardships at the northern tip of modern-day San Francisco in June 1776. They immediately claimed the peninsula for Spain. (Ironically, their claim of allegiance to Spain occurred only about a week before the 13 English-speaking colonies of North America's eastern seaboard, a continent away, declared their independence from Britain.) Their headquarters was an adobe fortress, the Presidio, built on the site of today's park with the same name. The settlers' church, built a mile to the south, was the first of five Spanish missions later developed around the edges of San Francisco Bay. Although the name of the church was officially Nuestra Señora de Dolores, it was dedicated to St. Francis of Assisi and nicknamed San Francisco by the Franciscan priests. Later, the name was applied to the entire bay.

In 1821, Mexico broke away from Spain, secularized the Spanish missions, and abandoned all interest in the Indian natives. Freed of Spanish restrictions, California's ports were suddenly opened to trade. The region around San Francisco Bay supplied large numbers of hides and tallow for transport around Cape Horn to the tanneries and factories of New England and New York. The prospects for prosperity persuaded an English-born sailor, William Richardson, to jump ship in 1822 and settle on the site of what is now San Francisco. To impress the commandant of the Presidio, whose daughter he loved, Richardson converted to Catholicism and established the beginnings of what would soon became a thriving trading post and colony. Richardson named his trading post Yerba Buena (or "good herb"), because of a species of wild mint that grew there, near the site of today's Montgomery Street. (The city's original name was recalled with endless mirth 120 years later during San Francisco's hippie era.) He conducted a profitable hide-trading business and eventually became harbormaster and the city's first merchant prince. By 1839, the place was a veritable town, with a mostly English-speaking populace and a saloon of dubious virtue.

Throughout the 19th century, armed hostilities between English-speaking settlers from the eastern seaboard and the Spanish-speaking colonies of Spain and Mexico erupted in places as widely scattered as Texas, Puerto Rico, and along the frequently shifting U.S.–Mexico border. In 1846, a group of U.S. Marines from the warship *Portsmouth* seized the sleepy main plaza of Yerba Buena, ran the U.S. flag up a pole, and declared California an American territory. The Presidio (occupied by about a

DATELINE

1542 Juan Cabrillo sails up the California coast.

1579 Sir Francis Drake lands near San Francisco, missing the entrance to the bay.

1769 Members of the Spanish expedition led by Gaspar de Portolá become the first Europeans to see San Francisco Bay.

1775 The *San Carlos* is the first European ship to sail into San Francisco Bay.

1776 Captain Juan Bautista de Anza establishes a presidio (military fort); San Francisco de Asís Mission opens.

1821 Mexico wins independence from Spain and annexes California.

1835 The town of Yerba Buena develops around the port; the United States tries unsuccessfully to purchase San Francisco Bay from Mexico.

1846 Mexican-American War.

1847 Americans annex Yerba Buena and rename it San Francisco.

1848 Gold is discovered in Coloma, near Sacramento.

dozen unmotivated Mexican soldiers) surrendered without a fuss. The first move the new, mostly Yankee citizenry made was to officially adopt the name of the bay as the name of their town.

The Gold Rush   The year 1848 was one of the most pivotal years in European history, with unrest sweeping through Europe and widespread disillusionment about the hopes for prosperity throughout the eastern coast of the United States. Stories about the golden port of San Francisco and the agrarian wealth of the American West filtered slowly east, attracting slow-moving groups of settlers. Ex-sailor Richard Henry Dana extolled the virtues of California in his best-selling novel *Two Years Before the Mast* and helped fire the public's imagination about the territory's bounty, particularly that of the Bay Area.

The first overland party crossed the Sierra and arrived in California in 1841. San Francisco grew steadily, reaching a population of approximately 900 by April 1848, but nothing hinted at the population explosion that was to follow. Historian Barry Parr has referred to the California gold rush as the most extraordinary event to ever befall an American city in peacetime. In time, San Francisco's winning combination of raw materials, healthful climate, and freedom would have attracted thousands of settlers even without the lure of gold. But the gleam of the soft metal is said to have compressed 50 years of normal growth into less than 6 months. In 1848, the year gold was first discovered, the population of San Francisco jumped from under 1,000 to 26,000 in less than 6 months. As many as 100,000 more passed through San Francisco in the space of less than a year on their way to the rocky hinterlands where the gold was rumored to be.

If not for the discovery of some small particles of gold at a sawmill that he owned, Swiss-born John Augustus Sutter's legacy would have been far less flamboyant. Despite Sutter's wish to keep the discovery quiet, his employee John Marshall leaked word of the discovery to friends. It eventually appeared in local papers, and smart investors on the East Coast took immediate heed. The rush did not start, however, until Sam Brannan, a Mormon preacher and famous charlatan, ran through the streets of San Francisco shouting, "Gold! Gold in the American River!" (Brannan, incidentally,

1849 In the year of the gold rush, San Francisco's population swells from about 800 to 25,000.

1851 Lawlessness becomes acute before attempts are made to curb it.

1869 The transcontinental railroad reaches San Francisco.

1873 Andrew S. Hallidie invents the cable car.

1906 The Great Earthquake strikes, and the resulting fire levels the city.

1915 The Panama Pacific International Exposition celebrates San Francisco's restoration and the completion of the Panama Canal.

1936 The Bay Bridge is built.

1937 The Golden Gate Bridge is completed.

1945 The United Nations Charter is drafted and adopted by the representatives of 50 countries meeting in San Francisco.

1950 The Beat Generation moves into the bars and cafes of North Beach.

1967 A free concert in Golden Gate Park attracts 20,000 people, ushering in the Summer of Love and the hippie era.

continues

bought up all the harborfront real estate he could get and cornered the market on shovels, pickaxes, and canned food, just before making the announcement that was heard around the world.)

A world on the brink of change responded almost frantically. The gold rush was on. Shop owners hung GONE TO THE DIGGINGS signs in their windows. Flotillas of ships set sail from ports throughout Europe, South America, Australia, and the East Coast, sometimes nearly sinking with the weight of mining equipment. Townspeople from the Midwest headed overland, and the social fabric of a nation was transformed almost overnight. Not since the Crusades of the Middle Ages had so many people been mobilized in so short a period of time. Daily business stopped; ships arrived in San Francisco and were almost immediately deserted by their crews. News of the gold strike spread like a plague through every discontented hamlet in the known world. Although other settlements were closer to the gold strike, San Francisco was the famous name, and therefore, where the gold-diggers disembarked. Tent cities sprung up, demand for virtually everything skyrocketed, and although some miners actually found gold, smart merchants quickly discovered that more enduring hopes lay in servicing the needs of the thousands of miners who arrived ill-equipped and ignorant of the lay of the land. Prices soared. Miners, faced with staggeringly inflated prices for goods and services, barely scraped a profit after expenses. Most prospectors failed, many died of hardship, others committed suicide at the alarming rate of 1,000 a year. Yet despite the tragedies, graft, and vice associated with the gold rush, within mere months San Francisco was forever transformed from a tranquil Spanish settlement into a roaring, boisterous boomtown.

Boomtown Fever   By 1855, most of California's surface gold had already been panned out, leaving only the richer but deeper veins of ore, which individual miners couldn't retrieve without massive capital investments. Despite that, San Francisco had evolved into a vast commercial magnet, sucking into its warehouses and banks the staggering riches that overworked newcomers had dragged, ripped, and distilled from the rocks, fields, and forests of western North America.

1974 BART's high-speed transit system opens the tunnel linking San Francisco with the East Bay.

1978 Harvey Milk, a city supervisor and America's first openly gay politician, is assassinated, along with Mayor George Moscone, by political rival Dan White.

1989 An earthquake registering 7.1 on the Richter scale hits San Francisco during a World Series baseball game, as 100 million watch on TV; the city quickly rebuilds.

1991 Fire rages through the Berkeley/Oakland hills, destroying 2,800 homes.

1993 Yerba Buena Center for the Arts opens.

1995 New San Francisco Museum of Modern Art opens.

1996 Former Assembly Speaker Willie Brown elected mayor of San Francisco.

2000 Pacific Bell Park (now AT&T Park), the new home to the San Francisco Giants, opens.

Investment funds were being lavished on more than mining, however. Speculation on the newly established San Francisco stock exchange could make or destroy an investor in a single day, and several noteworthy writers (including Mark Twain) were among the young men forever influenced by the boomtown spirit. The American Civil War left California firmly in the Union camp, ready, willing, and able to receive hordes of disillusioned soldiers fed up with the internecine war-mongering of the eastern seaboard. In 1869, the transcontinental railway linked the eastern and western sea-boards of the United States, ensuring the fortunes of the barons who controlled it. The railways, however, also shifted economic power bases as cheap manufactured goods from the east undercut the high prices hitherto charged for goods that sailed or steamed their way around the tip of South America. Ownership of the newly formed Central Pacific and Southern Pacific railroads was almost completely controlled by the "Big Four," all iron-willed capitalists—Leland Stanford, Mark Hopkins, Collis P. Hunting-ton, and Charles Crocker—whose ruthlessness was legendary. (Much of the bone-crushing labor for their railway was executed by low-paid Chinese newcomers, most of whom arrived in overcrowded ships at San Francisco ports.) As the 19th century came to a close, civil unrest became more frequent as the monopolistic grip of the railways and robber barons became more obvious. Adding to the discontent were the uncounted thousands of Chinese immigrants, who fled starvation and unrest in Asia at rates rivaling those of the Italians, Poles, Irish, and British.

During the 1870s, the flood of profits from the Comstock Lode in western Nevada diminished to a trickle, a cycle of droughts wiped out part of California's agricultural bounty, and local industry struggled to survive against the flood of manufactured goods imported via railway from the well-established factories of the East Coast and Midwest. Often, discontented workers blamed their woes on the now-unwanted hordes of Chinese workers, who by preference and for mutual protection had congregated into teeming all-Asian communities.

Despite these downward cycles, the city enjoyed other bouts of prosperity around the turn of the 20th century, thanks to the Klondike gold rush in Alaska and the Spanish-American War. Long accustomed to making a buck off gold fever, San

2002 The San Francisco Giants make it to the World Series but lose to the Anaheim Angels in Game 7.

2004 Thirty-six-year-old supervisor Gavin Newsom becomes the city's 42nd mayor and quickly makes headlines by authorizing City Hall to issue marriage licenses to same-sex couples. Six months later, the state supreme court invalidates 3,955 gay marriages.

2005 The new, seismically correct $202-million de Young Museum opens in Golden Gate Park.

2006 The 100-year anniversary of the Great Earthquake and fire of 1906 is commemorated, the greatest disaster ever to befall an American metropolis.

2007 A tiger escapes from its pen at the San Francisco Zoo, killing one man and injuring two others before the police shoot and kill it.

2008 The California Supreme Court overturns the ban on same-sex marriage, touching off short-lived celebrations at San Francisco City Hall. The ban is reinstated in an election later that year, added to the ballot as "Proposition 8."

continues

Francisco managed to position itself as a point of embarkation for supplies bound for Alaska. Also during this time emerged the Bank of America, which eventually evolved into the largest bank in the world. Founded in North Beach in 1904, Bank of America was the brainchild of Italian-born A. P. Giannini, who later funded part of the construction for a bridge that many critics said was preposterous: the Golden Gate.

The Great Fire   On the morning of April 18, 1906, San Francisco changed for all time. The city has never experienced an earthquake as destructive as the one that hit at 5:13am. (Scientists estimate its strength at 8.1 on the Richter scale.) All but a handful of the city's 400,000 inhabitants lay fast asleep when the ground beneath the city went into a series of convulsions. As one eyewitness put it, "The earth was shaking . . . it was undulating, rolling like an ocean breaker." The quake ruptured every water main in the city, and simultaneously started a chain of fires that rapidly fused into one gigantic conflagration. The fire brigades were helpless, and for 3 days, San Francisco burned.

Militia troops finally stopped the flames from advancing by dynamiting entire city blocks, but not before more than 28,000 buildings lay in ruins. Minor tremors lasted another 3 days. The final damage stretched across a path of destruction 450 miles long and 50 miles wide. In all, 497 city blocks were razed, or about one-third of the city. As Jack London wrote in a heart-rending newspaper dispatch, "The city of San Francisco is no more." The earthquake and subsequent fire so decisively changed the city that post-1906 San Francisco bears little resemblance to the town before the quake. Out of the ashes rose a bigger, healthier, and more beautiful town, though latter-day urbanologists regret that the rebuilding that followed the San Francisco earthquake did not follow a more enlightened plan. So eager was the city to rebuild that the old, somewhat unimaginative gridiron plan was reinstated, despite the opportunities for more daring visions that the aftermath of the quake afforded.

In 1915, in celebration of the opening of the Panama Canal and to prove to the world that San Francisco was restored to its full glory, the city hosted the Panama Pacific International Exhibition, a world's fair that exposed hundreds of thousands of visitors to the city's unique charms. The general frenzy of civic boosterism, however, reached

2009   The economic downturn has San Francisco in a financial tailspin, but amazingly, tourism dollars keep pouring in. After a dismal start, hotel occupancies resurge. Small businesses continue to struggle, however, battling high rents and a cash-strapped public.

2010   The San Francisco Giants baseball team wins the World Series against the Texas Rangers; thousands of fans fill Civic Center Plaza for the parade and celebration.

2011   Ed Lee is elected San Francisco's 43rd mayor.

2012   The San Francisco Giants beat the Detroit Tigers to win the World Series, again.

2013   California Governor, Jerry Brown, instructs county clerks to begin issuing same-sex marriage licenses after the U.S. Supreme Court strikes down "Prop 8."

its peak during the years just before World War I, when investments and civic pride might have reached an all-time high. Despite Prohibition, speakeasies did a thriving business in and around the city, and building sprees were as high-blown and lavish as the profits on the San Francisco stock exchange.

World War II The Japanese attack on Pearl Harbor on December 7, 1941, mobilized the United States into a massive war machine, with many shipyards strategically positioned along the Pacific Coast, including San Francisco. Within less than a year, several shipyards were producing up to one new warship per day, employing hundreds of thousands of people working in 24-hour shifts. (The largest, Kaiser Shipyards in Richmond, employed more than 100,000 workers alone.) In search of work and the excitement of life away from their villages and cornfields, workers flooded into the city from virtually everywhere, forcing an enormous boom in housing. Hundreds found themselves separated from their small towns for the first time in their lives and reveled in their newfound freedom.

After the hostilities ended, many soldiers remembered San Francisco as the site of their finest hours and returned to live there permanently. The economic prosperity of the postwar years enabled massive enlargements of the city, including freeways, housing developments, a booming financial district, and pockets of counterculture enthusiasts such as the beatniks, gays, and hippies.

The 1950s: The Beats San Francisco's reputation as a rollicking place where anything goes dates from the Barbary Coast days when gang warfare, prostitution, gambling, and drinking were major city pursuits, and citizens took law and order into their own hands. Its more modern role as a catalyst for social change and the avant-garde began in the 1950s when a group of young writers, philosophers, and poets challenged the materialism and conformity of American society by embracing anarchy and Eastern philosophy, expressing their notions in poetry. They adopted a uniform of jeans, sweaters, sandals, and berets, called themselves Beats, and hung out in North Beach where rents were low and cheap wine was plentiful. *San Francisco Chronicle* columnist Herb Caen, to whom they were totally alien, dubbed them *beatniks* in his column.

Allen Ginsberg, Gregory Corso, and Jack Kerouac had begun writing at Columbia University in New York, but it wasn't until they came west and hooked up with Lawrence Ferlinghetti, Kenneth Rexroth, Gary Snyder, and others that the movement gained national attention. The bible of the Beats was Ginsberg's "Howl," which he first read at the Six Gallery on October 13, 1955. By the time he finished reading, Ginsberg was crying, the audience was chanting, and his fellow poets were announcing the arrival of an epic bard. Ferlinghetti published *Howl*, which was deemed obscene, in 1956. A trial followed, but the court found that the book had redeeming social value, thereby reaffirming the right of free expression. The other major work, Jack Kerouac's *On the Road,* was published in 1957, instantly becoming a bestseller. (He had written it as one long paragraph in 20 days in 1951.) The freedom and sense of possibility that this book conveyed became the bellwether for a generation.

While the Beats gave poetry readings and generated controversy, two clubs in North Beach were making waves, notably the hungry i and the Purple Onion, where everyone who was anyone or became anyone on the entertainment scene appeared—Mort Sahl, Dick Gregory, Lenny Bruce, Barbra Streisand, and Woody Allen all worked here. Maya Angelou appeared as a singer and dancer at the Purple Onion. The cafes of North Beach were the center of bohemian life in the '50s: the Black Cat, Vesuvio, Caffe

Trieste and Tosca Cafe, and Enrico's Sidewalk Café. When the tour buses started rolling in, rents went up, and Broadway turned into strip club row in the early 1960s. Thus ended an era, and the Beats moved on. The alternative scene shifted to Berkeley and the Haight.

The 1960s: The Haight   The torch of freedom had been passed from the Beats and North Beach to Haight-Ashbury and the hippies, but it was a radically different torch. The hippies replaced the Beats' angst, anarchy, negativism, nihilism, alcohol, and poetry with love, communalism, openness, drugs, rock music, and a back-to-nature philosophy. Although the scent of marijuana wafted everywhere—on the streets, in the cafes, in Golden Gate Park—the real drugs of choice were LSD (a tab of good acid cost $5) and other hallucinogens. Timothy Leary experimented with its effects and exhorted youth to turn on, tune in, and drop out. Instead of hanging out in coffeehouses, the hippies went to concerts at the Fillmore or the Avalon Ballroom to dance. The first Family Dog Rock 'n' Roll Dance and Concert, "A Tribute to Dr. Strange," was given at the Longshoreman's Hall in fall 1965, featuring Jefferson Airplane, the Marbles, the Great Society, and the Charlatans. At this event, the first major happening of the 1960s, Ginsberg led a snake dance through the crowd. In January 1966, the 3-day Trips Festival, organized by rock promoter Bill Graham, was also held at the Longshoreman's Hall. The climax came with Ken Kesey and the Merry Pranksters Acid Test show, which used five movie screens, psychedelic visions, and the sounds of the Grateful Dead and Big Brother and the Holding Company. The "be-in" followed in the summer of 1966 at the polo grounds in Golden Gate Park, when an estimated 20,000 heard Jefferson Airplane perform and Ginsberg chant, while the Hell's Angels acted as unofficial police. It was followed by the Summer of Love in 1967 as thousands of young people streamed into the city in search of drugs and free love.

The '60s Haight scene was very different from the '50s Beat scene. The hippies were much younger than the Beats had been, constituting the first youth movement to take over the nation. Ironically, they also became the first generation of young, independent, and moneyed consumers to be courted by corporations. Ultimately, the Haight and the hippie movement deteriorated from love and flowers into drugs and crime, drawing a fringe of crazies like Charles Manson and leaving only a legacy of sex, drugs, violence, and consumerism. As early as October 1967, the "Diggers," who had opened a free shop and soup kitchen in the Haight, symbolically buried the dream in a clay casket in Buena Vista Park.

The end of the Vietnam War and the resignation of President Nixon took the edge off politics. The last fling of the mentality that had driven the 1960s occurred in 1974 when Patty Hearst was kidnapped from her Berkeley apartment by the Symbionese Liberation Army and participated in their bank-robbing spree before surrendering in San Francisco in 1975.

The 1970s: Gay Rights   The homosexual community in San Francisco was essentially founded at the end of World War II, when thousands of military personnel were discharged back to the United States via San Francisco. A substantial number of those men were homosexual and decided to stay on in San Francisco. A gay community grew up along Polk Street between Sutter and California streets. Later, the larger community moved into the Castro, where it remains today.

The modern-day gay political movement is usually traced to the 1969 Stonewall raid and riots in Greenwich Village. Although the political movement started in New York,

California had already given birth to two major organizations for gay rights: the Mattachine Society, founded in 1951 by Henry Hay in Los Angeles, and the Daughters of Bilitis, a lesbian organization founded in 1955 in San Francisco.

After Stonewall, the Committee for Homosexual Freedom was created in spring 1969 in San Francisco; a Gay Liberation Front chapter was organized at Berkeley. In fall 1969, Robert Patterson, a columnist for the *San Francisco Examiner,* referred to homosexuals as "semi males, drag darlings," and "women who aren't exactly women." On October 31 at noon, a group began a peaceful picket of the *Examiner.* Peace reigned until someone threw a bag of printer's ink from an *Examiner* window. Someone wrote "F--- the Examiner" on the wall, and the police moved in to clear the crowd, clubbing them as they went. The remaining pickets retreated to Glide Methodist Church and then marched on City Hall. Unfortunately, the mayor was away. Unable to air their grievances, they started a sit-in that lasted until 5pm, when they were ordered to leave. Most did, but three remained and were arrested.

Later that year, an anti-Thanksgiving rally was staged at which gays protested against several national and local businesses: Western and Delta airlines, the former for firing lesbian flight attendants, the latter for refusing to sell a ticket to a young man wearing a Gay Power button; KFOG, for its anti-homosexual broadcasting; and also some local gay bars for exploitation. On May 14, 1970, a group of gay and women's liberationists invaded the convention of the American Psychiatric Association in San Francisco to protest the reading of a paper on aversion therapy for homosexuals, forcing the meeting to adjourn.

The rage against intolerance was appearing on all fronts. At the National Gay Liberation conference held in August 1970 in the city, Charles Thorp, chairman of the San Francisco State Liberation Front, called for militancy and issued a challenge to come out with a rallying cry of "Blatant is beautiful." He also argued for the use of what he felt was the more positive, celebratory term *gay* instead of *homosexual,* and decried the fact that homosexuals were kept in their place at the three B's: the bars, the beaches, and the baths. As the movement grew in size and power, debates on strategy and tactics occurred, most dramatically between those who wanted to withdraw into separate ghettos and those who wanted to enter mainstream society. The most extreme proposal was made in California by Don Jackson, who proposed establishing a gay territory in California's Alpine County, about 10 miles south of Lake Tahoe. It would have had a totally gay administration, civil service, university, museum—everything. The residents of Alpine County were not pleased with the proposal. But before the situation turned really ugly, Jackson's idea was abandoned because of lack of support in the gay community. In the end, the movement would concentrate on integration and civil rights, not separatism. They would elect politicians who were sympathetic to their cause and celebrate their new identity by establishing National Gay Celebration Day and Gay Pride Week, the first of which was celebrated in June 1970 when 1,000 to 2,000 marched in New York, 1,000 in Los Angeles, and a few hundred in San Francisco.

By the mid-1970s, the gay community craved a more central role in San Francisco politics. Harvey Milk, owner of a camera store in the Castro, decided to run as an openly gay man for the board of supervisors. He won, becoming the first openly gay person to hold a major public office. He and liberal mayor George Moscone developed a gay rights agenda, but in 1978 both were killed by former supervisor Dan White, who shot them after Moscone refused White's request for reinstatement. White, a Catholic and former police officer, had consistently opposed Milk's and Moscone's more liberal policies. At his trial, White successfully pleaded temporary insanity caused by additives in his fast-food diet. The media dubbed it the "Twinkie defense," but it worked, and the murder charges against White were reduced to manslaughter. That day, angry and grieving, the gay community rioted, overturning and burning police cars in a night of rage. To this day, a candlelight memorial parade is held each year on the anniversary of Milk's death, and Milk's martyrdom remains both a political and a practical inspiration to gay candidates across the country.

The emphasis in the gay movement shifted abruptly in the 1980s when the AIDS epidemic struck the gay community. AIDS has had a dramatic impact on the Castro. While it's still a thriving and lively community, it's no longer the constant party that it once was. The hedonistic lifestyle that had played out in the discos, bars, baths, and streets changed as the seriousness of the epidemic sunk in and the number of deaths increased. Political efforts shifted away from enfranchisement and toward demanding money for social services. The gay community has developed its own organizations, such as Project Inform and Gay Men's Health Crisis, to publicize information about AIDS, treatments available, and safe sex. Though new cases of AIDS within the gay community are on the decline in San Francisco, it still remains a serious problem.

The 1980s: The Big One, Part Two   The '80s may have arrived in San Francisco with a whimper (compared to previous generations), but they went out with quite a bang. At 5:04pm on Tuesday, October 17, 1989, as more than 62,000 fans filled Candlestick Park for the third game of the World Series—and the San Francisco Bay Area commute moved into its heaviest flow—an earthquake of magnitude 7.1 struck. Within the next 20 seconds, 63 lives would be lost, $10 billion in damage would occur, and the entire Bay Area community would be reminded of its humble insignificance. Centered about 60 miles south of San Francisco within the Forest of Nisene Marks, the deadly temblor was felt as far away as San Diego and Nevada.

Though scientists had predicted an earthquake would hit on this section of the San Andreas Fault, certain structures that were built to withstand such an earthquake failed miserably. The most catastrophic event was the collapse of the elevated Cypress Street section of I-880 in Oakland, where the upper level of the freeway literally pancaked the lower level, crushing everything. Other structures heavily damaged included the San Francisco–Oakland Bay Bridge, shut down for months when a section of the roadbed collapsed; San Francisco's Marina district, where several multimillion-dollar homes collapsed on their weak, shifting bases of landfill and sand; and the Pacific Garden Mall in Santa Cruz, which was completely devastated.

President George H. W. Bush declared a disaster area for the seven hardest-hit counties, where 63 people died, at least 3,700 people were reported injured, and more than 12,000 were displaced. More than 18,000 homes were damaged and 963 others destroyed. Although fire raged within the city and water supply systems were damaged, the major fires sparked within the Marina district were brought under control within 3 hours, due mostly to the heroic efforts of San Francisco's firefighters.

After the rubble had finally settled, it was unanimously agreed that San Francisco and the Bay Area had pulled through miraculously well—particularly when compared to the more recent earthquake in northeast Japan, which killed thousands. After the San Francisco quake, a feeling of esprit de corps swept the city as neighbors helped each other rebuild and donations poured in from all over the world. Though it's been over 2 decades since, the city is still feeling the effects of the quake. That another "big one" will strike is inevitable: It's the price you pay for living on a fault line. But if there is ever a city that is prepared for a major shakedown, it's San Francisco.

The 1990s: The Dot.com Bubble During the 1990s, the nationwide recession influenced the beginning of the decade, while the quiet rumblings of the new frontier in Silicon Valley escaped much notice. By the middle of the decade, San Francisco and the surrounding areas were the site of a new kind of gold rush—the birth of the Internet industry.

Not unlike the gold fever of the 1800s, people flocked to the western shores to strike it rich—and they did. In 1999, the local media reported that each day 64 Bay Area residents were gaining millionaire status. Long before the last year of the millennium, real estate prices went into the stratosphere, and the city's gentrification financially squeezed out many of those residents who didn't mean big business (read: alternative and artistic types, seniors, and minorities who made the city colorful). New businesses popped up everywhere—especially in SoMa, where start-up companies jammed warehouse spaces.

As the most popular post-education destination for MBAs and the leader in the media of the future, San Francisco no longer opened its Golden Gate to everyone looking for the legendary alternative lifestyle—unless he or she could afford a $1,000 studio apartment and $20-per-day fees to park the car.

The new millennium was christened with bubbly in hand, foie gras and caviar on the linen tablecloth, and seemingly everyone in the money. New restaurants charging $35 per entree were all the rage, hotels were renovated, the new bayfront ballpark was packed, and stock market tips were as plentiful as million-dollar SoMa condos and lofts. Though there were whispers of a stock market correction, and inklings that venture capital might dry up, San Franciscans were too busy raking in the dough to heed the writing on the wall.

The Millennium When the city woke up from the dot.com party, San Franciscans found themselves suffering from a major new millennium hangover. In the early 2000s, dot.coms became "dot.bombs" faster than you could say "worthless stock options," with companies shuttering at a rate of several per day. The crash of the Internet economy brought with it a real estate exodus, and scads of empty live-work lofts sprouted up in SoMa. But from the ashes of the collapse grew the seeds of innovation, and by mid-decade, San Francisco was back on the cutting edge with a little search engine called Google. Wikipedia, YouTube, and new skyscrapers followed, holding steady even as Wall Street and big banks fell around their feet in 2008. It's an undeniable testament to the resilience and mettle of San Franciscans, who always seem to have an ace in the hole, even when things seem at their worst.

San Francisco in Popular Culture: Books, Films & Music

Getting acquainted with San Francisco through the work of authors and filmmakers will provide an extra dimension to your trip and perhaps some added excitement when you happen upon a location you recognize from a favorite cinematic moment or literary passage. San Francisco's own Chronicle Books publishes a great variety of material on the city, for children, cooks, art and architecture students, and readers of memoirs and fiction. One of Chronicle's best books to stimulate your interest and curiosity is *San Francisco Stories: Great Writers on the City,* edited by John Miller. This collection of short pieces covers the personal and the political as recalled by acclaimed authors including Mark Twain, Jack Kerouac, Tom Wolfe, and Amy Tan. To find out about a smaller, more intimate city, check out *Good Life in Hard Times: San Francisco in the '20s and '30s,* by former journalist and San Francisco native Jerry Flamm (published by Chronicle Books).

One of the more famous and beloved pieces of modern fiction based in San Francisco is Armistead Maupin's *Tales of the City* (published by Perennial). If you've seen the miniseries, and especially if you haven't, this is a "must read" for a leisurely afternoon—or bring it with you on the plane. Maupin's 1970s soap opera covers the residents of 28 Barbary Lane (Macondry Lane on Russian Hill was the inspiration), melding sex, drugs, and growing self-awareness with enormous warmth and humor.

A work of fiction featuring San Francisco during the gold rush is *Daughter of Fortune,* by acclaimed novelist and Marin County resident Isabel Allende (published by HarperTorch). Allende's depiction of life in California during the mid–19th century is vividly described and is one of the novel's strengths.

As one of the loveliest spots on the planet, San Francisco has been a favorite of location scouts since the beginning of the film industry. Hundreds of movies and television shows have been shot or placed in San Francisco, making the hills and bridges among the most recognized of backgrounds. It may be difficult to locate at your local video store, but the 1936 Clark Gable/Jeanette MacDonald romance, *San Francisco,* is lauded for its dramatic reenactment of the 1906 earthquake and for MacDonald's rendition of the song of the same name. *The Maltese Falcon* (1941), Dashiell Hammett's classic detective story, with Humphrey Bogart starring as Sam Spade, includes shots of the Bay Bridge, the Ferry Building, and Burritt Alley (above the Stockton Tunnel). John's Grill, mentioned in the novel, continues to flog its association with Hammett's hero from its location at 63 Ellis Street (btw. Stockton and Powell sts.).

Alfred Hitchcock's *Vertigo* (1958), starring James Stewart and Kim Novak, is admittedly an obvious choice on the list of great San Francisco films, but it's always worth viewing. Stewart plays a former detective hired to tail the wife of an old college friend, but the woman's identity is less than clear-cut. In the meantime, Stewart becomes obsessed with his prey as they make their way around the Palace of the Legion of Honor, Fort Point, Mission Dolores, and the detective's apartment at 900 Lombard Street. The city also fared well in the 1968 thriller *Bullitt,* starring a young Steve McQueen. Along with the hair-raising car chase over many hills, you'll see the Bay Bridge from a recognizable point on the Embarcadero, Mason Street heading north next to the Fairmont Hotel, the front of the Mark Hopkins Hotel, Grace Cathedral, and the fairly unchanged Enrico's Sidewalk Café.

For a change of pace and no tragic law-enforcement characters, screen the romantic comedy *What's Up, Doc?* (1972) with Barbra Streisand and Ryan O'Neal. Along with being very funny, it's got one of cinema's all-time classic car chase scenes, with shots of Lombard Street, Chinatown, and Alta Plaza Park in Pacific Heights. If you have kids to rev up, the 1993 comedy *Mrs. Doubtfire,* starring Sally Field and the city's favorite son, Robin Williams, shows San Francisco under blue skies and cable cars with plenty of room. The house where the character's estranged wife and children live is located in Pacific Heights at 2640 Steiner Street (at Broadway St.), in case you care to gawk.

Finally, *24 Hours on Craigslist* is a documentary that covers a day in the life of the Internet community bulletin-board phenom. The filmmaker posted an ad on Craigslist, followed up with a handful of volunteers—an Ethel Merman impersonator seeking a Led Zeppelin cover band; a couple looking for others to join a support group for diabetic cats; a single, older woman needing a sperm donor—and sent film crews to cover their stories. Unlike other films that show the physical splendors of San Francisco, *24 Hours on Craigslist* will give you a sense of the city's psyche, or at least offer an explanation of why non–San Franciscans think the place is populated with . . . um . . . unusual types.

Sounds of the '60s

During its heyday in the 1950s and 1960s, San Francisco was the place to be for anyone who eschewed the conventional American lifestyle. From moody beatniks to political firebrands, the city was a vortex for poets, writers, actors, and a bewildering assortment of free thinkers and activists. Drawn by the city's already liberal views on life, liberty, and the pursuit of happiness, thousands of the country's youth—including some of America's most talented musicians—headed west to join the party. What culminated in the 1960s was San Francisco's hat trick of rock legends: It was able to lay claim to three of the rock era's most influential bands—the Grateful Dead, Big Brother and the Holding Company and Janis Joplin, and Jefferson Airplane.

The Grateful Dead   Easily the most influential band to be spawned from the psychedelic movement of the 1960s, the Grateful Dead was San Francisco's own music guru. Described as the "house band for the famous acid tests that transformed the City by the Bay into one endless freak-out," the Dead's music was played simultaneously on so many stereo systems (and at such high volumes) that the group almost seemed to have set the tone for one enormous, citywide jam session.

Though the group disbanded in 1995 after the death of its charismatic lead vocalist, Jerry Garcia, the group's devoted fans had already elevated the Grateful Dead to cult empire status. Tie-dyed "Deadheads" (many of whom followed the band on tour for decades) can still be found tripping within the Haight, reminiscing about the good old days when the group never traveled with a sound system weighing less than 23 tons. In fact, more than any other band produced during the 1960s, the Grateful Dead were best appreciated during live concerts, partly because of the love-in mood that frequently percolated through the acidic audiences. Many rock critics remember with nostalgia that the band's most cerebral and psychedelic music was produced in the 1960s in San Francisco, but in the 1980s and 1990s, permutations of their themes were marketed in repetitive, less threatening forms that delighted their aficionados and often baffled or bored virtually everyone else.

For better or for worse, the Grateful Dead was a musical benchmark, expressing in new ways the mood of San Francisco during one of its drug-infused and most creatively fertile periods. But the days of the Dancing Bear and peanut butter sandwiches will never be quite over: Working from a proven formula, thousands of bands around the world continue to propagate the Dead's rhythmical standards, and several of the band's original members still tour in various incarnations.

But reading about the Grateful Dead is like dancing to architecture: If you're looking for an album whose title best expresses the changing artistic premises of San Francisco and the ironies of the pop culture that developed here, look for its award-winning retrospective *What a Long Strange Trip It's Been* at any of the city's record stores.

Big Brother and the Holding Company and Janis Joplin   The wide-open moral and musical landscape of San Francisco was almost unnervingly fertile during the 1960s. Despite competition from endless numbers of less talented singers, Texas-born Janis Joplin formulated much of her vocal technique before audiences in San Francisco. Her breakthrough style was first acknowledged at the Monterey Jazz

Festival in 1967. Audiences reached out to embrace a singer whose rasping, gravely, shrieking voice expressed the generational angst of thousands of onlookers. *Billboard* magazine characterized her sound as composed of equal portions of honey, Southern Comfort, and gall. She was backed up during her earliest years by Big Brother and the Holding Company, a group she eventually outgrew.

Warned by specialists that her vocal technique would ruin her larynx before she was 30, Janis wailed, gasped, growled, and staggered over a blues repertoire judged as the most raw and vivid ever performed. Promoters frantically struggled to market (and protect) Janis and her voice for future artistic endeavors but, alas, her talent was simply too huge for her to handle, the time and place too destructive for her raw-edged psyche. Her style is best described as "the desperate blues," partly because it never attained the emotional nonchalance of such other blues singers as Bessie Smith or Billie Holiday.

Parts of Janis's life were the subject of such lurid books as *Going Down with Janis,* and stories of her substance abuse, sexual escapades, and general raunchiness litter the emotional landscape of modern-day San Francisco. The star died of a heroin overdose at the age of 27, a tragedy still mourned by her thousands of fans, who continue to refer to her by her nickname, "Pearl." Contemporary photographs taken shortly before her death show a ravaged body and a face partially concealed behind aviator's goggles, long hair, and a tough but brittle facade. Described as omnisexual—and completely comfortable with both male and female partners—she once (unexpectedly) announced to a group of nightclub guests her evaluation of the sexual performance of two of the era's most visible male icons: Joe Namath (not particularly memorable) and Dick Cavett (absolutely fantastic). The audience (like audiences in concert halls around California) drank in the anecdotes that followed as "Gospel According to Janis."

Jefferson Airplane   In the San Francisco suburbs of the late 1960s, hundreds of suburban bands dreamed of attaining stardom. Of the few that succeeded, none expressed the love-in ethic of that time in San Francisco better than the soaring vocals and ferocious guitar-playing of Jefferson Airplane. Singers Grace Slick and Marty Balin—as well as bass guitar player Jack Casady—were considered at the top of their profession by their peers and highly melodic even by orchestral standards. Most importantly, all members of the band, especially Paul Kantner and Jorma Kaukonen, were songwriters. Their fertile mix of musical styles and creative energies led to songs that still reverberate in the minds of anyone who owned an AM radio during the late 1960s. The intense and lonely songs such as "Somebody to Love" and "White Rabbit" became the musical anthems of at least one summer, as American youth emerged into a highly psychedelic kind of consciousness within the creatively catalytic setting of San Francisco.

Although in 1989 the group reassembled its scattered members for a swan song as Jefferson Starship, the output was considered a banal repetition of earlier themes, and the energy of those long-faded summers of San Francisco in the late 1960s was never recovered. But despite its decline in its later years, Jefferson Airplane is still considered a band inextricably linked to the Bay Area's historic and epoch-changing Summer of Love.

WHEN TO GO

If you're dreaming of convertibles, Frisbee on the beach, and tank-topped evenings, change your reservations and head to Los Angeles. Contrary to California's sunshine-and-bikini image, San Francisco's weather is "mild" (to put it nicely) and can often be downright bone-chilling because of the wet, foggy air, and cool winds—it's really nothing like Southern California. **Summer,** the most popular time to visit, is often the coldest time of year, with damp, foggy days; cold, windy nights; and crowded tourist destinations. A good bet is to visit in spring or, better yet, autumn. Just about every **September,** right about the time San Franciscans mourn being cheated (or fogged) out of another summer, something wonderful happens: The thermometer rises, the skies clear, and the locals call in sick to work and head for the beach. It's what residents call "Indian summer." The city is also delightful during **winter,** when the opera and ballet seasons are in full swing; there are fewer tourists, many hotel prices are lower, and downtown bustles with holiday cheer.

Travel Attire

Even if it's sunny out, don't forget to bring a jacket and dress in layers; the weather can change almost instantly from sunny and warm to windy and cold—especially as you move between microclimates.

San Francisco's temperate, marine climate usually means relatively mild weather year-round. In summer, chilling fog rolls in most mornings and evenings, and if temperatures top 70°F (21°C), the city is ready to throw a celebration. Even when autumn's heat occasionally stretches into the 80s (upper 20s Celsius) and 90s (lower 30s Celsius), you should still dress in layers, or by early evening you'll learn firsthand why sweatshirt sales are a great business at Fisherman's Wharf. In winter, the mercury seldom falls below freezing and snow is almost unheard of, but that doesn't mean you won't be whimpering if you forget your coat. Still, compared to most of the state's weather conditions, San Francisco's are consistently pleasant, and even if it's damp and chilly, head north, east, or south 15 minutes and you can usually find sun again.

The coastal fog is caused by a rare combination of water, wind, and topography. The fog lies off the coast, and rising air currents pull it in when the land heats up. Held back by coastal mountains along a 600-mile front, the low clouds seek out any passage they can find. The easiest access is the slot where the Pacific Ocean penetrates the continental wall—the Golden Gate.

San Francisco's Average Temperatures (°F/°C)

	JAN	FEB	MAR	APR	MAY	JUNE	JULY	AUG	SEPT	OCT	NOV	DEC
Avg. High	56/13	59/15	61/16	64/18	67/19	70/21	71/22	72/22	73/23	70/21	62/17	56/13
Avg. Low	43/6	46/8	47/8	48/9	51/11	53/12	55/13	56/13	55/13	52/11	48/9	43/6

Holidays

Banks, government offices, post offices, and many stores, restaurants, and museums are closed on the following legal national holidays: January 1 (New Year's Day), the third Monday in January (Martin Luther King, Jr., Day), the third Monday in February (Presidents' Day), the last Monday in May (Memorial Day), July 4 (Independence Day), the first Monday in September (Labor Day), the second Monday in October (Columbus Day), November 11 (Veterans Day/Armistice Day), the fourth Thursday in November (Thanksgiving Day), and December 25 (Christmas). The Tuesday after the first Monday in November is Election Day, a federal government holiday in presidential-election years (held every 4 years).

San Francisco–Area Calendar of Events

For more information on San Francisco events, visit **www.onlyinsanfrancisco.com** for an annual calendar of local events, as well as **http://events.frommers.com**, where you'll find a searchable, up-to-the-minute roster of what's happening in cities all over the world.

FEBRUARY

Chinese New Year, Chinatown. Public celebrations spill onto every street in Chinatown, beginning with the "Miss Chinatown USA" pageant parade, and climaxing a week later with a celebratory parade of marching bands, rolling floats, barrages of fireworks, and a block-long dragon writhing in and out of the crowds. The action starts at Market and Second streets and ends at Kearny Street. Arrive early for a good viewing spot on Kearny Street. You can purchase bleacher seats online starting in December. Make your hotel reservations early. For dates and information, call *€* **415/340-3055** or visit www.chineseparade.com.

MARCH

St. Patrick's Day Parade, Union Square, and Civic Center. Everyone's an honorary Irish person at this festive affair, which starts at 11:30am at Market and Second streets and continues to City Hall. But the party doesn't stop there. Head down to the Civic Center for the post-party, or venture to the Embarcadero's Harrington's Bar & Grill (245 Front St.) and celebrate with hundreds of the Irish-for-a-day yuppies as they gallivant around the closed-off streets and numerous pubs. Sunday before March 17. For more information, visit **www.saintpatricksdaysf. com**.

APRIL

Cherry Blossom Festival, Japantown. Meander through the arts-and-crafts and food booths lining the blocked-off streets around Japan Center and watch traditional drumming, flower arranging, origami making, and a parade celebrating the cherry blossoms and Japanese culture. Call *€* **415/563-2313** for information. Mid- to late April.

San Francisco International Film Festival, around San Francisco with screenings at the Sundance Kabuki Cinemas (Fillmore and Post sts.), and at many other locations.

Begun in 1957, this is America's oldest film festival. It features close to 200 films and videos from more than 50 countries. Tickets are relatively inexpensive, and screenings are accessible to the public. Entries include new films by beginning and established directors, and star-studded tributes. For a schedule and to purchase tickets, visit **www.festivalsffs.org**. Mid-April to early May.

MAY

Cinco de Mayo Festival, Mission District. This is when the Latino community celebrates the victory of the Mexicans over the French at Puebla in 1862; mariachi bands, dancers, food, and revelers fill the streets of the Mission. The celebration is usually in Dolores Park (Dolores St. btw. 18th and 20th sts.). Contact the Mission Neighborhood Center for more information at *€* **415/206-0577** or www.sfcincodemayo.com.

Bay to Breakers Foot Race, the Embarcadero through Golden Gate Park to Ocean Beach. Even if you don't participate, you can't avoid this giant, moving costume party (which celebrated its 100th year in 2011) that goes from downtown to Ocean Beach. More than 75,000 entrants gather—many dressed in wacky, innovative, and sometimes X-rated costumes—for the approximately 7½-mile run. If you don't want to run, join the throng of spectators who line the route. Sidewalk parties, bands, and cheerleaders of all ages provide a good dose of true San Francisco fun. For more information, call *€* **415/864-3432,** or check their website, www.baytobreakers. com. Third Sunday of May.

Carnaval Festival, Harrison St. between 16th and 23rd Sts. The Mission District's largest annual event, held from 9:30am to 6pm, is a day of festivities that includes food, music, dance, arts and crafts, and a parade that's as sultry and energetic as the Latin American and Caribbean people behind it. For one of San Franciscans' favorite events, more than half a million spectators line the parade route, and samba musicians and dancers continue to entertain on 14th Street, near Harrison, at the end of the march, where you'll find food and craft booths, music, and more revelry. Call ✆ **415/206-0577** for more information. Celebrations are held Saturday and Sunday of Memorial Day weekend, but the parade is on Sunday morning only. See www. carnavalsf.org for more information.

JUNE

Union Street Art Festival, Pacific Heights along Union Street from Steiner to Gough streets. This outdoor fair celebrates San Francisco with themes, gourmet food booths, music, entertainment, and a juried art show featuring works by more than 250 artists. It's a great time and a chance to see the city's young well-to-dos partying it up. Call the **Union Street Association** (✆ **415/ 441-7055**) for more information or see www.unionstreetfestival.com. First weekend of June.

Haight-Ashbury Street Fair, Haight-Ashbury. A far cry from the froufrou Union Street Fair, this grittier fair features alternative crafts, ethnic foods, rock bands, and a healthy number of hippies and street kids whooping it up and slamming beers in front of the blaring rock-'n'-roll stage. The fair usually extends along Haight Street between Stanyan and Ashbury streets. For details, visit www.haightashburystreetfair. org. Second Sunday of June.

North Beach Festival, Grant Ave., North Beach. In 2009, this party celebrated its 55th anniversary; organizers claim it's the oldest urban street fair in the country. Close to 100,000 city folk meander along Grant Avenue, between Vallejo and Union streets, to eat, drink, and browse the arts-and-crafts booths, poetry readings, swing-dancing venue, and *arte di gesso* (sidewalk chalk art). But the most enjoyable parts of the event are listening to music and people-watching. Visit **www.sresproductions. com/north_beach_festival.html**. Saturday & Sunday, June 14 & 15, 2014.

Stern Grove Music Festival, Sunset District. Pack a picnic and head out early to join the thousands who come here to lie in the grass and enjoy classical, jazz, and ethnic music and dance in the grove, at 19th Avenue and Sloat Boulevard. The free concerts take place every Sunday at 2pm between mid-June and August. Show up with a lawn chair or blanket. There are food booths if you forget snacks, but you'll be dying to leave if you don't bring warm clothes—the Sunset District can be one of the coldest parts of the city. Call ✆ **415/252-6252** for listings or go to www.sterngrove. org. Sundays, mid-June through August.

San Francisco Lesbian, Gay, Bisexual, Transgender Pride Parade & Celebration, downtown's Market St. This prideful event draws up to one million participants who celebrate all of the above—and then some. The parade proceeds west on Market Street until it gets to the Civic Center, where hundreds of food, art, and information booths are set up around several soundstages. Call ✆ **415/864-0831** or visit www.sfpride.org for information. Usually the third or last weekend of June.

JULY

Fillmore Jazz Festival, Pacific Heights. July starts with a bang, when the upscale portion of Fillmore closes to traffic and the blocks between Jackson and Eddy streets are filled with arts and crafts, gourmet food, and live jazz from 10am to 6pm. For more information visit **www.fillmorejazzfestival. com**. First weekend in July.

Fourth of July Celebration & Fireworks, Fisherman's Wharf. This event can be something of a joke—more often than not, fog comes into the city, like everyone else, to join in the festivities. Sometimes it's almost impossible to view the million-dollar pyrotechnics from Pier 39 on the northern waterfront. Still, it's a party, and if the skies are clear, it's a darn good show.

San Francisco Marathon, San Francisco and beyond. This is one of the largest marathons in the world. It starts and ends at the Ferry Building at the base of Market Street, winds 26-plus miles through virtually every neighborhood in the city, and crosses the Golden Gate Bridge. For entry information, visit **www.thesfmarathon.com**. Usually the last weekend in July.

SEPTEMBER

Sausalito Art Festival, Sausalito. A juried exhibit of more than 20,000 original works of art, this festival includes music—provided by jazz, rock, and blues performers from the Bay Area and beyond—and international cuisine, enhanced by wines from some 50 Napa and Sonoma producers. Parking is impossible; take the ferry (www.blueand goldfleet.com) from Pier 41 to the festival site. For more information, call 🕐 **415/332-3555** or log on to www.sausalitoartfestival. org. Labor Day weekend.

Opera in the Park. Usually in Sharon Meadow, Golden Gate Park. Each year, the San Francisco Opera launches its season with a free concert featuring a selection of arias. Call 🕐 **415/861-4008** or visit www. sfopera.com to confirm the location and date. Usually the Sunday after Labor Day.

Folsom Street Fair, along Folsom St. between 7th and 12th sts, the area south of Market Street (SoMa, From11am to 6pm). This is a local favorite for its kinky, outrageous, leather-and-skin gay-centric blowout celebration. It's hard-core, so only open-minded and adventurous types need head into the leather-clad and partially dressed crowds. For info visit www.folsom streetfair.org. Last Sunday of September.

OCTOBER

Fleet Week, Marina and Fisherman's Wharf. Residents gather along the Marina Green, the Embarcadero, Fisherman's Wharf, and other vantage points to watch incredible (and loud!) aerial performances by the Blue Angels and other daring stunt pilots, as well as the annual parade of ships. Call 🕐 **650/599-5057** or visit www.fleet week.us for details and dates.

Artspan Open Studios, various San Francisco locations. Find an original piece of art to commemorate your trip, or just see what local artists are up to by grabbing a map to over 800 artists' studios that are open to the public during weekends in October and May. Visit www.artspan.org for more information.

Castro Street Fai, the Castro. Celebrate life in the city's most famous gay neighborhood. Call 🕐 **800/853-5950** or visit www. castrostreetfair.org for information. First Sunday in October, from 11am to 6pm.

Italian Heritage Parade, North Beach and Fisherman's Wharf. The city's Italian community leads the festivities around Fisherman's Wharf, celebrating Columbus's landing in America with a parade along Columbus Avenue. But for the most part, it's a great excuse to hang out in North Beach and people-watch. For more information, visit **www.sfcolumbusday.org**. Observed the Sunday before Columbus Day.

Halloween, the Castro. This once huge street party has been tamed down by city officials in recent years to curb violence and prevent the increasing influx of out-of-towners into the neighborhood. Castro denizens still whoop it up with music and drag costume contests, but if you go to gawk, you'll be disappointed. October 31.

Treasure Island Music Festival, Treasure Island. Bands and crowds take over this East Bay landfill island (and former U.S. Navy base) for the weekend. Free shuttle from AT&T Park. Visit **www.treasureisland festival.com**. Mid-October.

DECEMBER

The Nutcracker, War Memorial Opera House, Civic Center. The **San Francisco Ballet** (🕐 **415/865-2000**) performs this Tchaikovsky classic annually. (It was actually the first ballet company in America to do so.) Order tickets to this holiday tradition well in advance. Visit **www.sfballet.org** for information.

SantaCon, various San Francisco locations. Get into the holiday spirit and join thousands as they booze their way across the city. Dress up as Santa, Mrs. Clause, an elf, or your own interpretation for a full day of drinking, singing, and being merry. This is an adults-only pub crawl that, true to San Francisco style, includes nudity. The time, date, and location change annually and the details are released only a few days before the event, so follow SantaCon on twitter or check out the website at **www.santacon. info/San_Francisco-CA**.

WHERE TO STAY

Whether you want a room with a view or just a room, San Francisco is more than accommodating to its 15.7 million annual guests. Most of the city's 200-plus hotels cluster near Union Square, but some smaller independent gems are scattered around town. It's the savvy San Francisco traveler who avoids the heavily touristed areas such as Union Square and Fisherman's Wharf, and instead hangs his or her hat at the city's outlying (and quieter) districts such as the Marina and walks or takes public transportation into city central.

PRACTICAL MATTERS: THE HOTEL SCENE

4

Getting the Best Deal

In the listings in this chapter, I've tried to give you an idea of the kind of deals that may be available at particular hotels. All rates are real rates, as opposed to rack rates, and I was one click away from booking anything listed. Since there is no way of knowing what the offers will be when you're booking, consider these general tips:

Choose your season carefully. Room rates can vary dramatically—by hundreds of dollars in some cases—depending on what time of year you visit. Winter, from November through March, is best for bargains, excluding Thanksgiving, Christmas, and New Years, of course—though the days between Christmas and New Years can offer amazing deals, and these just happen to be some of the best shopping days all year in Union Square. Occupancy rates hover around 90 percent from June through October; rates adjust upwards accordingly. Bizarrely enough, when the city fills up, lesser quality hotels will often charge prices that are equal to or even higher than the luxury hotels are asking. It makes no sense, but it happens quite often. So it's important to NEVER try and assess the quality of a hotel by the price it's asking. Instead, read the reviews carefully and compare the prices you're being quoted to make sure you're not getting taken.

Remember to factor in the extras. Most folks simply look at the price when booking a room, without considering the value of the extras thrown in with a slightly more expensive place. For example, the Hotel Drisco (see p. 67) is a lovely place in Pacific Heights. At $285 per night, many might not even consider booking a room here. But when you factor in free parking (about a $50 value if you have a car), free heavy breakfast (worth at least $40 per couple), evening cocktails and hot appetizers (easily another $20 per couple), and free Wi-Fi ($10), all of a sudden it's as if you're only paying $165 for the room itself. For one of the finest hotels in

WHAT YOU'LL really PAY

With the average price for a double room topping $200 per night, and occupancy rates as high as 90 percent in peak season, getting a good deal on a bed in this city is a bit like playing roulette—you never know what number will come up. I have calculated the rates in this chapter by looking at what discounters are offering in three different seasons and then showing you the range, from low to high. I did not focus on any of the city's $12,000 per night suites—yes, we have them, and if you want one you'll likely find them in the more pricey properties listed in this book. But what this book is about, and what I have tried to focus on, are the best hotel values our city has to offer—in all price categories. By which I mean: interesting, unique properties that tell you a bit about the city you're visiting.

Though remember: you aren't coming to San Francisco for the hotels; you just sleep in the hotel. You are coming to taste fresh, juicy Dungeness crab at Fisherman's Wharf, hear the cling clang as the cable cars lumber improbably up the hills, and feel the wind whip your hair as you walk across our Golden Gate. Unless otherwise stated, all prices are for double rooms, and all properties offer free Wi-Fi.

the country, that's a darn good deal. Whenever possible, I have tried to focus on hotels that offer free breakfast, cocktails, nibbles, parking, and Wi-Fi—it adds up.

Stay in a hotel away from Fisherman's Wharf—or SoMa, Nob Hill, and Union Square for that matter. The advantages of staying in the popular tourist locations are overrated, particularly so when saving money is your object. Muni buses and, especially, the historic F-Line streetcars, can take you to most tourist sites in minutes. Even if you stay as far away as The Castro, you can be at the ferry launch for Alcatraz in about half an hour; your daily ride up and down Market Street on these old beauties will likely be a lovely lasting memory of your visit. You'll not only get the best value for your money by staying outside the tourist areas, in the residential neighborhoods where real San Franciscans live, but you'll have a better overall experience: you won't constantly be fighting crowds, you'll have terrific restaurants nearby and you'll see what life in the city is really like. Lodgings in The Castro, Haight-Ashbury, Civic Center, The Marina, and quiet Japantown offer particularly good savings.

Visit over a weekend. If your trip includes a weekend, you might be able to save big. Business hotels tend to empty out, and rooms that go for $300 or more Monday through Thursday can drop dramatically in cost, to as low as $150 or less, once the execs have headed home—these deals are especially prevalent in SoMa. Also, you'll find that Sunday nights are the least expensive, no matter the neighborhood. Check the hotel's website for weekend specials. Or just ask when you call. None of this applies in Fisherman's Wharf—it's always expensive there.

Do what they do in Europe and share a bathroom. What is the value of a private loo? In San Francisco, I'd say it's at least $100 per night. If the thought of "sharing" brings back dreaded memories of the high school locker room scene, don't worry; unless you are staying in a hostel, "sharing" usually means you can lock the door to the bathroom—as you would visiting a friends' house. The bathroom won't be in your room, it will be down the hall, and will be used by fellow guests.

Shop online. There are so many ways to save online and through apps, we've devoted an entire box to the topic. See p. 50.

Make deals with the chains. We have not focused on chain properties in this chapter. You pretty much know what you will get with a Hyatt, Hilton, or Holiday Inn, so we have tried to focus on smaller, unknown, independent properties with character—and a good local feel—to help enhance your travel experience. That said, the big brand names are usually in good locations, and can be a great deal as they are market sensitive. Because they hate to see rooms sit empty, they'll often negotiate competitive rates at the last minute and in slow seasons. Most chain hotels let the kids stay with parents for free using existing bedding and they accept loyalty points. Ask for every kind of discount; if you get an unhelpful reservation agent, call back—and try calling the local number. For your convenience, we have listed all of the major chains—including neighborhood, website, address, and local phone number—in a box on p. 54.

Avoid excess charges and hidden costs. Use your own cell phone, pay phones, or prepaid phone cards instead of dialing direct from hotel phones, which usually have exorbitant rates. And don't be tempted by minibar offerings: Most hotels charge through the nose for water, soda, and snacks—is a Diet Coke really worth $5? Unless you are a member of one of their elite groups, many large hotel chains charge a fortune for Wi-Fi; at smaller places, it is usually free. Most of the hotels listed below offer free Wi-Fi. For information about free Wi-Fi throughout the city, see p. 238. If a hotel insists upon tacking on an "energy surcharge" that wasn't mentioned at check-in, you can often make a case for getting it removed.

Buy a money-saving package deal. A travel package that combines your airfare and your hotel stay for one price may just be the best bargain of all. In some cases, you'll get airfare, accommodations, transportation to and from the airport, plus extras—maybe an afternoon sightseeing tour or restaurant and shopping discount coupons—for less than the hotel alone would have cost had you booked it yourself. Most airlines and many travel agents, as well as the usual booking websites (Priceline, Orbitz, Expedia) offer good packages to San Francisco.

Alternative Accommodations

Consider private B&B accommodations. Did you know you can rent a bed, a room, and sometimes a whole house or apartment, from a private owner? Think of it as a private B&B (though breakfast may or may not be included). This type of stay is usually much cheaper than a hotel room, it allows you to meet a friendly local, and it places you in a residential neighborhood where you live like a local, rather than a visitor. One of the best companies to use for this type of booking is AirBNB, though many also turn to the website www.bedandbreakfast.com. Be sure to get all details in writing and an exact price for the stay, including applicable taxes and fees, before booking.

Try a Home Exchange. As featured in the movie *The Holiday,* a home exchange is essentially a swap—Cameron Diaz's character stayed in a lovely cottage in England, while the owner of the cottage, Kate Winslet's character, stayed in Cameron's pad in Los Angeles. Romances happen, lives change, yada, yada, yada. If you are looking for romance, hoping to change your life, or, more than likely, just looking for an inexpensive way to stay somewhere, a home exchange might be just the thing for you. This is

TURNING TO THE internet or apps FOR A HOTEL DISCOUNT

Before going online, know what "flavor" of discount you're seeking. Currently, there are four types of online reductions—mystery property, direct with the hotel, agencies, and last minute.

- **Extreme discounts on sites where you bid for lodgings without knowing which hotel you'll get.** You'll find these on such sites as Priceline.com and Hotwire.com, and they can be real money-savers, particularly if you're booking within a week of travel (that's when the hotels get nervous and resort to deep discounts to get beds filled). As these companies use only major chains, you can rest assured that you won't be put up in a dump. For more reassurance, visit the website www.BetterBidding.com. On it, actual travelers spill the beans about what they bid on Priceline.com and which hotels they got. I think you'll be pleasantly surprised by the quality of many of the hotels that are offering these "secret" discounts to the opaque bidding websites.

- **Discounts on the hotel's website itself.** Sometimes these can be great values, as they'll often include such nice perks as free breakfast or parking privileges. Before biting, though be sure to look at the discounter sites below.

- **Discounts on online travel agencies as Hotels.com, Venere.com, Quikbook.com, Expedia.com, and the like.** Some of these sites reserve rooms in bulk and at a discount, passing along the savings to their customers. But instead of going to them directly, I'd recommend looking at such dedicated travel search engines as **Hipmunk.com, HotelsCombined.com, Momondo.com** and my favorite, **Trivago.com**. These sites list prices from all the discount sites as well as the hotels directly, meaning you have a better chance of finding a discount. *Note:* Sometimes the discounts these sites find require advance payment for a room (and draconian cancellation policies), so double check your travel dates before booking. Be extremely careful when one of these sites says "just a few blocks from Union Square," as you could find yourself stepping over homeless people and through drug dealers and prostitutes in the Tenderloin—which is just a few blocks from Union Square. Always read the reviews!! **Tingo.com**, a site founded by TripAdvisor, is another good source, especially for luxury hotels. Its model is a bit different than the others. Users make a pre-paid reservation through it, but if the price of the room drops between the time you make the booking and the date of arrival, the site refunds the difference in price.

- **Try the app HotelsTonight.com.** It only works for day of bookings, but WOW, does it get great prices for procrastinators and spontaneous people who decide to travel on a whim—up to 70 percent off in many cases. *A possible strategy:* make a reservation at a hotel, then on the day you're arriving try your luck with HotelsTonight.com. Most hotels will allow you to cancel without penalty, even on the date of arrival.

Yes, it's a lot of surfing, but with the potential to save hundreds of dollars over a few days, it can certainly pay off.

a great way for families on a budget to visit an expensive city. For more information, see the box on p. 72.

Stay in a Hostel. If the word "hostel" conjures up images of a wild, drunk, noisy, twenty-something party scene, think again. I'm a safety conscious, 48-year old soccer mom, and have stayed in hostels all over the world with my kids. They have loved the experience, and decided it would be boring to just sit with mom at breakfast (as at a regular hotel) when they can meet people from all over the world sitting at a community table. The hostel scene in San Francisco is a good deal. We've named the quiet, waterfront Hostelling International Fort Mason Hostel the "Best Value" and "Best View" in the city. See p. 68.

UNION SQUARE

This area is the Times Square of San Francisco and a shopper's delight: Macy's, Nordstrom, Neiman Marcus, Tiffany, and more.

Best For: Travelers who enjoy the hustle and bustle of a big city, walking everywhere, shopping, and riding the cable cars.

Drawbacks: Noisy, crowded, difficult street parking, outrageous hotel garage rates, panhandlers, and premium-location hotel rates.

Expensive

Hotel Triton ★★   East meets West at the corner of Grant and Bush streets. On the one side you have the upscale luxury shops and trendy restaurants of the world famous Union Square neighborhood; on the other, you'll find ancient men mixing ancient recipes with Chinese herbs, simple noodle shops and tea stands through the gates and under the red lanterns of old Chinatown. Where such opposites meet, you could not find a more ideal location for the anything-but-mundane Hotel Triton. Unlike any other hotel in the city, wild colorful murals cover the lobby, employees wear their own clothes instead of uniforms, the bathrobes are zebra-printed, and the evening wine reception features poetry and tarot card readings. (Don't drink wine? Your freebie will be the fresh baked cookies that are served every afternoon at 3pm.) Using bright colors and an eclectic collection of furniture, under the guise of their "individuality theme," Kimpton does a good job making you forget the fact that the rooms are a little small and dated. A few specialty rooms have been designed by such entertainers Kathy Griffin and Jerry Garcia—complete with many of the late great's original watercolors hanging on the walls. Another specialty room has a Haagen-Dazs ice cream theme, including a custom-designed ice cream cabinet filled daily with pints in an assortment of flavors. Dogs are not only welcomed, they are greeted with a message board announcing their arrival, and offered spa treatments.

342 Grant Ave. (at Bush St.). ✆ **415/394-0500.** www.hoteltriton.com. 140 units. From $143–$289. Parking $40, oversize vehicles $49. Cable car: Powell–Hyde or Powell–Mason line (2 blocks west). Pets friendly. **Amenities:** Cafe; 24-hr fitness center; room service; concierge; raid the mini bar (up to $10) and free Wi-Fi for Kimpton InTouch members (no charge to join).

Sir Francis Drake ★★★   If you are looking for a hotel with a little history, a little mystery, and lots of British pomp and circumstance, put the Sir Francis Drake at the top of your list. Located a few steps from Union Square, this landmark hotel has been in operation since 1928. Upon arrival, you'll be welcomed by fully costumed Beefeater doormen—Tom Sweeney, the city's most famous doorman, has been carrying bags here for over 30 years. Step inside where the impressive grand lobby welcomes you with high ceilings, ornate chandeliers, and swirling staircases. Kimpton Hotels (famous for putting lipstick on old properties) took over a few years ago, and immediately invested in a $20 million facelift. As with most historic hotels, the rooms are small but filled with rich wooden furnishings and striped wallpaper giving them a cushy, old European feel. Ask to sleep on a higher floor, away from the traffic noise and cling clanging cable cars. No visit to the Sir Francis Drake would be complete without a drink gazing out at the amazing city views from **Harry Denton's** infamous **Starlight Room** on the 21st floor. For a little mystery, try to decide if the lovely ladies at the **Sunday's a Drag Brunch** are men or women.

450 Powell St. (at Sutter St.). ℂ **415/392-7755.** www.sirfrancisdrake.com. 416 units. $150–$400. Valet parking $50. Cable car: Powell–Hyde or Powell–Mason line (direct stop). Pets welcome. **Amenities:** 2 restaurants; bar; concierge; exercise room; room service; raid the mini bar (up to $10) and free Wi-Fi for Kimpton InTouch members (no charge to join).

Westin St. Francis ★ If you are determined to sleep as close to Union Square as is humanly possible, then look no further than the Westin St Francis—the only hotel right on the square. Built in 1904 by "Bonanza King" Charles Crocker and his wealthy friends, the St. Francis has hosted a who's who of world famous celebrities including Mother Teresa, Helen Keller, Charlie Chaplin, Douglas Fairbanks, Mary Pickford, Queen Elizabeth, Emperor Hirohito, and Duke Kahanamoku, as well as a number of U.S. presidents. The Westin is made up of two buildings. The historic Landmark Building was built in 1904 (like almost everything else in the book, it was rebuilt after the 1906 earthquake and fires), fronts the square, and rooms feature turn-of-the-century charm including high ceilings and ornate crystal chandeliers. The 32-story Tower Building was built in 1972 and features five glass, spacious modern rooms, featuring larger bathrooms than their Landmark counterparts. Personally, I prefer the older, and more authentic, part of the hotel. The St. Francis is especially lovely around the holidays when executive pastry chef, Jean-Francois Houdre, is famous for creating the confectionary real estate concoctions displayed in the lobby—one year it might be a sugar castle, another a gingerbread village. Chocolate condo anyone?

335 Powell St. (btw. Geary and Post sts.). ℂ **415/397-7000.** www.westinstfrancis.com. 1,195 units. $179–$699. Children stay free w/parents when using existing bedding. Valet parking $57 ($7 more for SUV/larger vehicles). Cable car: Powell–Hyde or Powell–Mason line (direct stop). Pets under 40lbs. accepted. **Amenities:** 2 restaurants; concierge; elaborate health club and spa; room service; Wi-Fi ($15 per day).

Moderate

Hotel Diva ★★ Sleek and chic are words that come to mind when you walk into the lobby of this Personality Hotel. There is no hint of stuffy old Victorian charm here; it's all stainless, modern, and minimalist. Rooms are the same, with George Jetson furnishings and bright blue carpeting. Kids will go wild for the Little Divas Suite—a completely tricked out room featuring bunk beds, a computer, toys, games, a drawing table, Wii game, and—heaven help us—a karaoke machine. Parents, stay in the same room, just around the corner. Guest have use of the business and fitness centers 24/7.

Union Square Hotels

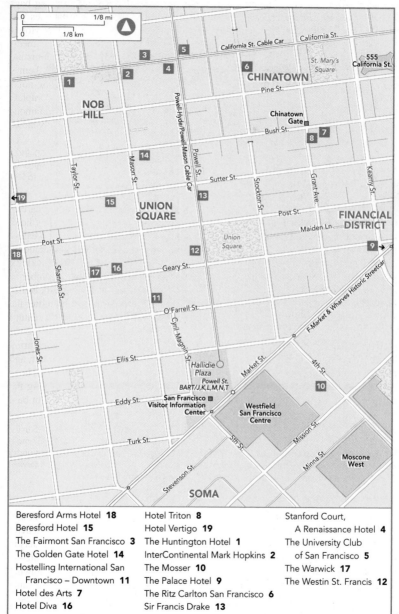

Beresford Arms Hotel **18**
Beresford Hotel **15**
The Fairmont San Francisco **3**
The Golden Gate Hotel **14**
Hostelling International San Francisco – Downtown **11**
Hotel des Arts **7**
Hotel Diva **16**

Hotel Triton **8**
Hotel Vertigo **19**
The Huntington Hotel **1**
InterContinental Mark Hopkins **2**
The Mosser **10**
The Palace Hotel **9**
The Ritz Carlton San Francisco **6**
Sir Francis Drake **13**

Stanford Court, A Renaissance Hotel **4**
The University Club of San Francisco **5**
The Warwick **17**
The Westin St. Francis **12**

NAME BRAND hotels

Because this is a small pocket guidebook with limited space, we chose to write about independent hotels that offer a uniquely San Francisco experience (or a really great deal). But we understand that many readers alleviate the cost of travel with free stays through hotel loyalty programs. So for those readers, we've compiled the following list of hotels, in all prices ranges, but not all areas (we only chose the ones we feel are well-located).

Hyatt (www.hyatt.com)
- Hyatt Regency **FiDi** ($381) 5 Embarcadero Center, ℂ **415/788-1234**
- **Fisherman's Wharf** ($305) 555 North Point St., ℂ **415/563-1234**
- **Union Square** Grand Hyatt ($235) 345 Stockton St., ℂ **415/398-1234**

Marriott (www.marriott.com)
- Courtyard **Downtown** ($169) 299 Second St., ℂ **415/947-0700**
- **Fisherman's Wharf** ($269) 1250 Columbus Ave., ℂ **415/775-7555**
- Courtyard **Fisherman's Wharf** ($299) 580 Beach St., ℂ **415/775-3800**
- JW Marriott **Union Square** ($239) 500 Post St., ℂ **415/771-8600**
- **Union Square** ($229) 480 Sutter St., ℂ **415/398-8900**
- Marquis **SoMa** ($179) 780 Mission St., ℂ **415/896-1600**

Starwood (www.starwoodhotels.com)
- Le Meridien **Embarcadero** ($469) 333 Battery St., ℂ **415/296-2900**
- Sheraton **Fisherman's Wharf** ($299) 2500 Mason St., ℂ **415/362-5500**
- St. Regis **SoMa** ($625) 125 Third St., ℂ **415/284-4000**
- W San Francisco **SoMa** ($446) 181 Third St., ℂ **415/777-5300**
- Westin Market St. **SoMa** ($436) 50 Third St., ℂ **415/974-6400**
- Westin St. Francis **Union Square.** ($296) 335 Powell St., ℂ **415/397-7000**

Restaurants, galleries, and high-end stores are all close by, as are the cable cars and historic F-Line streetcars.

440 Geary St. (btw. Mason and Taylor sts.). ℂ **415/885-0200.** www.hoteldiva.com. 116 units. From $144–$300. Pets welcome for $75 fee. Valet parking $40–$45. Bus: 38 or 38L. Cable car: Powell–Mason line. **Amenities:** Concierge; restaurant; 24-hr. exercise room; free Wi-Fi.

Hotel Vertigo ★   "Good Eeeeeevening." For Alfred Hitchcock buffs, there is no better place to stay than the Vertigo, the location of a few of the scenes of the movie by the same name. Though it was the Empire Hotel in the Hitchcock movie, fans will recognize the bay window where the Kim Novak's "Judy" gazed out in her green dress. Keeping with the Hitchcock theme, the rooms and lobby have been redone in a vintage 50's/60's style with period furniture, the signature tangerine and white colors from the movie's promotional materials, and wall art featuring the *Vertigo* spiral motif. The film plays constantly in the lobby where free morning beverages are offered along with wine on weekdays at 5:30pm. *Note*: Though not located in the Tenderloin per se, Hotel Vertigo is only a couple of blocks from this area of inner city blight. Make sure to ask

Hilton (www.hilton.com)

- **FiDi** ($275) 750 Kearney St.,
  © **415/433-6600**
- **Fisherman's Wharf** ($272) 2620
  Jones St., © **415/885-4700**
- **Union Square** ($234) 333
  O'Farrell St., © **415/771-1400**

Holiday Inn (www.holidayinn.com)

- **Civic Center** ($164) 50 Eighth
  St., © **415/626-6103**
- Express **Fisherman's Wharf**
  ($265) 550 North Point St.,
  © **415/409-4600**
- **Fisherman's Wharf** ($247) 1300
  Columbus Ave., © **415/
  771-9000**
- by **Nob Hill** ($197) 1500 Van
  Ness Ave., © **415/441-4000**

Best Western (www.bestwestern.com)

- **Fisherman's Wharf** ($263) 425
  North Point St., © **415/
  561-1100**
- by **Union Square** ($225) 121 Sev-
  enth St., © **415/626-0200**
- SoMa ($158) 580 Geary St.,
  © **415/441-2700**

Travelodge (www.travelodge.com)

- by **The Castro** ($158) 1707 Mar-
  ket St., © **415/621-6775**
- **Fisherman's Wharf** ($169) 1450
  Lombard St., © **415/673-0691**
- **Marina** ($144) 2230 Lombard St.,
  © **415/922-3900**
- **Marina** ($175) 2755 Lombard St.,
  © **415/931-8581**
- **North Beach** ($127) 1201 Colum-
  bus Ave., © **415/776-7070**

Days Inn (www.daysinn.com)

- **America's Best Value** (www.
  americasbestvalue.com)
- **Civic Center** ($146) 465 Grove
  St., © **415/864-4040**
- **Marina** ($93) 2322 Lombard St.,
  © **415/921-4980**
- **Marina** ($144) 2358 Lombard St.,
  © **415/922-2010**
- **SoMa** ($99) 10 Hallam St.,
  ©**415/431-0541**
- **Sunset** ($126) 2600 Sloat Blvd.,
  © **415/665-9000**

the concierge which way to walk when heading out sightseeing. As in any large city, use caution, especially late at night.

940 Sutter St. (btw. Leavenworth and Hyde sts.). © **415/885-6800.** www.hotelvertigosf.com. 102 units. From $119–$209. Rates include morning beverages in lobby, wine 5:30pm weekdays, mini fridges. Valet parking $35–$40. Bus: 2 or 3. **Amenities:** Concierge; small fitness center.

The Warwick ★   Set in the heart of the theater district, the old world charm of this boutique hotel is sure to satisfy visitors looking for a non-cookie cutter experience. Regular rooms feature canopied beds, hand-carved headboards, and antique furnishings; the 16 suites are all decked out in Louis XVI style. Though a little dated, and a little noisy, you can't get a much better deal on a hotel this close to Union Square. Guest are invited to enjoy complimentary afternoon coffee, tea, and cookies.

490 Geary St. (btw. Mason and Taylor sts.). © **415/928-7900.** www.warwicksf.com. 90 units. $134–$299. Parking $42, oversized vehicles $59. Bus: 2, 3, 27, or 38. Cable car: Powell–Hyde or Powell–Mason line. **Amenities:** Restaurant; concierge; access to nearby health club ($15 per day); room service; Internet $9.95 per day.

Inexpensive

Beresford Arms Hotel ★★★   As a low-cost hotel in the heart of downtown, the Beresford Arms is an especially good choice for large family groups: A family of up to seven can stay in a two-bedroom suite with a full kitchen, including a complimentary continental breakfast, afternoon wine, cheese, and cookies, for around $200, an excellent price for suites with these amenities. Listed on the National Register of Historic Places, the public areas have a '20's feel, complete with parlor furniture, white columns, elegant chandeliers and a grandfather clock. The regular rooms are also large, and all suites—not just the two bedrooms—have a kitchenette or wet bar. Want to bring Fido with you? No problem; pets are welcome. So what's the downside? It's a little dated, a little noisy, and the beds are not the most comfortable in the world. But wait—did I mention the price? Ah, what's a little traffic noise? *Note:* This is another hotel that's near to the Tenderloin, so you'll want advice on which direction to head when you leave the hotel.

701 Post St. (at Jones St.). © **415/673-2600.** www.beresford.com. 95 units. $99–$289 double. Parlor Suite $200. Extra person $20. Children 12 and under stay free in parent's room. Rates include continental breakfast, afternoon wine and tea. Valet parking $27. Bus: 2, 3, 27, or 38. Cable car: Powell–Hyde line. **Amenities:** Access to nearby health club ($10 per day).

Beresford Hotel ★   Like its sister hotel, the Beresford Arms (above), the Beresford Hotel is an inexpensive old Victorian hotel in the heart of the city, where pets are welcome and continental breakfast is complimentary. While the Beresford Arms is a bigger property with large suites and grand old public spaces, the Beresford Hotel could best be described as a lesser version of big sis. The rooms are small and standard; the lobby is compact and simple; and, as expected, the price is slightly lower. One thing the Beresford has on pretty big sis is its very own replica of an olde—with an "e" —English pub, the White Horse Tavern.

635 Sutter St. (near Mason St.). © **415/673-9900.** www.beresford.com. 114 units. $89–$165 double. Extra person $20. Rates include continental breakfast. Children 12 and under stay free in parent's room. Valet parking $27. Bus: 2, 3, 30, 38, or 45. Cable car: Powell–Hyde line. **Amenities:** Restaurant; access to nearby health club ($10 per day); free high-speed Internet access in kiosk in lobby.

The Golden Gate Hotel ★   Europeans love staying at this quaint inexpensive bed and breakfast in the heart of the city, where guests are greeted by everyone's favorite staff member, Pip, the ginger cat, who goes by the titles "Feline Overlord" and "Room Service Cuddle Provider." Rooms are small and cozy—read tiny. Decor is antiques, wicker, floral curtains, and wallpaper—think grandma's house. Coffee, tea, juice, and croissants are served in the parlor each morning and homemade cookies each afternoon.

775 Bush St. (btw. Powell and Mason sts.). © **415/392-3702.** www.goldengatehotel.com. 25 units. Double with shared bathroom from $135; with private bathroom from $190. Rates include continental breakfast and afternoon tea and cookies. Parking $30. Cable car: Powell–Hyde or Powell–Mason line. BART: Powell and Market. **Amenities:** Concierge.

Hostelling International San Francisco–Downtown ★   Stay a block from Union Square, surrounded by five star hotels, for as little as $30. Seriously? Not sure if you are into the shared-dorm-room-hostel-thing? Well, guess what? Private rooms start as low as $89 per night. Throw in a free continental breakfast and this deal is hard to pass up if your wallet is thin. So what if the sheet threadcount does not meet Ritz Carlton standards and you "only" get a bagel and coffee for breakfast; this is all about

BRING fido TO THE CITY

For dog lovers, our four-legged friends are like our children—though usually more obedient. A visit to San Francisco does not mean you have to leave Fido behind; a number of hotels will welcome your furry beast with open arms, or, I suppose, open paws. Weight restrictions, type of pet accepted, and number of pets allowed per person vary by hotel. Pet fees range from free to $50 per day to $100 per stay. Always confirm with the hotel before booking; policies can change at any time.

- **Hilton Union Square** welcomes dogs up to 75lbs. See p. 55.
- The **Argonaut Hotel** has no weight limit for dogs. See p. 65.
- **Hotel Kabuki** has no charge for pets. See p. 70.
- The **Sir Francis Drake Hotel** has no fee or weight restrictions. They offer pet beds, food, water bowls, and the pet can be a dog, a cat, or a lizard. See p. 52.
- At **Hotel Diva**, pets are welcome for a $25 per visit. See p. 52.
- The **Inn at the Presidio** charges a $40 one-time cleaning fee for guests with pets. See p. 67.
- The **Beresford** (see p. 56) and

sister hotel, **The Beresford Arms** (see p. 56), have no weight restrictions; call regarding fees.

- The **Mark Hopkins** has a max weight of 25lbs, and charges $50 per night. See p. 58.
- **The Palace Hotel** allows dogs up to 80lbs., and charges $100 per stay. Fido will be treated like a king and gets a bowl, a bed, and even a pet welcome kit. See p. 61.
- The **Ritz Carlton** allows teeny tiny dogs; call regarding weight limits. They have been known to offer a VIP—Very Important Pooch—Program. See p. 60.

Paws down, the best place for a dog in the city has to be **Hotel Triton**. There is no charge; there are no weight restrictions, and they provide bowls, beds, leashes, and plastic bags. Pet sitting, grooming, walking, and massage services are available for a fee. They even have a pet welcome board where your pet's name will be posted to greet him upon arrival.

For a city guide to dog friendly restaurants, parks, and beaches, as well as a complete list of all dog friendly hotels in the city, visit www.dogfriendly.com.

price for the location. And this hostel is by no means "slumming it." The lovely rooms have been recently renovated and offer a choice of a four-bed dorm (co-ed or gender specific) or private rooms (one to three people). You'll pay a little more for a private bathroom. Linens, towels, and lockers are free. All ages are welcome, though with free events ranging from beer tasting, to wine and cheese, to pizza-and-a-movie-night, not to mention the traffic outside, those seeking a quiet stay might want to consider the sister property located at Fisherman's Wharf (p. 68).

312 Mason St. (at O'Farrell St.). ℂ **415/788-5604.** www.sfhostels.org/downtown. 292 beds. Dorm beds $30–$45; private rooms $89–$135. HI membership required for $28 annual, or $3 per day. Rates include breakfast. Parking $17. Streetcar: F-Line. **Amenities:** Restaurant.

Hotel des Arts ★★ Guests seeking something different in a prime location—Union Square, Chinatown, and FiDi are just a few steps away—for a reasonable price, will love this art-gallery boutique hotel. With rooms and public spaces painted by local

BUNKING WITH THE big four
OR ONE OF THE bonanza kings

Let's start with the **"Big Four,"** who were railroad barons who controlled the city with money earned (some might say swindled) when they formed the Southern Pacific Railroad group and built the railroad connecting the nations two coasts. While all four had humble beginnings, with their new found wealth they quickly began competing to see who could build the largest, most extravagant home on Nob Hill—the only address of the city's moneyed elite. Though their homes burned to the ground after the 1906 earthquake, their legacy lives on with hotels, a park, and a church built on the sites.

Leland Stanford was president of the group, loved the limelight, and served as governor of California and U.S. Senator. After the passing of his 15-year-old son, Stanford converted his horse farm in Palo Alto into a university named for the boy. He loved to spend money and was first of the group to build on Nob Hill. At one point, he could brag his mansion had the largest private dining room in the West. On the site you'll find the aptly named **Renaissance Stanford Court Hotel ★** (905 California St. at Powell St.; **415/989-3500**; www.stanfordcourt.com; 393 units; $149–$429.) Compared to its illustrious Nob Hill neighbors below, the Stanford Court is a little worse for wear. Standard rooms are small and tired; the elevators are slow. Guests staying here are simply paying for the address; for a bit more money, you can have the address and then some at the places below.

Known as ruthless, **Collis P. Huntington** was vice president of the Big Four.

He spent time behind the scenes greasing palms and lobbying for favorable treatment of the group's interests with politicians. The site of his mansion is now Huntington Park (at California and Taylor sts.). He has a Nob Hill hotel named in his honor: **The Huntington Hotel ★** (1075 California St. btw. Mason and Taylor sts.; **415/474-5400;** www.huntington hotel.com; 136 units; $279–$500). A step above the Stanford Court, though not quite in the luxury league of the Mark Hopkins or Fairmont (below), the Huntington is a top quality boutique hotel. Rooms are large and tastefully decorated; the lobby is small and elegant. The hotel restaurant, called—what else?—**The Big Four** (✆ **415/474-5400;** www.big4restaurant.com) has walls covered with photos and historical objects commemorating the group, and serves fine delicacy tycoon-fare such as truffled lobster mac and cheese.

Considered the most frugal, it was only fitting that **Mark Hopkins** was the group's treasurer. Though he was happy living in small rented quarters on Sutter Street, his social climbing wife had other ideas. At a cost of $3 million dollars, she created a gothic, wooden fairytale castle, complete with towers and spires. Hopkins died just before it was completed and his wife lived there only a few years before moving to the East Coast. On the castle's site, you can sleep at the **Inter-Continental Mark Hopkins ★★** (1 Nob Hill at California and Mason sts.; ✆ **415/392-3434;** www.markhopkins. net; $295–$400). Hopkins' widow would approve of the hotel named after her husband. The lobby, with its thick carpets, high ceilings, and chandeliers is showy and grand; the rooms and suites—all with city views—feature rich woods and fine fabrics to keep even the most demanding widow comfortable. The Mark Hopkins, like the Fairmont below, is high-class luxury.

Charles Crocker was the group's construction supervisor—too bad he built his mansion out of wood. After the 1906 fire, the Crocker family donated the entire city block where their home had stood to the Episcopalian church, which built the beautiful **Grace Cathedral** (p. 116) on the site.

The Big Four's counterpoints—and I know, it's hard to keep all the rags-to-riches rapscallions of early San Francisco straight—were known as the **Bonanza Kings.** Four Irish buddies, they made their fortune on Comstock Lode—a silver mine near Virginia City, Nevada—their wealth far eclipsed that of the better-known Big Four.

Members **John William Mackay** and **William S. O'Brien** left little mark on San Francisco, whereas the mansion of partner **James C. Flood** can still be seen today at 1000 California Street on top of Nob Hill as home to the private Pacific-Union Club. Because it was built using Connecticut sandstone, it was one of the few structures in the area to survive the 1906 earthquake fires. You can't go inside, but you can take an up-close look from the street and admire the original bronze fence which still exists on three sides of the property.

The last Bonanza King partner, **James Fair,** died before he could build his mansion on Nob Hill. His daughters, Tessie and Virginia, built a hotel to honor their father, but, because they got in a little over their heads financially, had to sell to the Law brothers. Timing is everything though: the property changed hands on April 6, 1906, less than 2 weeks before the great quake. The hotel burned, though some of the structure survived. It was completely rebuilt with the help of architect, Julia Morgan—of Hearst Castle fame—and reopened 1 year to the date of the quake in 1907 as **The Fairmont San Francisco ★★★** (950 Mason St. at California St.; **415/772-5000;** www.fair mont.com/sanfrancisco; 591 units; $322–$775). Perched high atop Nob Hill, the grand old Fairmont is the last word in luxury—from the vaulted ceilings and Corinthian columns trimmed in gold in the opulent lobby, to the rooms featuring large marble bathrooms and walk-in closets. It's the last word in history too—the UN Charter was signed here in 1945, every U.S. president since Taft has slept here, and, probably most significant of all, it was here in the Venetian Room that Tony Bennett first crooned his tune "I Left My Heart in San Francisco."

But make no mistake, the Fairmont is not all pomp and circumstance. For a little wild and crazy, head down to the basement (the site of the Fairmont's original pool) and visit the whimsical **Tonga Room and Hurricane Bar** (p. 186), the original Rain Forest Cafe. Amidst regular "tropical rain storms," guests enjoy Asian fusion food and umbrella drinks while sitting in tiki huts—the perfect place to watch live music play on an "island" in the center of the pool.

and international emerging artists, it's just like sleeping in an art gallery. Some rooms scream edgy graffiti, others feature whimsical scenes. Should something strike your fancy, most of the art on the walls in the hallways is for sale. All guests enjoy complimentary continental breakfast, and every room has a fridge.

447 Bush St. (at Grant St.). ✆ **415/956-3232.** www.sfhoteldesarts.com. 51 units. Double with private bathroom $129; shared bathroom from $109. $15 for each extra person. Some rooms have 7-day minimums. Rates include continental breakfast. Nearby parking $30. Cable car: Powell–Hyde or Powell–Mason line. **Amenities:** Concierge.

NOB HILL

Most of the city's finest hotels are perched here. Nob Hill is where San Francisco's railroad and mining barons once lived and modern barons stay during their visits.

Best For: Wealthy travelers who prefer luxury accommodations. Easy access to cable cars.

Drawbacks: Very expensive hotels, steep hills (good luck in heels), and heavy traffic on California Street.

Expensive

The Ritz-Carlton, San Francisco ★★★ Aaaaaahhhh, The Ritz. The name alone evokes an image of luxury, a world of butlers and ballgowns, expensive champagne, European automobiles, and teeny white dogs that fit in your pocket. Housed in the 1909 Met Life building—ironic because Met Life repurchased the building in July 2013 for $161 million. Don't worry, Snoopy is going to continue to let Ritz manage the hotel! The Ritz Carlton has set the standard for formal, doting service since it opened on its Nob Hill perch back in 1991. As with every "old San Francisco" luxury hotel (even if they aren't that old), the Ritz has an impressive lobby featuring elegant furnishings, polished floors, stately columns, and chandeliers. Rooms are spacious and well-appointed. Guest amenities include a fitness center, spa, and an indoor pool. For dining, guests have a new option; **Parallel 37** opened in 2012 (chef Ron Siegel of French Laundry fame serves contemporary American cuisine). The **Lounge** features a legendary afternoon tea. Scoring an A+ in the categories of service, style, location, and amenities, it is no wonder the Ritz-Carlton San Francisco is regularly voted one of the world's best places to stay.

600 Stockton St. (at California St.). ✆ **415/296-7465.** www.ritzcarlton.com. 336 units. From $335–$688. Buffet breakfast $35. Pet friendly for dogs under 10lbs. Parking $62. Cable car: California St. line (direct stop). **Amenities:** 2 restaurants; 3 bars; concierge; outstanding fitness center; Jacuzzi; indoor pool; room service, gift shop, Wi-Fi in room $15 per day (no charge in bar and lobby areas).

Moderate

The University Club of San Francisco ★★ When it comes to value on Nob Hill, the University Club is a hotel you have to see to believe. Perched on Nob Hill, it's an elite private health and social club that opens its doors to guests looking for a room. The old San Francisco aura will lure you in—you know, the wood paneling, polished floors, and overstuffed leather furniture requisite of an old boys club. It's the type of place you'd expect to find a bespectacled gentleman seated in the lounge, book in his hand, wearing a tweed jacket with patches on the elbows and smoking a pipe, his golden lab laying faithfully at his feet. Well, tweed jackets with patches are allowed;

One of the city's most architecturally impressive hotels, the Mark has starred in numerous films. In Steve McQueen's famous cop thriller *Bullitt*, a suspect is spotted in the hotel's marble lobby. In Alfred Hitchcock's *Vertigo*, Jimmy Stewart can be spotted at the hotel's grand *porte-cochere* entrance (but vertigo prevents him from going to the Top of the Mark). The Mark also makes a cameo in Clint Eastwood's *Sudden Impact*. On Tuesdays all summer, the Mark screens these films, among others, on its rooftop with complimentary wine tasting. And, no, you do not have to be a hotel guest to partake. Call ✆ **415/616-6916** or check out www.markhopkins.net for details.

dogs and smoking are not. Rooms are big enough to add a rollaway bed for a third person or child. Perhaps the best perk is that guests have use of one of the finest gym facilities in the city, complete with exercise room, squash courts, yoga studio (with scheduled classes), steam, and sauna. Continental breakfast is included, as are killer views of the city. No club membership is required. To book a room, either call the hotel or send an email to reservations@univclub.com.

800 Powell St. (at California St.). ✆ **415/781-0900**. www.univclub.com. 16 units. 5 are suites with a sitting room. $200–$259. Children are free using existing bedding. Rates include continental breakfast. Limited parking $35 per day. **Amenities:** Restaurant and bar Tues–Fri only; gym; sauna.

SOMA

SoMa offers an eclectic mix of lodgings, from some of the highest thread counts in the city to budget motels. It's home to the Moscone convention center, MOMA, Yerba Buena Center for the Arts, and AT&T Park.

Best For: Baseball fans, conventioneers, foodies, clubbers, business travelers, and anyone with an affinity for the arts.

Drawbacks: Beware of seemingly great deals for hotels in sketchy areas. Long blocks mean long walks.

Moderate

The Palace Hotel ★★★   With all the lovely hotels to choose from for an overnight in San Francisco, the Palace is my absolute favorite. I've spent birthdays, anniversaries, New Years Eve, and other special occasions here over the years, and I never tire of this beautiful old girl. Originally built in 1875, back then, the Palace was once considered the largest, most expensive, luxurious hotel in the world, and, according to industrialist/philanthropist, Andrew Carnegie, she put The Grand in Paris to shame. Rebuilt completely after the 1906 quake, little has changed during the past 100-plus years. Entering the majestic lobby feels like a step back in time. As the only indoor historical landmark in the city, the stunning Garden Court, with marble columns, massive chandeliers, crowned by an atrium of over 80,000 panes of stained glass, will take your breath away. And though the Palace is the definition of elegant luxury, leave your ball gowns and tails at home; it is not the least bit pretentious. For a historic hotel, the rooms are a good size (even the least expensive standard rooms have enough space for

San Francisco Hotels

MARINA
Marina Green
Marina Blvd
Cervantes Blvd
North Point St.
Fort Mason
Bay St.
Francisco St.
Moscone Rec. Ctr.
Chestnut St.
Divisadero St.
Pierce St.
Avila St.
Mason St.
Richardson Ave.
Lincoln Blvd
101
San Francisco National Cemetery
THE PRESIDIO
7
4
5
6
101
Octavia St.
Franklin St.
Lombard St.
Greenwich St.
Filbert St.
COW HOLLOW
Union St.
Green St.
Vallejo St.
Broadway
Pacific Ave.
Laguna St.
Gough St.
Fillmore St.
Jackson St.
Washington St.
3
Scott St.
Alta Plaza
PACIFIC HEIGHTS
Lafayette Park
Buchanan St.
Presidio Golf Course
Clay St.
Sacramento St.
Lyon St.
Baker St.
California St.
Pine St.
Bush St.
16
15
PRESIDIO HEIGHTS
Maple St.
Cherry St.
Laurel St.
Walnut St.
Presidio Ave.
Lake St.
5th Ave.
Cornwall St.
Euclid Ave.
Sutter St.
Post St.
Japan Center
17
Commonwealth Ave.
Jordan Ave.
Palm Ave.
Parker Ave.
Spruce St.
Collins St.
Wood St.
Hamilton Sq.
Geary Blvd.
WESTERN ADDITION
Clement St.
Arguello Blvd.
O'Farrell St.
Ellis St.
Steiner St.
Eddy St.
Webster St.
Jefferson Square
1
RICHMOND
6th Ave.
4th Ave.
3rd Ave.
2nd Ave.
Anza St.
UNIVERSITY OF SAN FRANCISCO
Turk Blvd.
Masonic Ave.
Golden Gate Ave.
Fulton St.
Balboa St.
Willard St.
Cole St.
U.S.F.
McAllister St.
Divisadero St.
Alamo Square
Cabrillo St.
Stanyan St.
Grove St.
Central Ave.
Lyon St.
Hayes St.
Pierce St.
Fell St.
HAYES VALLEY
Fillmore St.
Laguna St.
Fulton St.
Conservatory of Flowers
John F. Kennedy Dr.
The Panhandle
Fell St.
Oak St.
Page St.
Waller St.
Hermann St.
GOLDEN GATE PARK
Shrader St.
Clayton St.
Ashbury St.
HAIGHT-ASHBURY
Haight St.
Buena Vista Park
Alpine Terr.
Duboce Park
Duboce Ave.
18
Kezar Dr.
21
22
Kezar Stadium
Frederick St.
Buena Vista Ave.
14th St.
Noe St.
Sanchez St.
Lincoln Wy.
Carl St.
15th St.
Castro St.
Church St.
Hugo St.
INNER SUNSET
Parnassus Ave.
Belvedere St.
Cole St.
Corona Heights Park
States St.
16th St.
Mission Dolores
Dolores St.
6th Ave.
5th Ave.
UNIVERSITY OF CALIFORNIA–SAN FRANCISCO
Carmel St.
17th St.
CASTRO
20
Castro Theatre
19
18th St.
Market St.
Dolores Park

0 | 1/2 mi
0 | 1/2 km

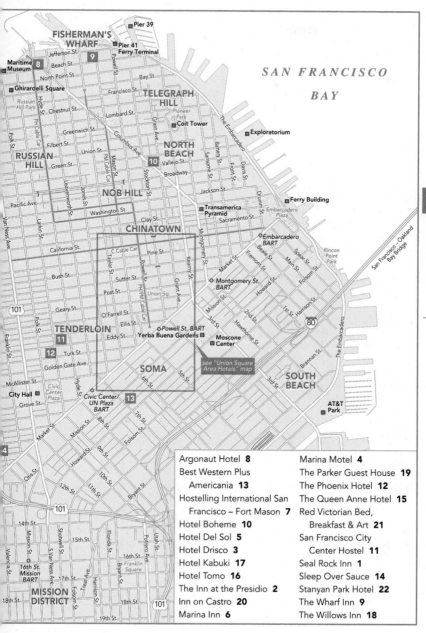

FISHERMAN'S WHARF
Pier 39
Pier 41
Ferry Terminal
Maritime Museum
8
9
Jefferson St.
Beach St.
North Point St.
Ghirardelli Square
Russian Hill Park
Bay St.
Francisco St.
TELEGRAPH HILL
Pioneer Park
Coit Tower
Chestnut St.
Lombard St.
Greenwich St.
Filbert St.
RUSSIAN HILL
Union St.
Green St.
NORTH BEACH
10
Vallejo St.
Broadway
Exploratorium
Pacific Ave.
NOB HILL
Jackson St.
Washington St.
Clay St.
CHINATOWN
Transamerica Pyramid
Sacramento St.
Ferry Building
Embarcadero Plaza
California St.
C Cable Car
Pine St.
Embarcadero BART
Rincon Point Park
Bush St.
Sutter St.
Union Sq.
Montgomery St. BART
Post St.
Geary St.
O'Farrell St.
Ellis St.
Powell St. BART
Yerba Buena Gardens
Moscone Center
TENDERLOIN
11
Turk St.
Eddy St.
Golden Gate Ave.
McAllister St.
City Hall
Civic Center Plaza
Grove St.
SOMA
see "Union Square Area Hotels" map
SOUTH BEACH
12
Civic Center/ UN Plaza BART
13
Market St.
Mission St.
Howard St.
Folsom St.
AT&T Park
4
Otis St.
MISSION DISTRICT
Franklin Square
16th St. Mission BART
18th St.
19th St.

SAN FRANCISCO BAY

San Francisco–Oakland Bay Bridge

Argonaut Hotel **8**	Marina Motel **4**
Best Western Plus	The Parker Guest House **19**
Americana **13**	The Phoenix Hotel **12**
Hostelling International San	The Queen Anne Hotel **15**
Francisco – Fort Mason **7**	Red Victorian Bed,
Hotel Boheme **10**	Breakfast & Art **21**
Hotel Del Sol **5**	San Francisco City
Hotel Drisco **3**	Center Hostel **11**
Hotel Kabuki **17**	Seal Rock Inn **1**
Hotel Tomo **16**	Sleep Over Sauce **14**
The Inn at the Presidio **2**	Stanyan Park Hotel **22**
Inn on Castro **20**	The Wharf Inn **9**
Marina Inn **6**	The Willows Inn **18**

THE most FAMILY-FRIENDLY HOTELS

Argonaut Hotel (p. 65)   Not only is it near all the funky kid fun of Fisherman's Wharf and the National Maritime Museum, but this bayside hotel also has kid-friendly perks like the opportunity for each child to grab a gift from the hotel's "treasure chest," a scavenger hunt, board games, kid-friendly movies, and a Wii game in the lobby.

Beresford Arms Hotel (p. 56)   The Parlor Suite can sleep up to a family of seven and comes with a full kitchen and dining room—all for around $200. The Junior Suite sleeps six and costs only $159. Located a few blocks from Union Square, this Victorian charmer is perfect for families on a budget wanting a little extra space.

The Fairmont San Francisco (p. 59)   While the glamorous lobby and spectacular city views will please parents, kids will be thrilled by the hotel's **Tonga Room,** a fantastically kitsch Disneyland-like tropical bar and restaurant where "rain" falls every 30 minutes.

Hotel Del Sol (p. 68)   It's colorful enough to represent a Crayola selection, but tots are more likely to be impressed by the "Kids are VIPs" program that includes a lending library, toys and movies, evening cookies and milk, a heated pool, and a nearby park. Parents will be happy to find a 2-bedroom family suite.

Hotel Diva (p. 52)   The sleek, mod Diva has all sorts of fun kid-friendly perks.

Check out SF's version of the Walk of Fame right outside the door, and definitely ask about their two-room Little Divas Suite, with bunk beds, drawing tables, and a TV loaded with kids' movies.

Hotel Kabuki (p. 70) features rooms with 2 double beds for as little as $139. Kids will be thrilled with the traditional Japanese decor.

Ritz Carlton (p. 60)   The Ritz has a Very Important Kid program with a kid-sized in-room tent for your room, coloring books, and milk and cookies at turndown.

Seal Rock Inn (p. 67)   Surrounded by parks, across the street from the beach, and just a few minutes from the zoo, this family-friendly hotel features suites with kitchenettes.

Stanyan Park Hotel (p. 74)   Plenty of elbowroom and a half-block walk to Golden Gate Park's Children's Playground make this a prime spot for crashing family style. But the biggest bonuses are the suites, which come with one or two bedrooms, a full kitchen, and a dining area.

Westin St. Francis (p. 52)   A classic San Francisco hotel down to its hospitality, the Westin welcomes the little ones with fun gifts and toys, including coloring books, crayons, and a rubber ducky. Kids love riding in the glass elevators.

a comfy chair to relax in and a desk set). The surprisingly high ceilings also help give the illusion that rooms are a little larger. Rates vary drastically; I have always found the best deals using AAA and booking direct through the hotel website.

2 New Montgomery St. (at Market St.). ✆ **415/512-1111.** www.sfpalace.com. 553 units. $169–$379 double. Extra person $40. Children 17 and under sharing existing bedding stay free in parent's room. Parking $59, oversized vehicles $64. Bus: All Market St. buses. Streetcar: All Market St. streetcars. Bart: Market. **Amenities:** 4 restaurants; bar; room service; concierge; health club w/ skylight-covered, heated lap pool; Jacuzzi; sauna; spa; free Wi-Fi in lobby; Wi-Fi in room $20 per day.

Inexpensive

The Best Western Plus Americana ★ Imagine if the folks who drew *The Jetsons* cartoon were to design a motel. The groovy decor would look just like it does at the Americana, a hip yet affordable lodging in the heart of the city. You wouldn't expect to get a heated outdoor swimming pool and reasonably sized and equipped gym for the nightly rates here, but you do get them. Add to all that laundry facilities, board games in each room and free Wi-Fi, and you have a prize pick.

121 7th St. (at Minna St.). ℭ **415/626-0200.** www.americaniahotel.com. 143 units. $126–$242 double. Pet friendly. Valet parking $30, $35 for oversize vehicles. Streetcar: F-Line. **Amenities:** Restaurant, fitness center, pool, laundry, dry cleaning, complimentary bikes based on availability.

The Mosser ★ Regular visitors wishing to stay in the SoMa area have to compete with the deep pockets of corporate guests attending events at the nearby Moscone Center. The result is that hotel prices in the area are generally high, and reasonably priced hotel rooms are like the proverbial needle in a haystack. The Mosser—a sophisticated modern hotel housed in a Victorian building—bucks this trend by offering top quality lodging at more than affordable prices. If you are willing to share a bathroom, the price gets even better. On the off chance you are tired of singing in the shower and hoping to get discovered, along with offering guests complimentary continental breakfast, and access to a nearby fitness center, the Mosser has an onsite recording studio.

54 Fourth St. (at Market St.). ℭ **415/986-4400.** www.themosser.com. 166 units, $110–$214 double with bathroom; $85–$144 double w/out bathroom. Rates include continental breakfast. Valet parking $35, $45 for oversize vehicles. Streetcar: F-Line, and all underground Muni. BART: All trains. **Amenities:** Restaurant; bar; concierge, access to Marriott fitness center and spa for $15 per day.

NORTH BEACH/FISHERMAN'S WHARF

North Beach is the birthplace of the Beat Generation, where Little Italy meets and mixes with Big China. It's home to boutique hotels, family-run restaurants, and a lively nightlife scene. Fisherman's Wharf is the heart of all the tourist action. You'll pay more to stay in this neighborhood, because it's where most visitors want to be.

Best For: Hopeless romantics, foodies, wannabe novelists, coffee lovers, chowder lovers, sea lion lovers.

Drawbacks: Tough parking, few hotel bargains, rowdy out-of-towners on weekend nights, and (family alert) plenty of porn on Broadway.

Expensive

Argonaut Hotel ★★★ If you have absolutely no patience for public transportation, don't give a damn about saving money, and want to walk right out your door into the heart of the all the tourist action, this nautical themed hotel is perfect for you. Owned by upscale Kimpton Hotels, the Argonaut is housed in the exposed red brick and wooden beams of the old 1908 Haslett warehouse. The good-sized rooms are navy and beige, decorated with tasteful nautical knickknacks, and feature complimentary Starbucks coffee. Kids love the treasure chest at the front desk; staff are thoughtful (when we stayed here a few years ago, they let my daughter pick out a little plastic something every time she walked by). With a Wii game in the lobby, games and movies to borrow, and Ghirardelli ice cream sundaes a short stroll around the corner, you know you will never be allowed to stay anywhere else if the little ones have a say. Your dog might not let you stay anywhere else either: the Argonaut is just a few minutes from a grassy walking area and the keep-the-leash-on beach across the street. After a long day playing and sniffing, your pup can come home to his own dog bed, dog toys, and even doggie room service. Each afternoon at 5pm, the hotel's Master Sommelier hand selects a few vintages for guests to enjoy at a hosted wine reception in the Living Room, a comfortable lounge area with a fireplace, plush red chairs, and all sorts of nautical paraphernalia mounted on the walls, such as maps, compasses, and wooden steering wheels. The nautical theme carries over to the **Blue Mermaid Chowder House & Bar,** open daily for breakfast, lunch and dinner in a sea-faring room of thick-hewn timber and braided ropes.

495 Jefferson St. (at Hyde St.). ✆ **415/563-0800.** www.argonauthotel.com. 252 units. $278–$369 double; $358–$639 quad. Rates include evening wine in the lobby. Pet friendly (no charge, no size limit). Parking $46, oversized vehicles $61. Bus: 30 or 47. Streetcar: F-Line. Cable car: Powell–Hyde line. **Amenities:** Restaurant; bar; concierge; in-room spa services; 24-hr fitness center, complimentary Wi-Fi and "raid the mini bar" program for Kimpton InTouch members (no charge to join).

Moderate

The Hotel Bohème ★ By definition, a bohemian is "a person who has informal and unconventional social habits, especially an artist or writer." And that about sums up the clientele here. Don't believe me? Beat Poet Allen Ginsberg was known to hang his hat here, apparently in room 204. Like the other guests, he likely prized the company he kept here and overlooked the fact that the rooms are tiny, the bathrooms even smaller, and steep steps connect them all. As for the decor: let's call it shabby chic but clean. But the neighborhood, with its Italian cafes, bookstores, and bars right out the door on lively Columbus Avenue, are superb; and complimentary sherry service each evening in the hotel lobby makes the atmosphere very social. Obviously, this isn't the place for everyone, but it might be just right for you.

444 Columbus Ave. (btw. Vallejo and Green sts.). ✆ **415/433-9111.** www.hotelboheme.com. 15 units. $174–$214 double. Rates include afternoon sherry. Parking at nearby public garages $30–$35. Bus: 12, 30, 41, or 45. Cable car: Powell–Mason line. **Amenities:** Concierge.

The Wharf Inn ★ Though this basic hotel might be a little dated, the Wharf Inn is the rare example of a really good deal right in the heart of Fisherman's Wharf. Pier 39, the cable car turnaround, and Boudin Bakery are all just steps away. And the digs? They're clean if frill-free. A helpful front desk staff, complimentary coffee, tea, and hot chocolate all day in the lobby, as well as free parking help most guests forgive the Wharf Inn's lack of style.

2601 Mason St. (at Beach St.). ✆ **415/673-7411.** www.wharfinn.com. 51 units. $127–$160. Free parking. Bus: 39 or 47. Streetcar: F-Line. Cable car: Powell–Mason or Powell–Hyde line.

THE MARINA/PACIFIC HEIGHTS/ PRESIDIO

This is where the college Greek crowd ends up after graduating. It's our top pick for staying at a reasonably priced hotel or motel and taking public transport to Union Square.

Best For: Eye candy, shopping, kid-friendly lodging, lively restaurant and bar scene, nonhill strolling, beach access.

Drawbacks: Few sightseeing attractions, and you'll need to take a taxi or bus (or a very long walk) to the city center.

SLEEPING seaside

Established in 1959, the **Seal Rock Inn** ★★ is San Francisco's only ocean-front motor inn. The perfect spot for a family stay, the inn is surrounded by parks and trails and sits across the street from the beach—great for relaxing but don't swim here; there is a nasty current. The zoo and Golden Gate Park are just a few minutes away. Rooms are large, and some feature kitchenettes or fireplaces; all have fridges and free parking. As of August 2013, the pool was temporarily closed (call ahead if a pool is important). The Seal Rock Inn (✆ **415/752-8000;** www.sealrockinn.com) is at 545 Point Lobos Ave. (at 48th Ave.). Double rooms range from $120 to $177. Two-night minimum on weekends and holidays. $10 per night for additional guests 16 and above; $5 for guests ages 1 to 15 years old.

Expensive

Hotel Drisco ★ The non-descript Hotel Drisco is a bit off the beaten path, quietly blending in with the multi-million dollar mansions of old-moneyed Pacific Heights. It's a place for guest seeking discreet, high-class service and amenities, without the showy feel of a big city luxury property. Guests enjoy generous rooms, many with commanding views of the city. Complimentary continental breakfast includes such delicacies as currant scones with lemon curd and clotted cream, local organic sheep's milk yogurt, and a selection of meats and cheeses. The evening wine reception allows guest to socialize while noshing on cheese, charcuterie, and a variety of hot hors d'oeuvres. Should you in fact decide to leave this serene enclave to go see the sights, shopping, restaurants, and nightlife are all only a few minutes away. Bikes are available to borrow on a first-come first-serve basis.

2901 Pacific Ave. (at Broderick St.). ✆ **415/346-2880.** www.hoteldrisco.com. 48 units. $285–$425. Rates include gourmet continental breakfast, afternoon tea and cookies, and evening wine, cheese, and hot hors d'oeuvre. Free street parking available. Bus: 3 or 24. **Amenities:** Concierge; exercise room and free pass to YMCA; room service.

Inn at the Presidio ★★★ If you prefer nature to the traffic, crowds, and sky-scrapers of a big city, yet still want to visit San Francisco, this former officers' quarters—converted to an inn in 2011—was created just for you. Set on over 1,400 acres of coastal dunes, forests, and prairie grasslands, guests arrive to find a stately red brick Georgian Revival-style building from back in the U.S. Army days when the Presidio played an important role defending the new territories on the West coast. Though Pershing Hall, as the inn was formerly called, is on the National Register of Historic Places, this is anything but a musty old boys club. Rooms are modern and elegant, featuring high ceilings and original moldings; most are suites with fireplaces; many have views of the bay. At almost 300 square feet, even the basic queen rooms are large by San Francisco hotel standards. Public spaces are warm and inviting; guests enjoy complimentary continental breakfast and an evening wine and cheese reception.

The inn has been such a success that in July 2013, Funston House—a Victorian-style home that used to house officers and their families—opened as a four-bedroom cottage that can be rented in part or as a whole by groups or extended families for $215–$1,000 per night. If you want to see the city sights, the PresidioGo shuttle offers rides downtown on weekdays; Muni buses serve the area daily. Though, with miles of hiking

ACCOMMODATIONS WITH free parking

Despite our exhortations to leave the driving to locals and use the public transportation system to get around, some of you will still want to drive the crazy streets of San Francisco, or at least arrive by car. But with parking fees averaging $45 to $60 a night at most hotels, the extra charges can add up for visitors with wheels. So if you're going to rent a car or bring your own, you might want to consider staying at one of these hotels that offers free parking:

- **Hostelling International San Francisco,** Fisherman's Wharf, below
- **Hotel Del Sol,** Marina District/ Cow Hollow, p. 68
- **Hotel Drisco,** Pacific Heights, p. 67 (no garage, but lots of free street parking)
- **Marina Motel,** Marina District/ Cow Hollow, p. 69
- **Phoenix Hotel,** Civic Center, p. 71
- **Seal Rock Inn,** Richmond District, p. 67
- **The Wharf Inn,** North Beach/ Fisherman's Wharf, p. 66

trails just out the door, a fire pit on the back deck, and rocking chairs on the front porch, you might not make it to Fisherman's Wharf.

Main Post, 42 Moraga Ave. (at Funston Ave.). ℂ **415/800-7356.** www.innatthepresidio.com. 26 units. From $215–$375; $25 extra person charge; no charge for children 15 and under. Rates include continental buffet breakfast, evening wine and cheese reception. Pet friendly $40 fee. Self parking $6. Bus: 28, 43, or PresidioGo shuttle bus.

Moderate

Hotel Del Sol ★★   Wonderful, colorful Hotel del Sol is strategically located in the family-friendly Marina District, just a couple of blocks from the bustling thoroughfare of Lombard Street. Children will be thrilled to know they are not far from the Disney Museum, and hiking trails of the Presidio, as well as the noise and excitement of Fisherman's Wharf. When little ones tire of touring, they can cool off in the hotel's sparkling outdoor heated pool. Two-bedroom family suites are available; make sure to ask about the "Kids-are-VIP's" program featuring books, toys, and movies. All guests are served a complimentary continental breakfast, and—could it get any better—parking is free.

3100 Webster St. (at Greenwich St.). ℂ **415/921-5520.** www.thehoteldelsol.com. 57 units. From $143–$224 double; $161–$296 suite. Rates include continental breakfast and free newspapers in the lobby. Free parking. Bus: 22, 28, 30, or 43. **Amenities:** Heated outdoor pool.

Inexpensive

Hostelling International San Francisco—Fort Mason ★★★   When some people hear "hostel," they automatically assume the place will be a noisy party scene, filled with young people trying to save a buck. Well, the hostel at Fort Mason is absolutely none of that. This lovely hostel is in a clean, quiet, and historic building on a bluff overlooking the bay. It boasts extraordinary views of Alcatraz and is just a few minutes' walk from The Marina and Fisherman's Wharf. The atmosphere is downright genteel and at $30 per night, including breakfast and parking, the price is more than right. That starting rate is for the co-ed, girls-only, and boys-only dorm rooms, but you can take advantage of the benefits of staying here—and there are many—by booking one of the few private doubles and triples. Linens and towels are provided, smoking and alcohol are not allowed; and quiet time is from 11pm–7am though there is no curfew (the front desk is staffed 24/7). No one is required to do any chores, but guests are asked to pick up after themselves, duh. Computer terminals (small fee), free Wi-Fi, a fully equipped kitchen, laundry facilities, and a lounge area with cushy sofas, a flat-screen TV, and a pool table are available for anyone to use. A free continental breakfast is served daily in Café Franco overlooking the water; inexpensive lunches and dinners are also available. The front desk can help book day trips, and an airport shuttle will pick you up or drop you off for only $14 each way (arrange online before your stay). This hostel is not only for youths—when I was there last, I met 20-something Swedish backpackers and 60-something Canadian visitors. Children under 7 have to be in a private room with their parents. Children 7 and older are allowed in the dorms as long as they are accompanied by a parent.

I truly wish I could say this place is the best kept secret in the city, but the word is already out. You need to book early, especially if you want one of the coveted private rooms with a view (Room 23, a triple with a 180 degree water view, is my personal favorite). Booking through the hostel website is straightforward and they guarantee the lowest rates or you save 25 percent. Sister properties are available at Union Square (p. 56) and Civic Center.

Fort Mason, Bldg. 240. ☎ **415/771-7277.** www.sfhostels.com/fishermans-wharf. 150 beds. Dorm beds $30–$42; private rooms $75–$109. Rates include breakfast. HI membership required $28 annual, or $3 per day. Free limited parking. Bus: 28, 30, 47, or 49. **Amenities:** Concierge services, cafe.

Marina Inn ★   Similar to the Marina Motel (below), this inexpensive inn is another great choice for budgeteers. Set in a 1920's Victorian building, the floral wallpaper and heavy pine furniture give the whole place a cozy, cottage-like feel. Rooms are cute and quaint, though a little noisy if close to busy Lombard Street (ask for a room in the back). When you consider the complimentary continental breakfast, with prices as low as $63 for a double, it's hard to find a better deal in the city. In fact, there isn't a better deal in the city.

3110 Octavia St. (at Lombard St.). ☎ **415/928-1000.** www.marinainn.com. 40 units. $63–$199 double. Rates include continental breakfast. No parking. Bus: 28, 30, or 49. **Amenities:** Concierge.

Marina Motel ★   This sweet and simple "auto courtyard" motel was built to cel-ebrate the opening of the Golden Gate Bridge in 1939, and has been owned by the same Gold Rush-era pioneer family ever since. Guests enter the property on a cobble-stone driveway, and pull their cars into a courtyard with cascading flowers, reminiscent of a European inn. They then park in their own private garage—unheard of at most San Francisco hotels, and, for that matter, most San Francisco houses too. Rooms are cozy (yes, small) and clean, though a little noisy if they front Lombard street (here's another one where asking for a room in the back pays off). All rooms have fridges, and com-plimentary coffee, tea, and hot chocolate. 17 of the units have fully equipped kitchens, making this a great choice for extended stays and families. Dogs are welcome. Trendy restaurants and cool shops on Chestnut and Union Streets are just a few blocks away.

2576 Lombard St. (btw. Divisadero and Broderick sts.). ☎ **415/921-9406.** www.marinamotel.com. 39 units. $109–$179 double; $119–$279 suite. Rates include discount coupons for nearby cafe. Pet friendly. Free covered parking. Bus: 28, 30, 43, 45, or 70.

JAPANTOWN & ENVIRONS

If you're staying in or near Japantown, it might be because you found a lodging deal you couldn't pass up. Though a few miles from the typical tourist sights, this historic neighborhood in and of itself is interesting and offers lots to see and do.

Best For: Central location for exploring the entire city (including the west side), Japanese culture, quiet lodgings, safe neighborhood. Great for families.

Drawbacks: Limited nightlife, a few miles from the main tourist hotspots.

Moderate

Hotel Kabuki ★★   And now for something completely different . . . While most hotels in San Francisco fall into the category of either Modern Contemporary, Victorian, Edwardian, or Motel Dumpian, Hotel Kabuki is none of these. Located in the center of quiet Japantown, this lovely property features zen gardens, minimalist rooms, lacquered furnishings, shoji screens, and deep soaking tubs—all elements of traditional Japanese decor. The koi pond outside is pure serenity, a welcome respite after a day of touring. Pets are welcome. Family-sized suites are available for well under $200. *Hint:* This hotel tends to give the best rates to those who book direct at www.hotelkabuki.com. Click "Specials" (top right) for massive discounts on breakfast, parking, and spa passes.

1625 Post St. (btw. Gough and Octavia sts.). ✆ **415/922-3200.** www.hotelkabuki.com. 218 units. $143–$224 double; $159–$309 quad. Extra person $20 over 18 yrs. Pet friendly. Valet parking $40; public garage $23. Bus: 2 or 3. **Amenities:** Restaurant; concierge; 24-hr. fitness room.

Hotel Tomo ★★   Where else would you expect to find an anime-themed hotel but in the heart of Japantown? Not quite sure what anime even is? It is a Japanese art form characterized by stark colorful graphics, vibrant characters with large doe-like eyes, and futuristic settings. The rooms at this Joie de Vivre property are high design, each with its own colorful wall mural by Heisuke Kitazawa, comfy beds and lots of light. Rooms are large by San Francisco standards, and offer guests a fridge and a Keurig coffee-maker. If you're just not sure where to dine in Japantown, **Mums,** the hotel's onsite restaurant, serves all-you-can-eat shabu-shabu and all-you-can-drink beer and sake.

1800 Sutter St. (at Buchanan St.). ✆ **415/921-4000.** www.hoteltomo.com. 125 units. $185–$295 double. Parking $29. Bus: 2 or 3. **Amenities:** Restaurant, fitness center, business center.

The Queen Anne Hotel ★   Do you believe in ghosts? Visitors at this historic hotel are certain it's haunted by a Miss Mary Lake, the former headmistress of the school that occupied this building 100 years ago. Her office was in room 410, and experts swear there is paranormal activity in the area. Scared away? Don't be. This "haunted hotel" is one of the best values in the city for those looking for unusually large guestrooms. Many room have fridges; all are furnished in beautiful, period antiques. In the morning, guests enjoy a complimentary and heavy breakfast including sausage and eggs; in the evening, complimentary tea and cookies encourage guests to congregate in the common area to trade ghost stories.

1590 Sutter St. (btw. Laguna and Webster sts.). ✆ **415/441-2828.** www.queenanne.com. 48 units. $109–$199 double; $145–$350 quad; $325–$459 suite for six. Extra person $10. Rates include continental breakfast, afternoon tea and sherry, morning newspaper. Parking $20. Bus: 2 or 3. **Amenities:** Concierge, airport shuttle service.

CIVIC CENTER/TENDERLOIN

This is another one of those locations where you get more bang for your hotel buck by commuting to the tourist hotspots. That being said, the Civic Center has a large homeless population; the Tenderloin has that and many drug addicts and dealers. Both areas can be on the sketchy side—you'll see more folks pushing shopping carts than baby carriages—so the use of caution is especially crucial late at night. But, there is safety in numbers; with the Asian Art Museum, the opera, ballet, symphony, and brand new SFJAZZ venue all close by, you'll rarely find yourself alone.

Best For: Folks seeking culture, and those who want to play wannabe rock star at the Phoenix Hotel.

Drawbacks: Expect panhandlers, and take taxis after dark.

Moderate

The Phoenix Hotel ★   Welcome to the unofficial local rock and roll sleeping hall of fame, a place favored by many, many musicians. Stay here and you just may sleep in the same bed as the Red Hot Chili Peppers, Moby, Keanu Reeves, Pearl Jam, Joan Jett, and David Bowie. Don't worry, the sheets have been changed. Rooms are colorful and noisy; all face the pool in the courtyard outside a la Melrose Place. Visiting entertainers, bands, and regular guests gather around the heated outdoor pool under the watchful eyes of a giant blue mosaic frog strumming a guitar. To help a poor musician catch a break, breakfast, parking, and Wi-Fi are free. Now, if only the walls could talk.

601 Eddy St. (at Larkin St.). ✆ **415/776-1380.** www.thephoenixhotel.com. 44 units. $129–$199 double; $129–$359 quad. Rates include continental breakfast and free weekday passes to Kabuki Springs & Spa. Free parking. Bus: 47. Streetcar: F-Line. **Amenities:** Bar, concierge, heated outdoor pool.

Inexpensive

San Francisco City Center Hostel ★   Located in a 1920's boutique hotel on the border of the Civic Center and Little Saigon in the Tenderloin District, this hostel can best be described as an inexpensive place with spotless rooms in a sketchy area. Ok, first let's address the area—it is a fact that the Tenderloin is home to addicts and homeless people. As with any large city, use extreme caution when walking after dark. The hostel itself feels very safe; guests are an eclectic mix of visitors from all over the world, including many international students who stay up to 9 months. Because the property used to be a regular hotel, each room has a private bathroom and houses 4-5 people in bunk beds. Private rooms with attached bathrooms are available for far less than you'd pay at a traditional hotel. There is a clean updated stainless kitchen for guests to use, as well as four different lounge areas stocked with books and games. **Ivy's Place,** the onsite cafe, is the main gathering place, serving free continental breakfast in the morning (for an extra $1, you can have all-you-can-eat eggs and pancakes), and beer, wine, and snacks in the evening. Guests bond and make new friends on organized pub crawls, dinners, movie nights, and walking tours.

685 Ellis St. (at Larkin St.). ✆ **415/474-5721.** www.sfhostels.org/city-center. 185 beds. Dorm beds from $27; private rooms from $89. HI membership required $28 annual, or $3 daily, rates include continental breakfast. Parking $24. Bus: 47. Streetcar: F-Line. **Amenities:** Kitchen, cafe.

Sleep Over Sauce ★   When the three Holsley brothers (Matt, Trip, and Nate), along with chef Ben Paula, opened Sauce restaurant in 2004, they never imagined they

WHY SETTLE FOR A HOTEL? ALMOST FREE
home exchanges

There are three types of home exchanges: simultaneous (you stay in someone's house while they stay in yours), non-simultaneous (you stay at someone's home, no one stays in yours), and a hospitality exchange (you stay in someone's home while they are there). Sound like a weird, new trendy idea? **Homelink** (www.homelink.org), one of the premier home exchange companies, has been in business for over 60 years. You pay a small fee to join (though you can take a look for free), and then connect with homeowners around the world.

I have never done a home exchange, but friends have, and swear by it. They say that by the time the exchange happens, they have emailed and spoken on the phone with their exchange partners so often, they feel like old friends. A quick glance shows lovely homes with spectacular views available in Nob Hill, Pacific Heights, and Telegraph Hill, as well as many other properties. Two more companies specializing in exchanges are **HomeExchange** (www.homeexchange.com), and **Intervac** (www.intervac.com). Most experts warn against using **Craigslist** for swaps, because it's had problems with scammers. Those clubs that charge a fee—and all those listed above do—are able to weed out the ne'er do wells.

would get into the hotel business a few years later. In 2009, when the space above the restaurant became available, they jumped on it; the result is a cozy urban guest house with eight rooms, a living room—complete with fireplace and cushy leather sofas, and a full service bar and restaurant. The simple guestrooms are decorated with wood trim and framed photos of past and present San Francisco, as well as kitschy chandeliers to add a little character. Beds are comfy; the bathrooms have been remodeled. Located in the center of the city, Sleep Over Sauce is an ideal central home base for visitors wanting to see more than just Fisherman's Wharf. Most of the city's performing arts venues, as well as the fabulous Asian Art Museum, are just a few minutes' walk away. The Mission District, Japantown, Castro, and Haight-Ashbury neighborhoods can be reached by Muni in a few minutes, and the historic F-line will take guests to Union Square and Fisherman's Wharf. Don't look for a front desk, guests check in at the bar.

135 Gough St. (at Lily St.). ✆ **415/621-0896.** www.sleepsf.com. 8 units. From $129 double; $234 suite. Some dates have 2-night minimum. Parking: city parking garages within a few blocks. Bus: 21. Streetcar: F-Line. **Amenities:** Restaurant, bar, business center.

CASTRO

This colorful neighborhood is symbolic of San Francisco's past and present as a city of anything goes. Most businesses (including accommodations) cater to LGBT customers, but everyone is welcome in this lively neighborhood. Though located a few miles from all of the tourist action, public transportation makes for an easy ride straight to the visitor meccas of Union Square and Fisherman's Wharf.

Best For: Excellent dining scene, great for people-watching, eclectic shops selling things you may not be able to buy in your hometown, and, best of all, unbelievable value for your hotel dollar.

Drawbacks: Minimal selection of hotel choices, noise and crowds on Pride and holiday weekends. Far from city center.

Moderate

The Parker Guest House ★★★ Rated one of the top guest houses in San Francisco by gay travel sites such as Spartacus and Purple Roofs, this lovely 1909 Edwardian B&B in the heart of the Castro is the perfect oasis to return to after a long day of sightseeing in the big city. Sip a glass of wine outside by the garden fountain at the daily complimentary social. Lounge by the fireplace, or, perhaps, in the library. Spacious rooms feature down comforters, terry robes, and period antiques.

520 Church St. (btw. 17th and 18th sts.). ℰ **415/621-3222.** www.parkerguesthouse.com. 21 units. From $159 double shared bathroom; $269 junior suite. Minimum stays on weekends and during events. Rates include extended continental breakfast and evening wine social. Self-parking $23. Bus: 22 or 33. Streetcar: J Church. **Amenities:** Steam room, gardens.

Inexpensive

Inn on Castro ★ Guests at this inn in the heart of the Castro have two choices when it comes to sleeping arrangements. The first is one of the self-catered apartments with a full kitchen; they sleep up to four comfortably. Mollie Stone's Grocery is just a short walk away. The second choice is a room in the regular, full service B&B, located in a restored Edwardian building filled with fresh flowers and original artwork. Bathrooms are shared or private, depending on which room you choose. Guests of the B&B rooms enjoy a complimentary full breakfast each morning; the hosted afternoon brandy service is always a good way to unwind and socialize. Either way you go, in the Castro, it's all about value for your money.

321 Castro St. (at Market St.). ℰ **415/861-0321.** www.innoncastro.com. 8 units, 2 w/bathroom across the hall; 6 apts. From $135 double w/shared bathroom; $250 2-bedroom apartment w/full kitchen suitable for 4. Rates include full breakfast and evening brandy. Streetcar: F, K, L, or M lines.

The Willows Inn ★ Yet another example of excellent value for your tourist dollar, the Willows is an old Edwardian building located in the center of the Castro, only a short streetcar ride away from all the sights. Though typically catering to the LGBT guest, all are welcome in this quaint B&B. Rooms vary in size and are priced accordingly; each has a vanity sink, though none have private bathrooms, again helping to keep the price down. Some rooms have chaise lounges or bay windows; all have bentwood willow furnishings, antique dressers or armoires, and colorful cozy duvets. Guests enjoy a complimentary continental breakfast including eggs, juice, yogurt, fruit, and coffee. Evening cocktails are hosted, encouraging guests to mingle and relax.

710 14th St. (near Church and Market sts.). ℰ **415/431-4770.** www.willowssf.com. 12 units, none w/bathroom. From $120 double; $160 triple; $170 quad. Rates include continental breakfast. Streetcar: F-Line.

HAIGHT–ASHBURY

San Francisco's summers of love are long gone, but open-minded folk wanting to escape the tourist scene and embrace eccentricity will dig the Haight.

Best For: Finding your inner hippie, an eclectic array of shops and restaurants with plenty of visual stimulation, close to Golden Gate Park.

Drawbacks: "Got change?" Young squatters begging for change on Haight Street get old real fast.

Moderate

Stanyan Park Hotel ★   This historic Victorian B&B is strategically located right across the street from all of the treasures of Golden Gate Park: the Japanese Tea Garden, the Conservatory of Flowers, the de Young Museum, and the California Academy of Sciences. It's ideal for families looking for a home base for exploring the western side of the city. One and two-bedroom apartments feature full kitchens, dining rooms, and living rooms. The guest rooms are comfortable and decorated with fine period antiques, reminiscent of a more genteel time. All guests enjoy complimentary continental breakfast.

750 Stanyan St. (at Waller St.). ℂ **415/751-1000.** www.stanyanpark.com. 36 units. From $175 doubles; $300 suite; $350 2-bedroom suite. Rates include continental breakfast. Rollaway $20; cribs free. Off-site parking available $18. Bus: 6, 33, 43, or 71. Streetcar: N-line.

Inexpensive

Red Victorian Bed, Breakfast & Art ★★   This fabulous bright red B&B in the Haight lets you take a trip back to the '60's without having to resort to psychedelic designer drugs. Artist in residence, Sami Sunchild—who just happens to be the owner as well—has personally designed 18 rooms to reflect San Francisco's Summer of Love history at her self-described "museum of living peace." Each of the 18 rooms has a different theme, and is decorated accordingly. "The Conservatory" room, so named in honor of the conservatory across the street in Golden Gate Park, is filled with white wicker, a floral bedspread, and a flower-filled window garden. The "Summer of Love" room has a tie-dye canopy over the bed, a real lava lamp, and '60's posters on the wall. Dedicated to saving the trees, "The Redwood Forest Room" features a wall covered in a scene from a redwood grove; guests sleep under a willow canopy. Regardless of the theme, most rooms include a private bathroom, all guests enjoy a continental breakfast.

1665 Haight St. (btw. Cole and Belvedere sts.). ℂ **415/864-1978.** www.redvic.com. 18 units, 4 w/ private bathroom. From $89 double w/shared bathroom; $149 double w/private bathroom; $179 suite. Rates include continental breakfast. Lower rates for stays of 3 days or more. Bus: 6 or 71. **Amenities:** Cafe.

WHERE TO EAT

San Francisco's restaurant scene is as varied as our weather. Unpredictable. Contrarian. Hot and cold. We attract some of the world's most talented chefs, drawn not only to the creative freedom that has always defined San Francisco's culinary scene, but also to the year-round access to Northern California's unparalleled abundance of organic produce, seafood, free-range meats, and wine. There's a reason Bon Appetit has named San Francisco the best for dining in the US for the past decade.

A small guidebook is not the place to write about every culinary experience to be encountered by the golden gate. How could it be? With more than 3,500 restaurants, San Francisco has more restaurants per capita than any other city in the United States.

Instead, we chose to write about just the can't-miss favorites, with a healthy mix of cuisines, price ranges, and neighborhoods. Some are brand new, yet already earning coveted foodie awards; others have been around forever—for a reason. We could not possibly write a guidebook about San Francisco without mentioning some of the pure-culinary-genius-over-the-top splurges that draw epicureans from around the world. And, to counter our reputation of being an expensive city to visit, we have included a few inexpensive dining experiences, delivering delicious food in interesting or historical surroundings, allowing you to keep some of your hard-earned money for cable car rides, and, perhaps, a trip to Alcatraz. Enjoy!

PRACTICAL INFORMATION

Although dining in San Francisco is almost always a hassle-free experience, here are a few things to keep in mind:

- **If you want a table at the restaurants with the best reputations,** you probably need to **book 6 to 8 weeks in advance** for weekends, and a couple of weeks ahead for weekdays.
- **If you can't get a reservation** at your favorite restaurant, don't hesitate to put your name on a **waiting list** a few weeks in advance. I have received that call from some of the popular places; just make sure to call back quickly—they mean business.
- **If there's a long wait for a table, ask if you can order at the bar,** which is often faster and more fun.
- **Don't leave *anything* valuable in your car** while dining, particularly in or near high-crime areas such as the Mission, downtown, or—believe it or not—Fisherman's Wharf. (Thieves know tourists with nice cameras and a trunk full of mementos are headed there.) Also, it's best to give the parking valet only the key to your car, *not* your hotel room.

on-line resources FOR DINING

Want to book your reservations online? Go to www.opentable.com, where you can reserve seats in real time.

For local food blogs, Grub Street (www.grubstreet.com) posts daily updates, and Marcia Gagliardi's **Table-hopper** (www.tablehopper.com) posts smart, gourmand observations every Tuesday and Friday.

While Los Angeles has "It" celebrities, San Francisco has "It" restaurants. To see what's hot during your visit (it may or may not stay hot), check **SF Eater's Heatmap** (www.sf.eater.com/tags/heat-map), updated monthly by popularity.

For an epic culinary scavenger hunt, or simply more dining ideas, see **7x7 Magazine's "The Big Eat 2013: In Photos"** (www.7x7.com/big-eat-2013). The list shows photos of specific dishes to hunt for like Sardine Chips at **Rich Table** (p. 92); Chicken Wings at **Aziza** (p. 98); Katsiki Youvetsi at **Kokkari** (p. 76); California State Bird at **State Bird Provisions** (p. 92); and Whole Wheat Flour Carrot Cake at **Farallon** (p. 81).

If you really want to nosh like a tech-savvy local, download the **Foodspotting** mobile app (www.foodspotting.com), which lets you photograph and tag your favorite foods. Look for 7x7's "Big Eat" list (and other lists within the app), and tag their recommended items as you eat them. You can also search for dishes others have tagged at restaurants near you to see what looks appetizing.

For a collection of restaurant reviews and suggestions by bloggers, diners, and critics like Zagat, SF Weekly, and the San Francisco Chronicle, check out **Urban Spoon** at www.urbanspoon.com. Just watch the dates; while most are current, some reviews are 10 years old.

For food trucks, your best bet is **Off the Grid**, a daily gathering of a half dozen or so trucks, usually from 11am to 2pm, and 5pm to 9pm, occasionally with live music. Check www.offthegridsf.com/markets) Otherwise, **Roaming Hunger** (www.roaminghunger.com) lists locations of food trucks, based on Twitter feeds.

Vegetarians won't have trouble finding dishes on a typical menu here, and you'll find a couple of restaurants marked "vegetarian" throughout this chapter. For vegan eats, consult **Happy Cow** (www.happycow.net)

- **No smoking.** It is against the law to smoke in any restaurant in San Francisco, even if it has a separate bar or lounge area. You're welcome to smoke outside; make sure to stay 20 feet away from any entryway.
- This ain't New York: **Plan on dining early.** Most restaurants close their kitchens around 10pm.
- **If you're driving to a restaurant, add extra time to your itinerary for parking,** which can be an especially infuriating exercise in areas like the Mission, downtown, the Marina, and, well, pretty much everywhere. Expect to pay at least $12 to $15 for valet service, *if* the restaurant offers it.
- **If you have to find parking, check out sfpark.org** (more on p. 234).

FINANCIAL DISTRICT

Kokkari ★★ GREEK/MEDITERRANEAN   Years ago, I spent a summer living on the Greek island of Santorini and fell head over heels in love with the food, the culture, and the simple way of life. I never thought I would recreate that experience without hopping on a plane, and then I found Kokkari. Exposed wood, earthen pottery, soft lighting, an open kitchen, and a large rotisserie fireplace, slowly roasting some sort of beast each day, all give Kokkari a warm, yet sophisticated, Mediterranean feel. And the food—eureka!—the food is superb. Highly recommended are such Hellenic classics as *horiatiki* (traditional Greek salad), *dolmathes* (stuffed grape leaves), baked feta, *moussaka* (eggplant, potato, lamb, yogurt béchamel), and any dish with lamb. If you are into Greek coffee, ask your server to take you back by the kitchen and show you how the coffee is made in an *ibrik,* and slowly heated in hot sand, Mediterranean style. Best seat in the house for two is just to the right of the fireplace.

200 Jackson St. (at Front St.). © **415/981-0983.** www.kokkari.com. Main courses $14–$28 lunch, $21–$45 dinner. Mon–Fri 11:30am–5:30pm; bar menu only 2:30–5:30pm; Mon–Thurs 5:30–10pm; Fri 5:30–11pm; Sat 5–11pm, Sun 5–10pm. Valet parking (dinner only). Bus: 1, 12. All Market St. buses, light rail, and streetcars.

Quince ★★ CALIFORNIAN/ITALIAN   Simple food from simple ingredients that's phenomenally tasty. Sounds like a, well, simple formula, but it's one that many chefs mess up. Not Michael Tusk, who honed his skills at the famed Chez Panisse (an iconic restaurant that pioneered this style of cooking). As is the trend with many fine-dining establishments in our "City by the Bay," diners have a choice of a four-course dinner menu ($95), or a tasting menu ($140, wine pairings $95) that changes frequently. Many of the dishes are Italian in origin (like the squab cannelloni with wild nettle, spring onion, and porcini mushroom); though the meaty entrees also shine (dry-aged side of beef with salt-crusted formanova beet, bone marrow, and nasturtium is a menu stand out, as is the suckling pig featuring turnip and whey). Leave room for dessert! I personally could live off the international cheese cart with tastings from France, Italy, and California. For the sweet tooth, the ganache, with salted cocoa nib toffee, candied hazelnut, and buttermilk sherbet is sure to satisfy. For a lighter dining experience, check out the bar menu which offers la carte items.

470 Pacific Ave. (at Montgomery St.). © **415/775-8500.** www.quincerestaurant.com. Bar menu $12–$60. Mon–Sat 5:30–10pm. Valet parking $12. Bus: 1, 10, 12, or 30.

The Slanted Door ★★ VIETNAMESE   Considered by many to be the best Vietnamese restaurant in America, Slanted Door is worth the wait if you are foolish enough to wing it without a reservation, as I have. Celebrity fans, including Mick Jagger, Keith Richards, Quentin Tarantino, Luke Wilson, and Gwenyth Paltrow, have been known to sneak in for a bite (we assume they don't need reservations). Using only fresh, local, organic ingredients to create mouth-watering specialties like grass-fed estancia shaking beef, and crispy imperial rolls, owner/chef, Charles Phan, is the darling of modern Vietnamese cuisine. Located in the happening Ferry Building, with walls of glass and a stellar view of The Bay Lights (see p. 110), Slanted Door is rightly one of the most popular restaurants in town.

1 Ferry Building (at the Embarcadero and Market). © **415/861-8032.** www.slanteddoor.com. Lunch main courses $12–$36; dinner dishes $18–$45; fixed-price lunch $48 and dinner $53–$65 (parties of 7 or more only). Daily 11am–10pm; bar only from 2:30–5:30pm. All Market St. buses, light rail, and streetcar.

Price Categories

The restaurants listed below are classified first by area, then by price, using the following categories: **Expensive,** dinner for $50 or more per person; **Moderate,** dinner from $35 per person; and **Inexpensive,** dinner less than $35 per person. These categories reflect prices for an appetizer, main course, dessert, and glass of wine.

Citywide Dining

Golden Gate Bridge

Fort Point

Mason St

101

San Francisco
National
Cemetery

THE PRESIDIO

PACIFIC OCEAN

Presidio
Golf
Course

1

Lincoln Blvd

Lincoln Park

SEACLIFF

Lake St

California Palace of
the Legion of Honor

California St

PRESIDIO
HEIGHTS

Clement St.

30th Ave.
26th Ave.
24th Ave.
20th Ave.
18th Ave.

12th Ave.

2nd Ave.

Warit

Spence St.

Laurel St.

Locust St.

Point Lobos Ave.
Geary Blvd.

Anza St.

2
3

4

Parker Ave.

46th Ave.
44th Ave.
42nd Ave.
40th Ave.
38th Ave.
36th Ave.
34th Ave.
32nd Ave.
28th Ave.
22nd Ave.
16th Ave.
Presidio Blvd.
10th Ave.
8th Ave.
6th Ave.
4th Ave.
Arguello Blvd.

Stanyan St.

1
48th Ave.

Balboa St.

RICHMOND

Cabrillo St.

Fulton St.

Conservatory
of Flowers
de Young John F. Kennedy Dr.
Museum

The Panhandle

Great Hwy

Spreckels L.

GOLDEN GATE PARK

Stow L.

Calif. Academy
of Sciences

HAIGHT-
ASHBURY

John F. Kennedy Dr.

Crossover Dr.

Kezar Dr.

Cole St.
Shrader St.

Middle Dr. West

Martin Luther King Jr. Dr.
Lincoln Wy.

Frederick St.
Carl St.

La Playa St.
47th Ave.
43rd Ave.
41st Ave.
39th Ave.

35th Ave.
Sunset Blvd.
33rd Ave.
31st Ave.
29th Ave.

Irving St.

Judah St.

1

17th Ave.
15th Ave.
13th Ave.
11th Ave.

7th Ave.

Parnassus Ave.

9th Ave.

Clarendon Ave.

Kirkham St.

INNER
SUNSET

SUNSET

Lawton St.

45th Ave.

Moraga St.

27th Ave.
25th Ave.
23rd Ave.
21st Ave.
19th Ave.

Woren Dr.

TWIN
PEAKS

Noriega St.

To San Francisco Zoo

Ortega St.

THE sun on your face AT BELDEN PLACE

San Francisco has always been woefully lacking in the alfresco dining department, which may or may not have something to do with the Arctic summer fog. But **Belden Place**—an adorable little brick alley in the heart of the Financial District—goes against that trend. A skinny walkway open only to foot traffic, it's a little bit of Paris just off Pine Street. Restaurants line the alley sporting big umbrellas, tables, and chairs, and, when the weather is agreeable, diners linger long after the lunch hour.

A handful of cafes line Belden Place and offer a variety of cuisines at moderate prices. There's **Cafe Bastille** ★, 22 Belden Place (✆ **415/986-5673**), a classic French bistro with a boho basement that serves excellent crepes, mussels, and French onion soup; it offers live jazz on Fridays. **Cafe Tiramisu** ★, 28 Belden Place (✆ **415/421-7044**), is a stylish Italian hot spot serving addictive risottos and gnocchi. **Plouf** ★ 40 Belden Place (✆ **415/986-6491**), specializes in big bowls of mussels slathered in your choice of seven sauces, as well as fresh seafood. **B44** ★, 44 Belden Place (✆ **415/986-6287**), serves up a side order of Spain alongside its revered paella and other seriously zesty Spanish dishes. **Brindisi** ★, 88 Belden Place (✆ **415/593-8000**), dishes out small plates of Mediterranean fare. New to the hood is **Sauce** ★, 56 Belden Place (✆ **415/397-8800**), which serves large portions of American comfort food.

Moderate

Bocadillos ★ SPANISH/BASQUE TAPAS   It has been said that a tapa—"lid" in Spanish—originated when bartenders placed a slice of ham or cheese over the top of a patron's drink to keep the flies away—or maybe they wanted to hide the smell of their cheap wine? However tapas began, the tradition of eating small amounts of food with a drink caught on, and expanded to sharing many small plates of food, and many drinks, with friends. So what do flies and cheap wine have to do with Bocadillo's? Absolutely nothing. At Bocadillo's, the wine is fine—so is the beer—and your tapa choices are far more advanced than a simple slice of protein. Basque favorites include Thai snapper ceviche with key lime and persimmon, quail with Moorish spices, bavette steak with chimichurri sauce, lamb burger with aioli and shallots, and patatas bravas with romesco sauce. For dessert, warm chocolate cake with banana ice cream is the house specialty—my only complaint is you have to share. The atmosphere is casual—meet new friends at the long communal table, or belly up to the bar. For a little privacy, try one of the bar tables or snag one of the few outdoor seats. Open for breakfast on weekdays.

710 Montgomery St. (at Washington St.). ✆ **415/982-2622.** www.bocasf.com. No reservations. Breakfast $5–$13; lunch and dinner tapas $7–$17. Mon–Fri 7am–10pm; Sat 5–10pm. Bus: 1 or 8X.

Tadich Grill ★ SEAFOOD   California was not even a state when Tadich Grill opened in 1849. It's the oldest, continuously run restaurant in San Francisco, owned by the Buich family since 1928. When you walk through the door, time stands still. From the dark wood, brass fixtures, long bar, and private booths, you get the feeling you are in an old boys club and expect to see deals being made under the haze of cigar smoke. If you can only try one dish here, know that people come from all over the world for Tadich's *cioppino:* a red stew chock full of scallops, clams, prawns, mussels, fish, and crab, served with garlic bread for dipping. Another specialty of the house is the Hangtown Fry, a mélange of eggs, bacon and deep fried oysters, scrambled together to make a dish the late Herb Caen—*Chronicle* journalist, unofficial mayor, and recipient of a Pulitzer Prize for being the "voice and conscience" of San Francisco—loved almost as much as the city itself. This special fry has been served continuously since the Gold Rush days, when miners who struck it rich would come in to enjoy one of the most expensive meals in the city. Finish your trip down memory lane with the simple rice pudding—the recipe has not changed in over 100 years.

240 California St. (btw. Battery and Front sts.). ✆ **415/391-1849.** www.tadichgrill.com. No reservations. Main courses $15–$49. Mon–Fri 11am–9:30pm; Sat 11:30am–9:30pm. All Market St. buses, light rail, and streetcars. BART: Embarcadero.

UNION SQUARE

Expensive

Farallon ★★ SEAFOOD   Giant jellyfish lamps float overhead from the arched, mosaic ceiling, tentacles dangling, lighting the way to your table. Kelp columns in amber hues rise from the floor, amidst 8-foot sea urchins and a giant clamshell. The underwater theme is everywhere, but no, this is not a tacky, Ariel–Disney experience. The decor here is downright stunning, as is the food. Owner/designer Pat Kuleto and owner/chef Mark Franz (both of Waterbar fame p. 83) have worked together to create a unique underwater fantasy in the former Elks Club building. As you might expect, the food is, well, fishy, too. Your picks could range from petrale sole with caviar butter to grilled Georges bank diver scallops (a melt-in-your-mouth treat). Sadly, my husband does not eat seafood, but was happy to dine on the petite filet of beef with red wine risotto in a pinot noir reduction, on a recent visit (so there are choices for the fish-averse). Desserts are also primo.

450 Post St. (at Powell St.). ✆ **415/956-6969.** www.farallonrestaurant.com. Advanced reservations recommended. Main courses $28–$36. Dinner Sun 5–9:30pm, Mon–Thurs 5:30–9:30pm, Fri–Sat 5:30–10pm, Happy hour daily 4:30–7pm. Limited valet parking. Cable car: Powell–Mason or Powell–Hyde line. BART: Powell St.

Gitane ★★ SPANISH   Gitane radiates passion and intensity with wild food to match its sensual, bordello-like interior. That means dishes that may scare more conservative diners, like the *cordero*: lamb tongue and crispy sweetbreads. It also means cuisine so authentically Andalusian, it would make your Spanish *abuela* weep, such as the lamb tartare with black olive puree and smoky eggplant; bacon "bon bons" of prunes and goat cheese wrapped in smoked bacon; or the paella with braised rabbit meatballs. For a more casual atmosphere, head to the bar or the outdoor bistro tables. A final perk: the Bay Area's largest selections of sherry and gypsy cocktails, plus a fine collection of Spanish, Portuguese, and California wines.

6 Claude Ln (at Bush or Sutter). ✆ **415/788-6686.** www.gitanerestaurant.com. Reservations only through www.opentable.com. Main courses $22–$34, 5-course tasting menu $65, wine pairing $45, Taberna bar menu $8–$22. Mon–Wed 5:30–10:30pm, bar open until midnight, Thurs–Sat 5:30–11:30pm, bar open until 1am. Bus: 2, 30, 31, or 45. BART: Montgomery St.

Inexpensive

Johnny Foley's Irish House ★ IRISH PUB   Foley's is as well known for its surprisingly good pub food (bangers and mash, fish and chips, cottage pie and the like) as it is for its famous dueling pianos downstairs. It's the perfect place to head if you're needing the comfort of a home away from home. Truly: there are 16 types of beer on tap, sports on the telly, and a good kids menu—what more would you need? Stop in, refresh, and get back out to the "grind" of heavy-duty sightseeing.

243 O'Farrell St. (at Cyril Magnin St.). © **415/954-0777.** www.johnnyfoleys.com. Main courses $15–$34. Daily 11:30am–1:30am, kitchen closes 10pm. Bus: 38. BART: Powell St.

SOMA

Expensive

Benu ★★ ASIAN FUSION   Housed in a heritage building in the heart of SoMa, a few minutes' walk from many of our cultural attractions and historic hotels, Benu represents the changing face of fine dining in San Francisco. With no dress code, no tablecloths, and no stuffy servers, it is truly all about the food. And though you can order a la carte, the tasting menu is the way to go if you want to experience the two Michelin stars awarded to chef Corey Lee's culinary wizardry (he's formerly of the famed French Laundry, see p. 221). Presented on custom-created porcelain designed specifically to show off the food, Lee has created an eclectic menu that might include choices as varied as potato salad with anchovy; thousand-year-old quail egg with ginger and nasturtium; monkfish liver on brioche; or salt and pepper squid. The faux shark fin soup with black truffle custard shows off Lee's ability to create daring combinations, as does the charcoal-grilled lamb belly with quinoa, pear, and sunflower. Plan to spend upwards of 3 hours basking in top quality food, wine, and service, in minimalist, serene surroundings.

22 Hawthorne St. (at Howard St.). © **415/685-4860.** www.benusf.com. Tasting menu $180, wine pairing $150, a la carte (Tues–Thurs only) main courses $26–$42. Tues–Sat 5:30–9pm. Valet parking $15. All Market St. buses, light rail, and streetcars.

Palace Hotel ★ AMERICAN   Two iconic dining spaces, set in one landmark hotel: You have a difficult choice to make when eating at the Palace Hotel. If you choose to go the elegant route, hit the Garden Court, the only indoor historic landmark in San Francisco (it was the former carriage entrance to the hotel and reopened as a restaurant after the 1906 earthquake). With an atrium ceiling, swirled marble columns, gilt finishes, and antique chandeliers, it offers a sumptuous step back in time. While you can dine here any day of the week, the over-the-top Sunday brunch is best: a smorgasbord of everything from crepes and omelets to a seafood station to dim sum and sushi.

For a more casual dining experience, step into the dark woods and rich leather seating at the **Pied Piper.** By the time this book goes to print, the name may have reverted back to Maxfield's Pied Piper Bar—for the 16-ft. mural created by Maxfield Parish in 1909. This masterpiece was quietly removed in early 2013 with a plan to sell it at auction for upwards of $5M; it will be returned shortly following an outcry from the good citizens of our metropolis, a call from the mayor, and a general threat to boycott the Palace altogether. Lesson learned: Do not mess with our culture! Whatever the place is called, the drinks are strong and the food is solid (think pizzas, burgers and steaks).

Palace Hotel, 2 New Montgomery St. (at Market St.). **Garden Court** © **415/546-5089.** www. sfpalace.com/garden-court. Sunday brunch (Jan–Nov) $85 adults, $45 children; Holiday brunch menus in Dec. Breakfast Mon–Fri 6:30–10:30am; Sat 6:30–11am; Sun 7–10am; Sunday brunch 10:30–1:30pm; Lunch Mon–Sat 11:30–2pm; Saturday afternoon tea seating 1pm or 1:30pm. **Pied Piper** © **415/546-5089.** www.sfpalace.com/pied-piper. Main courses $13–$35. Mon–Fri 11:30am–midnight; Sat 11am–midnight; Sun 10am–midnight. Valet parking $24 (up to 4 hours). All Market St. buses, light rail, and streetcars.

Waterbar ★★ SEAFOOD   With a stunning view of the Bay Bridge, an outdoor patio, $1 oysters from 11:30am to 5:30pm daily, and a fab weekend brunch (the exotic Bloody Mary comes complete with smoked bacon and jumbo prawns), Waterbar delivers just about everything a San Francisco visitor could want. Oh wait, did I mention the two floor-to-ceiling fish tank columns in the middle of the restaurant, filled with eels, fish, and other Pacific Ocean critters? A mini-aquarium! Consistent with San Francisco's current zeitgeist, the menu offers a wide variety of fresh, ethically sourced, seasonal seafood such as tomba tuna and king salmon—and it even tells you the tuna was snagged with a hook and line in Honolulu, and the salmon was caught trolling off of Half Moon Bay aboard a boat named *Two's Company*. Now that's sustainable! And if the fish and eels are not enough dining entertainment, Waterbar affords an excellent view of The Bay Lights—the world's largest LED light sculpture, celebrating the 75th anniversary of the Bay Bridge—scheduled to appear each evening from dusk until 2am through March 2015.

399 Embarcadero (at Harrison St.). ✆ **415/284-9922.** www.waterbarsf.com. Main courses $35–$42. Daily 11:30am–2pm and 5:30–10pm. Valet parking. Bus: 1, 12, 14, or 41. BART: Embarcadero.

Moderate

AsiaSF ★ ASIAN/CALIFORNIAN   Does it get more wonderfully, if stereotypically, "San Francisco" than this? At AsiaSF, dinner is served by world famous transgender stars, who perform hourly on the red runway bar and lip-sync show tunes between courses. (Despite the high kicks and sashays on a miniscule space, owner, Skip Young, says only two girls have actually fallen off the bar in their 15-year history.) The *menage a trois* menu is the way to go and that gets you three dishes (what were YOU thinking?) from a mouthwatering list, including sake steamed mussels, sesame steak salad, miso glazed king salmon served over black "forbidden" rice, truffled soba noodles, and "baby got back" ribs. It's a lot of fun and, believe it or not, kids are welcome at the first seating. Note: You must dine to see the show.

201 Ninth St. (at Howard St.). ✆ **415/255-2742.** www.asiasf.com. Main courses $12–$20. Dinner packages $35–$69. Wed only (a la carte menu) with $25 pp minimum. Sun, Wed, Thurs 7–10pm; Fri 7pm–2am; Sat 5pm–2am; cocktails and dancing until 2am on Fri–Sat. All Market St. buses, light rail, and streetcars. BART: Civic Center.

Inexpensive

SoMa StrEat Food Park ★★ FOOD TRUCKS   As the first permanent food truck plaza in San Francisco, SoMa StrEat Food Park is breaking new culinary ground in a city where that's a pretty tough thing to do. Here's how it works: each day 13 trucks roll in and serve lunch; some may stay on to serve dinner, others leave and their spot is given to a new truck. The only permanent truck is StrEat Brew, serving beer, wine, and sangria; and a $12 bottomless mimosa for the Sunday brunch crowd. With over 70 rotating vendors, with names like Curry Up Now, Seoul on Wheels, Adam's Grub Truck, and Chairman Bao, you are sure to find something you like, no matter when you show up. And this is not a roach coach scene at all. The food is high quality, the trucks are clean, music is playing, and there's covered seating, flat-screen tv's, restrooms, and free Wi-Fi. In fact, SoMa StrEat Food feels like one big party. Judging by the line outside the Del Popolo truck (it makes pizza with a real wood-fired oven), they are one of the most popular trucks in the park. With no tourist attractions close by, but easy public transportation access, this place is a destination in itself; come just to hang out and eat with the locals. Most vendors take credit cards; there's also an ATM on site.

428 11th St. (at Division St.). www.somastreatfoodpark.com. Main courses $5–$17. Mon–Fri 11am–3pm; Sat 11am–10pm; Sun 10am–5pm. Street parking. Bus: 9, 12, 27, or 47.

CHINATOWN—SO MANY choices!

San Francisco's **Chinatown** has the largest Chinese population outside of China; so it follows that we have lots of Chinese restaurants. It's hard to know which place to try—some look clean and inviting, with bright colored photos of yummy delicacies posted outside; others have sun-faded menus peeling off of dirty windows—but looks can be deceiving. Most places in **Chinatown** fall into the inexpensive category—so how do you choose? We think the following restaurants stand out from the pack.

Brandy Ho's Hunan Food ★ 217 Columbus Ave (© **415/788-7527;** www. brandyhos.com), is rightly known for its Three Delicacies—a main dish of scallop, shrimp, and chicken seasoned with ginger, garlic, and wine. Most dishes are served hot and spicy; just ask if you want the kitchen to tone it down.

Climb the steps at tiny **Hong Kong Clay Pot Restaurant** ★, 960 Grant Ave. (© **415/989-2638;** www.hongkong claypotrestaurant.com), and try—gee, what do you think? A clay pot filled with meat, seafood, or vegetables. Did you know the clay pots are soaked in water before cooking? When heated up, they release steam, making dishes that are extra moist and delicious. Yum!

R&G Lounge ★, 631 Kearny St (© **415/982-7877;** www.rnglounge. com), is a very popular three-story restaurant; best on the menu are the salt and pepper crab, and R&G special beef.

Great Eastern ★, 649 Jackson Street (© **415/986-2500;** www.greateasternsf. com), specializes in dim sum, as well as fresh seafood pulled from tanks lining the walls—Prez Obama stopped in here for takeout.

At **House of Nanking** ★★, 919 Kearny Street (© **415/421-1429**), abrupt and borderline rude waiters—half the fun of Chinatown—serve vegetarian dishes as well as perfect sesame chicken. The fish soup is stellar too, though you have to ask for it specially, as it's not on the English–language menu.

Hunan Home's ★★, 622 Jackson Street (© **415/982-2844**), known for their wicked hot and sour soup, and "Succulent Bread"—baked and then slightly deep fried, this locals' favorite was the winner of the "Best Bay Area Chinese Restaurant" in the *Chinese World Journal*.

NOB HILL/RUSSIAN HILL

Expensive

La Folie ★ FRENCH   A fixture on the dining scene since 1988, the "Grand Dame" of Russian Hill is the place to go if you're in the mood for a luxurious, if long, meal. Chef/owner Roland Passat was born in the Rhone–Alpes in France and honed his craft at cooking school in Lyon; his food is sauced, frilled and *tres* Gallic. Diners choose between the three ($80), four ($90), and five-course menu ($100) which feature such indulgences as asparagus soup with poached quail egg and lobster; or duck breast and duck confit *gateau* with brandied cherries and baby turnips. As a final performance, do not miss the huckleberry baked Alaska, and the Edam cheese soufflé. Portions are generous, so if you're trying to decide how many courses to pick, you may want to go with the smaller choices.

2316 Polk St. (btw. Green and Union sts.). © **415/776-5577.** www.lafolie.com. 3-course tasting menu $80; 4-course tasting menu $90; 5-course chef's tasting menu $100; vegetarian tasting menu $90. Mon–Sat 5:30–10:30pm. Valet parking. Bus: 12, 19, 27, 45, and 47.

Sons and Daughters ★★ AMERICAN   One Michelin star. Superb food made with ingredients straight from their Los Gatos farm. Reasonable prices for the zip code. Too good to be true? Thankfully, no. Chefs Matt McNamara and Teague Moriarty keep their tiny Nob Hill restaurant full with the perfect combination of a cozy atmosphere and beautifully presented food that tastes as good as it looks. A great place to celebrate a birthday or anniversary, sit by the fireplace and enjoy an evening of culinary delights on the seasonal tasting menu. Recent luscious offerings have included Tomales Bay miyagi oysters; Fort Bragg sea urchin; Berkshire pork with fennel and blackberry; and geranium ice cream with huckleberry and redwood clover. The staff is exceptionally friendly and approachable and they know the dishes well and are happy to accommodate any food allergies or dislikes. One last note: Don't even think of trying to park a car on the street around here. If you must drive, the Sutter/Stockton garage a block away is a good bet.

708 Bush St. (at Powell St.). ✆ **415/391-8311.** www.sonsanddaughterssf.com. Tasting menu $98, pairings $68. Wed–Sun 5–9:30pm. Bus: 1, 2, or 30. Cable Car: Powell–Hyde or Powell–Mason.

Moderate

Swan Oyster Depot ★★ SEAFOOD   Swan Oyster Depot opened in the current building in 1912, and little has changed since—and I mean little. Pull on a long, brass, fish-shaped door handle, and step across the cracked mosaic floor; there's no website, no computer system, no reservations on Open Table; you won't find over-the-top haute cuisine here. You will find 18 stools lined up in front of the original, worn, marble counter, paper napkins to wipe crab juice off your mug, and a friendly member of the Sancimino Family—owners since 1946—taking your order while wrapping fish for a take-home customer. As for the food: "If it's not fresh, we don't serve it," the counterman briskly explained to me when I inquired why they were out of crabs. That's the unofficial mantra and it works well for the all seafood menu. Recipes are simple—think steamed, raw or fried seafood, the terrific cocktail sauce house-made, the prices very reasonable, and the service gruffly charming. Eating here is a fun, old-timey experience—and needs to be as there's usually an hour wait to get in! If starving and tired of waiting, do what I have done, call in a take-out order while in line. Only cash and local checks accepted.

1517 Polk St. (btw. California and Sacramento sts.). ✆ **415/673-1101.** No reservations. Main courses $5–$45. Mon–Sat 10:30am–5:30pm. Bus: 1, 12, 19, 47, or 49. Cable Car: California.

Inexpensive

U-Lee ★★ CHINESE   Open beams of reclaimed wood and a warm, inviting decor? Nope. Award-winning wine list? Nope. Fresh, sustainable, ingredients grown on an organic farm, hand-picked in a kind manner? Probably not. Inexpensive, delicious food on Nob Hill? Yup. U-Lee is the proverbial hole in the wall, serving some of the best Chinese food in the city for the cost of parking at other places. Locals in the know, and visitors lucky enough to find it, come back again and again for hot and sour soup, General Tsao chicken, beef with asparagus, and pork fried rice. Did I mention the pot stickers? U-Lee's is known for succulent, juicy pot stickers the size of your fist. Portions are huge, so bring your appetite. And make sure to bring some of that good old fashioned stuff called cash; it is all they accept. Because parking is almost impossible around here, take the cable car; it stops right outside.

1468 Hyde St. (btw. Washington and Jackson sts.). ✆ **415/771-9774.** www.u-leesf.com. No reservations. $2–$9 per dish. Tues–Sun 11am–9pm. Bus: 1, 12, 27, or 49. Cable Car: Powell–Hyde.

NORTH BEACH/TELEGRAPH HILL

Expensive

Coi ★★ CALIFORNIAN   Coi (pronounced "kwa"), meaning tranquil, is the perfect respite from the bustle of the city. With two Michelin stars, self-taught chef, Daniel Patterson—known for his use of molecular gastronomy to create visually beautiful dishes—was the pioneer who started the current San Francisco trend of fixed price tasting menus—and people thought he was crazy. Each evening Coi offers only one tasting menu with 8-11 courses based on what is fresh and available. Selections might include charcoal roasted beets with blackberry, salted marrow fat and arugula; a chilled yellow squash soup with saffron, lime and nasturtium; a gently steamed wild kind salmon, stuffed with morels, peas and sorrel; and whipped coconut olive oil, rhubarb and blood orange to finish. Brilliant wine pairings are an additional $105 per person.

373 Broadway (at Montgomery St.). 🕿 **415/393-9000.** www.coirestaurant.com. Nightly menu $150–$175. Tues–Sat 5:30–9:30pm. Valet parking. Bus: 1, 8, 10, or 12.

Moderate

Original Joe's ★ ITALIAN   This San Francisco institution claims it has served everyone from "the head politician to the head prostitute"—presumably not at the same time, though you never know. First opened after the Great Depression by Tony Rodin, the restaurant is now run by his grandkids, John Duggan, and his sister, Elena, and they haven't changed it much. The menu still features a large selection of typical Italian comfort food in generous portion sizes, and at reasonable prices. By the way, this is not quite the original "Original Joes." That was located in the Tenderloin from 1937 until it was destroyed by a fire in 2007. The current Original Joe's re-opened in North Beach in 2012, but their loyal clientele followed and once you've had the parmigiana here, you'll understand why.

601 Union Street (at Stockton St.). 🕿 **415/775-4877.** www.originaljoessf.com. Main courses $11–$44. Mon–Fri 11am–10pm, Sat–Sun 9am–10pm. Bus: 30, 41, or 45.

Inexpensive

Pier 23 ★ SEAFOOD   With an awesome view of the bay, great food at great prices, and live music most evenings, don't let the rundown exterior keep you from trying this hidden gem on the Embarcadero. Ask the gravelly voiced hostess, Alicia, to get you a waterfront table, then dig into heavenly fish and chips, or a juicy black angus burger, while watching the boats sail by. A hearty brunch is served on weekends, and features a variety of dishes like huevos rancheros, whole roasted Dungeness crab, and a smoked salmon plate. Even the little ones will be happy; the kid's menu offers all the usual faves—grilled cheese, chicken strips, and more.

Pier 23 (on Embarcadero). 🕿 **415/362-5125.** www.pier23cafe.com. Main courses $12–$28. Weekdays 11:30am–10pm, Sat 10am–10pm, Sun 10am–9pm. Any Embarcadero light rail or streetcar.

FISHERMAN'S WHARF

Expensive

Forbes Island ★★★ FRENCH   How many people can say they had a fantastic meal . . . underwater? In a floating lighthouse? Tied up beside the city's famous barking sea lions? While the food might not rival Farallon or Gary Danko, the location

Chinatown & North Beach Restaurants

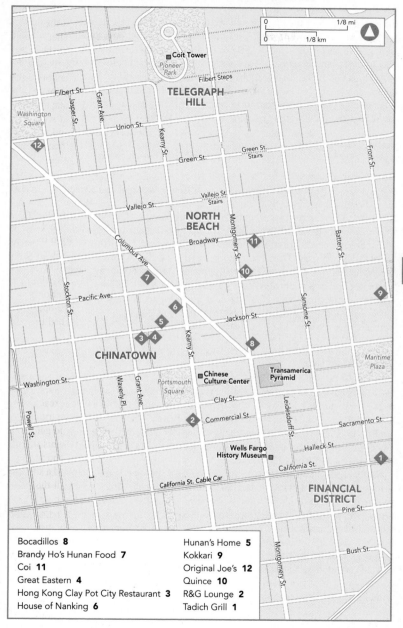

Coit Tower
Pioneer Park
Filbert Steps

TELEGRAPH HILL

Washington Square

Filbert St.
Jasper St.
Grant Ave.
Kearny St.
Union St.
Green St.
Green St. Stairs
Front St.

Vallejo St. Stairs
Vallejo St.

NORTH BEACH

Columbus Ave.
Broadway
Montgomery St.
Battery St.

Stockton St.
Pacific Ave.
Kearny St.
Jackson St.
Sansome St.

CHINATOWN

Washington St.
Waverly Pl.
Grant Ave.
Portsmouth Square
Chinese Culture Center
Transamerica Pyramid
Maritime Plaza

Powell St.
Clay St.
Leidesdorff St.
Commercial St.
Sacramento St.

Wells Fargo History Museum
Halleck St.
California St.

California St. Cable Car
FINANCIAL DISTRICT
Pine St.

Montgomery St.
Bush St.

Bocadillos **8**

Brandy Ho's Hunan Food **7**

Coi **11**

Great Eastern **4**

Hong Kong Clay Pot City Restaurant **3**

House of Nanking **6**

Hunan's Home **5**

Kokkari **9**

Original Joe's **12**

Quince **10**

R&G Lounge **2**

Tadich Grill **1**

alone warrants a visit to this unique, San Francisco institution. In the late 1970s, master carpenter, Forbes Kiddoo, spent 5 years building this 1600-square-foot floating home. After adding a beach, boulders, and 40-foot palm trees, Kiddoo dropped anchor across the bay in Sausalito, and might have lived there forever had new houseboat regulations not forced him to shove off. After drifting around for a few years (pun intended), and adding a 40-foot lighthouse in 1998, the island was towed to Pier 39, a license was obtained, and San Francisco's first and only floating lighthouse restaurant was born. As well as two daily fresh fish dishes, the menu includes tasty variations on risotto, lambchops, steaks and more. With a fire burning in the old fireplace, and the wood and brass interior, this underwater dining room is cozy, homey, and really cool. Though I get seasick easily, the gentle swaying at Forbes Island has never bothered me.

Free water shuttle is to the left of Pier 39 at "H" dock (the first dock to the left by the sidewalk). ℂ **415/951-4900.** www.forbesisland.com. Main courses $28–$39. Daily 5pm–close. Validated parking at Pier 39 garage. Bus: 47. All Embarcadero light rail and streetcars.

Restaurant Gary Danko ★★★ FRENCH   What has *not* been said about Gary Danko? James Beard Award winner for Best New Restaurant and Best Chef–California. Michelin stars. Five Star Mobil rating. Elegant atmosphere. Romantic, but not schmaltzy. Dedicated, professional servers, best in the city. Organic, sustainable, fresh food. Generous portions. Sophisticated, contemporary cuisine. Food that is sensible and luxurious, bright, fresh, and stunning. Very expensive, yes, but worth every penny.

It has all been said. Over and over and over. And it's all true. But what you likely haven't heard is what a downright friendly, unsnooty experience dining here can be. That's what Gary Danko is really about: true culinary genius in a down-to-earth environment. If there is one place to splurge with limited time and budget in San Francisco, this is it.

800 North Point Street (at Hyde St.). ℂ **415/749-2060.** www.garydanko.com. 3-course fixed-price menu $73; 4-course menu $93; 5-course menu $107. Daily 5:30–10pm. Valet parking. Bus: 30, 47, or 49. All Embarcadero light rail and streetcars. Cable car: Powell–Hyde.

Moderate

Buena Vista Cafe ★ AMERICAN   "Meet me at the B.V." has been a San Francisco catchphrase for decades—and for good reason. Buena Vista means "good view" in Spanish, and this classic certainly lives up to its name. Converted from a boarding house to a saloon in 1916, the setting was the perfect place for fishermen and dockworkers to take a break while watching the bay for, literally, "their ships to come in." When the fishing boats arrived, they could chug their drinks and quickly run down the hill to get back to work.

Seat yourself at an empty space at one of the large round communal tables by the window and laugh as 18-year veteran waitress, Katherine, flings napkins at you and scowls if, heaven forbid, you dare *not* order a famed Irish Coffee (see below). Don't worry; she won't bite. Serving breakfast all day, with a variety of fat burgers, sandwiches, salads, pasta, steaks, and crab cakes, a stop at the Buena Vista is a classic San Francisco activity for visitors—the cable car stops right outside. I personally love the crab eggs benedict, and the sourdough bread will literally make you drool for more.

Make sure to try the "national institution" Buena Vista Irish Coffee. The first Irish coffee served in America was crafted here by owner, Jack Koeppler, and Pulitzer–Prize winning travel writer, Stanton Delaplane, back in 1952.

2765 Hyde St. (at Beach St.). ℂ **415/474-5044.** www.thebuenavista.com. Main courses $28–$39. Mon–Fri 9am–2am, weekends 8am–2am, no food or children after 9:30pm. Bus: 47. All Embarcadero light rail and streetcars. Cable Car: Powell–Hyde.

Inexpensive

Crepe Cafe ★ FRENCH   What started as a food cart in Ghiradelli Square, has become a favorite in a permanent location on Pier 39. It serves up all the usual crepe toppings (sugar, Nutella, strawberries or savory crepes with ham, eggs, chicken) to some more unusual choices like pesto and avocado. People in the know carry their pancakey creation out the back door and find a seat on the wooden benches to watch chubby sea lions bark and fight for space on the docks.

Pier 39 (at Embarcadero). ℭ **415/318-1494.** Main courses $6–$10. Sun–Thurs 9am–9pm, Fri–Sat 9am–10pm. Bus: 47. All Embarcadero light rail and streetcars.

THE MARINA/PACIFIC HEIGHTS/ COW HOLLOW

Expensive

Atelier Crenn ★★ FRENCH/CALIFORNIAN   An atelier is a French workshop; chef Dominique Crenn (of Luce fame) uses hers to create artistic food fantasies, resulting in dishes that are so intricate and whimsical it's wrenching to "ruin them" by taking that first bite. This is poetic culinaria at its best, complete with poetry for menus, and artsy plating with food served on slabs of bark, slate, and eucalyptus branches. With four menus per year to reflect each of the seasons, you essentially have two choices—five signature courses ($95) with wine pairing ($85), or the Chef's Grand Tasting Menu ($180) with wine pairing ($150); on Saturdays, only the Grand Tasting Menu is available. Atelier Crenn is a once in a lifetime experience that you will talk about for years to come, whether you are saying "WTF?? I just don't get it. Where is the menu? What is this poetry stuff? I have no idea what I just ate. Two Michelin stars? These San Francisco people are crazy." (That would be my father.) Or, "That was the most unique, thought-provoking, perfect meal I will ever have the pleasure of eating." Either way, you will be talking.

3127 Fillmore St. (btw Pixley and Filbert sts.). ℭ **415/440-0460.** www.ateliercrenn.com. 5-course menu $95, wine pairings $85; Chef's grand tasting menu $180, wine pairings $150. Bus: 22, 30, 41, 43, or 45.

Moderate

Greens ★★ VEGETARIAN   Greens was, arguably, the first restaurant in the U.S. to take a gourmet approach to vegetarian food, both in its ambitious menu and its serene, all hand-carved wood decor and its oversized windows offering up one of the best water views in the city. (The restaurant is in a former warehouse at Fort Mason.) Its status remains untouched. Come here even if you're a devoted carnivore, the food is revelatory (truly, you won't miss meat); and jumps continents with ease, offering terrific all veggie-takes on Moroccan, Mexican, and Italian foods. There's even an extensive wine list and a "Greens to Go" menu for those who'd prefer to do a picnic on the Marina Green.

Bldg. A, Fort Mason Center (across from Safeway). ℭ **415/771-6222.** www.greensrestaurant.com. Main courses $17–$24; Sat fixed-price dinner $56, wine pairings $33; Sun brunch $13–$18. Tues–Sat 11:45am–2:30pm; Sun 10:30am–2pm; Evenings 5:30–9pm. Greens To Go Mon–Thurs 8:30am–7pm; Fri–Sat 8:30am–5pm; Sun 9am–4pm. Bus: 28 or 30.

"WHEN ARE WE GONNA BE THERE?" family-friendly restaurants

Does it make you cringe to think about sitting at a restaurant with your child for 3+ hours, while 18 expensive, organic, sustainable, farm-to-table courses are slowly served on rocks and bark, when all they really want is a bowl of buttered noodles?

Well, fear not—San Francisco is one of the best cities in the world to visit with children; we have lots of places to entertain and feed our hungry little guests.

Children love **Forbes Island** (p. 86), "H" dock beside Pier 39 because you have to take a water taxi to get there, you can climb up the lighthouse to spy on the barking sea lions, and you eat your dinner underwater. What's not to love?

My son's 11-year-old friend, Dylan, told me about his favorite dim sum place, **Ton Kiang** (p. 99), and to test it, a girlfriend and I took five kids (age 11–13). They enjoyed loudly voting "yay" or "nay" depending on the small plates offered every few minutes. Annie screamed when presented with deep fried chicken feet—the kids voted "nay".

Farallon (p. 81), with jellyfish lamps and kelp rising from the floor, it's an underwater fantasy perfect for budding little marine biologists; ordering from the a la carte menu means dinner does not have to be a 3-hour affair.

SoMa StrEat Food Park (p. 83) is a happening place to grab lunch with the kids, as 13 food trucks means there's bound to be something even the pickiest tot will like. Let them run free amongst the local dot com geniuses lunching here. Who knows? Maybe they will make a few future connections.

Little ones will love the swish swish of **Mums—Home of Shabu Shabu** (p. 91), where they can cook their own steak, noodles, and veggies in a bubbling cauldron, Harry Potter style.

Kids like getting up close to the sea creatures displayed in the **Swan Oyster Depot** (p. 85) window. Plus it's so small, loud, and crowded, if your child accidentally drops their bowl of chowder on the floor, no one will even notice.

One last thought for kids: Take them to one of our city's colorful Chinese restaurants—see the box **Chinatown—So Many Choices** on p.84. My kids' favorite, partially because they can hop off the cable car right outside, is **U-Lee's** Chinese (p. 85). Feed'em the potstickers, which are about the size of your fist ($1 each), and they should be content.

Ristobar ★★★ ITALIAN   In 2010, one of America's finest pastry chefs decided to focus on savory fare, and the competition learned they'd better watch out. That pastry chef is Gary Rulli and stepping into his *piazza*—note the stunning murals on the walls and ceilings—is like being enveloped into the arms of his wonderful Italian family. Gary and his wife Jeannie Rulli, serve *molto delizioso* food for a reasonable price. The menu takes you straight back to Gary's Italian roots: *zuppa* of asparagus puree with olive oil and crostini; Lombardian-style stuffed pasta with veal, prosciutto, pork tenderloin and pancetta; and the Chestnut pizza, with prosciutto, burrata, prawns, cherry tomatoes and arugula, are just a few of the specialties on offer. Most Friday and Saturday evenings, Gary is outside on the corner of Chestnut and Scott roasting lamb skewers. Though it will be hard, leave room for dessert—Angela's tiramisu is pure heaven.

2300 Chestnut Street (at Scott St.). ✆ **415/923-6464.** www.ristobarsf.com. Main courses $13–$29. Tues–Thurs 5:30–10pm, Fri 5:30–11pm, Sat 11am–11pm, Sun 11am–9pm. Bus: 22, 30, or 43.

Tacolicious ★ MEXICAN   Far from the cheesy taco joint the name implies, this is where the beautiful people go for beautiful Mexican food in the Marina. With high ceilings, modern lighting, warm green jewel tones on the walls, and nary a Mexican flag in sight, the only clue you've even entered a Mexican restaurant is the 120 types of tequila offered at the bar. To keep your girlish figure—and fit into the micro mini-skirt that seems to be a customer uniform here—try the Marina Girl Salad, featuring avocado, cucumber, and cotija cheese. And where there are girls in miniskirts, you usually find sports figures—SF Giants pitcher, Tim Lincecum, is a regular, swears by the carnitas, and brings his Giants teammates by on occasion. We're guessing they go for the tacos, which are made with a variety of fillings including summer squash, filet mignon, and the house specialty, guajillo braised beef short ribs. This place is so popular the owners have opened two more city locations in North Beach (1548 Stockton St.) and in the Mission (741 Valencia St.). No reservations.

2031 Chestnut St. (at Fillmore St.). © **415/346-1966.** www.tacolicious.com. Main courses $10–$18. Thurs–Sat 11:30am–midnight; Sun-Wed 11:30am–11pm. Bus: 22, 30, or 43.

Zushi Puzzle ★★ SUSHI   Don't bother showing up if you don't get a reservation in advance. San Francisco's finest sushi restaurant may look like a rundown neighborhood take-out Asian, but its chef is a true master, which means that even on a Tuesday at 10pm all seats will be taken. To try the best of the buttery, unusual fish they source from around the globe, go with nigiri rather than rolls. And real sushi aficionados should settle in for an *omakase* meal, which loosely translates to "let-grumpy-show-man-chef-Roger-Chong-slice-and-dice-and-make-whatever-he-feels-like-making-for-you." Chong—yes, he's a Chinese sushi chef—is the equivalent of the soup Nazi on Seinfeld; if you tell him what you like and he gives you something else, too bad (you'll probably love it; he's a sushi genius). Plus, what can you do? Chong is a big guy and has a sharp knife in his hand!

1910 Lombard St. (at Buchanan St.). © **415/931-9319.** www.puzzle.com. Rolls $4–$12, Nigiri (2 pc) $4–$8, Sashimi (8 pc) $13–$16, Omakse market price. Mon–Sat 5–10:30pm. Bus: 22, 30, or 43.

JAPANTOWN/WESTERN ADDITION
Moderate

Mums—Home of Shabu Shabu ★ JAPANESE   If you think Japanese food begins and ends with raw fish, think again. Mums specializes in "shabu shabu," a hearty but healthy cook-it-yourself meal that takes its name from the sound diners make as they swish paper-thin slices of beef, noodles, and assorted vegetables in a light broth (its said to have been created in the 13th century when Ghengis Khan needed to feed his soldiers quickly). As the meat cooks, the fat in it melts off and one person at the table skims it out of the broth with a long-handled sieve. Diners then dip the cooked meats, veggies, and noodles in one of two oil-light sauces, a ponzu, and a sesame sauce. The delicious simplicity of the food and the fun of cooking it makes Shabu Shabu a great choice for those traveling with kids.

Hotel Tomo, 1800 Sutter St. (at Buchanan St.). © **415/931-6986.** www.mumssf.com. All shabu shabu meals have a minimum of two people. Lunch set plate of shabu shabu is only available 11am–5pm $16, All-you-can-eat shabu shabu is available anytime $25, children $12–$15, with all-you-can-drink $43. Open daily 7am–10pm. Bus: 1, 2, 3, 22, or 38.

State Bird Provisions ★★★ CALIFORNIAN   If there's one restaurant that has been talked about more than any other place in the city, this is it. And for good reason, as it created a whole new category of food: American dim sum. Here, the food is wheeled around on carts and carried on trays—just like at your favorite Chinese restaurant—but instead of dumplings, you get exquisite, high-concept American small plates. Rock star chef Nicole Krasinski (you'll often see her in the open kitchen; she's the one in the cool red glasses) has a way with unusual food pairings, so you might find yourself dining on Nova Scotia oysters with spicy kohlrabi kraut and sesame seeds or croquettes created from rabbit and fontina cheese. Be careful: You may end up ordering far more than you planned; seeing those plates pass by is just so darn tempting. And though each plate is only $3 to $16, it does add up. Reservations are necessary up to 60 days in advance. If you don't have one, stand in line at 4:30pm, and wait for the doors to open at 5:30pm—you will eventually get seated; one third of the restaurant is set aside for walk-ins, including the chefs' counter—where I stood for my last meal.

1529 Fillmore Street (at O'Farrell St.). ℭ **415/795-1272.** www.statebirdsf.com. Bites $3–$16. Mon–Thurs 5:30–10pm, Fri–Sat 5:30–11pm. Bus: 1, 22, or 38.

CIVIC CENTER/HAYES VALLEY

Expensive

Rich Table ★★ CALIFORNIAN   Though Rich Table lost the 2013 James Beard Award for Best New Restaurant to State Bird Provisions (p. 92), finishing second in the country is not too shabby. And no wonder, as owners/chefs, Evan and Sarah Rich, have some serious cred behind them with years of combined experience at Michael Mina, Quince, and Coi. When they decided to launch their own restaurant, Evan and Sarah wanted an open kitchen and California casual decor to make people feel they have been invited into their home. It works. Employees have a laid back, but attentive style of service, fitting for the whole mi-casa-su-casa theme. The menu changes regularly depending on which ingredients are available, and the whims of the chefs. The sardine chips are a house favorite, as are the dried porcini mushroom doughnuts served with raclette. If you are hungry for more than a bite, unique crowd pleasers are oxtail tagliatelle; lamb tartare with charred eggplant and cucumber; pork belly; and spaghetti with English peas, goat cheese, and mint.

199 Gough Street (at Oak St.). ℭ **415/355-9085.** www.richtablesf.com. Main courses $17–$30, chefs picks $80, wine pairings $55. Sun, Mon, Wed, Thurs 5:30–10pm, Fri–Sat 5:30–10:30pm. Bus: 5, 9, 38, 47, or 49. Any Market St. light rail or streetcar.

Moderate

Plaj ★ SCANDINAVIAN   Located at the back of the Inn at the Opera, by the War Memorial Opera House, the Louise M. Davies Symphony Hall, and the new SFJAZZ Center, Plaj—San Francisco's first Scandinavian restaurant—is the perfect place to dine before a show. Small and intimate, this place radiates charm, from the bar at the center of the room with inviting nautical lights and brass foot rail, to the large fireplace, and the cushy, pillow-covered, leather sofas used for seating at some tables. Chef Robert Sundell, shows off his Swedish heritage with dishes such as traditional Swedish meatballs with lingonberrie; braised ox cheek with roasted beet root, fried onions, and horseradish; and a taste of herring with a trio of flavors. Wine buyer, Emi Maruyama, has created a progressive wine list with a focus on good value—most bottles are around $50. For the more adventuresome, try one of the homemade aquavits. Best seats in the house include Table 12 by the fireplace and Table 10 for a little more privacy. My only concern about Plaj is that the sofa seating is just a little too plush and comfy; after all that yummy food, you might just say "god natt"—"good night" in Swedish—and miss your show.

333 Fulton Street (inside Inn at the Opera). ✆ **415/294-8925.** www.plajrestaurant.com. Main courses $14–$26; Daily 5–11pm, kitchen closes 10:30pm Sun–Thurs. Bus: 5, 9, 38, 47, or 49. Any Market St. light rail or streetcar.

Inexpensive

Tommy's Joynt ★ AMERICAN   Here is the proof you can judge a book by its cover—the crazy murals outside are indicative of the flea-market-meets-my-father-in-law's-garage decor inside. A bizarre collection of bric-a-brac cover every square inch of this place, and range from a collection of giant German beer steins to rusty firearms to a stuffed buffalo head. Fine dining be damned, this is a no frills serious eatin' place. A heat lamp-warmed counter serves every type of carb and fat-laden comfort food you can think of, including corned beef, buffalo stew, and fancy pants roast beef. And for those who want to do some serious drinkin', Tommy's offers a variety of almost 100 beers and ciders from over 30 different countries.

11011 Geary Blvd. (at Van Ness Ave.). ✆ **415/775-4216.** www.tommysjoynt.com. Main courses $6–$10; Daily 10am–1:40am. Parking: free hour with validation, $5 for 2 hours. Bus: 38 or 90.

MISSION DISTRICT

Expensive

Central Kitchen ★ CALIFORNIAN   Thomas McNaughton, of upscale pizzeria **flour + water** fame (another fun place to go, it's at 2401 Harrison St.), has just opened this epitome of California–chic in the trendy Mission District. A covered garden patio provides alfresco dining space year round; the open kitchen sets the tone for a laid back, relaxed feel. In that kitchen, McNaughton creates delectables such as hen-liver mousse in a mulled-wine gelee; olive oil baked halibut; and seared squid with peas and peppercorn. My only complaint about Central Kitchen is that it is hard to find. The entrance is set back from the street, to the left of the McNaughton-owned market/café, Salumeria. Both share the 3000 address. Look up and left for the small, square "Central Kitchen" sign.

3000 20th Street (at Florida St.). ✆ **415/826-7004.** www.centralkitchensf.com. Main courses $16–$27, tasting menu $89, pairings $50. Mon–Thurs 5:30–10pm, Fri–Sat 5:30–11pm, Sun 5:30–9pm. Sunday brunch 10am–2:30pm. Bus: 22, 27, or 33.

Foreign Cinema ★★★ CALIFORNIAN   We've all heard the Mission District is the hip, trendy place to dine in San Francisco—it's easy to think it's all been done; there is nothing new to try. Well, aside from the fantastic food, this place gets an extra star just for the really cool new concept: eat dinner outside while foreign and indie flicks play on the side of a building. Little speaker boxes sit on each table ensuring diners can actually hear the movie. Way cool. Oh, and the food is primo, too. After slurping something down from the oyster bar, munch on dishes as varied as sea bass tartare and sesame fried Madras curry chicken. Sure beats popcorn at the movies!

2534 Mission St. (btw. 21st and 22nd sts.). ✆ **415/648-7600.** www.foreigncinema.com. Main courses $15–$30. Dinner Mon–Thurs 6–10pm; Fri–Sat 5:30–11pm; Sun 5:30–10pm; Weekend Brunch 11am–3pm; Bar opened until 2am nightly. Bus: 14.

Moderate

Blowfish Sushi ★ JAPANESE Chef Ritsuo Tsuchida comes from a long line of chefs in the family and makes us beg the question: Are others of his kin as crazy creative as he is? His pyramid of tartare is a triangular edifice of tuna, salmon, and avocado with a side of honey tartare and sweet garlic ginger soy sauce, served with house made potato chips. To make his Blowfish Sushi signature dish, the Ritsu Roll, Tsuchida quickly flash fries two types of tuna, avocado and masago, and serves it with a side of citrus ponzu sauce and Japanese dijon aioli. This is Asian fusion at its wildest (and that goes for the decor and ambience which consists of TV screens flashing anime, upbeat club music blasting, and cool artwork on the walls).

2170 Bryant St. (btw 19th and 20th sts.). ✆ **415/285-3848.** www.blowfishsushi.com. Main courses $17–$26. Lunch Mon–Fri 11:30am–2:30pm; dinner Mon 5–10pm; Tues 5:30–10pm; Wed–Thu 5:30–10:30pm; Fri–Sat 5:30–11pm; Sun 5:30–10pm. Bus: 27 or 33.

Delfina ★★ ITALIAN This warehouse-chic restaurant has been alive and kicking for over 15 years—that's a Grandpa by Mission District-restaurant-scene standards. The reason for its longevity in the fickle restaurant world must have something to do with their ability to serve basic food like roasted chicken with mushrooms and olive oil mashed potatoes, and make it taste so freaking good, patrons continuously return, drooling for more. For a more casual environment, Delfina's has an outdoor patio open from mid-March—October. If you want to get even more casual, without actually dining in your pajamas, try **Pizzeria Delfina** next door (3611 18th St.; ✆ **415/437-6800;** www.pizzeriadelfinasf.com). A second pizzeria is located at 2406 California Street in Pacific Heights, ✆ **415/440-1189.**

3621 18th St. (btw Dolores and Guerrero sts.). ✆ **415/552-4055.** www.delfinasf.com. Main courses $17–$80. Mon–Thurs 5:30–10pm; Fri–Sat 5:30–11pm; Sun 5–10pm. Bus: 14 or 22. Streetcar: J.

Gracias Madre ★★ VEGAN/MEXICAN It's a travel tragedy to go to San Francisco and not have Mexican food (a specialty, thanks to the city's thriving Latin population). It's possible to do so at Gracias Madre without busting your diet (if you're on one), as all the food here is vegan. Don't worry: After you've tasted soft corn tacos filled with garlicky greens or grilled eggplant, you won't miss pork and beef. Food preparations here are not too oily, featuring veggies grown at the restaurateur's own farm and subbing in dots of creamy nut cheese for dollops of fatty sour cream. Get here early, there's always a line out front. Organic beer, wine, and cocktails available.

2211 Mission St. (at 19th St.). ✆ **415/683-1346.** www.gracias-madre.com. Main courses $12–$16. Daily 11am–11pm; Happy hour 3–6pm. Bus: 14 or 22.

Local's Corner ★ SEAFOOD What's the "mother of invention"? In this case it would be a tiny kitchen. Because Local's Corner's is so small (and that goes for the seating area, too), it has room only for a convection oven, a few low-powered burners and a circulator bath. That means the food here (mostly seafood) is often cooked at low temperatures, or served in raw preparations or tenderized in that bath gizmo, which gives it all a very unique flavor profile (and wonderfully tender textures). What could have been an Achilles heal, is a strength, thanks to the creativity of the owners. We also like the kindly staff, who more than make up for the cramped quarters.

2500 Bryant St. (at 23rd). ✆ **415/800-7945.** www.localscornersf.com. Main courses $14–$25. Tues–Sat 8am–10pm; Sun 8am–2pm. Bus: 9, 10, 27, 33, 48, or 90.

Mission District & Castro Restaurants

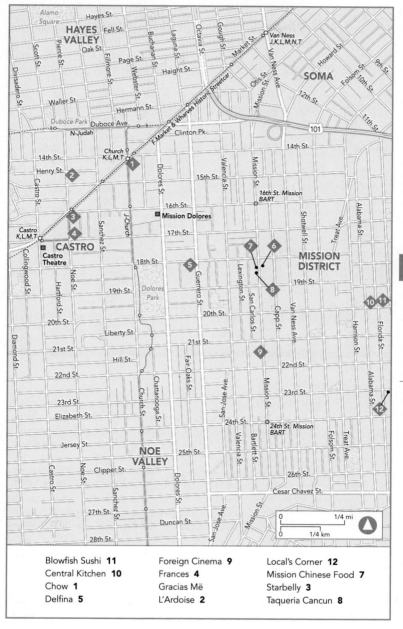

Blowfish Sushi **11**	Foreign Cinema **9**	Local's Corner **12**
Central Kitchen **10**	Frances **4**	Mission Chinese Food **7**
Chow **1**	Gracias Më	Starbelly **3**
Delfina **5**	L'Ardoise **2**	Taqueria Cancun **8**

ANYONE FOR sweet nothings?

After strolling across the Golden Gate Bridge, hiking up to Coit Tower, or walking through 6,000 years of history at the Asian Art Museum, you might feel the need for a sweet treat—here a are a few places sure to satisfy.

Bi-Rite Creamery and Bakeshop, 3692 18th St. (*(C)* **415/626-5600,** www.biritecreamery.com) uses organic ingredients to create mouthwatering ice cream with flavors like roasted banana and toasted coconut.

The Candy Store, 1507 Vallejo St. (*(C)* **415/921-8000,** www.thecandystoresf.com), is a candy boutique featuring confections from around the world, and nostalgic, old-fashioned treats.

The Crepe Café (p. 89), Pier 39 on The Embarcadero (*(C)* **415/318-1494**). Push your nose up against the window to watch the workers make delicious dessert crepes loaded with Nutella, caramel, strawberries, bananas, and whip cream.

Ghirardelli (p. 174), 900 North Point St. at Ghirardelli Square (*(C)* **415/474-3938,** www.ghirardelli.com) ice cream parlor and chocolate shop serving sweet treats for the last 160 years.

Miette, Ferry Building Marketplace Shop #10 (*(C)* **415/837-0300,** www.miette.com), is a pastry shop featuring treats like Parisian macaroons, chocolate eclairs, and lavender shortbread cookies.

Ristobar (p. 90), 2300 Chestnut St. (*(C)* **415/923-6464,** www.ristobarsf.com). Italian Master pastry chef, Gary Rulli, whips up some of the best desserts in San Francisco—try Angela's tiramisu.

The original **Swensen's Ice Cream,** 1999 Hyde St. (*(C)* **415/775-6818,** www.swensens.com) opened in 1948—pure old school indulgence.

Tcho (p. 170), Pier 17 on The Embarcadero (*(C)* **415/963-5090,** www.tcho.com). Sign up online to take a chocolate factory tour, learn the history of chocolate, and taste artisan samples. Or, just show up and sample.

Inexpensive

Mission Chinese Food ★★★ CHINESE   Eating here is an adventure and the first part is simply finding the place. Set in a rundown dump, it has a large yellow sign reading "Lung Shan Restaurant." Hmm. But if you peek in the cracked window, you'll see it's a bit more inviting inside, thanks to the large orange dragon snaking across the ceiling. The other clue you're in the right place: the long line snaking down the street. Believe it or not, this hovel is home to one of the most talked-about chefs in the country, Danny Bowien, who has made a name for himself with his bold mixtures of Chinese classics and iconic foods from other culinary traditions (Kung Pao pastrami, anyone?). But the food isn't just showy, it's scrumptious and has garnered Bowien a boatload of awards (including Rising Star Chef of the Year from the Beard Foundation). Personal fav is the salt cod fried rice. Portions are large and great for sharing. BYOB. No reservations.

2234 Mission St. (at 18th St.). *(C)* **415/863-2800.** www.missionchinesefood.com. Main courses $10–$18. Daily 11:30–3pm, 5–10:30pm, closed Wed. Bus: 14 or 22.

Taqueria Cancun ★★ MEXICAN   After a night on the town, visitors and locals looking for mouth-watering, cheap Mexican food walk, stagger, stumble, and shuffle into this tiny Mission taqueria, open nightly until the wee hours. Green, yellow, and red plastic cut-outs cover the ceiling; beer flags, guitars, and the Virgin Mary hang on bright yellow walls—the clientele is as decorated and colorful as the restaurant, and range from hipsters sporting seriously complex tattoos to slightly tipsy button-down finance guys. Along with the delicious scent of grilling meats, when I recently popped in there was a slight odor of marijuana in the air—for medicinal purposes I am sure. Overall this place feels like a rowdy college hangout for bigger, older kids. When you grab a table, chances are the last diner's yellow plastic food basket will still be sitting there—you'll wait a long time for someone to clear it; just take a seat and push it aside. If the line to order is long, don't worry, it moves quickly; this place is used to crowds. No wonder, the food is delicious; the Carne Asada Super Burrito for $6.50 is huge, juicy, and full of flavor; the steak charred to perfection. What a surprise—they only take cash. No reservations.

2288 Mission St. (btw. 18th and 19th sts.). ☏ **415/252-9560.** Main courses $5–$9. Weekdays 9:30am–1:30am, Fri–Sat 9:30am–2:30am. Bus: 14 or 22.

THE CASTRO & NOE VALLEY

Expensive

Frances ★★ CALIFORNIAN   With only 37 seats, this is a tiny restaurant, with a tiny menu—and one tiny Michelin star—that consistently delivers a huge dining experience. Five years after opening in the Castro, Melissa Perello's personal baby has remained a top place in the city, known for an eclectic menu that might include choices as varied as squid ink tagliatelle with calamari, meyer lemon and green garlic; or Sonoma duck breast with apricot, onion and kale. I felt like an addict after sampling the applewood smoked bacon beignets—you dip them in crème, fresh with maple and chive. I just want more! Another must try are the Panisse frittes—chickpea fritters with garlic green goddess and meyer lemon. For dessert, the lumberjack cake—apple, kumquat, Medjool dates, and maple ice cream—is a crowd pleaser, as is the interesting idea of selling the house red and white wines for the bargain price of $1 an ounce. Make a reservation up to 60 days in advance, or walk in and sit at the bar.

3870 17th St. (at Pond St.) ☏ **415/621-3870.** www.frances-sf.com. Main courses $18–$29. Tues–Thurs and Sun 5–10pm; Fri–Sat 5–10:30pm. Bus: 22, 24, or 33. Any Market St. light rail or streetcar.

Moderate

L'Ardoise ★★ FRENCH   When Dominique Crenn—of Atelier Crenn (p. 89) fame, smiles fondly and says she loves to drop in here for a late evening supper, you know this place is good—really good. Pronounced "lard wazz"—the French word for the large chalkboard listing the daily specials—this hidden Castro gem feels like an old Parisian bistro, with rich burgundy walls, plush carpet, heavy curtains, and dark wood. Yes, the mood is romantic, and the food a bit more special than usual. Take zee escargots: not satisfied with regular escargots, Clement serves them *en gueusaille*—in fried potato cups—with a garlic and parsley cream sauce. Favorite entrees are as Gallic, think coq au vin in red wine sauce with potato puree, bacon and pearl onions; and roasted rack of lamb with *pomme frites*, garlic and parsley butter. Add a bottle from the selective wine list, a cheese plate to finish, and you have an evening that is *parfait*.

151 Noe St. (at Henry St.). ☏ **415/437-2600.** www.lardoisesf.com. Main courses $17–$39. Tues–Thurs 5:30–10pm; Fri–Sat 5–10:30pm. Bus: 24. Any Market St. light rail or streetcar.

Starbelly ★ CALIFORNIAN   Etiquette says we are supposed to eat dinner and then think about dessert, but two of the desserts here are so deliriously good, I have to mention them first. One is a luscious salted caramel pot de crème with rosemary cornmeal cookies. You'll be temped to swirl your fingers round the mason-type jar it comes in to get every last drip of caramel. The second sweet treat is warm toffee cake, drenched in caramel sauce, served with Medjool dates and mascarpone cheese. Yum. Preceding the drool-worthy desserts at this small, laid back café (it has an outdoor patio for good-weather dining), are such American classics as burgers with house cut fries, pot pies, steaks, and a variety of thin-crust pizzas. Don't miss the microbrew beers, some imported from as far away as Belgium and Canada, others produced by local artisan breweries.

3583 16th St. (at Noe and Market sts.). © **415/252-7500.** www.starbellysf.com. Main courses $11–$24. Mon–Thurs 11:30am–11pm; Fri 11:30am–midnight; Sat 10:30am–midnight; Sun 10:30am–11pm. Bus: 22. Any Market St. light rail or streetcar.

Inexpensive

Chow ★ AMERICAN   Chow is the perfect place to fuel up without emptying your wallet. Think warm, upscale neighborhood diner with cool artwork, serving organic BLT sandwiches, cobb salads, and chicken noodle soup, and you get the Chow concept. Hungrier? Try spring pesto lasagna, grilled catch of the day, or beef pot roast for some rib-sticking fare. A hearty brunch is served (weekends only), and breakfast is served on weekdays. Beer and wine are available. There's usually a line to get in, but you can call the same day to put your name on the list and get an idea of wait times. (They will accept reservations for parties of 8 or more).

215 Church St. (near Market St.). © **415/552-2469.** www.chowfoodbar.com/church_location. Main courses $9–$16. Mon–Fri 8–11am; Sat–Sun brunch 8am–2pm; Lunch daily 11am–5pm; Sun–Thurs 5–11pm, Fri–Sat 5pm–midnight. Bus: 22 or 37. Any Market St. light rail or streetcar.

RICHMOND/SUNSET DISTRICTS

Yes, it's a long haul from downtown to "the Avenues," but these restaurants wouldn't be in the guidebook if they weren't worth the trip.

Moderate

Aziza ★★ MOROCCAN   If I didn't know better, I'd say "Aziza" must mean "exciting food" in English. Long hailed as one of the best Moroccan restaurants in the city—big deal, we don't have many—Aziza has moved up the ranks to be called one of the best restaurants in the city. Period. Owner/chef, Mourad Lahlou, has shot to the top by combining classic dishes from his native Marrakesh with unusual, local ingredients. To sample this alchemist's gold, you have to try his traditional basteeya (a sweet and savory pot pie dish) made with duck confit instead of the usual chicken. And who else would think to add Medjool date, celery, and parsley to lentil soup? Even the couscous, which can be bland in traditional preparations, is extra–tasty here, made with fig and urfa (a spicy Turkish pepper).

5800 Geary Blvd. (at 22nd Ave.). © **415/752-2222.** www.aziza-sf.com. Main courses $19–$29. Wed–Mon 5:30–10pm. Street and valet parking. Bus: 1, 28, or 38.

Cliff House ★ CALIFORNIAN/SEAFOOD   The Cliff House, which, yes, is perched high on the cliffs, with awe-inspiring views, is a classic cat with nine lives. In 1887 it was severely damaged by an explosion when an abandoned ship loaded with dynamite crashed on the rocks out front. In 1894, it was destroyed by a chimney fire. And after reopening in 1896, the building survived the 1906 earthquake only to burn to the ground in 1907.

Thank goodness the Cliff House has a few lives left. Dining here on the bluff, while the sun falls into the crashing Pacific, is a sublime way to experience the California Coast. The Cliff House offers three dining options: **Sutro's,** the more formal place (think rib-eye steaks and the like); the **Terrace Room,** famous for its extravagant Sunday brunch (to live harp music, no less); but my personal preference is the low-key **Bistro** which fits with the rugged beauty outside. Regardless of which option you choose, after dining, work off your calories with a stroll along the oceanfront paths. Don't miss the gift shop with historical photos and memorabilia of the Cliff House and the Sutro Baths.

1090 Point Lobos (at Merrie Way), ℂ **415/386-3330.** www.cliffhouse.com. **Bistro** main courses $9–26; **Sutro's** main courses $19–$39. **Terrace Room** brunch $49; children $25. **Bistro** Mon–Sat 9am–3:30pm; Sun 8:30–3:30pm; Dinner every evening 4:15–9:30pm; **Sutro's** Mon–Sat 11:30am–3:30pm; Sun 11am–3:30pm; Dinner every evening 5–9:30pm. **Terrace Room** Sun 10am–4pm. Valet parking after 5pm daily. Bus: 5 or 38.

Inexpensive

Burma Superstar ★ BURMESE Because of the no-reservations policy, and numerous stellar online reviews, the lines just keep getting longer at Burma Superstar. So show up early, leave your cell phone number, and browse the interesting shops on Clement Street. Getting a chance to try authentic Burmese cuisine (which itself is an intriguing mix of Indian, Chinese and Thai influences) is worth the wait. So what to order? The tea leaf salad is the "superstar" on the menu, though the chili lamb with coconut rice and veggie samosa soup come in a very close second and third. The Food Network featured another signature dish: the rainbow salad. My daughter claims she hates all vegetables and yet she loves this mix of 22 ingredients including noodles, papaya, tofu, onion, beans, cabbage, carrots, tomatoes, potatoes, dried shrimp and spices. By the way, most dishes can be prepared vegetarian.

309 Clement St. (at Fourth Ave.). ℂ **415/387-2147.** www.burmasuperstar.com. No reservations. Main courses $8–$16. Daily 11:30am–3:30pm; Sun–Thurs 5–10pm; Fri–Sat 5–10:30pm. Bus: 2, 38, or 44.

Ton Kiang ★★★ CHINESE/DIM SUM When my son's friend, Dylan, told me I had to try this dim sum house, I questioned just how much an 11-year-old knows, and then gave it a shot. That Dylan is a smart boy. If you love dim sum, Ton Kiang is hands down the best place in the city to nibble, and nibble, and nibble. Visitors and locals line up early for the chance to take a seat and browse the passing trays of delish pot stickers and dumplings filled with every imaginable combination of mushrooms, peas, spinach, cabbage, shrimp, scallops, pork, and crab. Some dim sum can be gummy or mushy, but not here. The *dai dze gao* (scallop and shrimp dumplings with cilantro), and *gao choy-got* (green chives and shrimp dumpling) are so crunchy, light and perfect, you will inhale them and keep asking for more. If dim sum is not your style, the regular menu, filled with delicacies from southeastern China—including clay pot casseroles and Peking duck—is always available. By the way, the hours on the website are incorrect; the hours below are correct.

5821 Geary Blvd. (btw. 22nd and 23rd aves.). ℂ **415/387-8273.** www.tonkiang.net. Dim sum $3–$7; main courses $10–$26. Mon–Thurs 10am–9:30pm; Fri 10am–10pm; Sat 9:30am–10pm; Sun 9am–9pm. Bus: 5 or 38.

6 | EXPLORING SAN FRANCISCO

S an Francisco's parks, museums, tours, and landmarks are favorites for travelers the world over and offer an array of activities to suit every visitor. But no particular activity or place makes the city one of the most popular destinations in the world. It's San Francisco itself—its charm, its atmosphere, its perfect blend of big metropolis with small-town hospitality. No matter what you do while you're here—whether you spend all your time in the touristy areas like Union Square or Fisherman's Wharf, or explore the outer neighborhoods—you're bound to discover the reason millions of visitors keep leaving their hearts in San Francisco.

A (Nearly) City-Wide Attraction

Cable Cars ★★★ Although they may not be San Francisco's most practical means of transportation, cable cars are certainly the best loved and are a must-experience when visiting. Designated official moving historic landmarks by the National Park Service in 1964, they clank up and down the city's steep hills like mobile museum pieces, tirelessly hauling thousands of tourists each day to Fisherman's Wharf and elsewhere at the brisk pace of 9 miles per hour.

As the story goes, London-born engineer Andrew Hallidie was inspired to invent the cable cars after witnessing a heavily laden carriage pulled by a team of overworked horses, slip and roll backwards down a steep San Francisco slope, dragging the horses behind it. Hallidie resolved to build a mechanical contraption to replace horses, and in 1873, the first cable car made its maiden voyage from the top of Clay Street. Promptly ridiculed as "Hallidie's Folly," the cars were slow to gain acceptance. One early onlooker voiced the general opinion by exclaiming, "I don't believe it—the damned thing works!"

Even today, many visitors have difficulty believing that these vehicles, which have no engines, actually work. The cars, each weighing about 6 tons, run along a steel cable, enclosed under the street on a center rail. You can't see the cable unless you peer straight down into the crack, but you'll hear its characteristic clickity-clacking sound whenever you're nearby. The cars move when the gripper (they don't call themselves drivers) pulls back a lever that closes a pincerlike "grip" on the cable. The speed of the car, therefore, is determined by the speed of the cable, which is a constant 9½ mph—never more, never less. The two types of cable cars in use hold a maximum of 90 and 100 passengers, and limits are rigidly enforced. The

The Secret to Catching Cable Cars

Here's the secret to catching a ride on a cable car: Don't wait in line with all the tourists at the turnaround stops at the beginning and end of the lines. Walk a few blocks up the line (follow the tracks) and do as the locals do: Hop on when the car stops, hang on to a pole, and have your $6 ready to hand to the brakeman (hoping, of course, that he'll never ask). **Note:** On a really busy weekend, however, the cable cars often don't stop to pick up passengers en route because they're full, so you might have to stand in line at the turnarounds.

best view (and the most fun) is from a perch on the outer running boards—but hold on tightly, especially around corners.

Hallidie's cable cars were imitated and used throughout the world, but all have been replaced by more efficient means of transportation. San Francisco planned to do so, too, but met with so much opposition that the cable cars' perpetuation was actually written into the city charter in 1955. The mandate cannot be revoked without the approval of a majority of the city's voters—a distant and doubtful prospect. San Francisco's three existing cable car lines form the world's only surviving system, which you can experience for yourself should you choose to wait in the often long lines (up to a 2-hr. wait in summer). For more information on riding them, see "Getting Around By Public Transportation" in chapter 12 on (p. 229).

Powell–Hyde and Powell–Mason lines begin at the base of Powell and Market sts. California St. line begins at the foot of Market St. at the Embarcadero. $6 per ride.

FISHERMAN'S WHARF

Few cities in America are as adept at wholesaling their historical sites as San Francisco, which has converted Fisherman's Wharf into one of the most popular tourist attractions in the world—over 14 million visit each year. Unless you come early in the morning to watch the few remaining fishing boats depart, you won't find many traces of the traditional waterfront life that once existed here—the only trolling going on at Fisherman's Wharf these days is for tourist dollars. Originally called Meiggs' Wharf, this bustling strip of waterfront got its present moniker from generations of fishermen who used to dock their boats here. A small fleet of 30 or so fishing boats still set out from here, but mostly it's one long shopping and entertainment mall that stretches from Ghirardelli Square at the west end to Pier 39 at the east. Accommodating a total of 300 boats, two marinas flank Pier 39 and house the sightseeing ferry fleets, including departures to Alcatraz Island. The most famous residents of Fisherman's Wharf are the hundreds of **California sea lions** (p. 109) hanging out, barking on the docks at Pier 39.

Some love Fisherman's Wharf (my family and I fall into this category); others can't get far enough away from it. I suppose it has much to do with one's tolerance for kitsch. Among the most popular sites at the Wharf are the **Ripley's Believe It or Not! Museum** at 175 Jefferson St (✆ **415/202-9850;** www.ripleysf.com) and the street performers who convene on the stage at Pier 39 (though sometimes it feels like the entire Embarcadero has become an unofficial stage). In the summer of 2014 two more happily cheesy attractions are set to open: **Madame Tussaud's** and the **San Francisco Dungeon** (both at 145 Jefferson St.).

Alcatraz Island **12**
Asian Art Museum **22**
AT&T Park **37**
The Bay Lights **36**
Cable Car Museum **27**
Cable Cars **25**
California Academy of Sciences **7**
California Historical
    Society Museum **42**
Cartoon Art Museum **41**
Castro Theater **18**
Children's Creativity Museum **38**
Chinatown Gate **24**
City Hall **21**
Coit Tower **32**
Conservatory of Flowers **9**
Contemporary Jewish Museum **45**
The de Young Museum **6**
The Exploratorium **33**
Ferry Building Marketplace **34**
GLBT History Museum **17**
Glide Memorial Church **23**
Golden Gate Bridge **10**

Golden Gate Fortune
    Cookie Factory **28**
Golden Gate Park **2**
Grace Cathedral **26**
Haas-Lilienthal House **14**
Japan Center **15**
Japanese Tea Garden **5**
The Legion of Honor **3**
Lombard Street **13**

Mission Dolores **19**
Museum of the African Diaspora **43**
Pacific Heritage Museum **30**
The Painted Ladies of
    Alamo Square **16**
Pier 24 Photography Museum **35**
Precita Eyes Mural Arts Center **20**
San Francisco Botanical Gardens
    at Strybing Arboretum **8**

However you feel about these sort of attractions—and they're only part of what you'll experience here—most agree that, for better or worse, Fisherman's Wharf has to be seen at least once in your lifetime. There are still some traces of old-school San Francisco character here to enjoy, particularly the convivial seafood street vendors who dish out piles of fresh Dungeness crab and sour dough bread bowls full of clam chowder from their steaming stainless steel carts. And, yes, you can hop on a boat and go fishing.

At Taylor St. and the Embarcadero. ℰ **415/674-7503.** www.fishermanswharf.org. Bus: 30, 39, 47, or 82X. Streetcar: F. Cable car: Powell–Mason line to the last stop and walk to the wharf. If you're arriving by car, park on adjacent streets or on the wharf btw. Taylor and Jones sts. for $16 per day, $8 with validation from participating restaurants.

Alcatraz Island ★★★ HISTORIC SITE   If you can only do one tour while in San Francisco, make it Alcatraz. Probably the most famous prison in America, if not the world, this was where the worst of the worst criminals were marooned to suffer and freeze in the Bay. The building has barely changed at all from its days as a "grey-bar hotel." It's like walking through the past.

A bit of history: In 1775, Juan Manuel Ayala was the first European to set foot on the island. He named it after the many *alcatraces,* or pelicans that nested here. From the 1850s to 1933, Alcatraz served as a military fortress and prison. In 1934, the government converted the buildings of the military outpost into a maximum-security civilian penitentiary, one of the roughest places to be incarcerated in history. Inmates suffered psychologically and emotionally. The wind howled through the windows, the concrete was chilly and dank, and everything good and right in the world was perennially located at an unreachable distance. Given the sheer cliffs, treacherous tides and currents, and frigid water temperatures, it was believed to be totally escape-proof. Among the famous gangsters who occupied cellblocks A through D were Al Capone; Robert Stroud, the so-called Birdman of Alcatraz (an expert in ornithological diseases); Machine Gun Kelly; and Alvin "Creepy" Karpis, a member of Ma Barker's gang. It cost a fortune to keep them imprisoned here because all supplies, including water, had to be shipped in. In 1963, after an apparent escape in which no bodies were recovered, the government closed the prison. It moldered abandoned until 1969, when a group of Native Americans chartered a boat to the island and symbolically reclaimed the island for the Indian people. They occupied the island until 1971—the longest occupation of a federal facility by Native Americans to this day—but eventually were forcibly removed by the government. (See www.nps.gov/archive/alcatraz/indian.html for more information on the Native American occupation of Alcatraz.) The next year the island was given over to the National Park Service, natural habitats were restored, and the wildlife that was driven away during the prison years began to return. Today, you can see black-crested night herons and other seabirds here on a trail along the island's perimeter.

Admission to the island includes a fascinating audio tour, *Doing Time: The Alcatraz Cellhouse Tour,* narrated by actual former convicts, who are less grizzled than you might guess; the main voice pronounces "escape" as "excape," as someone's adorable Midwestern grandpa might. Don't be shy about pausing the recording with the Stop button, otherwise it rushes you along a bit too quickly. And don't be afraid to break away after your first pass through Broadway (the main corridor) so that you can explore the recreation yard. Wear comfortable shoes (the National Park Service notes that there are a lot of hills to climb) and take a heavy sweater or windbreaker, because

SAN FRANCISCO BAY

Alcatraz Island	**14**
Alcatraz Landing at Pier 33	**13**
Aquarium of the Bay	**10**
Boudin at the Wharf	**6**
Cable Car Turnaround	**3**
California Sea Lions	**12**
Ghirardelli Square	**2**
Madame Tussaud's Wax Museum (Summer 2014)	**7**
Musee Mechanique	**5**
Pier 39	**11**
Ripley's Believe It Or Not! Museum	**9**
San Francisco Dungeon (Summer 2014)	**8**
San Francisco Maritime National Historical Park	**1**
USS Pampanito	**4**

even when the sun's out, it's cold and windy on Alcatraz. Although there is a beverage-and-snack bar on the ferry, the options are limited and expensive; you might want to bring your own snacks for the boat. Only water is allowed on the island.

Note: The excursion to Alcatraz is very popular and space is limited, so purchase tickets as far in advance as possible (up to 90 days) via the **Alcatraz Cruises** website at www.alcatrazcruises.com. You can also purchase tickets in person by visiting the Hornblower Alcatraz Landing ticket office at Pier 33. The first departure, called the "Early Bird," leaves at 9am, and ferries depart about every half-hour afterward until 4pm. Two night tours (highly recommended) are also available, offering a more intimate and wonderfully spooky experience.

For those who want to get a closer look at Alcatraz without going ashore, two boat-tour operators offer short circumnavigations of the island. (See "Self-Guided & Organized Tours" on p. 136 for complete information.)

Pier 33, Alcatraz Landing near Fisherman's Wharf. ℂ **415/981-7625.** www.alcatrazcruises.com. Admission (includes ferry trip and audio tour) $90 family ticket for 2 adults and 2 kids (not available for the night tour), $30 adults, $28 seniors 62+, $18 child 5–11, free 4 and under. Night tour prices slightly higher. Arrive at least 20 min. before departure time. Streetcar: F-Line.

LITTLE KNOWN FACTS ABOUT *"the rock"*

○ Although Burt Lancaster's film performance made the Birdman of Alcatraz famous as a gentle, nurturing soul, in reality, the guy was a psychotic maniac. What's more, he never had any birds at Alcatraz. Because prisoners here were refused special treatment, he was forced to give them up when he was transferred here.

○ No documented person ever escaped and survived it. The cliffs are too tough, the bay's water would cause rapid hypothermia, and there would be a strong likelihood of being swept under the Golden Gate and out to sea. In fact, no one is known to have survived an escape, or if they did, they were captured anyway.

○ Why haven't they turned some of the empty buildings into a historical resort? Mostly because the island is still operating on its antique sewer line, which is barely strong enough to support the guest restrooms and gift shop as it is. Any future restorations or development will probably require a new line, which has kept anyone from seriously trying. That didn't stop a group of activists from attempting to convince the government to convert the island from a museum into a "Peace Center," an idea that was soundly defeated in a 2008 referendum. Locals love their Rock as it is: harsh and creepy.

Aquarium of the Bay ★ AQUARIUM   Set streetside at Pier 39, this cool little aquarium is a quick tour kids love. With over 20,000 sea creatures swimming about, you'll see the usual eels, octopuses, and jelly fish; you can pat bat rays and leopard sharks at the touch pool, or check out the new otter exhibit. The highlight of the aquarium is the conveyor-belt floor that moves you along a clear tube through a 700,000 gallon tank while sharks, rays, and all sorts of fish swim frantically beside you and over your head. Though a little on the expensive side compared to other things to do in the city, the chance to take a photo of your child grinning wildly with a shark right behind them is priceless. Skip this site if you will visit the Monterey Bay Aquarium—there is no need to see both.

Pier 39, the Embarcadero at Beach St. (✆ **415/623-5300.** www.aquariumofthebay.com. Aquarium admission $22 adults, $13 seniors (65+) and children 4–12, free for children 3 and under; family (2 adults, 2 children) package $64. Behind-the-scenes tours for an additional $12–$25 per person. Summer open daily 9am–8pm; Fall/Spring 10am–7pm (8pm weekends); Winter 10am–6pm (7pm weekends). Closed Christmas. Parking: Pier 39 Garage across the street. Streetcar: F-Line.

Boudin at the Wharf ★ FACTORY TOUR   After more than 30 years of being simply a bread shop in the heart of Fisherman's Wharf, the Boudin Bakery was supersized a few years ago. The new, ultramodern, 26,000-square-foot flagship baking emporium is now nearly half a block long, housing not only their demonstration bakery but also offers a museum, gourmet marketplace, cafe, espresso bar, and restaurant. You can see it the bakery by guided tour. And you might want to just do that: the Boudin (pronounced Bo-*deen*) family has been baking sourdough French bread in San Francisco since the gold rush, using the same simple recipe and original "mother dough" for more than 150 years. About 3,000 loaves a day are baked within the glass-walled bakery; visitors can watch the entire process from a 30-foot observation window along Jefferson Street or from a catwalk suspended directly over the bakery (it's quite entertaining). You'll smell it before you see it: the heavenly aroma emanating from the bread ovens is purposely blasted out onto the sidewalk.

Fisherman's Wharf 160 Jefferson St. (btw. Taylor and Mason sts.). ⓒ **415/928-1849.** www.boudin bakery.com. Tours Wed–Mon 11:30am–6pm $3 for anyone 12 and over, 11 and under free when accompanied by an adult. Bus and streetcar: All Embarcadero lines.

Ghirardelli Square ★ This National Historic Landmark property dates from 1864, when it served as a factory making Civil War uniforms, but it's best known as the former chocolate and spice factory of Domingo Ghirardelli (pronounced *Gear*-ar-dell-y), who purchased it in 1893. The factory has since been converted into an unimpressive three-level mall containing 30-plus stores and five dining establishments. Street performers entertain regularly in the West Plaza and fountain area. Incidentally, the **Ghirardelli Chocolate Company** ★ still makes chocolate, but its factory is in a lower-rent district in the East Bay. Still, if you have a sweet tooth, you won't be disappointed at the mall's fantastic (and expensive) old-fashioned soda fountain; their "world famous" hot fudge sundae is good, too. (Then again, have you ever had a bad hot fudge sundae?) As if you need another excuse to laze the day away in this sweet spot, the square now boasts free Wi-Fi.

900 North Point St. (btw. Polk and Larkin sts.). www.ghirardellisq.com. Stores generally open daily 10am–9pm in summer; Sun–Fri 10am–6pm, Sat 10am–9pm rest of year. Chocolate store and ice cream parlor: ⓒ **415/474-3938.** www.ghirardelli.com. Sun-Thurs 10am–11pm, Fri–Sat 10am–midnight. Cable car: Powell–Hyde.

Musee Mechanique ★★ ARCADE Calling it a museum is stretching things, but the Musee Mechanique is certainly fun, and the mechanical-minded will find it fascinating. A warehouse of dozens of antique coin-operated penny arcade diversions, most of which you'll never encounter anywhere else, it began entertaining people back in the 1930s, when a guy named George Whitney was his generation's leading impresario of cheap entertainment. Today, it's maintained by his descendent Daniel Zelinsky, an aficionado of such amusements, who stuck with a high-art name for his low-art attraction and showcases most of his 300-strong collection here. Because it's located among the pap of the Wharf, it's easy to confuse this one as a tourist trap, but in fact, the lack of an admission fee (you'll part only with whatever change you deposit into the machines of your choice) prove that's not the case. Most of the machines require a few quarters to reveal their Coney Island–era thrills, and almost all of the machines are representatives of a form of mechanical artistry rarely found in working condition anywhere. My favorite machines are the Opium Den, a morality tale in which a diorama of smoking layabouts comes alive with serpents and demons, and the Bimbo Box, in which seven monkey puppets respond to your loose change by playing the Tijana Brass. The Guillotine is also macabre fun; its doors upon to reveal the bloodless beheading of a tiny doll. But the standout machine is creepy old Laffing Sal, a funhouse figure that pretty much roars with laughter (and horrifies small children) upon the dropping of a coin. Every day except Tuesday, Zelinsky is on hand, repairing and polishing his beloved machines; he wears a badge reading "I work here."

Pier 45 at Taylor Street. ⓒ **415/346-2000.** www.museemechanique.org. Mon–Fri 10am–7pm, Sat–Sun 10am–8pm. Free.

San Francisco Maritime National Historical Park ★ HISTORIC SITE/ MUSEUM Since 1962, the Hyde Street Pier has been lined with one of the world's

CITYPASS VS. GO SAN FRANCISCO CARD

Several outfits in town will try to sell you a card that grants you discounts at a variety of attractions and restaurants; some throw in transportation, too. They really *do* give when they promise, but there's a problem with most of these cards: They usually include deals on stuff you'd never normally want to see or have time to cram in. Visiting extra attractions in an effort to make a "discount card" purchase pay off is a classic way to derail your vacation out of a sense of obligation.

Our advice? Never buy a discount card without first mapping out the plans you have for your visit's days, because you will likely discover you'd spend more money obtaining the card than you'll make back in touring. Never buy a discount card, here or in any other city, on the spur of the moment.

That being said, some may pay off and those that allow you to skip the lines offer real value in terms of time saved. Here are the two we'd recommend you consider:

CityPass (www.citypass.com) is a 7-day Muni and cable car pass with unlimited rides. It also allots users 9 days to visit four (five if you opt for the de Young Museum and the Legion of Honor choice) top sights from a choice of eight—including Alcatraz and The Exploratorium. The attractions alone have a retail value of $148 for an adult, and the CityPASS costs $84. Throw in free Muni and cable cars for 7 days, and the savings add up. We think this is likely the better of the two options, as it only includes the sights most visitors want to see.

The **Go San Francisco Card** (www.smartdestinations.com) can be purchased for 1-7 days; the price varies depending on the number of days. It does not include Muni transportation, nor does it cover the Exploratorium. However, Alcatraz was recently added as an option *if* you buy a 3 or 5-day pass through Alcatraz itself (see website for details). For those interested in tours (including a tour of wine country) or traveling with children (it includes many sights that still interest them) it *might* be a worthwhile buy. Especially if you can snag an additional 15% discount or the $10 off code for liking them on Facebook.

best collections of rare working boats, maintained by the National Park Service's San Francisco Maritime National Historic Park. They include the Glasgow-built **Balclutha,** a gorgeous 1886 three-mated sailing ship that, most famously, appeared in the classic Clark Gable movie Mutiny on the Bounty; the **Eureka,** an 1890 paddlewheel ferryboat that was once the largest of its kind on earth; the Hercules, a 1907 tugboat that worked towing logs up the West Coast; and the lumber schooner **C.A. Thayer** from 1895. The Alma, built in 1891, was once one of many schooners that plied the many waterways of the Bay Area, but today, it's the only one left.

Although it's free to admire the boats from the dock, $5 will get you onto the Balclutha, the Eureka, and the Hercules as much as you want for a week (NPS passes work to get you on for free). All of the vessels are designated National Historic Landmarks and it's worth seeing them, particularly the Balclutha, a 300-foot square-rigger cargo ship that moved goods like grain and coal between San Francisco, England, and New Zealand from 1886–1939. Especially interesting are the tiny crew bunk beds up front and the lavish Captain quarters farther back. In 1899, the wife of the Balclutha's Captain Durkee gave birth to a baby girl while aboard the ship; they named the little one

India Frances as they were sailing between India and San Francisco at the time. For more tidbits of history, use your cell phone as an audio guide to the ships by calling ✆ 415/294-6754 and entering one of the 28 tour codes found at www.nps.gov/safr "plan your visit," "things to do," "cell phone audio tour."

Before heading to the boats, be sure to pop into the park's signature Maritime Museum—on Beach Street at Polk Street, shaped like an Art Deco ship, and filled with sea-faring memorabilia. The **Aquatic Park Bathhouse Building is** also known as **The Maritime Museum;** it's free to enter located at Beach and Polk Streets. Check out the maritime murals and sea faring memorabilia. Next stop is the **Visitor Center** (also free) at Hyde and Jefferson Streets for a look at "The Waterfront," a surprisingly impressive, informative, and interactive exhibit about San Francisco's waterfront history (really, even if you don't usually like history museums, you'll find this one compelling and so will your kids; allot a good 40 min. to see it). It provides a terrific "overture" before seeing the boats themselves. One more "floater," the USS *Pampanito* (see below), is also well worth a visit.

Visitor's Center: Hyde and Jefferson sts. (near Fisherman's Wharf). ✆ **415/447-5000.** www.nps.gov/safr. No fee for Visitor's Center. Tickets to board ships $5, free for children 16 and under. Visitor's Center and Hyde Street Pier: Open daily 9:30am–5pm. Maritme Museum: Polk and Beach sts. ✆ **415/561-7100.** No fee. Open daily 10am–4pm. Bus: 19, 30, or 47. The park is open daily except for Thanksgiving, Christmas, and New Year's Day. Cable car: Powell–Hyde St. line to the last stop.

Pier 39 ★★ MALL/NATURE AREA   Pier 39 is a multilevel waterfront complex that makes up the eastern boundary of Fisherman's Wharf. Constructed on an abandoned cargo pier, it is, ostensibly, a re-creation of a turn-of-the-20th-century street scene, but don't expect a slice of old-time maritime life here: Today, Pier 39 is a busy mall welcoming millions of visitors per year. You will find more than 90 stores (personal favorites include Lefty's, where you can buy things like left-handed scissors and coffee cups; Shell Cellar which carries nothing but shell stuff; and Candy Baron which offers barrels and barrels of candy, with, as my 11-year old son discovered, adult-themed candy hidden at the back right), 14 full-service restaurants, a two-tiered Venetian carousel, the Aquarium of the Bay (p. 106), Magowan's Mirror Maze, bungee jumping, and a stage for street performers who juggle, ride unicycles, and tell corny jokes. My kids love Trish's Mini Donuts, where you can put your nose on the glass and watch a machine drop blobs of batter into boiling oil and make tiny sugar powdered donuts.

Best of all, Pier 39 has the **California sea lions.** Twenty years ago, hundreds of sea lions took up residence on the floating docks, attracted by herring (and free lodging). They can be seen most days sunbathing, barking, and belching in the marina—some nights you can hear them all the way from Washington Square. Weather permitting, naturalists from Aquarium of the Bay offer educational talks at Pier 39 daily from 11am–4pm (Memorial Day thru mid-October) that teaches visitors about the range, habitat, and adaptability of the California sea lion. After their population ballooned to more than 1,700 in the fall of 2009 the sea lions abruptly abandoned the docks, disappointing some onlookers. They returned in 2010, and the docks are once again loaded with these slippery, noisy beasts playing king of the mountain.

Pier 39 is *the* place that some locals love to hate (present company excluded), but kids adore it. Considering Fisherman's Wharf, including Pier 39, is rated one of the top tourist attractions in the world, don't listen to the naysayers; go check it out for yourself and grab a bag of donuts.

If the thought of walking up and down San Francisco's brutally steep streets has you sweating already, considering renting a talking **GoCar** ★ instead. The tiny yellow three-wheeled convertible cars are easy and fun to drive—every time I see one of these things, the people riding in them are grinning from ear to ear—and they're cleverly guided by a talking GPS (Global Positioning System), which means that the car always knows where you are, even if you don't. The most popular computer-guided tour is a 2-hour loop around the Fisherman's Wharf area, out to the Marina District, through Golden Gate Park, and down Lombard Street, the "crookedest street in the world." As you drive, the talking car tells you where to turn and what landmarks you're passing. Even if you stop to check something out, as soon as you turn your GoCar back on, the tour picks up where it left off. Or you can just cruise around wherever you want (but not across the Golden Gate Bridge). There's a lockable trunk for your things, and the small size makes parking a breeze. Keep in mind, this isn't a Ferrari—two adults on a long, steep hill may involve one of you walking (or pushing). You can rent a GoCar for 1 hour ($59), or for as long as you want (every hour after the first is $49/hr.). You'll have to wear a helmet, and you must be a licensed driver at least 18 years old. GoCar has two rental locations at Fisherman's Wharf (431 Beach St.), and Union Square (321 Mason St.). For more information call ℂ **800/91-GOCAR** (46227) or 415/441-5695, or log onto their website at www.gocartours.com.

On the waterfront at the Embarcadero and Beach St. ℂ **415/705-5500.** www.pier39.com. Shops daily 10am–9pm, with extended hours during summer and on weekends. Restaurant hours vary. Parking: Pier 39 Garage across the street. One hour validated if dining at a full service restaurant. Bus: 8X, 39, or 47. Streetcar: F-Line.

USS Pampanito ★ HISTORIC SITE   This storied sub sank six Japanese ships during four tours of the Pacific in World War II. The vessel, which is not for the claustrophobic or the infirm, has been painstakingly restored to its 1945 condition by admirers, who also run a smart, war-themed gift shop on the dock alongside it. Thanks to their efforts, she's still seaworthy, although sadly, the last time she was taken out into the ocean was for the filming of the abysmal 1996 Kelsey Grammer film *Down Periscope.* How glory fades . . .

Pier 45, Fisherman's Wharf. ℂ **415/775-1943.** www.maritime.org. Admission $12 for ages 13 and older, $8 for seniors (62+) and students with ID, $6 for children 6 to 12, and free for children 5 and under. Open daily at 9am.

SOMA (SOUTH OF MARKET)

From Market Street to Townsend Street and the Embarcadero to Division Street, SoMa has become the city's cultural hub, with the Yerba Buena District as its core, SoMa boasts a large concentration of museums, centers for the arts, and nightclubs—and plays home base for the World Series winning San Francisco Giants.

The Bay Lights ★ LIGHT SHOW   If you stand at the waterfront anywhere along the Embarcadero, your natural tendency will be to look left, towards our beautiful Golden Gate Bridge. If it's after sunset, try looking right—at the much-less-fussed-over

Bay Bridge; you can't help but notice the moving lights. To celebrate 75 years of connecting San Francisco to the East Bay, the bridge has been covered with the world's largest LED light sculpture, in what has been called the perfect mix of art and technology.

Each evening from dusk–2am through March 2015. www.thebaylights.org.

California Historical Society ★ MUSEUM Established in 1871, and filled with a large collection of Californiana—including photos, documents, and fine art, this museum celebrates the diverse heritage that is California. Exhibits rotate, and have featured topics as varied as a celebration of the 75th birthday of the Golden Gate Bridge to local artists' impressions of homelessness. Check the website to see what is planned during your visit.

678 Mission St. (btw. Third and New Montgomery sts.). ✆ **415/357-1848.** www.californiahistorical society.org. Admission $5 suggested donation for adults. Children are free. North Baker Research Library Wed–Fri noon–5pm. Galleries Tues–Sun noon–5pm. Bus: 5, 9, 14, 30, or 45. Streetcar: F-Line or Metro to Montgomery St.

Cartoon Art Museum ★★ MUSEUM Major points go to this surprisingly good attraction for addressing what could be a tourist-trap topic with academic intelligence. In fact, it's probably not a place where young kids will have a good time unless they're steeped in pop art. Here, you'll tour several rooms of works by seminal and well-known comic artists, particularly ones whose efforts primarily appeared on newsprint. It began in 1987 with an endowment from Charles M. Schulz, the *Peanuts* creator and since then, it's kept busy with up to seven changing exhibitions every year, and it has published 20 books (so far) on the neglected topic of cartoon history (the gift shop is excellent).

655 Mission St. (near 3rd St). ✆ **415/227-8666.** www.cartoonart.org. Admission $7 adults, $5 students and seniors, $3 kids 6–12; Tues–Sun 11am–5pm. Streetcar: F-Line.

Children's Creativity Museum ★ MUSEUM/AMUSEMENT CENTER Also in Yerba Buena Gardens you'll find this innovative, hands-on multimedia, arts, and technology museum for children of all ages. Kids howl tunes to the karaoke machine, and make art projects from boxes and scraps of material. One of the most favorite stations is the "Claymation area" where visitors make clay figures and learn all about stop motion animation by making a quick movie, *Wallace and Gromit*–style. Next door is the fabulous 1906 carousel that once graced the city's bygone oceanside amusement park, Playland-at-the-Beach, and there's a Children's Garden, a cafe, and a fun store.

Children's Creativity Museum: 221 Fourth St. (at Howard St.). ✆ **415/820-3320.** www.creativity. org. General admission $11; free for children 2 and under. Tues–Sun 10am–4pm. Carousel: Open daily 10am–5pm. $4 per ride ($3 w/paid museum admission). Bus: 14, 30, or 45. Streetcar: Powell or Montgomery.

Contemporary Jewish Museum ★ MUSEUM Set in the heart of the Yerba Buena cultural hub, in the epitome of an "old meets new" building—think shiny blue boxes dropped from the sky onto the roof of the historic, red-brick Willis Polk-designed PG&E building—this museum is dedicated to the celebration of *L'Chaim* ("To Life"). Inside, under the skylights and soaring ceilings designed by celebrated architect Daniel Liebeskind, are displays of art, music, film, and literature that celebrate Jewish culture, history, and ideas. Past exhibit subjects have been as varied Curious George, Gertrude Stein, and Allen Ginsberg. Future exhibits include "Live Archive: Jason Lazarus" (through March 2014), and "To Build and be Built: Kibbutz

SoMa (South of Market)

EXPLORING SAN FRANCISCO

When asking for directions in San Francisco, be careful not to confuse numerical avenues with numerical streets. Numerical avenues (Third *Avenue* and so on) are in the Richmond and Sunset districts in the western part of the city.

Numerical streets (Third *Street* and so on) are south of Market Street in the eastern and southern parts of the city. Get this wrong and you'll be an hour late for dinner.

History" (through June 2014). When you're ready for a break from culture, nosh on bagels and lox, matzo ball soup, and smoked pastrami on rye at the Wise Sons Jewish Deli.

736 Mission St. (btw. Third and Fourth sts.). ✆ **415/655-7800.** www.thecjm.org. Admission $12 adults, $10 seniors/students. 18 and under free. $5 for all Thurs after 5pm. Free every first Tues of the month. Open Fri–Tues 11am–5pm, Thurs 1–8pm. Closed Passover, July 4, Rosh Hashanah, Yom Kippur, Thanksgiving, and New Year's Day. Bus: 5, 9, 14, 15, 30, or 45. Streetcar: F-line or Metro to Montgomery St.

Museum of the African Diaspora ★ MUSEUM   This one's what I call a Spinach Museum—you go because it's good for you, or you go on a school field trip, but it's less than satisfying as there are almost no artifacts, only ideas. The enterprise is designed to teach all the ways that people from Africa have enriched world culture, and there obviously are many. But, aside from the occasional special exhibit that hits the mark, this museum isn't as effective as it could be.

685 Mission St. (near 3rd St.). ✆ **415/358-7200.** www.moadsf.org. Admission $10, $5 for seniors, free for kids under 12. Wed–Sat 11am–6pm, Sun noon-5pm. Bus: 14, 30, or 45. Streetcar: Powell or Montgomery.

Pier 24 Photography ★★ MUSEUM   At 8,534-square-metres, this former warehouse-turned-museum is one of the largest galleries in the world devoted exclusively to photography and video. But even with this amount of space, the main worry here seems to be that it will get too crowded. So, in an eccentric move (hey, this is San Francisco, after all), the Pilara Foundation, which owns the institution, allows only 20 people in at a time. Meaning that if you don't make advance reservations online, you might not get a place during one of the 2-hour visiting slots (entry is free). And that would be a real shame, because its exhibits tend to be dazzling. In the past, they've featured iconic works by Diane Arbus, Man Ray, and Walker Evans—though you might never know those were the photographers: in an attempt to make the viewers' experience of the art more immediate and unfettered, the gallery posts no wall text whatsoever. Instead viewers can borrow a rather loosely organized gallery guide to lead them through the mazelike space. It's rather like an art scavenger hunt. Through May of 2014, the exhibit features massive landscapes, in an exhibit titled "A Sense of Place."

At Pier 24 (near Harrison St. and the Embarcadero). ✆ **415/542-7424.** www.pier24.org. Admission free, but advanced reservations are required. Mon–Thurs 9am–5pm. Streetcar: F-Line.

San Francisco Museum of Modern Art (SFMOMA) ★★★ MUSEUM   Closed until early 2016 for renovations and expansion, some of the SFMOMA's collections have been temporarily set up at the Contemporary Jewish Museum (p. 111), and the Legion of Honor (p. 134). See Mark di Suvero's giant sculptures at Crissy Field through May 25, 2014.

151 Third St. (2 blocks south of Market St., across from Yerba Buena Gardens). ℂ **415/357-4000.** www.sfmoma.org.

Yerba Buena Center for the Arts ★ ARTS COMPLEX   The **YBCA,** which opened in 1993, is part of the large outdoor complex that takes up a few city blocks across the street from SFMOMA, and sits atop the underground Moscone Convention Center. It's the city's cultural facility, similar to New York's Lincoln Center but far more fun on the outside. The Center's two buildings offer music, theater, dance, and visual arts programs and shows. James Stewart Polshek designed the 755-seat theater, and Fumihiko Maki designed the Galleries and Arts Forum, which features three galleries and a space designed especially for dance. As for the shows at the galleries, they're often slightly more risky—or even risqué (local cartoonist R. Crumb mounted an R-rated show here several years back). As a testament to its quality, the museum also mounts traveling versions of shows for other museums. The museum also curates a monthly series of video or film screenings that specializes in experimental film and documentaries, and you'll get in the galleries free with your ticket.

701 Mission St. ℂ **415/978-ARTS** (2787). www.ybca.org. Admission for gallery $10 adults; $8 seniors, teachers, and students; free children 5 and under. Free to all 1st Tues of each month. Open Thurs–Sat noon–8pm; Sun noon–6pm; first Tues of the month noon–8pm; closed major holidays. Contact YBCA for times and admission to theater. Bus: 14, 30, or 45. Streetcar: Powell or Montgomery.

Yerba Buena Gardens ★ GARDENS   Unless you're at Yerba Buena to catch a performance, you're more likely to visit the 5-acre gardens, a great place to relax in the grass on a sunny day and check out architecture, artworks, and a revolving sea of humanity. The most dramatic outdoor piece is an emotional mixed-media memorial to Martin Luther King, Jr. Created by sculptor Houston Conwill, poet Estella Majozo, and architect Joseph De Pace, it features 12 panels, each inscribed with quotations from King, sheltered behind a 50-foot-high waterfall. There are also several actual garden areas here, including a Butterfly Garden, the Sister Cities Garden (highlighting flowers from the city's 13 sister cities), and the East Garden, blending Eastern and Western styles. Don't miss the view from the upper terrace, where old and new San Francisco come together in a clash of styles that's fascinating. May through October, Yerba Buena Arts & Events puts on a series of free outdoor festivals featuring dance, music, poetry, and more by the San Francisco Ballet, Opera, Symphony, and others.

Located on 2 square city blocks bounded by Mission, Folsom, Third, and Fourth sts. www.yerba buenagardens.com. Free admission. Daily 6am–10pm. Contact Yerba Buena Arts & Events: ℂ **415/543-1718** or www.ybgf.org for details about the free outdoor festivals. Bus: 14, 30, or 45.

FIDI (FINANCIAL DISTRICT)

Though most of the buildings in the FiDi are filled with brokers and bankers doing deals, along the beautiful waterfront visitors will find a few of San Francisco's best attractions.

The Exploratorium ★★★ MUSEUM   Recently relocated from dark, dated quarters at the Palace of Fine Arts to hip, new concrete, and glass digs on Pier 15, the "world's greatest science museum"—according to *Scientific American* magazine—is cooler than ever. This museum is all about demonstrating scientific concepts . . . in a sneaky enough way that kids think they're just playing. Instead they learn about the properties of motion by swinging a pendulum through sand or watch a chicken's heart beating through a microscope onto an egg yolk. (***Warning:*** that exhibit may turn them off to scrambled eggs).

On my last visit here with my own children, we spent 5 hours here; no one wanted to leave. If kids need to refuel before going back to tormenting their siblings, the cafe has wonderful sandwiches, chowder, cookies, muffins, and drinks.

Pier 15 (on the Embarcadero). ℰ **415/528-4444.** www.exploratorium.edu. Admission $25 adults; $19 seniors (65+), youth 6-17, visitors with disabilities, and college students with ID; free for children 5 and under. Open Tues–Sun 10am–5pm, Wed also open 6pm–10pm (for 18+). Parking across the street for $5 per hour. Streetcar: F-Line.

Ferry Building Marketplace ★★★ HISTORIC SITE/MARKET   Set inside a restored, history-rich ferry terminal and featuring some of the most scrumptious food vendors on the planet, the Ferry Building, and its twice-weekly farmers market, are as much a tourist attraction as they are a food hall. Which makes sense as few cities in the U.S. provide such a bounty of gourmet fixings. To read my full review, go to p. 146. You'll learn about the history of the place on our walking tour (p. 146).

Ferry Bldg, the Embarcadero (at Market St.). ℰ **415/983-9030.** www.ferrybuildingmarketplace. com. Most stores daily 10am–6pm; restaurant hours vary. Bus: 2, 12, 14, 21, 66, or 71. Streetcar: F-Line. BART: Embarcadero. Farmer's Market Thursdays and Saturdays, 10am–2pm right on the Embarcadero outside the building.

Wells Fargo History Museum ★ MUSEUM   On paper, it sounds awfully dull, but in reality, the Wells Fargo Museum paints a vivid portrait of early California life by using the company's once-vital stagecoaches as a centerpiece. For generations, the Wells Fargo wagon was the West Coast's primary lifeline; if you didn't want to or couldn't afford to use it (a ticket from Omaha to Sacramento was $300), then you'd be forced to take a long boat trip around Cape Horn. The curators have done a good job bringing the past to life by including biographies of some of the grizzled drivers of the 1800s, posting plenty of old ads, allowing visitors to climb aboard a nine-seat wagon, furnishing a reproduction of a "mug book" of highway robbers from the 1870s, and even putting together a sort of "CSI": Stagecoach re-created investigation revealing how they'd catch thieves after the fact. Wells Fargo has lost a lot of its cache in American culture; the Western theme fascinated kids in the 1950s but faded soon after. This well-assembled, two-story museum (budget about 45 minutes) helps restore some of that imagination again. There's a free audio tour, too, although everything is so well-signed you won't need it.

420 Montgomery St. (at California St.). ℰ **415/396-2619.** www.wellsfargohistory.com. Free admission. Mon–Fri 9am–5pm. Closed bank holidays. Bus: Any to Market St. Cable car: California St. line. BART: Montgomery St.

NORTH BEACH/TELEGRAPH HILL

As one of the city's oldest neighborhoods, the history of North Beach and Telegraph Hill is as rich as the Italian pastries found in the numerous shops along Columbus Avenue.

Coit Tower ★ HISTORIC SITE   In a city known for its great views and vantage points, Coit Tower is one of the best. Located atop Telegraph Hill, just east of North Beach, the round stone tower offers panoramic views of the city and the bay. Completed in 1933, the tower is the legacy of Lillie Hitchcock Coit, a wealthy eccentric who left San Francisco a $125,000 bequest "for the purpose of adding beauty to the city I have always loved." Though many believe the tower is a fire hose–shaped homage to San Francisco firefighters (Coit had been saved from a fire as a child and became a lifelong fan and mascot for Knickerbocker Engine Co. #5), the tower is merely an expression of Coit's esteem; a memorial to firefighters lies down below in Washington Square Park. Inside the base of the tower are impressive and slightly controversial (by 1930s standards) murals entitled *Life in California* and *1934,* which were completed under the Depression-era Public Works Art Project. Depicting California agriculture, industry, and even the state's leftist leanings (check out the socialist references in the library and on the newsstands), the murals are the collaborative effort of more than 25 artists, many of whom had studied under Mexican muralist Diego Rivera. The only bummer: The narrow street leading to the tower is often clogged with tourist traffic. If you can, find a parking spot in North Beach and hoof it. The Filbert and Greenwich steps leading up to Telegraph Hill are one of the most beautiful walks in the city (p. 114).

Telegraph Hill. ℂ **415/362-0808.** Admission is free to enter; elevator ride to the top is $7 adults, $5 seniors (65+) and youth 12–17, $2 children 5–11. Daily 10am–5:30pm. Closes 4:30pm in winter. Closed major holidays. Parking: don't even think about it. Bus: 39.

NOB HILL

When the cable car started operating in 1873, this hill became the city's exclusive residential area. Newly wealthy residents who had struck it rich in the gold rush and the railroad boom (and were known by names such as the "Big Four" and the "Bonanza kings") built their mansions here, but they were almost all destroyed by the 1906 earthquake and fire. The only two surviving buildings are the Flood Mansion, which serves today as the **Pacific Union Club,** and the **Fairmont San Francisco** (see p. 59), which was under construction when the earthquake struck and was damaged but not destroyed. Today, the sites of former mansions hold the city's luxury hotels—the Inter-Continental **Mark Hopkins** (p. 58), the **Stanford Court** (p. 58), the **Huntington Hotel** (p. 58), and spectacular **Grace Cathedral** (see below), which stands on the Crocker mansion site. Nob Hill is worth a visit if only to stroll around delightful **Huntington Park** with its cherubic fountain (a copy of the Tartarughe fountain in Rome), attend a Sunday service at the cathedral, visit the **Cable Car Museum** (below), or ooh and aah your way around the Fairmont's spectacular lobby.

Cable Car Museum ★★ MUSEUM   You can tell you're near this museum by the distinctive smell that, to me, proclaims San Francisco more than any of its famous food dishes. It's like the combined aroma of grease and electrical discharge that follows the famous cable cars wherever they roll. Here, in this warehouse that combines a museum experience with a real inside look at the inner machinations of the system, four mighty winding machines work the underground cables that propel the entire system, and if there's a cable break, this is where engineers splice it back together using some seriously medieval-looking implements. From decks overlooking the roaring machines, you'll see the cables shoot in from the streets, wind around huge wheels, and be sent back underground to carry more tourists up the city hills. You'll find out how the whole system works, including a look at the gripping mechanism that every car extends below the street level. I find it remarkable to think that nearly every American city of size once had systems just like this, but now only San Francisco maintains this antique (1873) but highly functional technology.

Alongside the spectacle, there's a museum telling the story of how, in 1954, some parking garage builders persuaded citizens to somehow support the destruction of most of the cable car network, leaving us with what you see here today. The museum also focuses on the effort to save the cable cars in 1947 when Mayor Lapham announced it was time to get rid of this antiquated form of public transportation. Armed with her knitting needles and a few friends, Telegraph Hill matron, Friedel Klussmann, stepped in and spearheaded a successful grassroots effort to save the iconic moving landmarks. As she effectively said, "Mayor Lapham didn't stand a chance—there is nothing a politician hates more than a bunch of little old ladies marching to his offices with the media in tow." The Powell–Hyde turnaround at Fisherman's Wharf is now named for Ms. Klussman.

Whatever you do, don't miss the chance to go downstairs, under the entrance to the building, where, in the darkness, you can peer at the whirring 8-foot sheaves that hoist in the cables from their various journeys around the city. Now and then, a real cable car will stall as it attempts to navigate the intersection outside, where drivers have to let go of one cable and snag another, and a worker will have to drive out in a cart and give it a nudge. This may be my favorite museum in town, and there's no other museum around that is as distinctive to the city, but mysteriously, few tourists bother to go.

1201 Mason St. (at Washington St.). ✆**415/474-1887.** www.cablecarmuseum.org. Free admission. Apr–Sept daily 10am–6pm; Oct–Mar daily 10am–5pm. Closed Thanksgiving, Christmas, and New Year's Day. Cable car: Both Powell St. lines.

Grace Cathedral ★ RELIGIOUS SITE Although this Nob Hill cathedral, designed by architect Lewis P. Hobart, appears to be made of stone, it is in fact constructed of reinforced concrete beaten to achieve a stonelike effect. Construction began on the site of the Crocker mansion in 1928 but was not completed until 1964. Among the more interesting features of the building are its stained-glass windows, particularly those by the French Loire studios and Charles Connick, depicting such modern figures as Thurgood Marshall, Robert Frost, and Albert Einstein; the replicas of Ghiberti's bronze *Doors of Paradise* at the east end; the series of religious murals completed in the 1940s by Polish artist John De Rosen; and the 44-bell carillon.

Where Grace really stands out, however, is in the compassion of its congregation, in no finer display than in the Interfaith AIDS Memorial Chapel that's located to the right as you enter. Two weeks before his own death from the disease in 1990, pop artist Keith Haring completed a triptych altarpiece called *The Life of Christ.* The final 600-pound work in bronze and white gold patina sits in the chapel's place of honor. The church has been respecting and praying for AIDS victims ever since 1986, back when most people in our government were sitting on their hands even while this city was being devastated. A segment of the famous AIDS Memorial Quilt is displayed above the chapel; it's rotated on a regular basis with new pieces.

Next door at the associated Diocesan House (1055 Taylor St.), there's a small and pleasant sculpture garden as well as, inside, frequently a free exhibition of photography or art.

Along with its unique ambience, Grace lifts spirits with services, musical performances (including organ recitals and evensong, or evening prayer, on many Sun). A lovely place to pray, meditate, or simply look at the beautiful building, doors are open every day to everyone.

1100 California St. (btw. Taylor and Jones sts.). ✆**415/749-6300.** www.gracecathedral.org. Bus: 1 or 27. Cable Car: Powell–Hyde or Powell–Mason.

CHINATOWN

The first Chinese immigrants—fleeing famine and the Opium Wars—came to San Francisco in the early 1800s to work as laborers and seek a better life promised by the "Gold Mountain." By 1851, 25,000 Chinese people were working in California, and most had settled in San Francisco's Chinatown. For the majority, the reality of life in California did not live up to the promise. First employed as workers in the gold mines during the gold rush, they later built the railroads, working as little more than slaves and facing constant prejudice. Yet the community, segregated in the Chinatown ghetto, thrived. Growing prejudice led to the Chinese Exclusion Act of 1882, which halted all Chinese immigration for 10 years and severely limited it thereafter. The Chinese Exclusion Act was not repealed until 1943. Chinese people were also denied the opportunity to buy homes outside the Chinatown ghetto until the 1950s. Today, San Francisco's Chinatown—the oldest in North America—is the largest outside of Asia. Although frequented by tourists, the area continues to cater to Chinese shoppers, who crowd the vegetable and herb markets, restaurants, and shops. Tradition runs deep here, and if you're lucky, through an open window you might hear women mixing mah-jongg tiles as they play the centuries-old game. (*Be warned:* You're likely to hear and see lots of spitting around here, too—it's part of local tradition.)

With dragons (or are they lions?) at its base, the ornate, jade-roofed **Chinatown Gate** at Grant Avenue and Bush Street marks the entry to Chinatown. Red lanterns hang across the street and dragons slither up lamp posts. The heart of the neighborhood is Portsmouth Square, where you'll find locals playing board games or just sitting quietly. On the newly beautified and renovated Waverly Place, a street where the Chinese celebratory colors of red, yellow, and green are much in evidence, you'll find three **Chinese temples:** Jeng Sen (Buddhist and Taoist) at no. 146, Tien Hou (Buddhist) at no. 125, and Norras (Buddhist) at no. 109. If you enter, do so quietly so that you do not disturb those in prayer. A block west of Grant Avenue, **Stockton Street,** from 1000 to 1200, is the community's main shopping street, lined with grocers, fishmongers, tea sellers, herbalists, noodle parlors, and restaurants. Here, too, is the Buddhist Kong Chow Temple, at no. 855, above the Chinatown post office. Explore at your leisure. A Chinatown walking tour is outlined in chapter 7 on p. 150. Visit www.sanfranciscochinatown.com for more information.

Golden Gate Fortune Cookie Factory ★ FACTORY TOUR   Not much has changed at this tiny Chinatown storefront since 1963, when it opened. Three women sit at a conveyer belt, folding messages into thousands of fortune cookies—20,000 a day—as the manager invariably calls out to tourists, beckoning them to stroll in, watch the cookies being made, and buy a bag of 40 for about $3. Sure, there are other fortune cookie bakeries in the city, but this is the only one left where the cookies are still made by hand the old-fashioned way. You can purchase regular fortunes, unfolded flat cookies without fortunes, or, if you bring your own fortunes, they can create custom cookies.

56 Ross Alley. ✆ **415/781-3956.** Admission is free. Open daily 9am–7pm. Photos are 50¢.

UNION SQUARE

The square itself is found in the city block surrounded by Stockton, Post, Powell, and Geary Streets; the area is San Francisco's Rodeo Drive—blocks and blocks of some of the best hotels, restaurants, and shops to keep the serious connoisseur happy for days.

When you tire of consuming, or your credit cards max out, grab a latte—or a glass of wine—at one of the cafes in the square; sit outside, relax, and people watch—the show is free, and always entertaining.

Glide Memorial United Methodist Church ★★ CHURCH Back in the 1960s, Glide Memorial's legendary pastor, Texas-born Cecil Williams, took over this 1931 church and began his famed, 90-minute "celebration" services. Williams, who retired the pastorship but is usually on hand anyway, is a little like a kindly high school principal, and his services are a little like a late night TV talk show, accompanied by a skilled six-piece jazz band (Leonard Bernstein was a fan, and Quincy Jones still is), backed by a 100-plus-voice choir (the Glide Ensemble, and man they're good). He's a solid American institution, counting Oprah Winfrey, Maya Angelou, and Robin Williams among his fans, and having appeared by himself in the Will Smith movie *The Pursuit of Happyness.* His wife, Janice Mirikitani, a well-known city poet, has also been working at the church since 1969. Their messages, repeated throughout the service, are of diversity, compassion, ending racism, brotherhood, and acceptance, and it doesn't take long before the crowd is on its feet, clapping, swaying, and praying. The church operates 87 entities designed to help others in a city that desperately needs such outreach, from help with housing and health care to jobs training. Don't miss a service here; there's nothing else like it, and it's impossible to feel unwelcome. Services are at 9 and 11am; don't show up with less than 15 minutes to spare or you will almost certainly have to participate by TV from a fellowship hall, and that would be a shame.

330 Ellis St. (at Taylor St.). ✆ **415/674-6000.** www.glide.org. Services Sun at 9 and 11am. Bus: 27. Streetcar: Powell. BART: Powell.

The Pacific Heritage Museum ★ MUSEUM If Asian art is an interest for you, the grandiosely named Pacific Heritage Museum may have something modest to offer. Its several hushed rooms mount displays of artworks by Asian-descended artists, both living and dead, but for me, the most interesting aspect of the place is the exhibit, in the basement, that uncovers the structure of the Subtreasury Building that stood in this spot from 1875 and was destroyed after the '06 quake. Of course, the palatial Asian Art Museum (p. ##) is the most elaborate repository in town for this sort of work, and shouldn't be missed.

608 Commercial St. (at Montgomery St.). ✆ **415/399-1124.** Free. Tues–Sat 10am–4pm. Bus: 1, 8X, or 12.

MISSION DISTRICT

This vibrant, cultural neighborhood gets its name from the oldest building in San Francisco, the haunting Mission Dolores (see below). Once inhabited almost entirely by Irish immigrants, the Mission District is now the center of the city's Latino community as well as a mecca for young, hip residents. It's an oblong area stretching roughly from 14th to 30th streets between Potrero Avenue on the east and Dolores Avenue on the west. The heart of the community lies along 24th Street between Van Ness and Potrero avenues, where dozens of excellent ethnic restaurants, bakeries, bars, and specialty stores attract people from all over the city. The area surrounding 16th Street and Valencia Street is a hotbed for impressive—and often impressively cheap—vintage stores, artisanal coffee shops, restaurants and bars catering to the city's hipsters. The Mission District at night doesn't feel like the safest place (although in terms of creepiness, the Tenderloin, a few blocks off Union Sq., beats the Mission by far), and walking around the area should be done with caution, but it's usually quite safe during the day and is highly recommended.

For insight into the community, go to the **Precita Eyes Mural Arts Center,** 2981 24th St., between Harrison and Alabama streets (ⓒ **415/285-2287;** www.precitaeyes. org), and take one of the 2-hour tours conducted on Saturdays and Sundays at 1:30pm, where you'll see a slide show covering the history of the murals that cover many walls in the area and the mural painting process. After the slide show, your guide will show you murals on a 6-block walk. Group tours are available during the week by appointment. $20 adults, $10 seniors (65+) and college students, $6 youth (12-17), $3 under 12.

Another sign of cultural life in the neighborhood is the progressive Theatre Rhinoceros (www.therhino.org).

Mission Dolores ★★ CHURCH The history of this church, more formally known as Misíon San Francisco de Asís, is the history of the early city, and there is not other surviving building that is more intrinsic to the early days of the town's formation. The tale goes back to the storied summer of 1776, when this site, then an uninhabited grove, was selected for a mission in a network that ran up and down the coast. Its first Mass was celebrated under a temporary shelter. The current building dates from 1791 and is the oldest in town. For such a rich representative of a city that has lost so much of its history, this place is a rare glimpse into the not-so-distant past and the troubled origins of California. This adobe-walled building, with its 4-foot-thick walls and rear garden, is hushed and transporting, and a precious survivor from California's colonial days. It's also almost entirely original, having survived the 1906 quake by dint of good old-fashioned craftsmanship, and as you roam, you'll encounter gorgeous altars brought from Mexico during the days of the Founding Fathers. The trusses, lashed together with rawhide, are made of redwood, and in 1916, they were reinforced with steel.

Following the chapel and the sanctuary, the tour's path visits a modest museum in the back before proceeding outside. In its heyday, the mission was home to some 4,000 people, but of course, most of that land was long ago sold off; look for the diorama, built in 1939, for a clearer picture of how it was all laid out. The back garden contains the graves of California's first governor and the city's first mayor, as well as, shockingly, the bodies of at least 5,000 Indians who died "helping" (read: slaving for) the mission. Sad to say, while few people know about the mass extinction, the mission is famous for the one grave that isn't there: The headstone of Carlotta Valdes, which Kim Novak visits in the movie *Vertigo* (1958) was a prop. Around the same time (1952), the compound was named a Basilica, an honorary Church of the Pope, and in 1987, Pope John Paul II swung by for a visit.

16th St. (at Dolores St.). ⓒ **415/621-8203.** www.missiondolores.org. Suggested donation $5 adults, $3 seniors and children. Open May–Oct 9am–4:30pm; Nov–Apr 9am–4pm; Closed Thanksgiving, Easter, Christmas, and New Year's Day. Bus: 22. Streetcar: J.

ALAMO SQUARE

The Painted Ladies of Alamo Square ★ No, we are not referring to (ahem) that kind of painted ladies, anything but—these lovely ladies are of a different sort. San Francisco's collection of Victorian houses, known as the **Painted Ladies,** is one of the city's most famous assets. Most of the 14,000 extant structures date from the second half of the 19th century and are private residences. Spread throughout the city, many have been beautifully restored and ornately painted. The small area bordered by

Divisadero Street on the west, Golden Gate Avenue on the north, Webster Street on the east, and Fell Street on the south—about 10 blocks west of the Civic Center—has one of the city's greatest concentrations of Painted Ladies. One of the most famous views of San Francisco—seen on postcards and posters all around the city—depicts sharp-edged Financial District skyscrapers behind a row of Victorians. This fantastic juxtaposition can be seen from Alamo Square, in the center of the historic district, at Fulton and Steiner streets. A **Victorian Homes Historical Walking Tour** is a great way to stroll past, and learn about, more than 200 restored Victorian beauties; for more information, see p. 138. For a peek inside, check out the **Haas-Lilienthal House.** Built in 1886, this home is filled with period pieces and depicts a slice of life back in a more genteel time. All visitors must take a docent-led tour, which lasts about an hour. Reservations are not required.

2007 Franklin St. (at Washington St.). *C* **415/441-3000.** www.sfheritage.org. 1-hr. guided tour $8 adults, $5 seniors and children 12 and under. Wed and Sat noon–3pm; Sun 11am–4pm. (**Note:** Some Sat the house is closed for private functions, so call to confirm.) Bus: 1, 10, 12, or 47. Cable car: California.

CIVIC CENTER

Filled with dramatic Beaux Arts buildings, showy open spaces, one of the best museums in the city, and a number of performing art venues, the Civic Center neighborhood has always made me think of a European city.

Asian Art Museum ★★ MUSEUM   A jewel-encrusted, silver elephant throne, or *howdah,* from India. Miniature carved *netsuke*—the decorations hung on the tassels of a kimono box-pocket in Japan. A room full of jade about which Confucius effectively said "gold is good, but jade is better." Evil-looking rod puppets from Indonesia. Welcome to the largest collection of Asian art in the United States. With over 18,000 treasures from Asian countries as varied as China, Tibet, India, and The Middle East, and with items spanning a 6000-year history, the Asian Art Museum is the largest museum of its kind, in fact, in this hemisphere. The concept of a museum devoted solely to Asian culture began in 1960 when Chicago Industrialist, Avery Brundage, agreed to donate his personal collection of Asian art to the city of San Francisco. Over time, the collection outgrew its space in a wing of the de Young Museum, and Italian architect, Gae Aulenti (famed for the Musee d'Orsay in Paris and the Palazzo Grassi in Venice), was hired to convert San Francisco's former main library into a contemporary showcase. Skylights, glass, and concrete hold three stories of treasures sorted by country. To better understand what you're seeing, I highly recommend taking a free docent-led tour, on which you'll learn about the role of the elephant as the ancient SUV of India, the reason jade can't be chiseled and while looking at a Koran from the 14th century, find out what the word "Koran" means. A highlight: one of the only collections of Sikh art in the world. With items of different mediums—including furniture, statues, clothing, paintings, jewelry, and sculpture—the pieces are varied and intriguing, even for kids. The collections change regularly and there is usually a visiting exhibition; the $5 audio tour is well worth the price. The museum store has handsome gifts for surprisingly good prices, and Café Asia serves a fabulous Asian chicken salad.

200 Larkin St. (btw. Fulton and McAllister sts.). *C* **415/581-3500.** www.asianart.org. Admission $12 adults, $8 seniors, students (with college ID), youths 13–17, free for children 12 and under. Free first Sun of the month. Open Tues–Wed and Fri–Sun 10am–5pm; Thurs 10am–9pm. Closed Thanksgiving, Christmas, and New Year's Day. Bus: All Market St. buses. Streetcar: Civic Center.

free CULTURE

To beef up attendance and give indigent folk like us travel writers a break, almost all of San Francisco's art galleries and museums are open free to the public 1 day of the month, and several never charge admission. Use the following list to plan your week around the museums' free-day schedules; see the individual attraction listings in this chapter for more information on each museum.

FIRST TUESDAY
- Yerba Buena Center for the Arts (p. 113)
- de Young Museum (p. 126)
- Legion of Honor (p. 134)
- Contemporary Jewish Museum (p. 111)

FIRST SUNDAY
- Asian Art Museum (p. 120)

FREE RANDOM DAYS (CHECK INDIVIDUAL WEBSITES)
- Exploratorium (p. 113)
- California Academy of Sciences (p. 125)

ALWAYS FREE
- Cable Car Museum (p. 115)
- Glide Memorial United Methodist Church (p. 118)
- Musée Méchanique (p. 107)
- Maritime National Historical Park & Museum ($5 to board ships; p. 107)
- Wells Fargo History Museum (p. 114)

City Hall ★★ HISTORIC SITE   San Francisco's Beaux-Arts City Hall was not built to be just another city hall. No, it was created with a measure of chutzpah that far outmeasured what the city was worth at the time. Having crumbled during the '06 quake, residents wanted show the world that San Francisco was still an American powerhouse, so this current City Hall was designed (1915) to be as handsome, proud, and imposing as a government capital building. In fact, most visitors are shocked to learn that its mighty rotunda is *larger* than the one atop Congress in Washington, DC. (Only four domes are bigger: the Vatican, Florence's Duomo, St. Paul's in London, and Les Invalides in Paris). If America ever moves its capital to San Francisco, its governmental home is taken care of. Should another horrible earthquake strike—make that *when* one strikes—a 1999 seismic retrofit saw to it that the structure can swing up to 27 inches in any direction; if you look closely at the stairs entering the building, you'll notice they don't actually touch the sidewalk because the entire building is on high-tech springs that had to be slipped, two by two, beneath a structure that already existed and was conducting daily business.

City Hall's most imposing attraction is indeed its fabulously ornate rotunda, a blend of marble (on the lower reaches) and painted plaster (high up), swept theatrically by a grand staircase where countless couples pose daily for their "just married" shots right after tying the knot (Friday is the busiest day for that). You've probably seen this staircase before. It featured in one of the final shots of *Raiders of the Lost Ark* (1981) as a stand-in for the U.S. Capitol. It was here, in 2004, that thousands of gay couples queued to sign up for their weddings; the first couple in line was an octogenarian lesbian couple that had been together for 51 years. Also, in 1954, Joe DiMaggio and Marilyn Monroe were married here and posed for photos on these steps. Not all the famous happenings at City Hall have been so hopeful. In 1978, the famous assassination of Mayor George Moscone and city Supervisor Harvey Milk occurred in two places on the second floor; the resulting trial, in which their killer got a light sentence

If you're walking around San Francisco—especially Telegraph Hill or Russian Hill—and you suddenly hear lots of loud squawking and screeching overhead, look up. You're most likely witnessing a fly-by of the city's famous green flock of wild parrots. These are the scions of a colony that started out as a few wayward house pets—mostly cherry-headed conures, which are indigenous to South America—who found each other, and bred. Years later they've become hundreds strong, traveling in chatty packs through the city (with a few parakeets along for the ride), and stopping to rest on tree branches and delight residents who have come to consider them part of the family. To learn just how special these birds are to the city, check out the book *The Wild Parrots of Telegraph Hill*, or see the heartwarming movie of the same name.

because, as his lawyers said, he was high on junk food (the "Twinkie Defense") became a lynchpin of outrage for the gay rights movement. In the rotunda, look up: Sculptures of Adam and Eve can be seen holding up the official seal of the city.

Across the hall at the top of the grand staircase, the sumptuous Chamber of the Board of Supervisors is worth a peek if it's open; its walls of Manchurian oak, plaster ceiling created to mimic wood, and doors hand-carved by French and Italian craftsmen make this one of the most opulent rooms in the city. Sunshine laws dictate that it must be open to the public unless in a special session, so pop in for a gander. Better yet, drop in during one of its colorful meetings.

Also check out the Light Court off the main rotunda on the ground floor; there, you'll find the head of a statues of the Goddess of Progress; she was atop the prior City Hall, in fuller figure, but this is all that survives. The light bulb sockets in her hair were later additions. Free and well-done 45-minute tours are available Mon-Fri 10am, noon, and 2pm. Reservations are not needed for groups less than eight people.

Civic Center 1 Dr. Carlton B. Goodlett Place (Polk St. btw McAllister and Grove Sts.). © **415/554-6139.** www.sfgov.org/cityhall. City Hall open to the public daily Mon-Fri 8am–8pm, closed major holidays. Parking: metered or CityPark lot across the street. Bart: Civic Center.

RUSSIAN HILL

This quiet residential area with stunning views of the bay is home to one of the best known streets in the world.

Lombard Street ★ ICON   Known (erroneously) as the "crookedest street in the world," this whimsically winding block of Lombard Street between Hyde and Leavenworth Streets draws thousands of visitors each year (much to the chagrin of neighborhood residents, most of whom would prefer to block off the street to tourists). The angle of the street is so steep that the road has to snake back and forth to make a descent possible. The brick-lined street zigzags around the residences' bright flower gardens, which explode with color during warmer months. This short stretch of Lombard Street is one-way, downhill, and fun to drive. Take the curves slowly and in low gear, and expect a wait during the weekend. Save your film for the bottom where, if you're lucky, you can find a parking space and take a few snapshots. You can also take staircases (without curves) up or down on either side of the street. In truth, most locals don't understand what the fuss is all about. I'm guessing the draw is the combination of seeing such a famous landmark, the challenge of negotiating so many steep curves, and a classic photo op. *FYI:* Vermont Street, between 20th and 22nd streets in Potrero Hill, is even more crooked, but not nearly as picturesque.

JAPANTOWN

More than 12,000 citizens of Japanese descent (1.5% of the city's population) live in San Francisco, or Soko, as the Japanese who first emigrated here often called it. Initially, they settled in Chinatown and SoMa, along Stevenson and Jessie streets from Fourth to Seventh streets. After the earthquake in 1906, SoMa became a light industrial and warehouse area, and the largest Japanese concentration took root in the Western Addition between Van Ness Avenue and Fillmore Street, the site of today's Japantown, now over 100 years old. By 1940, it covered 30 blocks. In 1913, the Alien Land Law was passed, depriving Japanese Americans of the right to buy land. From 1924 to 1952, the United States banned Japanese immigration. During World War II, the U.S. government froze Japanese bank accounts, interned community leaders, and removed 112,000 Japanese Americans—two-thirds of them citizens—to camps in California, Utah, and Idaho. Japantown was emptied of Japanese people, and war workers took their place. Upon their release in 1945, the Japanese found their old neighborhood occupied. Most of them resettled in the Richmond and Sunset districts; some returned to Japantown, but it had shrunk to a mere 6 or so blocks.

Today, the community's notable sights include the **Buddhist Church of San Francisco,** 1881 Pine St. (at Octavia St.), www.bcsfweb.org; the **Konko-Kyo Church of San Francisco,** 1909 Bush St. (at Laguna St.); the **Sokoji–Soto Zen Buddhist Temple,** 1691 Laguna St. (at Sutter St.); **Nihonmachi Mall,** 1700 block of Buchanan Street between Sutter and Post streets, which contains two steel fountains by Ruth Asawa; and the **Japan Center** (p. 123) a Japanese-oriented shopping mall occupying 3 square blocks bounded by Post, Geary, Laguna, and Fillmore streets. At its center stands the five-tiered **Peace Pagoda,** designed by world-famous Japanese architect Yoshiro Taniguchi "to convey the friendship and goodwill of the Japanese to the people of the United States." Surrounding the pagoda, through a network of arcades, squares, and bridges, you can explore dozens of shops featuring everything from TVs and *tansu* chests to pearls, bonsai, and kimonos. **Kabuki Springs & Spa** (see the "Urban Renewal" box below) is the center's most famous tenant. But locals also head here for its numerous authentic restaurants, teahouses, shops, and the Sundance multiplex movie theater. There is often live entertainment on summer weekends and during spring's cherry blossom festival, including Japanese music and dance performances, tea ceremonies, flower-arranging demonstrations, martial-arts presentations, and other cultural events. The **Japan Center** (© **415/922-7765**) is open daily from 10am to midnight, although most shops close much earlier. To get there, take bus no. 2, or 3 (exit at Buchanan and Sutter sts.) or no. 22 or 38 (exit at the northeast corner of Geary Blvd. and Fillmore St.). For a complete list of Japantown events, shops, and restaurants, go to www.japantown.org.

HAIGHT–ASHBURY

Few of San Francisco's neighborhoods are as varied—or as famous—as Haight-Ashbury. Walk along Haight Street, and you'll encounter everything from drug-dazed drifters begging for change to an armada of the city's funky-trendy shops, clubs, and cafes. Turn anywhere off Haight, and instantly you're among the clean-cut, young urban professionals who can afford the steep rents in this hip 'hood. The result is an interesting mix of well-to-do and well-screw-you aging flower children, former Deadheads, homeless people, and throngs of tourists who try not to stare as they wander through this most human of zoos. Some find it depressing, others find it fascinating, but everyone agrees that it ain't what it was in the free-lovin' psychedelic Summer of Love. Is it still worth a visit? Not if you are here for a day or two, but it's certainly worth an excursion on longer trips, if only to visit the trend-setting vintage clothing stores on the street (p. 165).

THE CASTRO

Castro Street, between Market and 18th streets, is the center of what is widely considered the world's first, largest, and best-known gay community, as well as a lovely neighborhood teeming with shops, restaurants, bars, and other institutions that cater to the area's colorful residents. Among the landmarks are **Harvey Milk Plaza, The GLBT History Museum** (see below) and the **Castro Theatre** (www.castrotheatre. com), a 1930s movie palace with a Wurlitzer organ.

The gay community began to move here in the late 1960s and early 1970s from a neighborhood called Polk Gulch, which still has a number of gay-oriented bars and stores. Castro is one of the liveliest streets in the city and the perfect place to shop for gifts and revel in free-spiritedness. Go to www.mycastro.com for local events, and www.castromerchants.com for a list of specialty shops. Also, check out www.sanfrancisco.gaycities.com, another resource for local gay bars, restaurants, and events. www.nighttours.com/sanfrancisco has an interactive map listing gay clubs, saunas, cruise bars and, cruising areas.

The GLBT History Museum ★ MUSEUM   North America's first full-fledged gay history museum, set in a former storefront in the Castro, is tiny but formidable, and ultimately quite moving. Recent exhibits have included quirky recaps of the past 25 years of queer history (their term), with profiles of the first lesbians to marry legally in California (including the pantsuits they wore); a section on the importance of gay bars for the community (illustrated by a marvelously decorative collection of matchbooks); an exhibit on the gay-rights movement (with Harvey Milk's sunglasses and the kitchen table he politicked at); and displays about gays in the military, hate crimes, AIDS and gays of color, among other topics. The museum is not appropriate for children—"We want to show how the erotic pleasure can become political power," co-curator Amy Sueyoshi told me as I gaped at a collection of sex toys—but should intrigue anyone with an interest in contemporary history.

4127 18th St. (btw Castro and Collingwood sts.). © **415-621-1107.** www.glbhistory.org. Admission $5, free the first Wed of each month. Mon-Sat 11am–7pm, Sun noon-5pm. Streetcar: F-Line.

GOLDEN GATE PARK ★★★

Everybody loves **Golden Gate Park**—people, dogs, birds, frogs, turtles, bison, trees, bushes, and flowers. Literally, everything feels unified here in San Francisco's enormous arboreal front yard. Conceived in the 1860s and 1870s, this great 1,017-acre landmark, which stretches inland from the Pacific coast, took shape in the 1880s and 1890s thanks to the skill and effort of John McLaren, a Scot who arrived in 1887 and began landscaping the park. When he embarked on the project, sand dunes and wind presented enormous challenges. But McLaren had developed a new strain of grass called "sea bent," which he planted to hold the sandy soil along the *Firth of Forth* back home, and he used it to anchor the soil here, too. Every year the ocean eroded the western fringe of the park, and ultimately he solved this problem, too, though it took him 40 years to build a natural wall, putting out bundles of sticks that the tides covered with sand. He also built the two windmills that stand on the western edge of the park to pump water for irrigation. Under his brilliant eye, the park took shape.

Today the park consists of hundreds of gardens and attractions connected by wooded paths and paved roads. While many worthy sites are clearly visible, there are infinite treasures that are harder to find, so pick up information at **McLaren Lodge and Park Headquarters** (at Stanyan and Fell sts.; *C* **415/831-2700**) if you want to find the more hidden spots. It's open daily 8am–5pm and offers park maps for $3. Of the dozens of special gardens in the park, most recognized are **McLaren Memorial Rhododendron Dell,** the **Rose Garden, Botanical Gardens,** and, at the western edge of the park, a springtime array of thousands of tulips and daffodils around the **Dutch windmill.** In addition to the highlights described in this section, the park contains lots of recreational facilities: tennis courts; baseball, soccer, and polo fields; a golf course; riding stables; and fly-casting pools. The Strawberry Hill boathouse handles boat rentals. The park is also the home of the **de Young Museum** (see below) Across from the de Young, you will find the **California Academy of Sciences** (also below).

To get around inside the park on weekends and public holidays, a free shuttle service is provided. For a complete list of maps, attractions, gardens, events se www.golden-gate-park.com Enter the park at Kezar Drive, an extension of Fell Street; bus riders can take no. 5, 28, 29, 33, 37 or 71.

Park Highlights

California Academy of Sciences ★★ MUSEUM   Though it's been sitting in the middle of Golden Gate Park for over 150 years, with a $500 million renovation completed in 2008, this museum is anything but a dusty, old dinosaur. Today it features every type of "arium" imaginable to interest your budding little scientist, by which I mean an aquarium, a planetarium, a butterfly-arium, and a reptile-arium.

And what attractions they are! The planetarium is the largest digital planetarium in the world. In the nature section, by the entrance, the main attraction is Claude, a formidable albino alligator. Up a circular ramp, four stories high, is a rainforest where brightly colored frogs play peek-a-boo while butterflies flit around your head. Topping it all off, literally, is a 2.5 acre rooftop garden with 1.7 million plants and flowers. The only thing to complain about at the Academy of Science is the steep entrance fee: $35 for adults. As the "greenest" museum in the world, it is safe to say all that money isn't going towards the lighting bills, but I suppose Claude has to eat.

55 Concourse Dr., Golden Gate Park. *C* **415/379-8000.** www.calacademy.org. Admission $35 adults, $30 seniors (65+), youth 12-17, students (with ID), $25 children 4–11, free for children 3 and under. Free admission on random Sundays, watch the website. Mon–Sat 9:30am–5pm; Sun 11am–5pm. Closed Thanksgiving and Christmas. Bus: 5, or 44. Streetcar: N-Judah.

Conservatory of Flowers ★★ CONSERVATORY   Opened to the public in 1879, this glorious Victorian glass structure is the oldest existing public conservatory in the Western Hemisphere. But it's not just a place of historic interest: a $25-million renovation, including a $4-million exhibit upgrade, was completed a few years ago, and now the Conservatory is a cutting-edge horticultural destination with over 1,700 species of plants, including rare tropical flora of the Congo, Philippines, and beyond. In fact, this is one of only four public institutions in the U.S. to house a highland

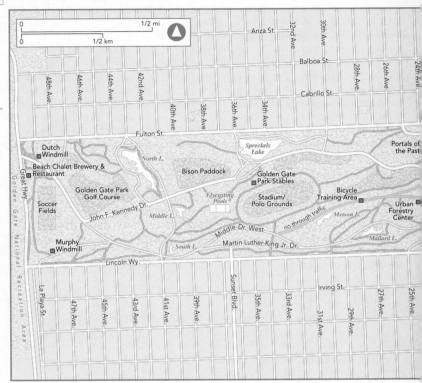

tropics exhibit. Its five galleries also host species from the lowland tropics, aquatic plants, the largest Dracula orchid collection in the world, and special exhibits. It doesn't take long to visit, but make a point of staying awhile; outside there are good sunny spots for people-watching as well as paths leading to impressive gardens. If you're around during summer and fall, don't miss the Dahlia Garden to the right of the entrance in the center of what was once a carriage roundabout—it's an explosion of colorful Dr. Seuss–like blooms.

100 John F Kennedy Dr. Golden Gate Park. 📞 **415/831-2090.** www.conservatoryofflowers.org. Admission is $7 adults; $5 youth (12-17), seniors (65+), and students with ID; $2 for children 5 to 11; and free for children 4 and under and for all visitors the first Tuesday of the month. Tues-Sun from 10am to 4:30pm.

de Young Museum ★★ MUSEUM   Built in 1894 for the California Midwinter International Exposition, the de Young has evolved from what was originally an eclectic collection of exotic oddities into a quality showcase of fine arts from around the world, many of which were donated by the Rockefeller Family. Permanent displays featuring North American art, and works from Oceania and Africa, have helped make the de Young one of the most-visited fine arts museums in North America. Exciting

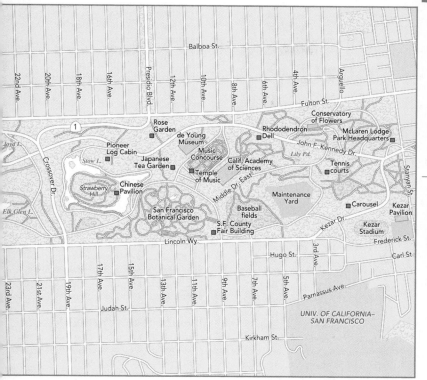

temporary exhibits change regularly—I've recently seen the treasures of King Tutankhamun and the dresses of Jean Paul Gaultier. Upcoming exhibits include a few of Elizabeth Taylor's baubles—among other pieces—at "The Art of Bulgari: La Dolce Vita & Beyond, 1950-1990" (Sept. 21, 2013–Feb. 17, 2014), "The Bay Bridge: A Work in Progress, 1933-1936" (Feb. 1, 2014–June 8, 2014), and "Modern Nature: Georgia O'Keefe and Lake George" (Feb. 15, 2014–May 11, 2014).

Be sure to climb up the 144-foot tower to the observation floor for a fantastic panoramic view of the city. As an added bonus, your de Young admission ticket can be used for same day entrance at the **Legion of Honor** (p. 134).

50 Hagiwara Tea Garden Dr. (inside Golden Gate Park, 2 blocks from the park entrance at Eighth Ave. and Fulton). ⏱ **415/750-3600.** www.deyoung.famsf.org. Admission adults $10, seniors (65+) $7, youths 13–17 and college students with ID $6, children 12 and under free. Free 1st Tues of the month. $2 discount for Muni riders with Fast Pass or transfer receipt. Tues–Sun 9:30am–5pm (Fri until 8:45pm [except Dec]). Closed New Year's Day, Thanksgiving, and Christmas. Bus: 5, 21, 44, or 71.

Japanese Tea Garden ★ GARDEN   John McLaren, the man who began landscaping Golden Gate Park, hired Makoto Hagiwara, a wealthy Japanese landscape designer, to further develop this garden originally created for the 1894 Midwinter

Relaxation and rejuvenation are raised to an art form in the City by the Bay. Here are six places you may want to try, for a massage, facial or what have you.

- **Kabuki Springs & Spa,** 1750 Geary Blvd. (*C* **415/922-6000;** www.kabukisprings.com), the Japan Center's most famous tenant, was once an authentic, traditional Japanese bathhouse. The Joie de Vivre hotel group bought and renovated it, however, and it's now more of a Pan-Asian spa with a focus on wellness. The deep ceramic communal tubs—at a very affordable $25 per person—private baths, and shiatsu massages remain. The spa is open from 10am to 10pm daily; joining the baths is an array of massages and ayurvedic treatments, body scrubs, wraps, and facials, which cost from $60 to $150.

- **Spa Radiance,** 3011 Fillmore St. (*C* **415/346-6281;** www.sparadiance.com), is an utterly San Francisco spa experience due to its unassuming Victorian surroundings and its wonderfully luxurious treatments such as facials, body treatments, massages, manicures, pedicures, Brazilian waxing, spray-tanning, and makeup application by in-house artists.

- A more posh and modern experience is yours at **International Orange,** 2044 Fillmore St., second floor (*C* **415/563-5000;** www.internationalorange.com). The self-described spa yoga lounge offers just what it says in a chic white-on-white space on the boutique-shopping stretch of Fillmore Street. They've also got a great selection of clothing and face and body products, including one of my personal favorites, locally made In Fiore body balms.

- In the St. Regis Hotel, **Remède Spa,** 125 Third St. (*C* **415/284-4060;** www.remede.com), has two whole floors dedicated to melting away all your cares, worries, kinks, and knots—not to mention primping. Expect wonderful massage, facials, manis and pedis, waxes, and more. A few doors down in the W Hotel is the city's outpost of New York's **Bliss Spa,** 181 Third St., fourth floor (*C* **877/862-5477;** www.blissworld.com). The hip version to St. Regis's chic, it offers a similar spa menu, including wedding specialties.

- Just over a decade old, **Tru,** 750 Kearny St. (*C* **415/399-9700;** www.truspa.com), is a sleek, modern-day spa with options that go way beyond your average hot stone massage. Signature treatments include oxygen facials and one of the world's only tropical rainforest water treatment room—a full-immersion experience involving steam, tropical rainstorms, and a 100-gallon-a-minute waterfall. It's located inside the Hilton Hotel, between Union Square and the Financial District.

Exposition. It's a quiet place with cherry trees, shrubs, and bonsai crisscrossed by winding paths and high-arched bridges over pools of water. Focal points and places for contemplation include the massive bronze Buddha (cast in Japan in 1790 and donated by the Gump family), the Buddhist wooden pagoda, and the Drum Bridge, which, reflected in the water, looks as though it completes a circle.

75 Hagiwara Tea Garden Dr. Golden Gate Park. *C* **415/752-1171.** www.japaneseteagardensf.com. Open daily 9am–6pm (4:45pm in winter months). Mon, Wed, Fri free admission before 10am, otherwise $7 adult, $5 senior (65+) and youth (12-17), $2 child (5-11), free toddler (4 and under).

San Francisco Botanical Gardens at Strybing Arboretum ★ GARDEN
More than 8,000 plant species grow here on 55 acres, among them some ancient plants in a special "primitive garden," rare species, and a grove of California redwoods. Check website for a variety of free docent-led tours.

1199 9th Ave., Golden Gate Park ☎ **415/661-1316** or visit www.strybing.org. Admission is $7 for adults, $5 for youth (12-17) and seniors (65+), $2 children (5-11), free under 5, $15 Family (2 adults and all children under 17). Open daily 9am–7pm (5pm in winter months).

Strawberry Hill/Stow Lake ★ NATURE AREA   Rent a boat and cruise around the circular Stow Lake as painters create still lifes, joggers pass along the grassy shoreline, ducks waddle around waiting to be fed, and turtles sunbathe on rocks and logs. Strawberry Hill, the 430-foot-high artificial island and highest point in the park that lies at the center of Stow Lake, is a perfect picnic spot; it boasts a bird's-eye view of San Francisco and the bay. It also has a waterfall and peace pagoda. For the **Stow Lake Boathouse,** call ☎ **415/386-2531.** Boat rentals are available daily 10am to 4pm, weather permitting; you can rent a rowboats ($14/hour), pedal boats ($19/hour), and electric boats ($29/hour) with a $5 deposit.

50 Stow Lake Dr., Golden Gate Park. ☎ **415/386-2531.** www.stowlakeboathouse.com. Mon–Fri 10am–7pm, Sat–Sun 9am–7pm (weather permitting).

THE PRESIDIO

In October 1994, the Presidio passed from the U.S. Army to the National Park Service and became one of a handful of urban national parks that combines historical, architectural, and natural elements in one giant arboreal expanse. (It also contains a previously private golf course and a home for George Lucas's production company.) The 1,491-acre area incorporates a variety of terrain—coastal scrub, dunes, and prairie grasslands—that shelter many rare plants and more than 200 species of birds, some of which nest here.

This military outpost has a 220-year history, from its founding in September 1776 by the Spanish under José Joaquin Moraga to its closure in 1994. From 1822 to 1846, the property was in Mexican hands.

During the war with Mexico, U.S. forces occupied the fort, and in 1848, when California became part of the Union, it was formally transferred to the United States. When San Francisco suddenly became an important urban area during the gold rush, the U.S. government installed battalions of soldiers and built Fort Point to protect the entry to the harbor. It expanded the post during the Civil War and during the Indian Wars of the 1870s and 1880s. By the 1890s, the Presidio was no longer a frontier post but a major base for U.S. expansion into the Pacific. During the war with Spain in 1898, thousands of troops camped here in tent cities awaiting shipment to the Philippines, and the Army General Hospital treated the sick and wounded.

By 1905, 12 coastal defense batteries were built along the headlands. In 1914, troops under the command of Gen. John Pershing left here to pursue Pancho Villa and his men.

The Presidio expanded during the 1920s, when Crissy Army Airfield (the first airfield on the West Coast) was established, but the major action was seen during World War II, after the attack on Pearl Harbor. Soldiers dug foxholes along nearby beaches, and the Presidio became the headquarters for the Western Defense Command. Some 1.75 million men were shipped out from nearby Fort Mason to fight in the Pacific; many returned to the Presidio's hospital, whose capacity peaked 1 year at 72,000 patients. In the 1950s, the Presidio served as the headquarters for the Sixth U.S. Army and a missile defense post, but its role slowly shrank. In 1972, it was included in new legislation establishing the Golden Gate National Recreation Area; in 1989, the Pentagon decided to close the post and transfer it to the National Park Service.

Today, the area encompasses more than 470 historic buildings, a scenic golf course, a national cemetery, the **Walt Disney Family Museum** (see below), several good restaurants, miles of hiking and biking trails, scenic overlooks, beaches, picnic sites, and a variety of terrain and natural habitats. The National Park Service offers docent and ranger-led tours, as well as a free shuttle called "PresidioGo." For more information, call the **Presidio Visitors Center** at © **415/561-4323,** or visit www.nps.gov/prsf. Take bus no. 28, 29, or 43 to get there.

Golden Gate Bridge ★★★ ICON   Very few cities possess an icon that so distinctly pronounces, "I'm here." New York has the Statue of Liberty, Sydney has its Opera House, but nothing makes you sigh "San Francisco" like the elegant profile of the stupendous **Golden Gate Bridge,** which links the city peninsula to the forests of Marin County.

It's not just an emblem. It was also an epic engineering feat that, when it was completed in 1937, changed the city from a clunky, ferry-dependent one to one of the motor age. President Franklin Roosevelt, in Washington, pushed a button and opened it to traffic, and what was then the world's longest suspension bridge went into service, as it has been reliably ever since (although now it's the second-longest in the country). It cost $26 million—less today than what it would cost to destroy it in an action movie, as so often happens. On the big day, cars paid 50¢, and pedestrians surrendered a nickel to thrill to the sight of deadly swirl of rushing currents far below. In an era when strides in steel and engineering measured a country's worth, this was a potent symbol of power. And it still impresses; it's tough to look down from its span and watch the waters roil angrily without being a little thankful that the wonders of engineering have the ability to make modern life so comfortable.

The bridge also has a dark side; is it the site of a suicide every 1 or 2 weeks (see the documentary *The Bridge* for a troubling look at some of them).

The bridge is not named for its color—it's red, after all, not yellow—or even after the miners of old, but for the channel below, which was originally named by knowing sailors after the treacherous Golden Horn in Turkey. Depending on the weather or the time of day, the stately bridge presents a different personality. That mutable color, known to its 38 ever-busy painters as "international orange," can appear salmon in daylight or clay red as the sun goes down. (It was originally going to be gunmetal grey, like the Bay Bridge, but folks fell in love with the red hue of the primer coat.) Wisely, the architects worked wonders in figuring out how to integrate the bridge with the landscape and not obliterate everything that led up to it, as usually happened in the 1930s. Consequently, getting a good snap of the thing isn't as easy as you'd think.

There's a pathway across the east side bridge for pedestrians (5am–9pm in summer, 5am–6pm in winter) that is on the best side for fantastic city views (the other side takes in the Pacific), but as you can imagine, it gets crowded on weekends. Unfortunately, the bridge isn't easy to reach on foot, as its entry on the San Francisco side is tangled up among the confusing and unfriendly roadways of the Presidio. The six-lane bridge, built to 1937 proportions, isn't the easiest or safest place to take photographs from your car, either although plenty of tourists snarl traffic in the effort. Instead, planners have also been intelligent enough to construct a viewing deck, complete with a restroom, at the bridge's northern end that is accessible no matter from which direction

Span: 6,450 feet
Total length: 8,981 feet
Completion date: May 28, 1937
Cost: $35 million
Date paid in full: July 1971
Engineer: Joseph B. Strauss
Road height: 260 feet
Tower height: 746 feet
Swing span: 27 feet
Deepest foundation: 110 feet under water

Cable thickness: 37 inches
Cable length: 7,650 feet
Steel used: 83,000 pounds
Concrete used: 389,000 cubic yards
Miles of wire cable: 80,000
Gallons of paint annually: 10,000
Color: international orange
Rise (in cold weather): 5 feet
Drop (in hot weather): 10 feet
Traffic: 3 million vehicles per month
Toll: $6 (southbound only)

you're coming on the 101. I prefer using it on the way into town, because visitors from southbound traffic must use a walkway that goes underneath the bridge, giving them a unique second perspective of its structural underpinnings. Try to show up earlier in the day, when the sun is unlikely to ruin your shots. If you do go on the bridge, for an extra thrill, be in the middle when a boat goes underneath; freighters are exhilarating when seen from above, and the regular tourist sightseeing boats bob helplessly for an amusing moment as they turn around in the teeming waters; sometimes, you can hear their passengers shout in alarm.

Hwy. 101 N. www.goldengatebridge.org. $6 electronic toll when driving south, cash no longer accepted. Bridge-bound Golden Gate Transit buses (𝒞 **511**) depart hourly during the day for Marin County. No toll northbound.

The Walt Disney Family Museum ★ MUSEUM   While this relatively new arrival on the cultural scene features the expected collection of Walt Disney memorabilia, the museum is really more of a tribute to the life of the man behind the mouse. It takes a serious look at Walt Disney's personal life, including his childhood in Kansas City, his move to California with nothing but $40 in his pocket and a dream, and explains how he and his brother, Roy, decided to launch Disney Bros. Studio. The most moving room is the gallery filled with thoughts and condolences from around the world when Mickey's creator passed away in 1966. But it's not a downer, and children will enjoy the visit. How could they not with all of the character sketches on display, including the earliest known drawings of Mickey Mouse, and original art from feature films like *Fantasia* and *Dumbo*?

In the Presidio, Main Post, 104 Montgomery St. (at Sheridan Ave.). 𝒞 **415/345-6800.** www.walt disney.org. Admission $20 adults, $15 for students with valid IDs and seniors 65 and over, $12 for children 6–17. Wed–Mon 10am–6pm. Bus: 28 or 43.

GOLDEN GATE NATIONAL RECREATION AREA

The largest urban park in the world, GGNRA makes New York's Central Park look like a putting green, covering three counties along 28 miles of stunning, condo-free shoreline. Run by the National Park Service, the Recreation Area wraps around the northern and western edges of the city, and just about all of it is open to the public with no

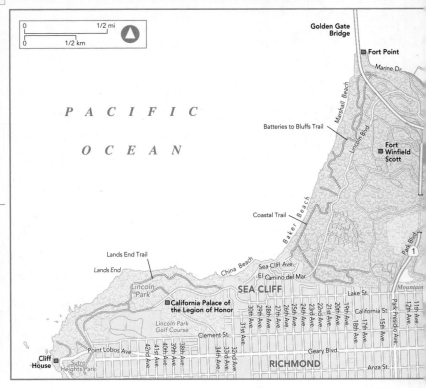

access fees. The Muni bus system provides transportation to the more popular sites, including Aquatic Park, Cliff House, Fort Mason, and Ocean Beach. For more information, contact the **National Park Service** (© **415/561-4700;** www.nps.gov/goga). For more detailed information on particular sites, see the "Getting Outside" section, later in this chapter.

Here is a brief rundown of the salient features of the park's peninsula section, starting at the northern section and moving westward around the coastline:

Aquatic Park, adjacent to the Hyde Street Pier, has a small swimming beach, although it's not that appealing (and darned cold).

Fort Mason Center, from Bay Street to the shoreline, consists of several buildings and piers used during World War II. Today they hold a variety of museums, theaters, shops, and organizations, and **Greens** vegetarian restaurant (p. 89), which affords views of the Golden Gate Bridge. For information about Fort Mason events, call © **415/345-7500** or visit www.fortmason.org. The park headquarters is also at Fort Mason.

Farther west along the bay at the northern end of Laguna Street is **Marina Green,** a favorite local spot for kite flying, jogging, and walking along the Promenade. The St. Francis Yacht Club is also here.

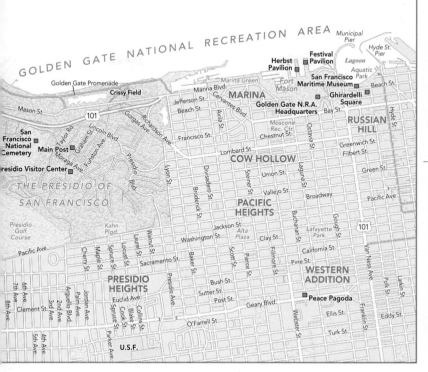

Next comes the 3½-mile paved **Golden Gate Promenade ★**, San Francisco's best and most scenic biking, jogging, and walking path. It runs along the shore past **Crissy Field** (www.crissyfield.org) and ends at Fort Point under the Golden Gate Bridge. Be sure to stop and watch the gonzo windsurfers and kite surfers, who catch major wind here, and admire the newly restored marshlands. **The Crissy Field Warming Hut Café and Bookstore (*©* 415/561-4030)** is open daily from 9am to 5pm (9am–7pm summer weekends) and offers yummy, organic soups, salads, sandwiches, coffee drinks, and a good selection of outdoor-themed books and cards.

Fort Point ★ (*©* 415/556-1693; www.nps.gov/fopo) was built between 1853 and 1861 to protect the narrow entrance to the harbor. It was designed to house 500 soldiers manning 126 muzzle-loading cannons. By 1900, the fort's soldiers and obsolete guns had been removed, but the formidable brick edifice remains. Fort Point is open Fri–Sun from 10am to 5pm (summer daily except Wednesday), and guided tours and cannon demonstrations are given at the site once or twice a day on open days, depending on the time of year.

Lincoln Boulevard sweeps around the western edge of the bay to **Baker Beach,** where the waves roll ashore—a fine spot for sunbathing, walking, or fishing. Hikers can follow the **California Coastal Trail** from Fort Point along this part of the coastline to Lands End (visit www.presidio.gov/explore/trails).

A short distance from Baker Beach, **China Beach** is a small cove where swimming is permitted. Changing rooms, showers, a sun deck, and restrooms are available.

A little farther around the coast is **Land's End ★**, looking out to Pyramid Rock. A lower and an upper trail offer hiking amid windswept cypresses and pines on the cliffs above the Pacific.

Still farther along the coast lie **Point Lobos,** the ruins of **Sutro Baths** (www.sutro baths.com), and the **Cliff House** (p. 98). The Cliff House which recently underwent major renovations, has been serving refreshments to visitors since 1863. It's famed for its views of Seal Rocks (a colony of sea lions and many marine birds) and the Pacific Ocean. Immediately northeast of Cliff House you'll find traces of the once-grand Sutro Baths. Built by mayor, Adolph Sutro, in 1896 as a bathing facility for the smelly masses without indoor plumbing, the baths turned into a swimming facility that was a major summer attraction accommodating up to 24,000 people. It burned down in 1966. See photos of the baths and a life-sized model in an antique Speedo inside the Cliff House.

A little farther inland at the western end of California Street is **Lincoln Park,** which contains a golf course and the spectacular **California Palace of the Legion of Honor Museum** (see below).

Though technically not inside the GGNRA, the **San Francisco Zoo** (p. 135) is located across the street where Sloat Blvd. meets the Great Highway.

At the southern end of Ocean Beach, 4 miles down the coast, is **Fort Funston** (*©* **415/561-4323**), where there's an easy loop trail across the cliffs. Here you can watch hang gliders take advantage of the high cliffs and strong winds. It's also one of the city's most popular dog parks. Check out the webcam at www.flyfunston.org/newwebcam.

Farther south along Route 280, **Sweeney Ridge** affords sweeping views of the coastline from the many trails that crisscross its 1,000 acres. From here the expedition led by Don Gaspar de Portolá first saw San Francisco Bay in 1769. It's in Pacifica; take Sneath Lane off Route 35 (Skyline Blvd.) in San Bruno.

The GGNRA extends into Marin County, where it encompasses the Marin Headlands, Muir Woods National Monument, and Olema Valley behind the Point Reyes National Seashore. See chapter 10 for information on Marin County and Muir Woods.

California Palace of the Legion of Honor ★★ The most beautiful museum in San Francisco sits perched high on the headlands with a stellar view of the Golden Gate Bridge. Built in 1924, in the Beaux-arts style, the Legion of Honor is a ¾ replica of the Palais de la Legion d'Honneur in Paris, and serves as a memorial to the 3600 California soldiers who lost their lives fighting on the battlefields of France in World War I. Though the setting alone makes this beaut a must-visit, the collections and ever-changing exhibits of classical art and artifacts are sure to please the fine arts connoisseur . . . and Alfred Hitchcock buffs: pivotal scenes from *Vertigo* were filmed here. Filled with 4000 years' worth of treasures, the focus is on ancient, and European, art and paintings, plus you'll find one of the largest collections of prints and drawings in the United States. Auguste Rodin's 1904 cast bronze sculpture "The Thinker" can be admired in the Court of Honor. Saturdays and Sundays at 4pm, visitors can hear Ernest Skinner's 1924 pipe organ reproducing the sounds of a full orchestra; it is considered one of the finest pipe organs in the world. Paintings, drawings and bronzes of Henri

ESPECIALLY FOR kids

San Francisco is one of the best cities in the world to visit with children. While some kids might want to visit our fine arts museums and cultural sights, for the others, we have burping sea lions, an underwater restaurant, and a grumpy old man in Chinatown passing out fortune cookies and threats. The following attractions appeal to all kids:

- **Alcatraz Island** (p. 104)
- **Aquarium of the Bay** (p. 106)
- **Cable Car Museum** (p. 115)
- **Cable Cars** (p. 100)
- **California Academy of Sciences** (p. 125)
- **Chinatown Walk** (p. 150)
- **The Exploratorium** (p. 113)
- **Forbes Island Restaurant** (p. 86)
- **Ghirardelli Ice Cream** (p. 96)
- **Golden Gate Bridge** (p. 130)
- **Golden Gate Park** (p. 124)
- **Golden Gate Fortune Cookie Factory** (p. 117)

- **Fisherman's Wharf** (p. 101)
- **Maritime National Historical Park** (p. 107)
- **Musee Mechanique** (p. 107)
- **Pier 39 and the California Sea Lions** (p. 109)
- **Ripley's Believe It or Not** (p. 101)
- **San Francisco Zoo** (p. 135)
- **Tcho Chocolate Factory Tour** (p. 170)
- **Uncle Gee in Chinatown** (p. 154)
- **Walt Disney Family Museum** (p. 131)
- **Yerba Buena Ice Skating, Bowling & Children's Creativity Center** (p. 113)

The website www.sfrecpark.org is an excellent resource for recreation centers, pool and parks; www.sfkids.org is another good resource for child-friendly activities.

Matisse on loan while the SFMOMA undergoes renovations will be on display at the exhibit "Matisse from SFMOMA" Nov. 9, 2013–Sept. 7, 2014. As an added bonus, if you would like to see more fine arts treasures, your ticket is valid for same-day entrance to the de Young museum (p. 126) in Golden Gate Park.

100 34th St. (at Clement St.), Lincoln Park. (C) **415/750-3600.** www.legionofhonor.famsf.org. Admission $10 adults, $7 seniors (65+), $6 youth 13-17 and students (with ID), free children 12 and under. Additional fees may apply for special exhibitions. Free admission first Tuesday of the month. Tues–Sun 9:30am–5:15pm. Closed Thanksgiving, Christmas, and New Year's Day. Bus: 1, 18, or 38.

San Francisco Zoo ★ Located between the Pacific Ocean and Lake Merced in the southwest corner of the city, the San Francisco Zoo, which once had a reputation for being a bit shoddy and out-of-date, has come a long way in recent years. Though grown-ups who are into wildlife will enjoy the visit, it's really aimed at kids, who get a kick out of attractions like the hands-on Children's Zoo, the flock of shockingly pink flamingos, the giant anaconda, the recently restored Carousel, and the ageless Little Puffer train.

Founded at its present site near the ocean in 1929, the zoo is spread over 100 acres and houses more than 930 animals, including some 245 species of mammals, birds, reptiles, amphibians, and invertebrates. Exhibit highlights include the **Lipman Family Lemur Forest,** a forest setting for five endangered species of lemurs from

Madagascar; **Jones Family Gorilla World,** a tranquil haven for a family group of western lowland gorillas; **Koala Crossing,** which connects to the Australian Walkabout exhibit with its kangaroos, wallaroos, and emu; **Penguin Island,** home to a large breeding colony of Magellanic Penguins; and the **Primate Discovery Center,** home to rare and endangered monkeys. **Puente al Sur (Bridge to the South)** has a pair of giant anteaters and some capybaras. The **Lion House** is home to rare Sumatran and Siberian tigers and African lions. **African Savanna** is a 3-acre mixed-species habitat with giraffes, zebras, antelopes, and birds. Check the website for a daily schedule of animal feeding times.

The 6-acre **Children's Zoo** offers kids and their families opportunities for close-up encounters with rare domestic breeds of goats, sheep, ponies, and horses in the Family Farm. Touch and feel small mammals, reptiles, and amphibians along the Nature Trail and gaze at eagles and hawks stationed on Hawk Hill. Don't miss a visit to the fascinating Insect Zoo or the Meerkat and Prairie Dog exhibit, where kids can crawl through tunnels and play in sand, just like these amazing burrowing species.

There's a coffee cart by the entrance as well as two decent cafes inside, definitely good enough for a bite with the kids (though the lines can be long and slightly confusing if you're handling food and kid duty at the same time).

Great Highway btw. Sloat Blvd. and Skyline Blvd. ✆ **415/753-7080.** www.sfzoo.org. Admission $15 adults, $12 for seniors (65+), $9 children 4-14, free for children 3 and under. San Francisco residents receive a discount. Daily 10am–5pm. Parking $8 weekdays, $10 weekends and holidays. Bus: 23 or 18. Streetcar: L from downtown Market St. to the end of the line.

SELF-GUIDED & ORGANIZED TOURS

The 49-Mile Scenic Drive ★★

This self-guided, 49-mile drive is an easy way to orient yourself and to grasp the beauty of San Francisco and its extraordinary location. Beginning in the city, it follows a rough circle around the bay and passes virtually all the best-known sights, from Chinatown to the Golden Gate Bridge, Ocean Beach, Seal Rocks, Golden Gate Park, and Twin Peaks. Originally designed for the benefit of visitors to San Francisco's 1939 and 1940 Golden Gate International Exposition, the route is marked by blue-and-white sea gull signs. Although it makes an excellent half-day tour, this mini-excursion can easily take longer if you decide, for example, to stop to walk across the Golden Gate Bridge or to have tea in Golden Gate Park's Japanese Tea Garden.

If you are in the area, the **San Francisco Visitor Information Center,** (www.sanfrancisco.travel), at Powell and Market streets, distributes free route maps, which are handy since a few of the Scenic Drive marker signs are missing. Otherwise, they have a great pdf map you can download on their website. Try to avoid the downtown area during the weekday rush hours from 7 to 9am and 4 to 6pm.

Walking Tours

Do not miss the opportunity to take one of the 80-plus absolutely free walking tours offered in rotation by **San Francisco City Guides ★★★** (✆ 415/557-4266; www.sfcityguides.org), a simply terrific volunteer organization that runs up to a dozen tours a day, from 10am to 2pm, all around town. You don't need to make a reservation; just show up at the place and time listed online on its home page, where the weekly

Paul Blart "Mall Cop" alert! Segways are those weird-looking upright scooters you've probably seen on TV. The two-wheeled "human transporter" is an ingenious electric-powered transportation device that uses gyroscopes to emulate human balance. After the free 30-minute lesson, riding a Segway becomes intuitive: lean forward, go forward; lean back, go back; stand upright, stop. Simple. The **San Francisco Electric Tour Company** offers Segway-powered narrated 2-hour tours—choose from Wharf and Waterfront, Golden Gate Park, Chinatown–Little Italy–Wharf night tour, and, for advanced riders, the Hills and Crooked Streets tour. For $70 it's not a bad deal, and it's the closest you'll come to being a celebrity (*everyone* checks you out). **Note:** You must be at least 12 years old, between 100-250lbs, and can't be pregnant to join the tour. No heels, sandals or flip-flops. For more information, log onto www.sfelectric tour.com or call ℂ **415/474-3130.**

schedule is kept up-to-date by the group's single paid employee. Tours are free, but at the end your guide, who will be someone who loves and studies the city and wants to share that love, will pass around an envelope and hope for a few bucks. Some of the cooler tours include a walk through the historic Palace Hotel; City Scapes and Public places, on which you'll discover hidden rooftop gardens and little-known financial museums downtown; a retelling of the history of the Mission Dolores neighborhood, one of the city's most historic; and Gold Rush City, which takes in the stomping grounds of the original '49ers. Most of the city's great attractions, from Coit Tower to Fisherman's Wharf, will have a tour dedicated to their explication. Tours are probably the city's best bargain, and they're an inviting way to see some windswept places you may not want to go to alone, including along the walkway of the Golden Gate Bridge and the Fort Mason complex. Some 21,000 people a year take advantage of this terrific service, and frugal city buffs could easily fill their vacations with two or three a day.

Cruisin' the Castro (ℂ **415/255-1821;** www.cruisinthecastro.com) is an informative historical tour of San Francisco's most famous gay quarter, concentrating on the contribution of the gay community to the city's political maturity, growth, and beauty. This fun and easy walking tour is for all ages, highlighting gay and lesbian history from 1849 to present. Stops include America's only Pink Triangle Park and Memorial, the original site of the AIDS Quilt Name Project, Harvey Milk's residence and photo shop, the Castro Theatre, and the Human Rights Campaign and Action Center. Tours run Monday through Saturday from 10am to noon and meet at the Rainbow Flag at the Harvey Milk Plaza on the corner of Castro and Market streets above the Castro Muni station. Reservations are required. The tour costs $30 per adult, $25 for children 5 to 12.

The **Haight-Ashbury Flower Power Walking Tour** (ℂ **415/863-1621**) explores hippie haunts with Pam and Bruce Brennan (aka "Hippy Gourmet"). You'll revisit the Grateful Dead's crash pad, Janis Joplin's house, and other reminders of the Summer of Love in 2½ short hours. Tours begin at 10:30am on Tuesdays and Saturdays, Thursday at 2pm, and Fridays at 11am. The cost is $20 per person, kids 9 and under are free. Reservations are advised. Purchase tickets online at www.haightashburytour.com

To explore the less-touristy side, and get the hidden nooks and crannies of China-town, sign up with **Wok Wiz Chinatown Walking Tours & Cooking Center,** 250 King St., Ste. 268 (ℂ **650/355-9657;** www.wokwiz.com). Founded over 2 decades ago by the late author and cooking instructor Shirley Fong-Torres, its guides today are all Chinatown natives, who speak fluent Cantonese, and are intimately acquainted with the neighborhood's history, folklore, culture, and food. Tours are conducted daily from 10am to 1pm and include a seven-course dim sum lunch (a Chinese meal made up of many small plates of food). There's also a less expensive tour that does not include lunch. Since groups are generally held to a maximum of 15, reservations are essential. Prices (including lunch) are $50 for adults and $35 for children (6-10); without lunch, prices are $35 and $25, respectively. Tickets can be purchased online at www.wokwiz. com. Wok Wiz also operates an **I Can't Believe I Ate My Way Through Chinatown** tour which starts with breakfast, moves to a wok shop, and stops for nibbles at a vegetarian restaurant, dim sum place, and a marketplace, before taking a break for a sumptuous authentic Cantonese luncheon. It's offered on most Saturdays, takes 3½ hours, and costs $90 per person ($50 for children), food included. The city mourns the loss of Shirley, who passed away in 2011.

Finally, for a tour of the areas where tour busses are foribidden, try Jay Gifford, **Victorian Homes Historical Walking Tour** (© 415/252-9485; www.victorianhome walk.com). As you might guess, the tour concentrates on architecture though Jay, a witty raconteur and San Francisco resident for more than 2 decades, also goes deeply into the city's history—particularly the periods just before and after the great earthquake and fire of 1906. You'll stroll through Japantown, Pacific Heights, and Cow Hollow. In the process, you'll see more than 200 meticulously restored Victorians, including the sites where *Mrs. Doubtfire* and *Party of Five* were filmed. Tours run daily and start at 11am rain or shine; cost is $25 per person (cash only).

Bike Tours

Several Fisherman's Wharf companies compete for biking business and frankly, there doesn't seem to be much difference between them, either in price, or quality of the rental equipment. They are **Blazing Saddles Bike Rentals and Tours** (© 415/202-8888; www.blazingsaddles.com), **Bay City Bike Rentals** (© 415/346-2453; www. baycitybike.com) and **San Francisco Bike Rentals** (© 415/922-4537; www.bikerental sanfrancisco.com). The last one also has shops at the Ferry Building and in the Haight.

Along with rentals, the first two offer identical, guided bike tours over the Golden Gate Bridge, and down into Sausalito ($55 for adults, $35 for kids 11 and under on both). The guided portion of the tour ends in Sausalito, and you are then free to ride more, eat lunch, browse the shops, and take the ferry back at your leisure. (*Note:* the $11 ferry ride back to Pier 39 is not included in the price, but the two companies can sell you the ticket if you want one—or you can ride back!). Tours start at 10am and take about 3 hours; helmets, locks, maps, and a safety training class are all included.

Boat Tours

One of the best ways to look at San Francisco is from a boat bobbing on the bay. There are several cruises to choose from, and land/cruise options available online. Regardless of which you take, bring a jacket; it can be freezing cold on the bay.

Blue & Gold Fleet, Pier 39, Fisherman's Wharf (© 415/705-8200; www.blueandgold fleet.com), offers a range of options including a 60-minute tour of the bay that follows along the historic waterfront, a 90-minute cruise around Alcatraz Island, and a "guaranteed to get soaked" bay adventure on the flame-covered RocketBoat. Prices for tours range from $28 for an adult on one of the cruises to $50 for a combo ticket of a cruise

QUACK! splash

San Francisco Duck Tours—those weird looking amphibian cars that drive around the city and then plunk into the bay for a water tour—have absolutely no historical importance or redeeming value. Oh well; judging by the grinning masses sitting inside blowing their duck whistles, no one seems to care. Try a tour on one, especially if you have kids in tow. 2766 Taylor St. (at Jefferson St.); *©* **877/887-8225;** www.sanfranciscoducks.com; $35 adults, $25 kids (4–17).

plus the RocketBoat. Ferries are available to Sausalito, Tiburon, and Angel Island for $17–$22 roundtrip (adults), $10–$14 (kids and seniors), free 5 and under.

The **Red & White Fleet,** established in 1892, departs daily from Pier 43½ (*©* **415/673-2900;** www.redandwhite.com), and offers a number of bay cruise tours including the 90-minute "Bridge 2 Bridge" ($36 adults, $24 kids 5–17, free 5 and under), 2-hour "Sunset" ($58 adults, $40 kids 5–17, free under 5), and "Golden Gate" ($28 adults, $18 kids 5–17, free under 5).

Bus Tours

San Francisco's public transportation system can be hard to master for newbies, so these Hop On/Hop Off tours fill a niche, especially for those looking to see just the major sites. A number of different combinations are offered, by a number of different companies and none is significantly better than the others. So look at your needs: do you want a funky old trolley or an open double-decker bus? A tour that crosses the Golden Gate Bridge and visits Sausalito? Look, too, at how many stops are en route; and how often the busses leave. In the off-season, that might be just twice a day, making a hop-on, hop-off tour more "stay on" (study the bus schedules before booking!). Companies to compare include **Big Bus Tours** (www.bigbustours.com), **City Sightseeing San Francisco** (www.city-sightseeing.us), and **The San Francisco Sightseeing Company** (www.sanfranciscosightseeing.com). Prices vary depending on the tour. *Tip:* A second day of hopping on and off can often be added for only a few more dollars, though many people find 1 day on these buses is more than enough.

Air Tours

San Francisco Seaplane Tours is the Bay Area's only seaplane tour company, a good choice for thrill-seekers. For more than 60 years, this locally owned outfit has provided its customers a bird's-eye view of the city, flying directly over San Francisco at an altitude of about 1,500 feet. Sights you'll see during the narrated excursions include the Golden Gate and Bay Bridges, Alcatraz, Tiburon, and Sausalito. Half the fun, however, is taking off and landing on the water (which is surprisingly smooth). Trips depart from Mill Valley; the company offers complimentary shuttle pickup at Pier 39. Prices range from $189 per person for the 30-minute Golden Gate Tour to $249 for the 40-minute Champagne Sunset Flight, which includes a bottle of bubbly and a cozy backseat for two. Children's rates are available, and cameras most welcome. For more information or reservations, call *©* **415/332-4843** or log onto www.seaplane.com.

Equally thrilling (and perhaps more so if you've never been in a helicopter) is a tour of San Francisco and the bay via **San Francisco Helicopters.** The $175 ($135 child) Vista package includes free shuttle pickup from your hotel or Pier 39, and a 20-minute

A whale OF A TALE

Not many people outside of California know about the Farallon Islands, nor do many people get to visit up close. The entire Gulf of Farallones National Marine Sanctuary is off-limits to civilians, so visitors must gaze from the deck of a fishing or whale-watching boat if they want a peek firsthand.

This veteran eco-tourism company offers trips out to the desolate outcropping of rock off the coast of San Francisco that is home to birds, sea lions, seals, dolphins, and the ever-present great white shark. Typically on the search for migrating gray, humpback, or blue whales, expeditions leave from Pier 39 at 8am sharp and pass underneath the majestic Golden Gate Bridge on the 27-mile trip out to the islands. A crew of trained naturalists accompany each voyage, and will stop at the first sign of water spouts on the 5- to 6-hour trips.

For more information on the different tours offered, call (C) **415/331-6267** or visit www.sfbaywhalewatching.com.

tour that takes you over the city, and past the Golden Gate and Bay Bridges, and Alcatraz Island. After takeoff, the pilot gives a narrated tour and answers questions while the background music adds a bit of Disney-ride quality to the experience. *(Tip:* The view from the front seat is the best.) Picnic lunch and sunset dinner packages are available as well. For more information or reservations, call (C) **650/635-4500** or log onto www.sfhelicopters.com.

A BART Tour

One of the world's best commuter systems, **Bay Area Rapid Transit (BART)** runs along 104 miles of rail, linking 43 stations between San Francisco, Millbrae, and the East Bay. Under the bay, BART runs through one of the longest underwater transit tubes in the world. This link opened in September 1972, 2 years behind schedule and 6 months after the general manager resigned under fire.

The people who run BART think so highly of their trains and stations that they sell a $5.20 **"Excursion Ticket,"** which allows you, in effect, to "sightsee" the BART system, or basically ride it. "Tour" the entire system as much as you like for up to 3 hours; you must exit at the station where you entered. (If you get out anywhere else along the line, the gate instantly computes the normal fare.) For more information, call (C) **415/989-BART** (2278) or visit www.bart.gov, where you can also download trip plans directly to your iPod, PDA, or wireless.

GETTING OUTSIDE

Half the fun in San Francisco takes place outdoors. If you're not in the mood to trek it, there are other things to do that allow you to enjoy the surroundings.

BEACHES   Most days it's too chilly to hang out at the beach, but when the fog evaporates and the wind dies down, locals love to hit the sands. On any truly hot day, thousands flock to the beach to worship the sun, build sand castles, and throw a ball around. Without a wet suit, swimming is a fiercely cold endeavor and is not recommended. In any case, dip at your own risk—there are no lifeguards on duty and San Francisco's waters are cold and have strong undertows. On the South Bay, **Baker**

Beach is ideal for picnicking, sunning, walking, or fishing against the backdrop of the Golden Gate (most fisherman do catch and release here, due to pollution in the Bay). **Ocean Beach,** at the end of Golden Gate Park, on the westernmost side of the city, is San Francisco's largest beach—4 miles long. Just offshore, at the northern end of the beach, in front of Cliff House, are the jagged Seal Rocks, inhabited by various shorebirds and a large colony of barking sea lions (bring binoculars for a close-up view). To the left, Kelly's Cove is one of the more challenging surf spots in town. Ocean Beach is ideal for strolling or sunning, but don't swim here—tides are tricky, and each year bathers drown in the rough surf.

Stop by Ocean Beach bus terminal at the corner of Cabrillo and La Playa streets to learn about San Francisco's history in local artist Ray Beldner's whimsically historical sculpture garden. Then hike up the hill to explore **Cliff House** and the ruins of the **Sutro Baths.** These baths, once able to accommodate 24,000 bathers, were lost to fire in 1966.

BIKING   The San Francisco Parks and Recreation Department maintains two city-designated bike routes. One winds 7½ miles through Golden Gate Park to Lake Merced; the other traverses the city, starting in the south, and continues over the Golden Gate Bridge. These routes, however, are not just for bicyclists, who must exercise caution to avoid crashing into pedestrians. A bike map is available from the San Francisco Visitor Information Center, at Powell and Mason streets, for $3 (p. 245), and from bicycle shops all around town.

Ocean Beach has a public walk- and bikeway that stretches along 5 waterfront blocks of the Great Highway between Noriega and Santiago streets. It's an easy ride from Cliff House or Golden Gate Park.

Avenue Cyclery, 756 Stanyan St., at Waller Street, in the Haight (℗ **415/387-3155;** www.avenuecyclery.com), rents bikes for $8 per hour or $30 per day. It's open daily 10am to 6pm. For cruising Fisherman's Wharf and the Golden Gate Bridge, your best bet is **Blazing Saddles** (℗ **415/202-8888;** www.blazingsaddles.com), which has five locations around Fisherman's Wharf. Bike rentals start at $32 per day, and include maps, locks, and helmets; tandem bikes are available as well. They even have electric bikes if you don't have the energy to pedal but want to say you went biking. Reservations are not necessary. *Hint:* make a reservation online for a 10% discount.

BOATING   At the **Golden Gate Park Boathouse** (℗ **415/386-2531;** www.stow-lakeboathouse.com) on Stow Lake, the park's largest body of water, you can rent a boat by the hour and steer over to Strawberry Hill, a large, round island in the middle of the lake, for lunch. There's usually a line on weekends. The boathouse is open Monday to Friday 10am to 7pm, and weekends 9am to 7pm, weather permitting. Rowboats ($14/hour), pedal boats ($19/hour), and electric boats ($29/hour) are available with a $5 deposit.

CITY STAIR CLIMBING   Many health clubs have stair-climbing machines and step classes, but in San Francisco, you need only go outside. The following city stair climbs will give you not only a good workout, but seriously stunning neighborhood, city, and bay views as well. Check www.sisterbetty.org/stairways for a list of stairways—with photos—in locations all over the city. The **Filbert Street Steps,** between Sansome Street and Telegraph Hill, are a particular challenge. Scaling the sheer eastern face of Telegraph Hill, this 377-step climb winds through verdant flower gardens and charming 19th-century cottages. Napier Lane, a narrow, wooden plank walkway, leads to Montgomery Street. Turn right and follow the path to the end of the cul-de-sac,

Getting Outside

EXPLORING SAN FRANCISCO

When Eric Kipp, a certified yogi, conceptualized his wildly popular concept of Hiking Yoga, he aimed to bring tourists and locals alike out and about for some fresh air, intense cardio, and fantastic city views. Kipp's 90-minute urban treks, which take place several times a day, mostly on weekend days, depart from the clock tower at the Ferry Building and wind their way up to Coit Tower and around Telegraph Hill. Routes vary, but the formula is always the same:

Participants enjoy intense and fast-paced hill hiking—this is no leisurely walk in the park—while stopping at four stations throughout the city for a series of yoga poses. The program, which originated in San Francisco in 2007, was such a hit, Kipp has now taken it to more than a dozen cities. For information or a schedule of hikes, call © **415/261-3641** or visit www.hikingyoga.com. Reservations are required, and each session costs $20. Package deals are available.

where another stairway continues to Telegraph's panoramic summit and Coit Tower. The **Lyon Street Steps,** between Green Street and Broadway, were built in 1916. This historic stairway street contains four steep sets of stairs totaling 288 steps. Begin at Green Street and climb all the way up, past manicured hedges and flower gardens, to an iron gate that opens into the Presidio. A block east, on Baker Street, another set of 369 steps descends to Green Street.

GOLF   San Francisco has a few beautiful golf courses. One of the most lavish is the **Presidio Golf Course,** 300 Finley Road at the Arguello Gate (© **415/561-4653;** www. presidiogolf.com). Greens fees range from $49 (5pm start, no cart) to $145 (weekend morning with a cart) for non-residents. There are also two decent municipal courses in town. The 18-hole **Harding Park,** 99 Harding Road (at Skyline Blvd.; © **415/664-4690;** www.tpc.com/tpc-harding-park-golf), charges greens fees of $155 per person Monday through Thursday, $175 Friday through Sunday. Opened in 1925, and home to the Charles Schwab Cup Championship, it was completely overhauled in 2002, and the new Harding has been getting rave reviews ever since. In 2004, it was named by *Golf* magazine as the number-two best municipal golf course in America; in 2009 it hosted the President's Cup. The course, which skirts the shores of Lake Merced, is a 6,743-yard, par-72. You can also play the easier Fleming 9 Course at the same location. The 18-hole **Lincoln Park Golf Course,** 300 34th Avenue (at Clement St.; © **415/221-9911;** www.lincolnparkgc.com), charges greens fees of $38 per person Monday through Thursday, $42 Friday through Sunday, with rates decreasing after 3pm. It's San Francisco's prettiest municipal course, with terrific views and fairways lined with Monterey cypress and pine trees. The 5,181-yard layout plays to par 68, and the 17th hole has a glistening ocean view. This is the oldest course in the city and one of the oldest in the West. It's open daily at daybreak.

HANDBALL   The city's best handball courts are in Golden Gate Park, opposite Seventh Avenue, south of Middle Drive East. Courts are available free, on a first-come, first-served basis.

PARKS   In addition to **Golden Gate Park** and the **Golden Gate National Recreation Area** (p. 124 and 131, respectively), San Francisco boasts more than 2,000 acres of parkland, most of which is perfect for picnicking or throwing around a Frisbee.

Smaller city parks include **Buena Vista Park** (Haight St. btw. Baker and Central sts.), which affords fine views of the Golden Gate Bridge and the area around it and is also a favored lounging ground for gay trysts; **Ina Coolbrith Park** (Taylor St. btw. Vallejo and Green sts.), offering views of the Bay Bridge and Alcatraz; and **Sigmund Stern Grove** (19th Ave. and Sloat Blvd.) in the Sunset District, which is the site of a famous free summer music festival.

One of my personal favorites is **Lincoln Park,** a 270-acre green space on the northwestern side of the city at Clement Street and 34th Avenue. The **Legion of Honor** is here (p. 134), as is a scenic 18-hole municipal golf course (see "Golf," above). But the best things about this park are the 200-foot cliffs that overlook the Golden Gate Bridge and San Francisco Bay. To get to the park, take bus no. 38 from Union Square to 33rd and Geary streets, and then walk a few blocks.

RUNNING   The **Bay to Breakers Foot Race** ★ (© **415/864-3432;** www.baytobreakers.com) is an annual 7½-mile run from downtown to Ocean Beach. About 80,000 entrants take part in it, one of San Francisco's trademark events. Costumed participants and hordes of spectators add to the fun. The event is held on the third Sunday of May to May 18, 2014.

The **San Francisco Marathon** takes place annually at the end of July or first weekend in August. This year, it will take place July 27, 2014. For more information, call © **888/958-6668** or visit www.thesfmarathon.com.

Great **jogging paths** include the entire expanse of Golden Gate Park, the shoreline along the Marina, and the Embarcadero.

TENNIS   The **San Francisco Parks and Recreation Department** maintains more than 132 courts throughout the city. Almost all are available free, on a first-come, first-served basis. For an interactive map with addresses, directions, parking, and restroom information, check out www.sfrecpark.org/recprogram/tennis-program. An additional 21 courts are available in **Golden Gate Park,** which cost around $5 for 90 minutes. Check the website for details on rules for reserving courts (www.golden-gate-park.com/tennis.html).

WALKING & HIKING   The **Golden Gate National Recreation Area** offers plenty of opportunities. One incredible walk (or bike ride) is along the Golden Gate Promenade, from Aquatic Park to the Golden Gate Bridge. The 3½-mile paved trail heads along the northern edge of the Presidio out to Fort Point, passing the marina, Crissy Field's restored wetlands, a small beach, and plenty of athletic locals. You can also hike the Coastal Trail all the way from the Fort Point area to Cliff House. The park service maintains several other trails in the city. For more information or to pick up a map of the Golden Gate National Recreation Area, stop by the park service headquarters at Fort Mason; enter on Franklin Street (© **415/561-4700**). A number of pdf maps are available at www.nps.gov/goga/planyourvisit/maps.htm.

Although most people drive to this spectacular vantage point, a more rejuvenating way to experience **Twin Peaks** is to walk up from the back roads of U.C. Medical Center (off Parnassus Ave.) or from either of the two roads that lead to the top (off Woodside or Clarendon aves.). The best time to trek is early morning, when the city is quiet, the air is crisp, and sightseers haven't crowded the parking lot. Keep an eye out for cars, however, because there's no real hiking trail, and be sure to walk beyond the lot and up to the highest vantage point.

CITY STROLLS

Hills schmills. Don't let a few steep slopes deter you from one of San Francisco's greatest pleasures—walking around the neighborhoods and exploring the city for yourself. Here are a couple of introductory walks that hit the highlights of my favorite neighborhoods for touring on foot.

WALKING TOUR 1: THE EMBARCADERO & LOWER MARKET STREET

START:	**At the Ghandi statue behind the southern end of the Ferry Building, located at the northern end of Market Street.**
PUBLIC TRANSPORTATION:	**Bart: Embarcadero. Muni: J,K,L,M,N,T. Street-car: F-Line**
FINISH:	**Union Square.**
TIME:	**Allow 1 hour, plus time spent in attractions and on tangents.**
BEST TIMES:	**Start the tour hungry, one of the first stops will be the food stalls of the Ferry Building Marketplace. The prime times are Tuesday and Thursday 10am to 2pm, and Saturday 8am to 2pm, when regular opening hours are augmented by a farmer's market. Otherwise, streets are at their most lively during business hours.**
WORST TIMES:	**There's no bad time however; on weekends, the energy drains from the area.**
HILLS THAT COULD KILL:	**None.**

As long as anyone can remember, Market Street has been the spine of the city, and it remains its most important thoroughfare, cutting an oddball diagonal path through the traditional grid layout that rules the rest of downtown. From the 1800s to today, it was the avenue by which the city moved and breathed, where its most important banks and hotels clustered, where the streetcars and ferries headed, and even today, where all the major political and social parades march. To walk down its span, twice as wide as most other streets around here, is to wander through the city's tumultuous history, from boomtown to shakedown to the classy Financial District that dominates it today. Illogical as it seems, the section of Market Street between the Bay and (roughly) Van Ness Avenue is often called "Lower" Market despite the fact it appears higher up on maps than its other end, which threads through hills of Twin Peaks, southwest of the Castro.

Union Square Walking Tour

1 Gandi Statue
2 Ferry Building
3 Justin Herman Plaza
4 California Street
5 Boudin Bakery
6 Palace Hotel
7 Lotta's Fountain
8 Maiden Lane
9 Union Square

1 The Ferry Dock

The thing that will probably catch your eye the most is the mighty San Francisco–Oakland Bay Bridge. From here, you'll get a panorama of its western spans. That massive stone support beneath the roadway between the two suspension towers (526 ft. tall each) was, during construction, the tallest structure in town. Few people appreciate that it was completed just 6 months after the more famous Golden Gate—and at greater expense. The Bay Bridge lands nearly 5 blocks south, where it pours its 280,000 daily cars onto the 101, and where a new crop of skyscrapers is changing deep Soma into something worth visiting again.

The statue of Mohandas Gandhi standing in the middle of the square didn't make it here without some controversy, which is not atypical of this town. First, people accused its donor of some shady dealings and said that the city shouldn't accept the gift. Then others objected to the work's placement behind the Ferry Building, which some considered undignified. Make amends for all the whining by enjoying the bronze sculpture now.

Enter the back of the Ferry Building.

2 The Ferry Building

You are now entering the former baggage area for ferry passengers, now a 65,000 square-foot food marketplace. The boutique gourmet shops here are self-explanatory, and I encourage you to wander around, tasting things you've never tried before. Everything sold at stores here is from a Bay Area provider, so you're certain to eat something you probably can't get anywhere else in the world.

For nearly 100 years, from the Gold Rush to the Great Depression, the only way to get to San Francisco from the north and the east was by ferry—there were no bridges—and some 100,000 people a day poured through this building. This grand terminal was inspired by the craze for monumental, proto-Roman civic buildings inspired by Chicago's Columbian Exposition of 1893; it opened in 1898. For many years, this building symbolized San Francisco to the rest of the world. Then, it was as proud as a cathedral, with mosaic floors, ceramic and brick arches, and skylights. It managed to limp through the great quake of '06 by virtue of the firemen having just enough equipment to hose it down with Bay water. The Golden Gate Bridge, and the freedom it gave motorists, made the terminal obsolete, and its decline was swift. By the 1950s, this space had been brutalized by modern renovations and carved into office space. Some 90% of the floor under your feet was plastered with mastic or linoleum. For 50 years, this 660-foot-long space, called The Nave, was lost, but a celebrated renovation project, completed in 2003 and costing a reported $90 million, reintroduced it to some of its former glory.

Exit the building and look straight down Market Street as it heads southwest. Feel free to cross the few lanes of traffic and the tram tracks until you reach the bricky park on the right-hand corner as Market Street begins.

3 Justin Herman Plaza

Imagine this place in the latter part of the 1800s. First, the shoreline was further inland—pretty much wherever you see flat land, it was then water, and the gradual buildup of scuttled ships and landfill eventually created the present-day coast. The activity in those days was frenetic. San Francisco was the most important city in the West—Los Angeles was a nothing town, Seattle too—and in both directions, the shore would have been clogged with masted vessels and teeming with sailors and longshoremen. The quays were a jumble of saloons and chandlers and off-color hotels. And in between them, industrial railway tracks threaded their way in and out of warehouses and along the waterfront.

Now put yourself into the mind of the cataclysmic events of April 1906, the Great Earthquake. Imagine searing conflagrations pouring out of every window of every office building and smoke turning day into night. An entire city was ablaze. Thousands of people fled their homes and dragged a ludicrously impractical set of their best worldly possessions—jewelry boxes, desks, full armoires—down Market Street in the hope of making it to the city of Oakland and beyond. Astonishingly, there were no riots, no ugly scenes of pandemonium, just dazed and determined faces. When these now-homeless wanderers reached this place, they were told that they could only bring what they could carry in their arms. Countless people lost everything.

The nastiness didn't end with that chapter. When the era of waterfront trade died, so did the wharves. San Francisco's elders failed to prepare for container shipping, and Oakland poached much of its business while this city's docks became largely derelict. So as happened to so many waterfronts, locals simply wrote it off. In 1957, when Americans still believed the car was the talisman for a bright future, a two-level highway was plowed along the Embarcadero, darkening everything and cutting off the Ferry Building from the rest of the city. It took the so-called Lomo Prieta quake of 1989 to slap some sense into the town. The shaking damaged the highway so badly that it was dismantled, and the city's reconnection with its precious waterfront fostered a renaissance.

You may also cross paths with some antique-looking trams rolling through this intersection. Their history, and the story of their operation, is told at a free museum south across this plaza on Steuart Street.

In the park around you, take a moment to notice the angular concrete tubes of the so-called Vaillancourt Fountain (1971), which was despised as hideous upon its opening and isn't much more popular today. Local support eroded when people learned the message of the piece was to support a free Québec—hardly a Bay Area issue worthy of such a prominent location. The 710-ton tangle still routinely dodges efforts to demolish it, and the city pays $70,000 a year to pump water through it partly because, as one politician said in 2004, when it's dry, homeless people shelter there. Makes you wonder what kind of shelter $70,000 would buy.

Continue down Market Street.

4 California Street

The concrete building towering above the cable car terminus is the Hyatt (p. 54), which was also derided in its day but is now accepted as a landmark in brutalist architecture. Duck inside to the third-floor atrium lobby, which is seventeen dizzying stories tall; it's one of the city's most dramatic indoor spaces next to Grace Cathedral.

Across Market Street from here, at 101 Market, is the San Francisco branch of the Federal Reserve (© 415/974-3252; http://frbsf.org), which runs intermittent tours and has an extensive collection of antique American currency. Arranging a visit would be a hassle except for anyone fascinated with finance, but there is a quick exhibition in the lobby's west end (how to spot a counterfeit, that sort of thing) that might be worth a few minutes' dabble.

Continue down (up?) Market Street, staying on the right-hand (northern) side.

5 California to Montgomery Streets

The going gets faster now. Three blocks on, where Market, Battery, and Bush streets converge, you'll find the Mechanics Monument, a tribute to laborers created in 1901 by sculptor Douglas Tilden, who happened to be both deaf and mute. Made of bronze, it somehow made it through the 1906 fire (there are some striking archival photos of this statue standing proudly amidst a field of rubble), but it's fun to imagine that the flames burned off all the clothes of the manly men depicted. Only in San Francisco would an ironworker let any of his bits dangle. (Guess what? Locals were scandalized by this artwork, too—they objected to the nudity.)

Just behind the intersection of Sutter and Sansome streets, the Romanesque, 22-floor tower at 111 Sutter (1927) was the location of detective Sam Spade's office in The Maltese Falcon. For years, the beautiful geometric painting of birds on the ceiling of its lobby was hidden by layers of accumulated cigarette smoke and soot, but a renovation restored the architectural glories of this building, which was designed by the same men behind the Waldorf-Astoria in Manhattan. Past the elevators, you'll find a small exhibition, assembled by an enthusiastic employee named Tony (ask if he's handy; he's often in the lobby) that includes background on the building and Sam Spade, plus an original finial that was removed from the parapet.

Proceed to Montgomery. Douglas Tilden, he of the naked ironworkers, also created this statue, unveiled in 1897 to commemorate Californian statehood, which came about in 1850. It originally stood where Mason reaches Market but was shifted here in 1977. Strangely, its western side has an octopus on it; I suspect it's a reference to the Southern Pacific Railroad, which at the time was often likened to the animal because of its many-tentacled reach and strangling death-grip on anything that crossed its path. It would have been strange to include a jab at a major company on a public monument of this sort, but it would also be typical of San Francisco's habit of thumb-nosing the powerful. And I suppose it's no stranger than smelting something in your birthday suit.

Cross Market Street where you can. Continue down Market Street.

Boudin Bakery & Café ☕

Opposite where Montgomery and Post come together at Market, you'll see a branch of the Boudin Bakery & Café (619 Market St.; *(* **415/281-8200;** closed weekends) sourdough bread bakery. The restaurant that previously occupied its building refused to sell to developers, so a dull office tower was simply built around it. The café inside makes for a good coffee (and bread) break, should you need one. Outside of the lunch rush, you'll find lines here much shorter than they are at the Boudin at Fisherman's Wharf.

6 New Montgomery Street

Before the Quake, the area south of Market Street, or Soma, was an overcrowded, filthy depository for the working class, famous for block upon block of tumble-down homes. This area was known as "South of the Slot," a reference to the cable car route that then plied Market—think of it as the "wrong" side of the tracks. The fire following the Quake claimed nearly everything in Soma, and the area was rebuilt with equally depressing warehouses and factories. To this day, despite some notable developments (such as the open spaces at the Yerba Buena Gardens a block away from here at Third and Mission Streets), the area's mood still suffers.

The handsome, bulky building on the corner, at 50 New Montgomery Street, is the famous Palace Hotel, which upon its original construction in 1875 was the best and grandest hotel in America west of the Mississippi, and an icon of San Francisco wealth and pride. Every room had its own bathroom, a novelty even among luxury properties, and rooms could communicate by interconnected pneumatic tubes. A who's who of the Gilded Age stayed here, including Oscar Wilde, Ulysses S. Grant, and Teddy Roosevelt. Tenor Enrico Caruso was famously sleeping here on the night of the Quake, and King David Kalakaua, one of Hawaii's final monarchs, died here, ultimately delivering the kingdom into the hands of the United States. The building survived the quake intact, and might have weathered the subsequent fire—it had its own cistern but employees were too liberal with the water, leaving little for the firemen.

The present building (1909; anyone is welcome in its lobby, so go on in to explore) is still plenty grand, and it isn't without its own colorful history. The luncheon celebrating the establishment of the United Nations was held in its Garden Court, under its spectacular, 63,000-paned glass ceiling. In 1923, President Warren G. Harding died (many say mysteriously) in the Presidential Suite upstairs and was embalmed in its bathtub. This would also be the time to check out the gorgeous Maxfield Parrish mural located behind the hotel's Pied Piper Bar inside Maxfield's (p. 185). There was some debate if the bar would remain named "Maxfield's" when the hotel owners quietly snuck the mural out with plans to put it up for auction in May 2013. The public outcry was huge, with the good citizens of our metropolis threatening to boycott The Palace if the painting was not returned. Happily, the treasure was brought home to great fanfare in August 2013. The door to the bar is beside the Market Street entrance. Just outside its entrance in the Promenade, you'll find a case displaying memorabilia about the mural, including the original 1909 commission for $6,000. That was money well spent: The artwork is now estimated to be worth between $3-$5 million.

Exit the hotel at Market Street and turn left.

7 Lotta's Fountain

Cross Market to check out the little column at the confluence of Market, Geary, and Kearny streets. It's Lotta's Fountain. The sign here would lead you to believe that the reason to cherish this column is because a once-famous opera singer performed here 1 day in 1910, but in fact, this is the oldest monument in the city, erected in 1875 as a gift by a singer and dancer, Lotta Crabtree, who rose to fame performing for gold miners. And for many years, this intersection was so much considered the center of town that its three major newspapers were headquartered here; survivors of the '06 quake also met here annually until there were none left alive. Today, sadly, this once-central icon, although recently rehabilitated, has sunk into obscurity with locals.

Turn right at Kearny Street and walk a short block to Maiden Lane. Turn left onto it.

8 Maiden Lane

If you were here 125 years ago, you'd find a thoroughfare for prostitution (hence the winking name—its original name was Morton Street) along Maiden Lane. It has risen substantially in the world. Today, it's a desirable address for top-of-the-line labels and boutiques.

Halfway down this block on the right, stop in front of the tan, brick, windowless edifice with fanned brickwork around its doorway (1948). This building, Frank Lloyd Wright's only San Francisco effort, now housing a fine arts dealer specializing in Asian antiquities (it welcomes visitors), has a ramped interior that even a non-student of architecture can recognize as clearly a forerunner to his Guggenheim Museum in New York City.

Walk to the end of Maiden Lane to Stockton Street. There will be a park directly in front of you. Turn left to the intersection of Geary Street.

9 Union Square

Unlike New York City's Union Square, an important plaza which was named for the fact it sits at the confluence, or union, of several major avenues, this one was named just before the Civil War to demonstrate support for the Union of American States—California was never a slave state. The granite Corinthian column in the middle, the Dewey Monument, was dedicated in 1903 by Teddy Roosevelt to commemorate the war dead of the Spanish-American war, and it somehow made it through the 1906 disasters untoppled. But both Union Squares were and are important gathering places for the city residents in times of stress. After the Quake, thousands of residents camped out here as their city burned down.

Duck into the Neiman-Marcus that stands opposite you, kitty-corner to the park; its gorgeous stained-glass dome was salvaged from the City of Paris department store that stood here previously (and was destroyed after an epic city protest to preserve it).

On the opposite side of the square, on Powell Street at Geary along the cable car tracks, you can't miss the proud bulk of the luxury St. Francis Hotel (main building: 1908, plus a tacky, incongruous tower added in 1971), which like the Palace has long occupied a prestigious position in city culture. Like the famous Astor Hotel in New York, the St. Francis in its heyday was known for a clock that stood in its lobby, which became a well-known meeting public place. Unlike the demolished Astor, though, the St. Francis still has it. Explore its ornate marble-and-mirror lobby—the hotel employs a staff historian who keeps the walls stocked with vintage photographs (including several by Ansel Adams), thank-you notes from luminaries, and newspaper stories.

It was in a suite at the St. Francis where silent film star Fatty Arbuckle, who rivaled Chaplin for fame, hosted a party that ended in a young actress' death; although Fatty wasn't there at the time, the massive trials and their publicity ruined him, and modern movie censoring was instituted in response to the public fear of Hollywood debauchery. Here, too, was where, in 1950, one of the next greatest stars of the era, Al Jolson, died while playing cards in his suite. And in 1975, revolutionary Sara Jane Moore fired at President Gerald Ford as he left the building. She got out of prison in 2007.

WALKING TOUR 2: CHINATOWN: HISTORY, CULTURE, DIM SUM & THEN SOME

START:	**Corner of Grant Avenue and Bush Street.**
PUBLIC TRANSPORTATION:	**Bus no. 2, 3, 9X, 30, 38, 45, or 76.**
FINISH:	**Commercial Street between Montgomery and Kearny streets.**
TIME:	**2 hours, not including museum or shopping stops.**
BEST TIMES:	**Daylight hours, when the streets are most active.**
WORST TIMES:	**Early or late in the day, because shops are closed and no one is milling around.**
HILLS THAT COULD KILL:	**None.**

This tiny section of San Francisco, bounded loosely by Broadway and by Stockton, Kearny, and Bush streets, is said to harbor one of the largest Chinese populations outside Asia. Daily proof is the crowds of Chinese residents who flock to the herbal stores, vegetable markets, restaurants, and businesses. Chinatown, specifically Portsmouth Square, also marks the original spot of the city center. On this walk, you'll learn why Chinatown remains intriguing to all who wind through its narrow, crowded streets, and how its origins are responsible for the city as we know it.

Chinatown & North Beach Walking Tours

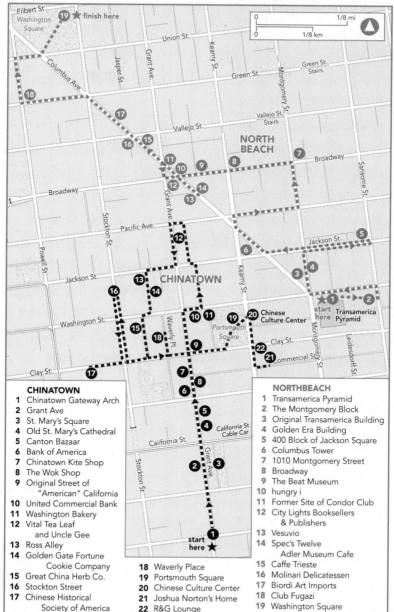

CHINATOWN

1 Chinatown Gateway Arch
2 Grant Ave
3 St. Mary's Square
4 Old St. Mary's Cathedral
5 Canton Bazaar
6 Bank of America
7 Chinatown Kite Shop
8 The Wok Shop
9 Original Street of
   "American" California
10 United Commercial Bank
11 Washington Bakery
12 Vital Tea Leaf
   and Uncle Gee
13 Ross Alley
14 Golden Gate Fortune
   Cookie Company
15 Great China Herb Co.
16 Stockton Street
17 Chinese Historical
   Society of America

18 Waverly Place
19 Portsmouth Square
20 Chinese Culture Center
21 Joshua Norton's Home
22 R&G Lounge

NORTHBEACH

1 Transamerica Pyramid
2 The Montgomery Block
3 Original Transamerica Building
4 Golden Era Building
5 400 Block of Jackson Square
6 Columbus Tower
7 1010 Montgomery Street
8 Broadway
9 The Beat Museum
10 hungry i
11 Former Site of Condor Club
12 City Lights Booksellers
   & Publishers
13 Vesuvio
14 Spec's Twelve
   Adler Museum Cafe
15 Caffe Trieste
16 Molinari Delicatessen
17 Biordi Art Imports
18 Club Fugazi
19 Washington Square

To begin the tour, make your way to the corner of Bush Street and Grant Avenue, 4 blocks from Union Square and all the downtown buses, where you can't miss the:

1 Chinatown Gateway Arch

Many Chinese villages have their own gateways, and bowing to tradition, so do many Chinatowns around the world. This one, to me, is very much an emblem of San Francisco's Chinatown. That's because it's not even Chinese, but Pan-Asian. It was a gift from modern-day Taiwan.

Once you cross the threshold, you'll be at the beginning of Chinatown's portion of:

2 Grant Avenue

This is a mecca for tourists who wander in and out of gift shops that offer a variety of junk interspersed with quality imports.

But all of this is today's Chinatown. Before rampant landfilling, this area was closer to the wharves, and Chinese residents could easily get back and forth from here to work on the docks. In 1849, there were only 54 Chinese here, but by 1876, there were 116,000 in the state. They mined for treasure. They broke their backs building the railroad. For their pains, they were despised, overtaxed, and excluded. In the late 1800s, this area would have been teeming with prostitutes, many young teens who were brought here as virtual slaves. As for the men, the so-called "coolies"—a bastardized word derived from the Chinese words for "rent" and "muscle"—they had slightly more protection in the form of benevolent societies, where acclimated Chinese helped them negotiate for jobs. But to booming San Francisco industry, these men were just as disposable as the girls.

The great earthquake of 1906 changed everything. The whole district was wiped out. The rebuilt Chinatown was more civilized than the old one, full of benevolent societies and churches rather than opium dens and saloons—although the buildings were still mostly owned by Western men, not Chinese. A local businessman named Look Tin Eli recognized that the squalor of the old Chinatown gave his neighbors an image problem, so he arranged to make buildings more tourist-friendly, decorating them with false pagodas and sloping roofs. At a time when the vast majority of Americans never left their home country, coming here felt like venturing to the Orient. The ruse worked, and today, Chinatown retains both its stage-set appearance and its fascination for visitors.

Tear yourself away from the shops and turn right at the corner of Pine Street. Cross to the other side of Pine and on your left you'll come to:

3 St. Mary's Square

The 14-foot metal-and-granite statue of Dr. Sun Yat-sen, the founder of the Republic of China, was the work of sculptor, Beniamino Bufano whose life-long dream was, according to the New York Times, to carve the face of U.S. President Franklin Delano Roosevelt on Mount Rushmore. Let's hope getting to create this likeness of the heroic Sun Yat-sen (he led the rebellion that ended the reign of the Qing Dynasty) was a happy second prize for him. It's appropriate the statue is here: during Sun Yat-sen's exile in San Francisco (before the revolution in 1916), he often whiled away the hours in this square. Visit early in the morning and you may see locals practicing tai chi here.

Walk to the other end of the square, toward California Street, turn left, cross California Street at Grant Street, and you'll be standing in front of:

4 Old St. Mary's Cathedral

Here stands the state's first building to be built as a cathedral, which it was from 1854 to 1894. Because the city began with such meager resources and fires were rampant, the oldest churches here are not the prettiest. The interior of this one is no exception, mostly because it was gutted by two catastrophic blazes—one being the Quake's. The shell of the building is original, but the inside dates to the days of Donna Reed. It was here, in 1902, that America's first mission for indigent Chinese immigrants was established; food was served, English taught, and charity otherwise available for anyone who was suffering in the New World.

Step inside to find a written history of the church and turn-of-the-20th-century photos of San Francisco.

Upon leaving the church, take a right, walk to the corner of Grant Avenue and California Street, and go right on Grant. Here you'll find a shop called:

5 Canton Bazaar

Of the knickknack and import shops lining Grant Avenue, this has the most comprehensive selection, including a boatload of Chairman Mao memorabilia for fans of kitsch; it's located at 616 Grant Ave.

Continue in the same direction on Grant Avenue and cross Sacramento Street to the northwest corner of Sacramento and Grant. You'll be at the doorstep of the:

6 Bank of America

Look up: even chain banks use traditional Chinese architectural style here. Notice the dragons subtly portrayed on many parts of the building.

Head in the same direction (north) on Grant Avenue to 717 Grant Ave:

7 Chinatown Kite Shop

A popular neighborhood fixture, owned by the same family since 1969, the Kite Shop offers an assortment of flying objects, including lovely fish kites, nylon or cotton windsock kites, hand-painted Chinese paper kites, wood-and-paper biplanes, pentagonal kites and even design-it-yourself options.

Cross Grant Avenue to 718 Grant Ave:

8 The Wok Shop

Here's where you can purchase just about any cleaver, wok, cookbook, or vessel you might need for Chinese-style cooking in your own kitchen.

When you come out of the Wok Shop, go right. Walk past Commercial Street and you'll arrive at the corner of Grant Avenue and Clay Street; cross Clay and you'll be standing on the:

9 Original Street of "American" California

Here an English seaman named William Richardson set up the first tent in 1835, making it the first place that an Anglo set up base in California.

Continue north on Grant Avenue to Washington Street. Turn right and at 743 Washington St. you will be standing in front of the former Bank of Canton, now known as the:

10 United Commercial Bank

This building boasts the oldest (from 1909) Asian-style edifice in Chinatown. After the earthquake, the city fathers were contemplating moving Chinatown to the outskirts of the city. The construction of this three-tiered pagoda-style building (it once housed the China Telephone Exchange) convinced these powerful men that the neighborhood had the potential to lure tourists and so Chinatown remained where it was.

You're probably thirsty by now, so follow Washington Street a few doors down (east); on your right-hand side, at 733 Washington St., you will come upon:

11 Washington Bakery & Restaurant ☕

No need to have a full meal here—the service can be abrupt. Do stop in, however, for a little potable adventure: snow red beans with ice cream. The sugary-sweet drink mixed with whole beans and ice cream is not something you're likely to have tried elsewhere, and it happens to be quite tasty.

Head back to Grant Avenue, cross Washington Street, and follow the east side of street 2 blocks to 1044 Gran Avenue:

12 Vital Tea Leaf

Stop here for tea and Gee—Uncle Gee, that is. The grouchy owner, who stands on the sidewalk luring passersby in with good-natured insults and jokey threats (along with the occassional fortune cookie) will introduce you to dozens of varieties of tea. And yes, tastings are part of the experience. You'll come in a stranger, but you leave feeling like part of the family (I promise).

Leave Vital Tea Leaf, make a left, cross Jackson Street and cross Grant Street, walk to Ross Alley, make a left into the alley

13 Ross Alley

These alleys, in the bad old days, were rife with gambling, brothels, drug dealing, and worse. Duncombe Alley, off Pacific, was famous for its opium dens. St. Louis alley, also off Pacific, was known for its slave market, where naked girls were auctioned off to pimps. It's all so hard to picture today, but thankfully, it's over. So have a cookie.

As you follow the alley south, on the left side of the street you'll encounter the:

14 Golden Gate Fortune Cookie Company

Located at 56 Ross Alley, this store is worth a stop if only for the glimpse of workaday Chinatown that is so rarely afforded to outsiders. It's little more than a tiny place where three women sit at a conveyer belt, folding messages into warm cookies as the manager invariably calls out to tourists, beckoning them to buy a big bag of the fortune-telling treats and come in and try a sample. You can purchase regular fortunes, unfolded flat cookies without fortunes, or, if you bring your own fortunes, make custom cookies. Photos inside the factory cost 50¢.

As you exit the alley, cross Washington Street, take a right heading west on Washington, and you're in front of the:

15 Great China Herb Co.

Herbs and roots and mysterious powders, oh my! For centuries, the Chinese have come to shops like this one to cure all types of ailments, plus ensure good health and a long life. Thankfully, unlike owners in many similar area shops, Mr. and Mrs. Ho speak English, so you will not be met with a blank stare when you inquire what exactly is in each box, bag, or jar arranged along dozens of shelves. And the answers should be truly fascinating. A wonderful place to browse.

Take a left upon leaving the store and walk to:

16 Stockton Street

This is my favorite part of Chinatown, and the part that most closely resembles a typical urban street in an older Chinese city, with sidewalk produce stands, fish markets, and bakeries. Some of the greasy spoons display the roasted meats of the day in their windows, head and all—the sight repulses some Westerners, but many Chinese customers know how to tell at a glance whether the quality of the inventory is high today. You'll also notice that the signs in the shop windows aren't in English as often as they are on Grant Avenue; that's because this is an active shopping street for everyday sundries, particularly for older Chinese-born residents.

Here, you should take your time and wander into the groceries to see what non-endemic produce is for sale. You'll find durian, starfruit, lychee, and other fruits they don't have at your local Winn-Dixie, and you'll have to swim through crowds of Asian folks to get to them. Happily, shopkeepers, though displaying a businesslike manner, are generally willing to explain any product for which you can't read the label.

One noteworthy part of this area's history is **Cameron House** (actually up the hill at 920 Sacramento St., near Stockton St.), which was named after Donaldina Cameron (1869–1968). Called Lo Mo, or "the Mother," by the Chinese, she spent her life trying to free Chinese women who came to America in hopes of marrying well but who found themselves forced into prostitution and slavery. Today, the house still helps women free themselves from domestic violence.

At 1068 Stockton St. you'll find **AA Bakery & Café,** an extremely colorful bakery with Golden Gate Bridge–shaped cakes, bright green and pink snacks, moon cakes, and a flow of Chinese diners catching up over pastries. **Gourmet Delight B.B.Q.,** at 1045 Stockton St., is another recommended stop; here, barbecued duck and pork are supplemented by steamed pigs' feet and chicken feet. Everything's to go, so if you grab a snack, don't forget napkins. Head farther north along the street and you'll see live fish and fowl awaiting their fate as the day's dinner.

Meander south on Stockton Street to Clay Street and turn west (right) onto Clay. Continue to 965 Clay St. (Make sure you come Tues–Fri noon–5pm or Sat 11am–4pm.) You've arrived at the:

17 Chinese Historical Society of America Museum

Founded in 1963, this museum (© **415/391-1188**) has a small but fascinating collection illluminating the role of Chinese immigrants in American history, particularly in San Francisco and the rest of California.

Artifacts on display—and they're more interesting to see than they are to read about—include a shrimp-cleaning machine, 19th-century clothing and slippers of the Chinese pioneers, Chinese herbs and scales, historic hand-carved and painted shop signs, and a series of photographs that document the development of Chinese culture in America.

The museum is open Tuesday through Friday from noon to 5pm and Saturday and Sunday from noon to 4pm. Admission is $5 for adults, $3 for college students with ID and seniors, and $2 for kids 6 to 17.

Retrace your steps, heading east on Clay Street back toward Grant Avenue. Turn left onto:

18 Waverly Place

Also known as "the Street of Painted Balconies," Waverly Place is probably Chinatown's most popular side street or alleyway because of its colorful balconies and architectural details—a sort of Chinese-style New Orleans street. At 125 Waverley, you'll find the building housing **Tin Hou Temple.** Founded in 1852, it's the oldest Chinese temple in America. Visitors are welcome, although it's polite to remove your shoes when you go inside to inspect its carvings, traditional architectural details, and altar, portions of which survived the 1906 blaze. It's customary to leave a few dollars in the red envelopes on the front table. The temple, serene and wafting with incense, is on the top floor and there's no elevator. (By the way, this kind of house of worship isn't so common here; there are more Chinese Christians in Chinatown than there are Buddhists.)

Once you've finished exploring Waverly Place, walk east on Clay Street, past Grant Avenue, and continue until you come upon the block-wide urban playground that is also the most important site in San Francisco's history.

19 Portsmouth Square

This very spot was the center of the region's first township, which was called Yerba Buena before it was renamed San Francisco in 1847. Around 1846, before any semblance of a city had taken shape, this plaza lay at the foot of the bay's eastern shoreline. There were fewer than 50 non–Native American residents in the settlement, no substantial buildings to speak of, and the few boats that pulled into the cove did so less than a block from where you're standing.

In 1846, when California was claimed as a U.S. territory, the marines who landed here named the square after their ship, the USS *Portsmouth.* (Today a bronze plaque marks the spot where they raised the U.S. flag.)

Yerba Buena remained a modest township until the gold rush of 1849 when, over the next 2 years, the population grew from under 1,000 to over 19,000, as gold seekers from around the world made their way here. When the square became too crowded, long wharves were constructed to support new buildings above the bay. Eventually, the entire area became landfill. That was almost 150 years ago, but today the square still serves as an important meeting place for neighborhood Chinese—a sort of communal outdoor living room.

Throughout the day, the square is heavily trafficked by children and—in large part—by elderly men, who gamble over Chinese cards and play chess. If you arrive early in the morning, you might come across people practicing tai chi.

It is said that Robert Louis Stevenson used to love to sit on a bench here and watch life go by. (At the northeast corner of the square, you'll find a monument to his memory, consisting of a model of the *Hispaniola,* the ship in Stevenson's novel *Treasure Island,* and an excerpt from his "Christmas Sermon.")

Once you've had your fill of the square, exit to the east at Kearny Street. Directly across the street, at 750 Kearny St., is the Holiday Inn. Cross the street, enter the hotel, and take the elevator to the third floor, where you'll find the:

20 Chinese Culture Center

This center is oriented toward both the community and tourists, offering display cases of Chinese art and a gallery with rotating exhibits of Asian art and writings that are often worth a look-see. The center is open Tuesday through Friday from 9:30 to 4pm, Saturday 10am to 4pm.

When you leave the Holiday Inn, take a left on Kearny Street and go 3 short blocks to Commercial Street. Take a left onto Commercial and note that you are standing on the street once known as the site of:

21 Joshua A. Norton's Home

Every town has its eccentric local celebrities, and San Francisco likely has had more than its share. But few are as fondly remembered as "Emporer Joshua Norton."

Norton was born around 1815 in the British Isles and sailed as a young man to South Africa, where he served as a colonial rifleman. He came to San Francisco in 1849 with $40,000 and proceeded to double and triple his fortune in real estate. Unfortunately for him, he next chose to go into the rice business. While Norton was busy cornering the market and forcing prices up, several ships loaded with rice arrived unexpectedly in San Francisco's harbor. With rice market was suddenly flooded, Norton was forced into bankruptcy. He left San Francisco for about 3 years and must have experienced a breakdown (or revelation) of some sort, for upon his return, Norton thought he was an emperor. In fact, he called himself: "Emperor of the United States and Protector of Mexico," and used to walk around the streets in an old brass-buttoned military uniform, sporting a hat with a "dusty plume."

He lived in a fantasy world, but instead of ostracizing him, San Franciscans embraced him and gave him free meals. When Emperor Norton died in 1880 (while sleeping at the corner of California St. and Grant Ave.), approximately 10,000 people passed by his coffin, which was bought with money raised at the Pacific Union Club, and more than 30,000 people participated in the funeral procession.

From here, if you've still got an appetite, you should go directly to 631 Kearny St. (at Clay St.), home of the R&G Lounge.

22 R&G Lounge 🍽

The R&G Lounge is a sure thing for tasty $5 rice-plate specials, chicken with black-bean sauce, and gorgeously tender and tangy R&G Special Beef.

Otherwise, you might want to backtrack on Commercial Street to Grant Avenue, take a left, and follow Grant back to Bush Street, the entrance to Chinatown. You'll be at the beginning of the Union Square area, where you can catch any number of buses (especially on Market St.) or cable cars, or do a little shopping. Or you might backtrack to Grant, take a right (north), and follow Grant to the end. You'll be at Broadway and Columbus, the beginning of North Beach, where you can venture onward for our North Beach tour (see below).

GETTING TO KNOW NORTH BEACH

START:	**Intersection of Montgomery Street, Columbus Avenue, and Washington Street.**
PUBLIC TRANSPORTATION:	**Bus no. 10, 12, 30X, or 41.**
FINISH:	**Washington Square.**
TIME:	**3 hours, including a stop for lunch.**
BEST TIMES:	**Monday through Saturday between 11am and 4pm.**
WORST TIMES:	**Sunday, when shops are closed.**
HILLS THAT COULD KILL:	**The Montgomery Street hill from Broadway to Vallejo streets; otherwise, this is an easy walk.**

Along with Chinatown, North Beach is one of the city's oldest neighborhoods. In the 1800s, one of its main thoroughfares, Pacific Avenue, was considered to be the spine of the notorious Barbary Coast area. Think of a wooden shantytown leading down to a bustling, curved wharf. Over time, the settlement grew, but it always retained its male-heavy population and its rough profile. Respectable men with families didn't come out West to seek their fortunes during the Gold Rush; that was the province of drifters, opportunists, and poor laborers. San Francisco was founded by these men.

And North Beach (especially Pacific Avenue) was a den of sin, pleasure, and crime. Routinely, young men on a night of carousing at the saloons and opium dens would pass out and wake up the next day on a ship already well out to sea, where they'd be forced to join the crew for months on end until they'd be able to return home. This impression-by-kidnapping method was called being "shanghaied," it often involved drugs slipped surreptitiously into beer, and it was so common that the police barely kept track of incidents. The brilliant underworld journalist Herbert Asbury, famous today for his book *Gangs of New York,* wrote in his *The Barbary Coast* that the period was "the nearest approach to criminal anarchy that an American city has yet experienced."

The Barbary Coast is now gone. Because of the fire, barely a plank of the original place remains. The land is also no longer on the coast, thanks to subsequent landfilling. But the Barbary Coast's 70-odd year reign gave San Francisco its reputation as a devil-may-care town of hedonistic inclinations, a reputation it no longer deserves but which persists among people who have never actually visited.

North Beach became the city's Italian district when Italian immigrants moved "uphill" in the early 1870s, crossing Broadway from the Jackson Square area and settling in. They quickly established restaurants, cafes, bakeries, and other businesses familiar to them from their homeland.

The "Beat Generation" helped put North Beach on the map, with the likes of Jack Kerouac and Allen Ginsberg holding court in the area's cafes during the 1950s. Although most of the original Beat poets are gone, their spirit lives on in North Beach, which is still a haven for bohemian artists and writers. The neighborhood, thankfully, retains its Italian village feel; it's a place where residents from all walks of life enjoy taking time for conversation over pastries and frothy cappuccinos.

If there's one landmark you can't miss, it's the familiar building on the corner of Montgomery Street and Columbus Avenue, the Transamerica Pyramid (take bus 30X or 41 to get there).

1 Transamerica Pyramid

Petitions and protests greeted the plan to build this unusual skyscraper, but once it was completed it immediately became a beloved fixture of the skyline. Noted for its spire (which rises 212 ft. above the top floor) and its "wings" (which begin at the 29th floor and stop at the spire), this pyramid is San Francisco's tallest building. You might want to take a peek at one of the rotating art exhibits in the lobby or go around to the right and into ½-acre Redwood Park, which is part of the Transamerica Center.

The Transamerica Pyramid occupies part of the 600 block of Montgomery Street, which once held a historic building called:

2 The Montgomery Block

Originally four stories high, the Montgomery Block was the tallest building in the West when it was built in 1853. San Franciscans called it "Halleck's Folly" because it was built on a raft of redwood logs that had been bolted together and floated at the edge of the ocean (which was right at Montgomery St. at that time). The building was demolished in 1959 but is remembered as the power center of old San Francisco. Its tenants included artists and writers of all kinds, among them Jack London, George Sterling, Ambrose Bierce, Bret Harte, and Mark Twain. This is a picturesque area, but there's no particular spot to direct you to. It's worth looking around, however, if only for the block's historical importance.

From the southeast corner of Montgomery and Washington streets, look across Washington to the corner of Columbus Avenue to 4 Columbus Ave which is the:

3 Original Transamerica Building

A Beaux Arts flatiron-shaped building covered in terra cotta, this old-fashioned beauty was built in 1909 as a bank. Today, the building houses a Church of Scientology.

Cross Washington Street and continue north on Montgomery Street to no. 730:

4 Golden Era Building

Erected around 1852, this San Francisco historic landmark building is named after the literary magazine *The Golden Era,* which was published here. Some of the young writers who worked on the magazine were known as "the Bohemians"; they included Samuel Clemens (better known as Mark Twain) and Bret Harte (who began as a typesetter here). Backtrack a few dozen feet and stop for a minute to admire the exterior of the annex, at no. 722, which, after years of neglect and lawsuits, has finally been stabilized and is going to be developed. The Belli Annex, as it is currently known, is registered as a historic landmark.

Continue north on Washington Street and take the first right onto Jackson Street. Continue until you hit the:

5 400 Block of Jackson Square

Here's where you'll find some of the only commercial buildings to survive the 1906 earthquake and fire. The building at 415 Jackson St. (ca. 1853) served as headquarters for the Ghirardelli chocolate company from 1855 to 1894. The Hotaling Building (no. 451) was built in 1866 and features pediments of cast iron applied over the brick walls. At no. 441 is another of the buildings that survived the disaster of 1906. Constructed between 1850 and 1852 with ship masts for interior supporting columns, it served as the French Consulate from 1865 to 1876.

Cross the street and backtrack on Jackson Street. Continue toward the intersection of Columbus Avenue and Jackson Street. Turn right on Columbus and look across the street for the small triangular building at the junction of Kearny Street and Columbus Avenue, Columbus Tower (also known as the Sentinel Building).

6 Columbus Tower

Also known as the Sentinel Building, it survived the Quake by virtue of being under construction at the time. The Kingston Trio owned it in the 1960s, when it went to seed; at the time, the basement contained a recording studio where the Grateful Dead recorded its second album. The movie director Francis Ford Coppola owns the building now; upstairs are the offices for the production company he started (now co-owned by his son Roman and his daughter, *Lost in Translation* director, Sofia). Downstairs, he sells his Napa and Sonoma county wines and there's also a little slightly overpriced but good European-style bistro, Café Zoetrope.

Continue north on Columbus Avenue and then turn right on Pacific Avenue. After you cross Montgomery Street, you'll find brick-lined Osgood Place on the left. A registered historic landmark, it is one of the few quiet—and car-free—little alleyways left in the city. Stroll up Osgood and go left on Broadway to:

7 1010 Montgomery St.

This is where Allen Ginsberg lived when he wrote his legendary poem, "Howl," first performed on October 13, 1955, in a converted auto-repair shop at the corner of Fillmore and Union streets. By the time Ginsberg finished reading, he was crying and the audience was going wild. Jack Kerouac proclaimed, "Ginsberg, this poem will make you famous in San Francisco." He underestimated the poem's impact, obviously.

Now head back to:

8 Broadway

The old Barbary Coast frolic hasn't completely died out—it limps along here, along Broadway between Columbus and Montgomery Street, where a fleet of XXX stores and go-go houses continue to attract men at all hours. Strange to think of a porno-shop block as having a long and established heritage, but this one does.

Keep walking west on Broadway and a little farther up is the current location of the:

9 The Beat Museum

You can purchase "Howl" and other Beat works and memorabilia at this museum, which has among its collections a $450 first edition of "On the Road" and a replica of Kerouac's 1949 Hudson. The car was featured in Walter Salles "On the Road" film adaptation (2012) and is on permanent loan from the director. Tickets to the museum within the store are $8 ($5 students and seniors).

10 hungry i

Now a seedy strip club (at 546 Broadway), the original hungry i (at 599 Jackson St., which is under construction for senior housing) was owned and operated by the vociferous "Big Daddy" Nordstrom. If you had been here while Enrico Banducci was in charge, you would have found only a plain room with an exposed brick wall and director's chairs around small tables. A who's who of nightclub entertainers performed at the original hungry i, including Lenny Bruce, Billie Holiday (who sang "Strange Fruit" there), Bill Cosby, Richard Pryor, Woody Allen, and Barbra Streisand.

At the corner of Broadway and Columbus Avenue, you will see the:

11 Former Site of the Condor Club

The city's topless scene got its start in 1964 in this tan building with green cornice and a lower floor of arched brick. The owner, looking for something to liven up his club, asked the chief of police if his waitresses could loosen their bikini tops. They did, and toplessness wasn't far behind. The mayor at the time tolerated it by saying "fun is part of our city's heritage." Within days, every club in the vicinity had also gone topless.

But the person who gets the most credit, to this day, is the copiously chested Carol Doda, who danced a dozen shows nightly at the Condor and was profiled in Tom Wolfe's *The Pump House Gang*. Only around 20 at the time, Doda is still a fixture on the San Francisco scene, now as a chanteuse and the owner of a store in the Marina district (at 1850 Union St.). What does she sell? Bras.

Note the bronze plaque claiming the Condor Club as BIRTHPLACE OF THE WORLD'S FIRST TOPLESS & BOTTOMLESS ENTERTAINMENT.

When you leave the Condor Sports Bar, cross to the south side of Broadway. Note the mural of jazz musicians painted on the entire side of the building directly across Columbus Avenue. Diagonally across the intersection from the Condor Sports Bar is:

12 City Lights Booksellers & Publishers

Founded in 1953, this is one of the best and most historic bookstores in the country, a triangular building stuffed with volumes, particularly hard-to-find ones by fledgling presses. Back in the 1950s, its owner, Lawrence Ferlinghetti, decided that good books didn't have to be expensive, and he set about publishing new writers who he thought deserved to be read. One of his choices was *Howl and Other Poems* by Allen Ginsberg. The book's homoerotic overtones scandalized some, and the resulting obscenity trial (which the poet won) made Ferlinghetti's bookstore nationally famous among both literary types and civil liberties defenders. By the 1960s, the Beat writers, a restless lot, had moved on, mostly taking their jazz-and-poetry evenings with them, but North Beach was indelibly stamped with their reputation.

Upon exiting City Lights bookstore, turn right, cross aptly named Jack Kerouac Street, and stop at 255 Columbus Ave, which is:

13 Vesuvio

Because of its proximity to City Lights bookstore, this bar became a favorite hangout of the Beats. Dylan Thomas used to drink here, as did Jack Kerouac, Ferlinghetti, and Ginsberg. The building dates from 1913, but maintains the same quirky decor it had during the beat era. It is an excellent example of pressed-tin architecture.

Facing Vesuvio across Columbus Avenue is another favorite spot of the Beat Generation:

14 Spec's Twelve Adler Museum Cafe

Located at 12 Saroyan Place, this is one of the city's funkiest bars, a small, dimly lit watering hole with ceiling-hung maritime flags and exposed brick walls crammed with memorabilia. Within the bar is a minimuseum that consists of a few glass cases filled with mementos brought by seamen who frequented the pub from the '40s and onward.

From here, walk back up Columbus Avenue across Broadway to Grant Avenue. Turn right on Grant and continue until you come to Vallejo Street. At 601 Vallejo St. (at Grant Ave.) is:

15 Caffe Trieste

Generally acknowledged to be the king of the North Beach cafés, Trieste makes a mean espresso—in fact, it claims to have served the first one in the neighborhood back in the 1950s when it opened. Its paneled dining area is the kind of place where you're encouraged to linger for hours, and many do. Some of the Beats hung here, shaking off their hangovers, and Francis Ford Coppola is said to have fashioned the screenplay to his *The Godfather* at the tables.

Look across Columbus where you'll see the famed:

16 Molinari Delicatessen

This deli, located at 373 Columbus Ave., has been selling its pungent, air-dried salamis since 1896. Ravioli and tortellini are made in the back of the shop, but it's the sandwiches and the mouthwatering selection of cold salads, cheeses, and marinades up front that captures the attention of most folks. One Italian sub is big enough for two hearty appetites.

Continue in the same direction on Columbus until you reach 412, home of:

17 Biordi Art Imports

This store has carried imported hand-painted majolica pottery from the hill towns of central Italy for more than 50 years. Some of the colorful patterns date from the 14th century. Biordi handpicks its artisans, and its catalog includes biographies of those who are currently represented.

Walk north to the lively intersection of Columbus and Green St. and go left to #678, the home of:

18 Club Fugazi

For many years, Fugazi Hall has been staging the zany and whimsical musical revue *Beach Blanket Babylon.* The show evolved from Steve Silver's Rent-a-Freak service, which consisted of a group of partygoers who would attend parties dressed as any number of characters in outrageous costumes. The fun caught on and soon became *Beach Blanket Babylon,* now the longest-running musical revue in the nation.

If you love comedy and enormous hats, you'll love this show. I don't want to spoil it for you by telling you what it's about, but if you get tickets and they're in an unreserved-seat section, you should arrive fairly early because you'll be seated around small cocktail tables on a first-come, first-served basis. (Two sections have reserved seating, four don't, and all of them frequently sell out weeks in advance; however, sometimes it is possible to get tickets at the last minute on weekdays.) You'll want to be as close to the stage as possible. This supercharged show (p. 180 for more information) is definitely worth the price of admission.

19 O'Reilly's Irish Pub 🍺

Head back the way you came on Green Street. Before you get to Columbus Avenue, you'll see this pub, at 622 Green St., a homey watering hole that dishes out good, hearty Irish food and a fine selection of beers (including Guinness, of course) that are best enjoyed at one of the sidewalk tables. Always a conversation piece is the mural of Irish authors peering from the back wall. How many can you name?

As you exit O'Reilly's, turn left, cross Columbus Avenue, and then take a left onto Columbus. Proceed 1 block northwest to:

20 Washington Square

The Romanesque church on its northern side, Saints Peter and Paul Church (1924), is most often cited as the background of some shots of Marilyn Monroe and Joe Dimaggio (who grew up about a block from here) after their wedding in 1954. (They actually got married at City Hall—the images were just for publicity.) In true literary North Beach style, the Italian motto on the façade quotes not the Bible but Dante's *Paradise,* from *The Divine Comedy.* About a third of the congregation these days is of Chinese extraction.

The statue of Ben Franklin in the square—why are there so few statues of Ben in America, by the way?—was a gift (1879) from a dentist, Henry Cogswell, who made a mint in the gold rush. An avid teetotaler, he built such statues, fitted with fountains, across the country in an effort to get people to drink water instead of beer or liquor. North Beach was lucky; usually, the statue was of him, glass of water proffered in an outstretched hand.

So where's the beach of North Beach? Gone. When sailors first got here, the shoreline was actually around Taylor Street, 2 blocks west. So deep beneath your feet, North Beach's beach, now dry, still lies. Landfill erased it, but the name stuck.

Your walking tour is over, but your tour of North Beach can be just beginning, if you like, for this park is its unofficial heart, and there are dozens of shops, bakeries, and restaurants in the blocks around here. Enjoy!

SHOPPING

Like its population, San Francisco's shopping scene is incredibly diverse. Every style, era, fetish, and financial status is represented here—not in huge, sprawling shopping malls, but in hundreds of boutiques and secondhand stores scattered throughout the city. Whether it's a pair of Jimmy Choo shoes, a Chanel knockoff, or Chinese herbal medicine you're looking for, San Francisco's got it. Just pick a shopping neighborhood, wear some sensible shoes, and you're sure to end up with at least a few take-home treasures.

THE SHOPPING SCENE

Major Shopping Areas

San Francisco has many shopping areas, but the following places are where you'll find most of the action.

Union Square & Environs   San Francisco's most congested and popular shopping mecca is centered on Union Square and bordered by Bush, Taylor, Market, and Montgomery streets. Most of the big department stores and many high-end specialty shops are here, including **Bloomingdales** (at 4th and Market sts.), **Brooks Brothers** (Post St. at Grant Ave.), **Macy's** (at Stockton and O'Farrell), **Neiman Marcus** (at Stockton and Geary), and **Nordstrom** (Market at 5th sts.). Be sure to venture to Grant Avenue, Post and Sutter streets, and Maiden Lane. This area is a hub for public transportation; all Market Street and several other buses run here, as do the Powell–Hyde and Powell–Mason cable car lines. You can also take the Muni streetcar to the Powell Street station.

Chinatown   When you pass through the gate to Chinatown on Grant Avenue, say goodbye to the world of fashion and hello to a swarm of cheap tourist shops selling everything from linen and jade to plastic toys and $2 slippers. But that's not all Chinatown has to offer. The real gems are tucked away on side streets or are small, one-person shops selling Chinese herbs, original art, and jewelry. Grant Avenue is the area's main thoroughfare, and the side streets between Bush Street and Columbus Avenue are full of restaurants, markets, and eclectic shops. Stockton Street is best for food shopping (including live fowl and fish). Walking is the way to get around, because traffic through this area is slow and parking is next to impossible. Most stores in Chinatown are open longer hours than in the rest of the city (see box), from about 10am to 10pm. Take bus no. 1, 9X, 15, 30, 41, or 45.

Jackson Square   A historic district just north of the Financial District's Embarcadero Center, this is the place to go for the top names in fine furniture and fine art. More than a dozen dealers on the 2 blocks between Columbus and Sansome streets specialize in European furnishings from

Store hours are generally Monday through Saturday from 10am to 6pm and Sunday from noon to 5pm. Most department stores stay open later, as do shops around Fisherman's Wharf, the most heavily visited area (by tourists).

Sales tax in San Francisco is 9.5%, which is added on at the register. If you live out of state and buy an expensive item, you might want to have the store ship it home for you. You'll have to pay for shipping, but you'll escape paying the sales tax. Most of the city's shops can wrap your purchase and ship it anywhere in the world. If they can't, you can send it yourself, either through **UPS** (**(** **800/742-5877**), **FedEx** (**(** **800/463-3339**), or the U.S. Postal Service.

the 17th to the 19th centuries. And here you'll encounter earlier than usual with most shops only open Monday through Friday from 9am to 5pm and Saturday from 11am to 4pm. Bus: 1, 3, 8, or 10.

Union Street Union Street, from Fillmore Street to Van Ness Avenue, caters to the upper-middle-class crowd. It's a great place to stroll, window-shop the plethora of boutiques, try the cafes and restaurants, and watch the beautiful people parade by. Take bus no. 22, 41, 45, 47, 49, or 76.

Chestnut Street Parallel and a few blocks north, Chestnut Street is a younger version of Union Street. It holds endless shopping and dining choices, and an ever-tanned, superfit population of postgraduate singles who hang around cafes and scope each other out. Take bus no. 22, 28, 30, 43, or 76.

Fillmore Street Some of the best shopping in town is packed into 5 blocks of Fillmore Street in Pacific Heights. From Jackson to Sutter streets, Fillmore is the perfect place to grab a bite and peruse the high-priced boutiques, crafts shops, and incredible housewares stores. (Don't miss Zinc Details; p. 172.) Take bus no. 1, 2, 3, 4, 12, 22, or 24.

Haight Street Green hair, spiked hair, no hair, or mohair—even the hippies look conservative next to Haight Street's dramatic fashionistas. The shopping in the 6 blocks of upper Haight Street between Central Avenue and Stanyan Street reflects its clientele. It offers everything from incense and European and American street styles to furniture and antique clothing. Bus nos. 6, 7, 66, and 71 run the length of Haight Street, and nos. 33 and 43 run through upper Haight Street. The Muni streetcar N-line stops at Waller Street and Cole Street.

SoMa Although this area isn't suitable for strolling, you'll find almost all the discount shopping in warehouse spaces south of Market. You can pick up a discount-shopping guide at most major hotels. Many bus lines pass through this area.

Hayes Valley While most neighborhoods cater to more conservative or trendy shoppers, lower Hayes Street, between Octavia and Gough streets, celebrates anything vintage, chic, artistic, or downright funky. With new shops opening frequently, it's definitely the most interesting new shopping area in town, with furniture and glass stores, thrift shops, trendy shoe stores, and men's and women's clothiers. You can find lots of great antiques shops south on Octavia Street and on nearby Market Street. Take bus no. 16AX, 16BX, or 21.

The Mission In just the last few years a treasure trove of fashionable and funky stores have popped up on 16th and 17th streets in the Mission, as well as along Valencia Ave. If you want a lamp created from a plaster bust of Caesar, an erudite book or a dress designed by a local, here's where to head. Bus: 12, 14, 22, or 49.

SHOPPING A TO Z

Antiques

Bonhams Part of a world-renowned chain of auction houses, the goodies here are international, ranging from exquisite ancient Japanese screens to Hopi pottery to art deco jewelry and more. Open Mondays through Fridays, 9am-5pm. 220 San Bruno Ave. (at 16th St.). © **800/223-2854** or 415/861-7500. www.bonhams.com/location/sf

Therien & Co. Once a showroom primarily for Scandinavian, French, and eastern European antiques, in the past few years they've expanded to include Mid-century Modern furniture, as well. You'll find both the real thing and replicas here, as well as made-to-order furniture. Mondays through Fridays 10am–5pm. 411 Vermont St. (at 17th St.). © **415/956-8850.** www.therien.com.

Art

For the latest on what artists are showing at the town's galleries, go online to www. sfbayareagalleryguide.com.

Catharine Clark Gallery In fall of 2013, this beloved contemporary art gallery (a specialist in video and media art) moved to the Portrero Hill neighborhood to enlarge its space. Which means that now would-be buyers will be able to see even more work by California's up-and-coming artists (the majority of exhibits focus on local artists). Shows change every 6 weeks. Open Tuesday through Friday 10:30am to 5:30pm and Saturday 11am to 5:30pm. Closed Sunday and Monday. 248 Utah St. (btw. 15th and 16th sts.). © **415/399-1439.** www.cclarkgallery.com.

Fraenkel Gallery Photography is the focus here; world-class artists from around the globe are featured in shows that change every 2 months. Open Tuesday through Friday 10:30am to 5:30pm and Saturday 11am to 5pm. Closed Sunday and Monday. 49 Geary St. (btw. Grant Ave. and Kearny St.), 4th floor. © **415/981-2661.** www.fraenkelgallery.com.

Hang Only Bay Area artists are exhibited at Hang. Since many are at the beginning of their careers, prices for pieces tend to be more affordable than usual. Open 10am-6pm Mondays through Saturdays and noon to 5pm on Sundays. 567 Sutter St. © **415/434-4264.** www.hangart.com.

Meyerovich Gallery A blue chip gallery, Meyervoich concentrates on selling the works of such modern masters as Chagall, Matisse, Miró, and Picasso. A Contemporary Gallery, across the hall, features works by Lichtenstein, Stella, Motherwell, and Hockney. Open Monday through Friday 10:30am to 6:30pm and Saturday 10:30am to 5pm. Closed Sunday. 251 Post St. (at Stockton St.), 4th floor. © **415/421-7171.** www.meyerovich.com.

Books

Argonaut Book Shop When Alfred Hitchcock walked into this book store while filming the movie *Vertigo,* he said something to the effect of "This is exactly what a book store should look like," and promptly recreated every detail of the store on his movie set in Hollywood. This antiquarian book shop specializes in California history, American West, rare books, as well as maps, prints, and photographs. Open 9am to 5pm Mondays through Saturdays and 10:30 am to 4pm on Saturdays. 1786 Sutter St. (at Jones St.). ℂ **415/474-9067.** www.argonautbookshop.com.

Book Passage Run by the ebullient Elaine Petrocceli, this bookstore in the Ferry Building may be small but its wonderfully well-curated, meaning you're sure to find something entertaining to read here. Book Passage is also known for its excellent author events and writer's conferences, both in San Francisco, and in its main store in Corte Madera. Open 9am-8pm Mondays through Fridays, 9am to 7pm on weekends. Ferry Building Marketplace (at the Embarcadero and Market St.). ℂ **415/835-1020.** www.bookpassage.com.

The Booksmith A true gem, with erudite, hand-written recommendations for books dotting the shelves, this Haight store may not be huge, but it has a smartly put together collection of books and more than 1,000 different magazines on sale. Mondays through Saturdays open 10am to 10pm, Sundays 10am to 8pm.1644 Haight St. (btw. Clayton and Cole sts.). ℂ **800/493-7323** or 415/863-8688. www.booksmith.com.

City Lights Booksellers & Publishers The city's iconic bookstore—once owned by Lawrence Ferlinghetti, the renowned Beat Generation poet—is still going strong. The three-level store is particularly good for art, poetry, and political paperbacks, though it also carries more mainstream books. Open daily until midnight. 261 Columbus Ave. (at Broadway). ℂ **415/362-8193.** www.citylights.com.

Green Apple Books A massive purveyor of both new and used books—the store boasts more than 160,000 tomes!—it's an excellent resource for those seeking special books, like modern first editions; and rare graphic comics. We also have to give kudos to the knowledgeable and friendly staff, who will help you find whatever you need *Note:* There's a separate music, fiction, and DVD annex next door. Hours are 10am-10:30pm Sunday through Friday, 10am-11:30pm on Saturday. 506 Clement St. (at Sixth Ave.). ℂ **415/387-2272.** www.greenapplebooks.com.

Books Inc. Holding the title "The West's Oldest Independent Bookseller," **Books Inc.,** established in 1857, is living proof an indie book seller can adapt, survive, and even prosper, despite Gold Rush busts and booms, numerous earthquakes, The Great Depression, fires, death, bankruptcy, and, most important (and probably toughest of all), the rapidly changing bookselling climate. Owners Margie and Michael Tucker have created a warm, inviting environment, hosting book clubs, author events, and travel lit groups—everyone is welcome to attend. The chain has four city locations, as well as two **Compass Books** at San Francisco International Airport. Hours vary by store, but most open and 10am and close no earlier than 7pm, seven days a week (with the Castro store open until 10pm nightly). Marina: 2251 Chestnut St. (btw. Scott and Pierce Sts.). ℂ **415/931-3633.** Castro: 2275 Market St. (at 16th St.). ℂ **415/864-6777.** Presidio Heights: 3515 California St. (at Locust St.) ℂ **415/221-3666.** Opera Plaza: 601 Van Ness (btw. Turk St. and Golden Gate Ave.) ℂ **415/776-1111.** SFO Airport: Terminals 2 and 3. www.booksinc.net.

Cigars

Occidental Cigar Club Hinton Rowan Harper, an 1800s Gold Rush-era writer, once remarked he'd seen "the purest liquor, the best segars (sic), the finest tobacco, the prettiest courtezans (sic)" and it was his "unbiased opinion that California can and does furnish the best bad things that are available in America." I haven't seen any courtesans here, but if you are looking for a fine stogie with a tumbler of rare scotch, and a legal smoking room to enjoy your treasures, step inside. Though the name implies it is a private club, Occidental is open to the public. A varied selection of premium cigars make good souvenirs to remember your time in the Sin City of the West. Daily noon-1am. 471 Pine St. (at Kearney St). ℂ **415/834-0485.** www.occidentalcigarclub.com.

Vendetta Men's Apparel & Vintage Cuban Cigars Vendetta's motto is "living well is the best revenge" and owner, Bruce Rothenberg, is all about the finer things in life. This is more than evident at his shop in Nob Hill's Fairmont Hotel, where he sells high quality items like fine Italian caps and Persol sunglasses. But Bruce's real specialty, his baby if you will, are the pre-embargo Cuban cigars he lovingly sells to customers with the reluctance of someone selling his offspring. He knows the history of these babies, dating from 1947–1962, and assures that, like a fine wine, they only get better—more complex and more character—with age. As one of the only (if not the only) stores in the country selling Cubans, you will pay the price for one of these rare stogies—cigars range from $125–$250. Bruce has added a separate smoking room with a cushy sofa for a few guests to light up and enjoy their purchases. Don't worry, if the Cubans are a little out of your price range, he carries Dominican and Nicaraguan cigars for a fraction of the price. Open Tuesday through Saturday, noon through 7pm. Fairmont Hotel, 950 Mason (btw. California and Sacramento sts.). ℂ **415/397-7755.** www.vendettablu.com.

Fashion
MEN'S FASHIONS
Cable Car Clothiers Since 1939, this gentleman's store has been helping San Francisco's elite look their most dashing. Selling everything from three button suits to fedoras to pocket squares, they source the best from around the world for their clientele and that even goes for the more esoteric buys, like wool hosiery from France and cotton underwear from Switzerland. Mondays through Fridays 9am to 6pm, Saturdays open 11am-5pm. Closed Sundays. 200 Bush St. (at Sansome St.). ℂ **415/397-4740.** www.cablecarclothiers.com.

Citizen Clothing Ben Sherman, Jack Spade, Fred Perry. No, that isn't who's shopping here. It's a very partial list of the swank brands this Castro shop carries to keep the neighborhood fellows looking dapper. Topnotch service is another hallmark of the store. Open daily 10am-8pm. 536 Castro St. (btw. 18th and 19th sts.). ℂ **415/575-3560.**

UNISEX
A-B Fits The solution for those who've given up finding a flattering pair of jeans, this North Beach boutique specializes in finding denim that, well, fits. Doing so requires a broad range of options and a dedicated staff. Luckily, A-B Fits has both—the shop carries over 100 styles of jeans and the salespeople are true experts at their highly specialized trade. Open Monday through Saturday 11:30 am-6:30pm and Sundays from noon to 6pm. 1519 Grant Ave. (at Union and Filbert sts.). ℂ **415/982-5726.** www.abfits.com.

Goorin Brothers Fabulous hats, for both men and women, are the stock in trade of this three-store chain. You'll find funky straw fedoras here (made by local artists), modern cloth cloches in all colors, porkpie hats, cowboy hats, and wide-brimmed hats perfect for fashionable garden parties (or gardening). Open Sundays through Fridays 11am to 8pm and Saturdays 11am to 9pm. 1612 Stockton St., 111 Geary St., and 1446 Haight St. ℂ **415/426-9450.** www.goorin.com.

Jeremy's   Fashionistas flock to Jeremy's because they can scoop up top-of-the-line name brand clothing here at bargain basement prices. Jeremy's fills its shelves with shirts, dresses, trousers, you name it, that were either used in window displays at big department stores, were created as samples, or are overstocks (they simply didn't sell last season). So these are NOT second-hand clothes or cheap knock-offs, but the real thing, just for far less than one usually pays. This place is a true treasure trove. Monday through Saturday open 11am to 6pm and Sundays from noon to 6pm. 2 S. Park (btw. Bryant and Brannan sts. at Second St.). ✆ **415/882-4929.** www.jeremys.com.

MAC   Nope, not the makeup store. The name stands for Modern Appealing Clothing, and that about sums up what's being sold here. The owners source attractive and (sometimes) unusual pieces from around the world—Belgium's Dries Van Noten and Martin Margiela, New York's John Bartlett, and local sweater sweetheart Laurie B, to name a few—and then helps customers arrange them into drop-dead gorgeous outfits. And happily, prices are *slightly* kinder at MAC than they are in the other trendy shops of the area. Open Mondays through Saturdays 11am-7pm and Sundays noon to 6pm. 387 Grove St. (at Gough St.). ✆ **415/863-3011.**

Marine Layer   Comfort is Marine Layer's *raison d'etre.* The firm makes simple shirts—t's, polos, button downs, cardigans, and hoodies—that feel already broken in (like you've had them for years). They do this by using a special blend of pima cotton and micro modal. And best of all, all of their products are made in the U.S.A. (unlike 95% of the clothing we buy in this country). As for the look of the clothes: I'd call these layering pieces, basics, basically. Open daily 10am to 7pm. 2209 Chestnut St. and 498 Hayes St. ✆ **415/346-2400.** www.marinelayer.com.

Wilkes Bashford   The couture boutique that first introduced Armani to the U.S. underwent a total facelift in 2012, making this elegant temple of commerce even more hoity toity. The fashions are primarily from France and Italy, and services include custom fittings on-site, free wine and coffee, and the advice of a staff of expert stylists. *Tip:* If you just can't stomach paying $6,000 for a blouse, shop here in February when the warehouse sale is held, and prices drop . . . a hair. Open Monday through Saturday 10am-6pm. 375 Sutter St. (at Stockton St.). ✆ **415/986-4380.** www.wilkesbashford.com.

WOMEN'S FASHIONS

emily lee   Not everyone is 22 and a size 2. For those who like to look stylish, but have bodies that are, well, like the majority of our bodies, emily lee offers artsy, generously cut duds that make most everyone look good. Among the designers sold here: Blanque, Eileen Fisher, Flax, Ivan Grundahl, and Three Dots. Open Monday through Friday 10am-6pm, Saturdays 9:30am to 5:30pm. 3509 California St. (at Locust St.). ✆ **415/751-3443.**

440 Brannan Studio Showroom   In this massive factory space, local designers sell limited edition lines to the public; you'll sometimes see one stitching a hem or constructing a jacket in the back. In business since 1998, the Studio's been an incubator for a number of talented San Francisco designers. While it does carry menswear, the vast majority of these unique, and often really fun and funky creations, are for women. Closed Sundays. 440 Brannon St. (near Zoe St.). ✆ **415/957-1411.** www.440Brannan.com.

RAG   And this being an ultra-creative city, here's a second collective of local designers where you can buy one-of-a-kind outfits. RAG stands for Residents Apparel Gallery, and it's a co-op shop for 55 new to newish designers to showcase their trousers, blouses, t-shirts, and dresses. Prices are low; fashions are forward, youthful, and of the moment. Daily 11:30am-7pm. 541 Octavia St. (btw. Hayes and Grove sts.). ✆ **415/621-7718.** www.ragsf.com.

Sunhee Moon   Clothing the "modern day Audrey Hepburn" is the goal of local designer SunHee Moon, and with her eye for color and fit, I'd say she's succeeding. Her dresses, which come in a variety of streamlined shapes and delicious colors, will likely become a staple of your wardrobe. Moon creates equally flattering separates: sleek pants, tailored and/or draped tops, and quirkily patterned skirts. And prices, while not low, are more than reasonable for clothing this sturdy, yet chic. Open Monday through Friday noon to 7pm and weekends noon to 6pm. 3167 Thirteenth St. and 1833 Fillmore St. ✆ **415/928-1800.** www.sunheemoon.com.

Consignment & Vintage Stores

Good Byes   The style-conscious citizens of San Francisco consign their cast-offs to this shop, meaning the quality of the goods is high, but the prices often surprisingly low (we've seen $350 pre-owned shoes going for just $35 here). Menswear is the focus at this store; womenswear is in a separate boutique across the street. Open Monday through Saturday 10m-6pm and Sunday 10am-5pm. 3464 Sacramento St. and 3483 Sacramento St. (btw. Laurel and Walnut sts.). ✆ **415/346-6388** (men's) and 415/674-0151 (women's). www.goodbyessf.com.

La Rosa   Specializing in clothes from the 1940s through the 1960s, this long-established store (founded in 1978) has a lot of great buys for folks who enjoy vintage fashions. Rumor has it that Dita Von Teese shops here regularly. Their sister store, **Held Over,** features less expensive and more modern duds (some are sold for $12 per pound!). It's located at 1543 Haight St., near Ashbury (✆ **415/864-0818**). Both open daily 11am to 7pm. 1711 Haight St. (at Cole St.). ✆ **415/668-3744.**

Food

Cowgirl Creamery Cheese Shop   Arguably one of the farms that pioneered the artisanal cheese craze, the small-production Cowgirl Creamery has its headquarters up in Point Reyes. Their city outpost is located in the Ferry Building Marketplace and offers all their signature cheeses—robust Red Hawk to smooth, creamy Mt. Tam. Open Monday through Friday 10am to 7pm, Saturday 8am to 6pm, Sunday 11am to 6pm. Ferry Building Marketplace, no. 17. ✆ **415/362-9354.** www.cowgirlcreamery.com.

Molinari Delicatessen   You can't help but take your camera out when you walk into this North Beach institution dating back to 1896. It's a food sensory overload. Everywhere you look, shelves, counters, and rafters are filled with jars of colorful sauces, olive oils, cheeses, and imported wines. Did I mention the salami? All sizes of red and white salamis hang from strings, creating a savory curtain. Molinari's is the perfect place to grab a thick meat-stuffed sandwich and picnic supplies; I recommend taking your feast to Washington Square Park 2 blocks away at Columbus and Union Streets. Open Monday through Friday 9am to 5:30 pm and Saturday 7:30am to 5:30pm.   373 Columbus St. (at Vallejo St.). ✆ **415/421-2337.**

Tcho Chocolate   Mmmmmmm, chocolate! And it has a social conscience, to boot. While there are lots of chocolate shops in the city where you can buy a sweet treat, Tcho is far more than just another candy store. It offers free, 1-hour factory tour (online

AMAZING grazing: THE FERRY BUILDING

As much a sightseeing attraction as a place to buy and consume food, the **Ferry Building Marketplace** and its corollary **Farmers' Market** (one of the most highly acclaimed farmers' markets in the United States) are tangible proof that people who live in San Francisco lead tastier lives than the rest of the nation (sorry, but it's true!). The produce looks like it was taken from a still-life painting (it's organic and sourced from small family farms), the meats and fish are super-fresh and the quality and variety of specialty goods—many of which you may never have encountered before (who knew balsamic vinegar is sometimes clear!)—will blow your mind.

Saturday mornings is the best time to stop by, as the farmer's market is in its full glory, playing host to local meat ranchers, artisan cheese makers, bread bakers, specialty food purveyors, and farmers. Some are picked for the 10:30am **Meet the Farmer** event, a half-hour interview created to give the audience in-depth information about how and where their food is produced. Then, at 11am, Bay Area chefs give cooking demonstrations using ingredients purchased that morning from the market. (And yes, tastings are given out, as are recipes.) Several local restaurants also have food stalls selling their cuisine—including breakfast items—so don't eat before you arrive.

The Marketplace is open daily and features Northern California's best gourmet food outlets including Cowgirl Creamery's Artisan Cheese Shop, Recchiuti Confections (amazing chocolate), Acme Breads, Hog Island Oysters, famed Vietnamese restaurant the Slanted Door, Imperial Tea Court (where you'll be taught the traditional Chinese way to steep and sip your tea), and a myriad of other restaurants, delis, gourmet coffee shops, specialty foods, and wine bars.

The Ferry Building Marketplace is open Monday through Friday from 10am to 6pm, Saturday from 9am to 6pm, and Sunday from 11am to 5pm. The Farmers' Market takes place year-round, rain or shine, every Tuesday and Thursday from 10am to 2pm and Saturday 8am to 2pm. The Ferry Building is located on the Embarcadero at the foot of Market Street (about a 15-min. walk from Fisherman's Wharf). Call ✆ **415/693-0996** for more information or log onto www.ferry plazafarmersmarket.com or www.ferry buildingmarketplace.com.

reservations required) which includes serious sampling. You'll also learn about the widespread problem of slavery in the chocolate biz. Who knew? If you don't do the tour, drop in for a sweet treat. Now, if they could just take out the calories. Open Monday through Friday 9m to 5:30pm, 10am-5:30pm on weekends. Pier 17. ✆ **415/981-0189.** www.tcho.com. Tours daily 10:30am and 2pm; no children under 8 allowed. Open Mon–Fri 9am–5:30pm; Sat–Sun 10am–5:30pm. Bus: 2, 12, 14, 21, 66, or 71. Streetcar: F-Line. BART: Embarcadero.

Z. Cioccolato A sweet-tooth wonderland, Z offers 40 flavors of fresh fudge, plus saltwater taffy, classic brands of candies of all sorts, and such novelty items as candy bras or g-strings. A decadent North Beach store that's sure to satisfy. Open Monday through Wednesday 10am to 10pm, Thursday and Sunday 10am to 11pm and Friday through Saturday 10am-midnight. 474 Columbus Ave (at Green St.). ✆ **415/395-9116.** www. zcioccolato.com.

Gifts

Art of China   Since 1974, this shop has been selling refined Chinese exports, so no plastic here! Instead you'll find genuine collectibles, from elegant hand-carved Chinese figurines to cloissine, porcelain vases and decorative items (and jewelry) created from ivory, quartz, and jade. Hours vary. 839–843 Grant Ave. (btw. Clay and Washington sts.). ℂ **415/981-1602.** www.artsofchinasf.com.

Cost Plus World Market   It sometimes feels like the entire world is on sale at this Fisherman's Wharf store (it's right at the cable car turnaround). You'll find biscuits from Australia and inlaid stools from India, artisanal beers from across the U.S. (they let you build your own six-pack so you can do a tasting), funky shower curtains, you name it! They have it here, usually in a foreign brand you haven't seen before and at a price that's more than fair. World Market is open Monday through Saturday from 10am to 9pm and Sunday from 10am to 7pm. 2552 Taylor St. (btw. North Point and Bay sts.). ℂ **415/928-6200.** www.worldmarket.com.

Dandelion   Paperweights and trivets, bookends and multi-colored garden trowels, 90 different teapots—these are just some of the pretty and well-designed goods on sale at Dandelion, many imported from India and Japan. If you can't find a gift here, well, you've got extraordinarily finicky friends. The store is closed Sunday and Monday, except during November and December, when it's open daily. Hours are 10am to 6pm. 55 Potrero Ave. (at Alameda St.). ℂ **415/436-9200.** www.tampopo.com.

Good Vibrations   Just what it sounds like, this is a sex-toy shop but one that's not at all, well, skeevy, thanks to the open, non-judgemental attitude of the staff (who own the place, incidentally; this is a woman-owned, worker owned co-operative). And if you're not in the market for any new gadgets, stop by to see the on-site vibrator museum. 603 Valencia St. (at 17th St.). ℂ **415/522-5460** or 800/BUY-VIBE (289-8423) for mail order. A 2nd location is at 1620 Polk St., at Sacramento St. (ℂ **415/345-0400**), and a 3rd is at 2504 San Pablo Ave., Berkeley. (ℂ **510/841-8987**). www.goodvibes.com.

Nest   It's hard to categorize Nest as it carries everything from throws and handmade quilts to flowy Boho dresses and sleepwear. What ties it all together is the impeccable taste of the owner, and the fact that you won't find a lot of these items anywhere else. This one's fun to just browse, even if the prices stop you from buying. Open Sunday through Thursday 10am to 9pm and Friday through Saturday 10am to 11pm. 2300 Fillmore St. (at Clay St.). ℂ **415/292-6199.** www.nestsf.com.

New People World   More than just a store, New People World is a $15-million complex dedicated to modern Japanese culture, both its zen side and its over-the-top, *anime* wackiness. In the basement is a THX-certified theater to showcase Japanese cinema; the other floors (there are five altogether) feature a nail salon, a crumpet and tea shop, a boutique dedicated to cute gadget cases, two clothing stores, and the Super-Frog art gallery. But back to those fashion stores, because they carry items you likely won't find anywhere else in North America. Like Lolita clothes (dresses for grown women that are made to look like outfits a toddler would wear; don't ask) and Sou Sou shoes, which are the classic, form-fitting Japanese shoes that come with an indent between the big toe and the rest of the toes (and here are done in all sorts of wacky, modern patterns). Hours vary by store, but more are open daily 11am to 7pm. 1746 Post St. (btw. Buchanan St. and Webster St.). No phone. www.newpeopleworld.com.

Housewares/Furnishings

Alessi Functional yet whimsical—that about describes the kitchen utensils of Italian designer Alberto Alessi (love his spiderlike lemon squeezer), and this is his North American flagship. It's a great place to find a gift, though most end up getting something for themselves, too, like a silver beaver shaped pencil sharpener or one of their oh-so-cute kettles. 424 Sutter St. (at Stockton St.). ✆ **415/434-0403.** www.alessi.com.

Biordi Art Imports Exquisite Italian majolica pottery is the lure here. Some use it to eat off of, but it's so pretty my guess is most buyers take those plates, bowls, and other items and stick them on the wall for decoration. The owner has been importing these hand-painted collectibles for 60 years. Open Monday through Saturday 10am to 6pm. 412 Columbus Ave. (at Vallejo St.). ✆ **415/392-8096.** www.biordi.com.

Gump's Those who need a special item for a special event come here, and have been doing so since 1861 when the store was founded. The service is legendary, many items can't be found anywhere else, and Gumps carries everything from jewelry to vases to Asian antiques. The store is particularly popular with engaged couples who register here for just the right set of silverware, or covetable throw pillows. The store also has an unusually good and large collection of Christmas ornaments. Monday through Saturday 10am to 6pm, Sunday noon to 5pm. 135 Post St. (btw. Kearny St. and Grant Ave.). ✆ **800/766-7628** or 415/982-1616. www.gumps.com.

Propeller For furniture that's alternately spikey and blocky, but always ultra-contemporary, head to this serene, sky-lit shop. Owner/designer Lorn Dittfeld handpicks pieces, promising that they are "built and offered by people with a stake in your happiness." Those people include up-and-coming designers from around California and the globe. Open Monday through Saturday 11am-7pm and Sunday noon to 5pm. 555 Hayes St. (btw. Laguna and Octavia sts.). ✆ **415/701-7767.** www.propellermodern.com.

The Wok Shop Every implement ever created for Chinese cooking is available in a store that goes well beyond woks. I'm talking cleavers, circular chopping blocks, dishes, oyster knives, bamboo steamers, strainers, and more. The shop also does a steady trade in aprons, linens, and baskets, again, all fabricated in China. The store is open daily from 10am to 6pm. 718 Grant Ave. (at Clay St.). ✆ **415/989-3797.** www.wokshop.com.

Zinc Details Celebrating 20 years in 2013, this high-style furniture and knick knack store just about defines the San Francisco aesthetic, with alternately hip, colorful and quirky pieces to dress up any home. While many of the furniture items come from such international brands as Knoll, a portion are made specifically for the store. Open Monday through Saturday 11am to 7pm and Sunday from noon to 6pm. 1905 Fillmore St. (btw. Bush and Pine sts.). ✆ **415/776-2100.** www.zincdetails.com.

Jewelry

Dianne's Old & New Estates Ask a local where they got their lovely engagement ring and they're likely to glow . . . and mention Dianne's. The shop literally has baubles for all tastes from fine antique jewels to more contemporary pieces. It also have a very forgiving payment policy: you can buy jewelry on layaway here, paying no interest whatsoever for the first 12 months. Open Monday through Saturday 11am to 6pm and Sunday 11am to 5pm. 2181A Union St. (at Fillmore St.). ✆ **888/346-7525** or 415/346-7525. www.diannesestatejewelry.com.

Foggy Notion   Everything is made on site here, from the somewhat punky jewelry to the ecologically friendly fragrance products. And to make the place even more eclectic, it also sells classic vinyl records. Open Wednesdays through Saturdays from noon to 7pm and Sundays from 11am to 6pm. 275 Sixth Ave. ☏ **415/683-5654.** www.foggy notion.com

Union Street Goldsmith   Made in San Francisco jewels, for those who like a more casual, contemporary look. Many of the pieces feature vibrantly colorful stones. The staff will also create custom designs for those who ask. Open Monday through Saturday 11am to 5:45pm and Sunday from noon to 4:45 pm. 1909 Union St. (at Laguna St.). ☏ **415/776-8048.** www.unionstreetgoldsmith.com.

Pirate Supplies

826 Valencia/Pirate Supply Store   When "A Heartbreaking Work of Staggering Genius" author, Dave Eggers, wanted to set up a literary salon to inspire young people to write, the city said his space was zoned for retail. Naturally, he opened a pirate supply store. Pick up a bottle of "Scurvy be Gone" or tattoo remover. Stock up on eye patches or glass eyes. When you order your custom hook, make sure to specify whether it is for the right or left hand. All proceeds from the store support up and coming young writers who hone their craft in the classroom in the back. Open daily from noon to 6pm. 826 Valencia St. (btw. 19th St. and Cunningham Lane). ☏ **415/642-5905.** www.826valencia.org.

Shoes

Bulo   Fashion-forward footwear from such cutting edge designers as Donald J. Pliner, Yuko Imanishi, and Bed Stu draws shoppers to this small store. In addition to shoes, Bulo now sells belts, socks, wallets, jewelry, and shoe care products. Open Monday through Saturday 11am to 7pm and Sunday from noon to 6pm. 418 Hayes St. ☏ **415/255-4939.** www.buloshoes.com.

Paolo Shoes   There really is a Paolo here (Paulo Iantorno) and he's more than just a shop owner. He actually designs the store's sexy footwear—colorful wedges and towering stilletos for women and funky purple suede ankle boots for men have been among the recent selections—and then sends his designs to Italy to be handcrafted. But what might make these shoes so unique is they're not only creative and colorful, they're actually comfortable—even the pumps! A worthy investment if you like to treat your tootsies well. Open Monday through Saturday 11am to 7pm and Sunday from noon to 6pm. 524 Hayes St. ☏ **415/552-4580.** A 2nd location is at 2000 Fillmore St. (☏ **415/771-1944**). www.paoloshoes.com.

Shopping Centers & Complexes

Crocker Galleria   Modeled after Milan's Galleria Vittorio Emanuele, this glass-domed, three-level pavilion, about 3 blocks east of Union Square, features around 40 high-end shops with expensive and classic designer creations. Fashions include Aricie lingerie, Gianni Versace, and Polo/Ralph Lauren. Closed Sunday. 50 Post St. (at Kearny St.).☏ **415/393-1505.** www.shopatgalleria.com.

Ghirardelli Square   This former chocolate factory is one of the city's quaintest shopping malls and most popular landmarks. It dates from 1864, when it served as a factory making Civil War uniforms, but it's best known as the former chocolate and spice factory of Domingo Ghirardelli (say "*Gear*-ar-dell-y"). A clock tower, an exact replica of the one at France's Château de Blois, crowns the complex. Inside the tower, on the mall's plaza level, is the fun Ghirardelli soda fountain. It still makes and sells small amounts of chocolate, but the big draw is the old-fashioned ice-cream parlor. Stores range from a children's club to a perfumery, cards and stationery to a doggie boutique. The main plaza shops' and restaurants' hours are 10am to 6pm Sunday through Thursday and 10am to 9pm Friday and Saturday, with extended hours during the summer. The square has recently undergone a major face-lift, which not only jazzed up its appearance a bit, but brought free Wi-Fi to the area. Along with elegant Vietnamese restaurant Ana Mandara, there's now an English tea experience (Crown & Crumpet), wine bar (Cellar360), cupcake bakery, and more. 900 North Point St. (at Polk St.). ✆ **415/775-5500.** www.ghirardellisq.com.

Pier 39 This bayside mall also happens to have stunning views. To residents, that pretty much wraps up Pier 39—an expensive spot where out-of-towners go to buy souvenirs and greasy fast food. For vacationers, though, Pier 39 does have some redeeming qualities—fresh crab (in season), playful sea lions, phenomenal views, and plenty of fun for the kids. If you want to get to know the real San Francisco, skip the cheesy T-shirt shops and limit your time here to one afternoon, if at all. Located at Beach St. and the Embarcadero.

Westfield San Francisco Centre Opened in 1988 and given a $460-million expansion in 2006, this ritzy 1.5-million-square-foot urban shopping center is one of the few vertical malls (multilevel rather than sprawling) in the United States. Its most attractive feature is a spectacular atrium with a century-old dome that's 102 feet wide and three stories high. Along with Nordstrom (p. 164) and Bloomingdale's (p. 164) department stores and a Century Theatres multiplex, there are more than 170 specialty stores, including Abercrombie & Fitch, Herve Leger, bebe, Juicy Couture, J. Crew, and Movado. The bottom level is sprinkled with probably the best food-court fare you've ever had, along with a gourmet market and deli, and a fast-service (but not fast food) outlet for Charles Phan's Slanted Door, called Out the Door. 865 Market St. (at Fifth St.). ✆ **415/512-6776.** www.westfield.com/sanfrancisco.

Toys

The Chinatown Kite Shop This delightful Chinatown classic sells all sorts of kites from ones you design yourself to color-saturated fish kites, windsocks, hand-painted Chinese paper kites, wood-and-paper biplanes, pentagonal kites, and more. All of it makes great souvenirs and decorations. Open daily from 10am to 8pm. 717 Grant Ave. (btw. Clay and Sacramento sts.). ✆ **415/989-5182.** www.chinatownkite.com.

Travel Goods

Flight 001 The store for jetsetters, it sells you the coolest of luggage tags, TSA-Friendly manicure sets, sleek travel pillows, and all sorts of other gadgets that will make your flight home that much more comfortable and/or fun. Open Monday through Saturday 11am to 7pm and Sunday from 11am to 6pm. 525 Hayes St. (btw. Laguna and Octavia sts.). ✆ **415/487-1001.** A 2nd location is out in Berkeley at 1774 4th St. ✆ **510/526-1001**). www.flight001.com.

Wine & Sake

True Sake   Some 150 different brands of sake are available at this specialty store, many of which, owner Beau Timken claims, are available at no other retail store in the U.S. Don't be intimidated if you know nothing about sake: the informed staff will help you make the best decision to suit your tastes and won't just push the pricier varieties (in fact, many of the bottles here are surprisingly affordable). Open Sunday through Tuesday from noon to 6pm and Wednesday through Saturday from noon to 7pm. 560 Hayes St. (btw. Laguna and Octavia sts.). ℂ **415/355-9555.** www.truesake.com.

Wine Club San Francisco   The Wine Club is a discount warehouse that offers excellent prices on more than 1,200 domestic and foreign wines. If you can't find your favorite on sale, the well-informed staff should be able to find you a similar tipple. Open Monday through Saturday from 10am to 7pm and Sunday from 10am to 6pm. 953 Harrison St. (btw. Fifth and Sixth sts.). ℂ **415/512-9086.** www.thewineclub.com.

NIGHTLIFE & ENTERTAINMENT

For a city with fewer than a million full-time inhabitants, San Francisco boasts an impressive after-dark scene. Dozens of piano bars and top-notch lounges augment a lively dance-club culture, and skyscraper lounges offer dazzling city views. The city's arts scene is also extraordinary: The opera is justifiably world renowned, the ballet is on its toes, and theaters are high in both quantity and quality. In short, there's always something going on in the city, and unlike in Los Angeles or New York, you don't have to pay outrageous cover charges or wait to be "picked" to be a part of the scene.

For up-to-the-minute nightlife information, turn to the *San Francisco Weekly* (www.sfweekly.com) and the *San Francisco Bay Guardian* (www.sfbg.com), both of which run comprehensive listings. They are available for free at bars and restaurants and from street-corner boxes all around the city. *Where* (www.wheresf.com), a free tourist-oriented monthly, also lists programs and performance times; it's available in most of the city's finer hotels. The Sunday edition of the *San Francisco Chronicle* features a "Datebook" section, printed on pink paper, with information on and listings of the week's events. If you have Internet access, it's a good idea to check out www.citysearch.com or www.sfstation.com for the latest in bars, clubs, and events. And if you want to secure seats at a hot-ticket event, either buy well in advance or contact the concierge of your hotel and see if they can swing something for you.

Tix Bay Area (also known as **TIX**; ✆ **415/430-1140;** www.tixbayarea.org) sells half-price tickets on the day of performances and full-price tickets in advance to select Bay Area cultural and sporting events. TIX is also a Ticketmaster outlet and sells Gray Line tours and transportation passes. Tickets are primarily sold in person with some half-price tickets available on their website. To find out which shows have half-price tickets, call the TIX info line or check out their website. A service charge, ranging from $1.75 to $6, is levied on each ticket depending on its full price. You can pay with cash, traveler's checks, Visa, MasterCard, American Express, or Discover with photo ID. TIX, located on Powell Street between Geary and Post streets, is open Tuesday through Friday from 11am to 6pm, Saturday from 10am to 6pm, and Sunday from 10am to 3pm. *Note:* Half-price tickets go on sale at 11am the day of the performance.

You can also get tickets to most theater and dance events through **City Box Office,** 180 Redwood St., Ste. 100, between Golden Gate and McAllister streets off Van Ness Avenue (✆ **415/392-4400;** www.cityboxoffice.com). MasterCard and Visa are accepted.

Tickets.com (© 800/225-2277; www.tickets.com) sells computer-generated tickets (with a hefty service charge of $3–$19 per ticket!) to concerts, sporting events, plays, and special events. **Ticketmaster** (© 415/421-TIXS [8497]; www.ticketmaster.com) also offers advance ticket purchases (also with a service charge).

For information on local theater, check out **www.theatrebayarea.org**. For information on major league baseball, pro basketball, and pro football, see "Professional Sports Teams" later in this chapter on p. 188.

And don't forget that this isn't New York: Bars close at 2am, so get an early start if you want a full night on the town in San Francisco.

THE PERFORMING ARTS

Special concerts and performances take place in San Francisco year-round. **San Francisco Performances** ★★ (www.performances.org), has brought acclaimed artists to the Bay Area for more than 30 years. Shows run the gamut from chamber music to dance to jazz. Performances are in several venues, including the Herbst Theater and the Yerba Buena Center for the Arts. The season runs from late September to June. Tickets cost from $15 to $96 and are available through **City Box Office** (© 415/392-4400) or through the San Francisco Performances website.

Classical Music & Opera

San Francisco Opera ★★★   Welcome to the second largest opera company on the continent. It's also one of the most courageous: along with presenting the classics, in lavish, huge productions, the SFO commissions new works each year. Sometimes these fresh operas can be quite controversial, such as the fall of 2013 adaptation of the Stephen King novel "Dolores Claiborne" by American composer Tobias Picker. All productions have English supertitles. The performance schedule is a bit of an odd one, with the season starting in September and lasting 14 weeks. It then takes a break for a few months before starting again in June for 2 months. It's usually possible to get the less coveted seats as late as the day of performance (though prime seats can go months in advance). War Memorial Opera House, 301 Van Ness Ave. (at Grove St.). © **415/864-3330** (box office). www.sfopera.com. Tickets $15–$250; standing room $10 cash only; student rush $25.

San Francisco Symphony ★★★   Michael Tilson Thomas is perhaps the most celebrated living American conductor and he holds the baton here. Thanks in part to his leadership, the roster is full of world-class soloists, world-premier pieces and high-quality performances. Davies Symphony Hall, 201 Van Ness Ave. (at Grove St.). © **415/864-6000** (box office). www.sfsymphony.org. Tickets $15–$156.

Free Opera

Every year, the **San Francisco Opera** stages a number of free performances, beginning with Opera in the Park every September to kick off the season. They follow it with occasional free performances throughout the city as part of the Brown Bag Opera program. Schedule details can be found on the company's website at **www.sfopera.com**.

Theater

American Conservatory Theater (A.C.T.) ★★★   This is, quite simply, one of the best theater companies in the U.S., with peerless acting, design and show-selecting chops. Since its debut in 1967 a number of big names have "trod the boards" here, including Annette Bening, Denzel

Washington, Danny Glover, and Nicolas Cage. The A.C.T. season runs September through July and features both classic and contemporary plays. Its home is the stupendously beautiful (and viewer-friendly) **Geary Theater,** built in 1910. It's a national historic landmark. Performing at the Geary Theater, 415 Geary St. (at Mason St.). 2015 Addison St., Berkeley. © **415/749-2ACT (2228).** www.act-sf.org. Tickets $20-$140.

Berkeley Repertory Theater ★★★ Across the bay, this theater was founded in 1968 and has been mopping up awards ever since. It rivals A.C.T. in the quality of its shows, though sometimes skews a bit more avante garde. Contemporary plays are offered throughout the year, usually Wednesday through Sunday. 2025 Addison St,. Berkeley. © **510/647-2900.** www.berkeleyrep.org. Tickets $55-$81.

The Magic Theatre ★★ Sam Shepard was a longtime artist-in-residence at the Magic, premiering his plays *Fool for Love* and *True West* here. That should give you an idea of the quality of work here (it's usually quite high). The company has been performing since 1967. Performing at Building D, Fort Mason Center, 2 Marina Blvd. (at Buchanan St.). © **415/441-8822.** www.magictheatre.org. Tickets $20–$60; discounts for students, educators, and seniors.

Theatre Rhinoceros ★ Founded in 1977, this was America's first theater created to address GLBT themes and stories. It's still going strong. The theater is 1 block east of the 16th Street/Mission BART station. 2926 16th St. © **866/811-4111.** www.therhino.org. Tickets $15–$30.

Dance

Top traveling troupes like the Joffrey Ballet and American Ballet Theatre make regular appearances in San Francisco. Primary modern dance spaces include **Yerba Buena Center for the Arts,** 701 Mission St. (© 415/978-2787; www.ybca.org); the **Cowell Theater,** at Fort Mason Center, Marina Boulevard at Buchanan Street (© 415/345-7575; www.fortmason.org); and the **ODC Theatre,** 3153 17th St., at Shotwell Street in the Mission District (© 415/863-9834; www.odcdance.org). Check the local papers for schedules or contact the theater box offices for more information.

San Francisco Ballet ★★★ This venerable company (founded in 1933), is the oldest professional ballet company in the United States and is still regarded as one of the country's finest. Along with its beloved *Nutcracker,* it performs a varied repertoire of full-length contemporary and classic ballets. The Season generally runs February through May, with *Nutcracker* performances in December. War Memorial Opera House, 301 Van Ness Ave. (at Grove St.). © **415/865-2000** for tickets and information. www.sfballet.org. Tickets $18–$266.

COMEDY & CABARET

BATS Improv ★ Born out of the improvisational comedy craze that swept the U.S. in the '80s, this is one of the last West Coast companies standing. Their emphasis is on what's called "long form" improv, which means shows are geared towards creating a coherent story line, rather than just 2 minute bursts of weirdness (though the audience is encouraged to yell out ideas throughout the performance). On some nights, teams compete for improv trophies. Main Company shows are Fridays and Saturdays at 8pm; student performance ensemble shows are Sundays; the times varies each week. Reservations and discount tickets available through their website. Remaining tickets are sold

ATTEND A pirate DINNER PARTY

And no, you won't have to wear an eye patch. A group called Ghetto Gourmet (www.theghet.com) began by throwing what it calls a "pirate restaurant" at someone's apartment in Oakland. Today, much more popular, it calls itself a "wandering supperclub," which means that the chefs and locations change each time it goes on. These nomadic restaurants, which serve between 3 and 11 courses (really!), are a social trend that have been slowly growing in the Bay Area and elsewhere, despite their potential for hygienic issues. They garner their members by putting the word out on the Web, so you've got to belly up to the keyboard at home before filling your belly in SF. Their dedication to local ingredients and top methods make this a cool choice for genuine foodies. In fact, two clubs that started around the same time, Digs Bistro of Oakland and Radio Africa in San Francisco, are now a real restaurants. Don't think you can just roll up and attend; these events book up weeks ahead of time, so it's essential that you stay on top of the website for new announcements.

Other outfits do the same thing, but each has their own rules about membership, and they may balk if they hear you're not from the area. Still, it's worth a try: along with TheGhet (see above), try **Sub Culture Dining Experience** (www. thescdsf.com). Best may be **EatWith. com**, which is a service that helps visitors find locals to dine with, in their homes (for a small fee, usually $25, but sometimes up to $50 for more elaborate meals). Eat With meals will tend to be smaller: you, your host, and up to 6 others.

at the box office the night of the show. Performing at Bayfront Theatre at the Fort Mason Center, Building B no. 350, 3rd floor. ✆ **415/474-6776.** www.improv.org. Tickets $5–$22.

Beach Blanket Babylon ★★ The longest-running musical revue in America, this beloved cabaret-style show—playing since 1974—is pure San Francisco filled with bawdy humor, campy sexual flirtation, and a devil-may-care attitude. Everyone should see it at least once—as recently, Prince Charles and Camilla did.

The show's name doesn't describe what you'll see, except possibly the "Babylon" part; it's left over from its debut incarnation, when the theatre was filled with sand and audience members had their hands slapped with Coppertone lotion. Some 12,000 performances and 4.8 million tickets later, the show's toothless political commentary and mild sexual innuendo hit just the right spot for an evening out. Everything about it is pleasingly silly, from the silly plots to the songs (mostly radio standards in 1-minute bursts) and the impersonations (Honey Boo Boo made a recent appearance).

The show's main claim to fame, besides its longevity, are the huge wigs and hats, which are as tall as the proscenium will allow. The climactic bonnet, an illuminated and mechanized city skyline, requires a hidden scaffolding to support. Sophomoric? Absolutely. But few evening entertainments in America do it so cheerfully and so boisterously. Performances are Wednesday and Thursday at 8pm, Friday and Saturday at 6:30 and 9:30pm, and Sunday at 2 and 5pm, check the website for additional Tuesday shows in July. Club Fugazi, 678 Beach Blanket Babylon Blvd. (Green St. at Powell St.). ✆ **415/421-4222.** www.beachblanketbabylon.com. Tickets $25–$130. Bus: 9X, 20, 30, or 45. Cable car: Powell–Mason.

Cobb's Comedy Club ★★   Some of the hottest names—Sarah Silverman, David Spade, Tracy Morgan—perform here, and there's not a bad seat in the house. Cover varies by act and there's a two-drink minimum (the drinks, alas, are far weaker than the line-ups). Shows are held Wednesday, Thursday, and Sunday at 8pm, Friday and Saturday at 8 and 10:15pm. 915 Columbus Ave. (at Lombard St.). ✆ **415/928-4320.** www. cobbscomedyclub.com. Cover $15–$60. 2-beverage minimum.

Martuni's ★★   As you might imagine from the fun name, a tongue-in-cheek take on a slurred drink order, this cheerful bar serves from a long list of well-poured cocktails. Skilled singers and piano players hold sway in back, making it the best place in the city to catch casual, but classy cabaret-style performances. 4 Valencia St. (at Market St.). ✆ **415/241-0205.** Cover and hours vary.

Punch Line Comedy Club ★   This is the biggest comedy club in San Francisco so it often gets the biggest names (think Emo Philips or Louis C.K). Showcase night is Sunday, when 15 comics take the mic. Doors always open at 7pm and shows are Sunday through Thursday at 8pm, Friday and Saturday at 8 and 10pm (18 and over; two-drink minimum). 444 Battery St. (btw. Washington and Clay sts.), plaza level. ✆ **415/397-4337** or 397-7573 for recorded information. www.punchlinecomedyclub.com. Cover: Tues–Thurs $16; Fri–Sat $20; Sun $13. Prices are subject to change for more popular comics, maxing out at a price of $45. 2-beverage minimum.

THE CLUB & MUSIC SCENE

The greatest legacy from the 1960s is the city's continued tradition of live entertainment and music, which explains the great variety of clubs and music enjoyed by San Francisco. The hippest dance places are south of Market Street (SoMa), in former warehouses; the artsy bohemian scene centers are in the Mission; and the most popular cafe culture is still in North Beach.

Drinks at most bars, clubs, and cafes follow most big-city prices, ranging from about $7 to $14, unless otherwise noted.

Rock, Jazz, Blues & Dance Clubs

In addition to the following listings, see "Dance Clubs," below, for (usually) live, danceable rock.

Bimbo's 365 Club ★★   Perhaps the most stylish place to catch a musical performance, Bimbo's is lushly draped in curtains, evoking a 1940s dance hall. Open since 1951 (though in a different venue originally), it's one of those rare institutions that's still hip, probably because it books a wide variety of acts, usually all quite good. Grab tickets in advance at the box office, which is open Monday through Friday, 10am to 4pm. 1025 Columbus Ave. (at Chestnut St.). ✆ **415/474-0365.** www.bimbos365club.com.

The Boom Boom Room ★★   Opened by the venerated Mississippi bluesman John Lee Hooker, in the last years of his life, it wasn't just his business but his hangout. In the mid-20th century, Filmore street was the most important scene for West Coast blues, and it still has street cred as a blues hall (though it now does roots music, too, ranging from New Orleans funk to trance jazz). Open Tuesday through Sunday until 2am. 1601 Fillmore St. (at Geary Blvd.). ✆ **415/673-8000.** www.boomboomblues.com. Cover varies from free to $15.

Bottom of the Hill ★ One of the few places in town to offer a ton of all-ages shows, it's the savvy programming (and excellent sound system) here that brings in the crowds. You'll hear everything from indie punk to rockabilly to hard funk, all topnotch. Doors open nightly around 8:30pm; bar closes a tad before 2am. Kitchen open until midnight most nights. 1233 17th St. (at Missouri St.). ⓒ **415/621-4455.** www.bottomofthehill. com. Cover $8–$50.

Cafe du Nord ★★ A valued indie-band lounge, Café du Nord was built in 1907, and during Prohibition it was known as a down-and-dirty speakeasy. It still retains many of its Victorian touches, including lots of moody wood walls and a 40-foot-long mahogany bar. The music picks here are mixed, with Café du Nord hosting visiting bluegrass artists, local singer songwriters and R&B bands and even punk groups. 2170 Market St. (at Sanchez St.). ⓒ **415/861-5016.** www.cafedunord.com. Cover $8–$15. Food $5–$9.

The Fillmore ★ Though concert halls around the nation are now called the Fillmore, this is the original. It's a treasure of San Francisco history. In the 1960s it was the heartbeat of San Francisco counter-culture, where legendary promoter Bill Graham booked the Grateful Dead, Jefferson Airplane, Janis Joplin and Led Zeppelin. While it's no longer a crucible of what's next, it's still an excellent place to see a show and small enough (1250 capacity for most shows) that you can stand in the back, near the bar, and still be satisfied. 1805 Geary Blvd. (at Fillmore St.). ⓒ **415/346-6000.** www.thefillmore. com. Tickets $23–$62.

Great American Music Hall ★★ Acts and audiences alike dig this saloon-like ballroom (opened in 1907). It's sized just right for listening to music and with its frescoed ceilings and marble columns, the beauty of the place sometimes outshines the music. But not often, because the programming tends to be solid. Over the years, acts who have played here have ranged from Duke Ellington and Sarah Vaughan to Arctic Monkeys, the Radiators, and She Wants Revenge. All shows are all ages (ages 6 and up) so you can bring your family, too. You can purchase tickets online or over the phone (ⓒ **888/233-0449**) for a $4 to $5 service fee. Or download a form from the website and fax it to ⓒ **415/885-5075** with your Visa or MasterCard info; there is a service fee of $2 per ticket. Stop by the box office to purchase tickets directly the night of the performance for no charge (assuming the show isn't sold out), or buy them online at www.gamhtickets.com or Tickets.com (ⓒ **800/225-2277**). 859 O'Farrell St. (btw. Polk and Larkin sts.). ⓒ **415/885-0750.** www.musichallsf.com. Ticket prices and starting times vary; call or check website for individual show information.

Ruby Skye ★ If you can name DJ's as if they were mainstream celebrities, this is the club for you. You'll appreciate its colossal size, and the massive crowd that come to writhe on the floor most nights of the week. Ruby Skye is set in a beautiful Art Nouveau space, dating to its original incarnation as an 1890's theater, invokes a pleasing baroque energy, even if some of the details have been obliterated by a misguided renovation. Be sure to call or check the website to make sure there isn't a private event taking place. 420 Mason St. (btw. Geary and Post sts.). ⓒ **415/693-0777.** www.rubyskye.com. Cover $10–$25.

SFJAZZ ★ As the only structure in the country built just for jazz, this brand new, $64 million dollar building is a must-visit for music fans. Yes, it's mostly jazz, though gospel brunches to Ethiopian blues bands have also been on the bill. I'd be lying if I said I was a huge jazz fan, but actually loved the evening I recently spent at this new cool-cat pad. We started with dinner and drinks at the full-service cafe by Charles Phan

DRINKING & SMOKING laws

The drinking age is 21 in California, and bartenders can ask for a valid photo ID, no matter how old you look. Some clubs demand identification at the door, so it's a good idea to carry it at all times. Once you get through the door, however, forget about cigarettes—smoking is banned in all California bars. The law is generally enforced and though San Francisco's police department has not made bar raids a priority, people caught smoking in bars can be—and occasionally are—ticketed and fined. Music clubs strictly enforce the law and will ask you to leave if you light up. If you must smoke, do it outside. Also, the dreaded last call for alcohol usually rings out at around 1:30am, since state laws prohibit the sale of alcohol from 2 to 6am every morning. A very important word of warning: Driving under the influence of alcohol is a serious crime in California, with jail time for the first offense. You are likely to be legally intoxicated (.08% blood alcohol) if you have had as little as one alcoholic drink an hour. When in doubt, take a taxi.

of Slanted Door (p. 77) fame, and then sat back in our seats to enjoy. There are no bad seats in the house, each one has great sound and a great view. Last minute tickets are often available. 201 Franklin St. (at Fell St.). ℂ **866/920-5299.** www.sfjazz.org. Tickets range from $5 to $200. Bart: Civic Center.

Yoshi's Jazz Club ★★   Rarely does jazz get such a grand setting (28,000-square feet!) as this club, which houses not one, but two sterling venues. The front is more of a walk-in scene, the back more for concerts, but for 3 decades this has been the jazz premier club in town. It'll be interesting to see if SF Jazz cuts into its cache (or programming oomph). But then SF Jazz doesn't have an on-site sushi chef. 1330 Fillmore St. (at Eddy St.). ℂ **415/655-5600.** www.yoshis.com.

THE BAR SCENE

Finding your kind of bar in San Francisco has a lot to do with which district it's in. The following is a *very* general description of what types of bars you're likely to find throughout the city:

- o **Marina/Cow Hollow** bars attract a yuppie post-collegiate crowd.
- o The opposite of the Marina/Cow Hollow crowd frequents the **Mission District** haunts.
- o **Haight-Ashbury** caters to eclectic neighborhood cocktailers and beer-lovers.
- o The **Tenderloin,** though still dangerous at night (take a taxi), is now a new hot spot for serious mixologists.
- o Tourists mix with conventioneers at **downtown** pubs.
- o **North Beach** serves all types, mostly tourists.
- o **Russian Hill**'s Polk Street has become the new Marina/Cow Hollow scene.
- o The **Castro** caters to gay locals and tourists.
- o **SoMa** offers an eclectic mix from sports bars to DJ lounges.

The following is a list of a few of San Francisco's more interesting bars. Unless otherwise noted, these bars do not have cover charges.

cocktails WITH A VIEW

Harry Denton's Starlight Room
★★★ The namesake here isn't some socialite dandy who was kicking up his spats. He's alive, spunky, and not even that old—he just decorates and runs his romantic aerie as if he expects Joan Blondell and Dick Powell to stroll in any minute. There are few better places to raise a stylish drink with an unspoiled panorama of one of the world's greatest cities. Most stay for dinner and dancing, but it's possible to simply come and enjoy a drink at the bar (though on nights that there's live music, you'll pay a cover charge). *Tip:* Come dressed to impress (no casual jeans, open-toed shoes for men, or sneakers), or you'll be turned away at the door. Atop the Sir Francis Drake Hotel, 450 Powell St., btw Post and Sutter St., 21st floor. (C) 415/395-8595. www.harrydenton.com. Cover $10. Tues–Thurs 6pm–midnight, Fri–Sat 6pm–1:30am, Sun 11am–3:30pm.

Top of the Mark ★★★ A 19th-floor bar doesn't sound like much, but considering in this case it's in a building that's already atop Nob Hill, and adding the fact that it's one of the most famous bars in the country, both the view and the mood are high. Floor-to-ceiling windows take in the kind of panorama that makes people want to move to this city: Golden Gate Bridge, Coit Tower, Alcatraz, and beyond, all in a smart, upper-class setting. The operators regularly close the space for private parties, so call ahead to make sure it's open on the night you wish to go. From Tuesday to Saturday, musical acts are booked—mostly jazz or other styles that make nice background—and covers are surprisingly cheap. Dinner is pricey, so we'd recommend just coming by for the tipple. In the Mark Hopkins InterContinental, 1 Nob Hill Place (btw. California and Mason sts.). (C) 415/616-6199. www.topofthemark.com. Cover $15. Mon–Thurs and Sun 5pm–midnight, Fri–Sat 4pm–1am.

SoMa, Downtown, Tenderloin & FiDi

Bar Agricole ★★★ In mixology circles the name Thad Vogler carries major weight. He's the drink master behind this chic bar, which has lighting that makes even the most haggard look dewy, an elegant skylight, a heated patio for all-weather outdoor tippling and a swell SoMa location. As for the cocktails, they're created from hard-to-source small batch liquors; the bar food is darn good too, a mix of Northern European and Californian cuisine. 355 11th St. (near Folsom St.). (C) **415/355-9400.** www.baragricole.com. Mon–Thurs 6–10pm, Fri–Sat 5:30–11pm, Sun 11am–2pm.

Bourbon & Branch ★★ Meet San Francisco's modern day speakeasy. Yup, you have to present a password to get in, though that's not to keep the police away. The folks behind Bourbon & Branch are determined to create an adult atmosphere, which means only those who have reservations are admitted, so that the place doesn't get too crowded. Those who get in the unmarked door (look for the address) choose from an extensive and creative cocktail list, sitting in one of the sexiest lounges in town. There's even a speakeasy within the speakeasy (even harder to get into!) called Wilson & Wilson, which offers a $30 tasting flight of cocktails. 501 Jones St. (at O'Farrell St.). (C) **415/346-1735.** www.bourbonandbranch.com. Daily 6pm–2am.

Edinburgh Castle ★ An oldie but a goodie (founded in 1958), this Scottish pub has the finest selection of single-malt scotches in the city as well as a number of unusual British ales on tap. Beloved of ex-pats (and Britophiles), the decor is filled with U.K. brit-a-brac, and the bar menu includes—what else—fish and chips. "The Castle" is also notable for the author readings and performances it hosts each week, some of which have featured famous writers. 950 Geary St. (btw. Polk and Larkin sts.). ℰ **415/885-4074.** www.castlenews.com. Mon–Fri 5pm–2am, Sat–Sun 1pm–2am.

Maxfield's Pied Piper Bar ★★★ It's not an inexpensive outing, but seeing as it's one of the most famous bars in the city, you should at least raise a ginger ale at this storied watering hole where one of the city's greatest art treasures, a mural of the Pied Piper by Maxfield Parrish, presides over the woody, dusky bar. (After a fight it's back where it should be; see p. 82 for more on that). Bartenders know how to mix a classic drink here, but I hope they also know jujitsu, because the painting behind them is now valued at between $3-$5 million. In the Palace Hotel, 2 New Montgomery St. at Market; ℰ **415/512-1111.** www.maxfields-restaurant.com. Mon–Fri 11:30am–midnight, Sat 11am–midnight, Sun 10am–midnight.

Terroir Natural Wine Merchant ★★★ With its rustic wooden beams and a library loft—not to mention a selection of natural wines to rival any Napa or Sonoma store—this is the oenophile's Shangri-la. Sit at the bar and get an education about the art, science, and soul of the winemaking process. Owners Luke, Billy, and Dagan will be happy to tell you everything you ever wanted to know about wine. Not in the mood for a lesson and prefer to simply relax? Head upstairs to the lounge and flip through a book, or play a game (board games are available), while you savor the nectar of the gods. Add in cheese and charcuterie and you probably won't want to return to your hotel. 1116 Folsom St. (btw. 7th and 8th sts.). ℰ **415/558-9946.** www.terroirsf.com. Mon–Thurs 2pm–midnight, Fri–Sat noon–2am, Sun 2–9pm.

Fisherman's Wharf, Russian Hill, Nob Hill & North Beach

Buena Vista Café ★ It's considered a modern tradition to visit Buena Vista Cafe to order a $7.25 Irish Coffee (coffee and whiskey), which was conceived here in 1952 by a local travel writer (hurrah!). This punch-packing quaff lures hordes of tourists before they wobble toward the cable car turnaround across the street. You may not want to hear how the bartender gets the cream to float—it's aged for 2 days before use. Some 2,000 are served each day in high season, which means you will probably have to wait for a table on a weekend afternoon (better, probably, to come at night; it's open until 2am). These beverages are indeed delicious, and the publike setting is classic without being snooty. 2765 Hyde St. (at Beach St.). ℰ **415/474-5044.** www.thebuenavista.com. Daily 9am–2am.

The Saloon ★ A true dive, this is supposedly the oldest bar in the city and it certainly looks (and smells) like it. Floors are but worn planks, staff are grizzled and hairy, and the story goes that this place managed to survive the conflagration of 1906 by offering the firefighters free booze. There's live music every night—mostly blues and jazz. Don't come expecting a cruisey scene; come for down-and-dirty music and cheap whiskey. 1232 Grant Ave. (at Columbus St.). ℰ **415/989-7666.** Music cover $5–$15 Fri–Sat. Daily noon–2am.

The Tonga Room & Hurricane Bar ★★★ This sublime and one-of-a-kind club has my heart for being utterly ridiculous. Every half-hour in this dim, Polynesian-themed fantasia, decorated with rocks and 12-foot tikis, lightening strikes, thunder rolls out and rain falls above the pond in the middle of it all (once the hotel's indoor pool). Of course, it's a gimmick and naturally, you'll pay a lot for a cocktail here, but it's fun anyway. During happy hour (Wed–Fri, 5–7pm), there's a list of strong, tropical drinks sold at a discount, and if you throw down just $10 you get unleashed on a heat lamp lit buffet of egg rolls and other grub, served beneath the rigging on the deck of an imaginary ship. There's a full menu, too, but people tend to take advantage of that later in the night, when musicians take the small stage in the middle of the room. In the Fairmont Hotel, 950 Mason St. (at California St.). ☎ **415/772-5278.** www.tongaroom.com. Wed–Thurs and Sun 5–11:30pm, Fri–Sat 5pm–12:30am.

Vesuvio ★★★ A generous pour, a trinket-stuffed decor, a cozy vibe, and a friendly attitude (despite its illustrious history) all make Vesuvio a go-to North Beach drinkery. It was opened in 1948, just in time to catch all the dissolute Beat writers as they staggered in and out of City Lights, located directly across Jack Kerouac Alley from its front door. In fact, this is where Kerouac spent many a night toxifying his liver. I guess that makes this bar a monument to alcoholism—how many bars wear that rep with honor? If you can get a table upstairs, do, because it overlooks the bar below, making it prime for people-watching, and it's romantic and secluded, making it prime for nuzzling. 255 Columbus Ave. (at Broadway). ☎ **415/362-3370.** www.vesuvio.com. Daily 6am–2am.

The Marina, Cow's Hollow

The Ice Cream Bar ★★ Nightlife doesn't get much more playful than it does at this ice cream emporium/bar, where yes, you can get alcohol or sweet treats or mix them together. Intrepid mixologists are at the helm here and they've created seriously delicious recipes for their dessert drinks. For those not into sweets, they also serve a wide selection of beer, wines, and artisanal cocktails (made with liquors and syrups the staff infuse on site). As for the look of the place, it's classic ice cream parlor, down to the 1930's era soda pumps that are still in use. 815 Cole St. (btw Frederick and Carl St.). ☎ **415/742-4932.** www.icecreambarsf.com. Mon–Thurs and Sun noon–10pm, Fri–Sat noon–11pm.

Nectar Wine Lounge ★ Few places in the city, or in North America for that matter, have as copious a menu when it comes to wine: 50 are available by the glass (from all around the globe) and a good 800 by the bottle. Just as impressive are the handsome crowd this hip, industrial-chic watering hole draws. It's a nice place to linger. 3330 Steiner St. (at Chestnut St.). ☎ **415/345-1377.** www.nectarwinelounge.com. Mon–Wed 5–10:30pm, Thurs–Sat 5pm–midnight, Sun 5–10pm.

Perry's★ Made famous by *Tales of the City,* this is not the crazy pick-up scene it was in the book. Still, locals and visitors alike enjoy chilling at the dark mahogany bar. An attached dining room offers up all sorts of simple food (think burgers or grilled fish) should you be feeling peckish. 1944 Union St. (at Laguna St.). ☎ **415/922-9022.** www.perryssf.com. Mon–Wed 7:30am–10pm, Thurs–Sat 7:30am–11pm, Sun 8:30am–10pm.

Press Club ★ You come here if you don't think you'll make it to Wine Country on this trip. Calling itself "urban wine tasting bar" the huge space features eight separate bars which are often manned by reps from regional Northern California wineries (the list of wineries rotates and these sellers are always happy to ship home cases for you, should you enjoy your glass). Gourmet small bites (including Cowgirl Creamery cheese plates), elbow room, and a mellow soundtrack make the Press Club quite popular among the 35-plus crowd. 20 Yerba Buena Lane (near Market St.). 📞 **415/744-5000.** www. pressclubsf.com. Mon-Thurs 4pm-11pm, Fri-Sat 2pm-midnight, Sun 2pm-9pm.

The Mission & Haight–Ashbury

Alembic ★★★ This tiny bar has become known for the skill of its bartenders, heavily tattooed gents who mix up wonderfully creative concoctions like the "Vasco de Gama" which blends Islay Scotch and Buffalo Trace bourbon with an apple syrup spiked with garam masala spices. They also do well by such classics as Manhattan's and Old Fashioned, plus the bar food is darn plush (house cured salmon—yum!). 1725 Haight (at Cole St.). 📞 **415/660-0822.** www.alembicbar.com. Daily noon-2am.

Shotwell's ★★ Don't believe the barflies who will tell you that the name of this place comes from the bullet holes in the back bar here. Nobody quite seems to know the origin of the bullet holes (the name comes from the nearby street), which probably isn't surprising considering this watering hole was founded in 1891. Today, it's a mellow (no more gun fights!) place to hang, with a pool table, pinball machines, and a wide selection of beers from across the globe. 3349 20th St. (near Shotwell). 📞 **415/648-4104.** www.shotwellsbar.com. Daily 4:30pm-2am.

Zeitgeist ★★ A dive bar that has been claimed and overtaken by energetic hipsters, Zeitgeist serves more than 20 types of German beer, most of them dead cheap. Come in good weather if you can, because the mellow beer-garden vibe is half the appeal. Don't miss the bloody mary. Cash only. 199 Valencia St. (at Duboce Ave.). 📞 **415/255-7505.** Daily 9am-2am.

GAY & LESBIAN BARS & CLUBS

Check the free weeklies such as the *San Francisco Bay Guardian* and *San Francisco Weekly* for listings of events and happenings around town. The *Bay Area Reporter* is a gay paper with comprehensive listings, including a weekly community calendar. All these papers are free and distributed weekly on Wednesday or Thursday, and can be found stacked at the corners of 18th and Castro streets and Ninth and Harrison streets, as well as in bars, bookshops, and other stores around town. See "LGBT Travelers," in chapter 12, beginning on p. 238, for further details on gay-themed guidebooks. Also check out the rather homely but very informative site titled "Queer Things to Do in the San Francisco Bay Area" at www.sfqueer.com, or www.gaywired.com for more gay happenings.

Badlands ★ Aaaah to be young. The barely legal Abercrombie crowd comes here to dance under the giant disco ball and suck back happy hour two-for-one cocktails. Videos blast the music played by the DJ while lights flash. It's one noisy, energetic party filled with a crowd that wants to meet and greet. 4121 18th St. (at Castro). 📞 **415/626-9320.** www.badlands-sf.com. Happy hour Mon–Sat 3–8pm.

Diva's Nightclub and Bar ★★ Located in the Tenderloin, all is not as it appears at this transgender-friendly dance and drag bar. Want to go back to school? Naughty schoolgirls appear each Wednesday at 10pm. The Diva Darlings take center stage each Thursday at 10pm. With dance floors, regular shows, and numerous bars, this three-story club filled with beautiful girlz can best be described as a party palace. 1081 Post St. (btw Polk and Larkin Sts.). 📞 **415/928-6006.** www.divassf.com. Open 6am–2am.

In the mood for drag queens with a slice of quiche? Harry Denton's Starlight Room (p. 184) hosts a weekly **Sunday's a Drag** brunch performance, where divas perform female impersonation acts and lip-sync Broadway tunes. The "brunch with an attitude" has two seatings every Sunday at noon and 2:30pm. The price of brunch is $45 per person, which includes entertainment, brunch, coffee, tea, and fresh juices. For reservations call © **415/395-8595** or e-mail reservations@harrydenton.com.

440 Castro ★★   A warm and fuzzy bear bar for the Levi's and leather crowd, most cruise between the video bar downstairs to the dark intimate bar up a few stairs in the back. Always popular, Monday is Underwear Night; Tuesday features $2 beers all day and night. No matter the day, drinks are always strong and cheap. Regular contests like the Battle of the Bulge, are a great way to meet new friends. 440 Castro St. (btw 17th and 18th). © **415/621-8732.** www.the440.com. Open daily until 2am.

The Lexington Club ★★★   San Francisco's premier lesbian bar features a full roster of events, an always-busy pool table, cheap drinks and a chill atmosphere. For those on the prowl, it's also commended for having an "eye candy" clientele (and bartenders). 3464 19th St. (btw. Lexington and Valencia sts.). © **415/863-2052.** www.lexington club.com. Daily 3pm-2am.

The Lookout ★   With two walls of glass and a massive deck looking down on the heart of the Castro, this karaoke bar is a good place to dance and belt out your best rendition of "I Will Survive." Nightly DJ's and a weekly drag show add to the excitement. If all that dancing and drag leaves you hungry, you don't have to lose your spot in line for the karaoke machine; the Lookout serves surprisingly good food. 3600 16th St. (at Market St.). © **415/431-0306.** www.lookoutsf.com. Open daily until 2am. Kitchen closes at 9:30pm and is closed on Tuesdays.

Twin Peaks Tavern ★★   Known locally as the gay "Cheers," Twin Peaks was the first gay bar in the country to unblock the floor to ceiling windows and let the world see just what was going on inside. It sits at the corner of Market and Castro, the true heart of the gay community, though otherwise you probably wouldn't even know this was a gay bar. In a culture that often worships youth and beauty, Twin Peaks is an oldie but goodie—and tends to attract an older crowd. The 1880's building survived the earthquake and recently gained historic landmark status. 401 Castro St. (at Market St.). © **415/864-9470.** www.twinpeakstavern.com. Hours vary, so call.

PROFESSIONAL SPORTS TEAMS

The Bay Area's sports scene isn't just about the Giants; it includes several major professional franchises. Check the local newspapers' sports sections and team websites for daily listings of local events. Along with each teams' website, www.tickets.com and www.stubhub.com are two good places to hunt for tickets.

AT&T Park ★★ If you're a baseball fan, you'll definitely want to schedule a visit to the magnificent AT&T Park, home of the San Francisco Giants and hailed by the media as one of the finest ballparks in America. From April through October, an often sellout crowd of 40,800 fans packs the $319-million ballpark—which has a smaller, more intimate feel than Candlestick Park (where the 49ers play) as well as prime views of San Francisco Bay—and roots for the National League's Giants.

During the season, regular tickets to see this World Series winning team play can be expensive and hard to come by (www.sfgiants.com). Bleacher and standing room only seats are a cheaper option. If you can't get bleacher seats, you can always join the "knothole gang" at the Portwalk (located behind right field) to catch a free glimpse of the game through cutout portholes into the ballpark. In the spirit of sharing, Portwalk peekers are encouraged to take in only an inning or two before giving way to fellow fans.

One guaranteed way to get into the ballpark is to take a **guided tour of AT&T Park** and go behind the scenes where you'll see the press box, the dugout, the visitor's clubhouse, a luxury suite, and more. All tours run daily at 10:30am and 12:30pm. Ticket prices are $20 for adults, $15 for seniors (55+), $10 for kids 12 and under, free for active military (with ID) and kids 2 and under. There are no tours on game days, and limited tours on the day of night games. To buy tickets online log onto www.sfgiants.com, click on "AT&T Park" at the bottom, and then "AT&T Park Tours" from the drop-down list. At the southeast corner of SoMa at the south end of the Embarcadero (bounded by King, Second, and Third sts.). ✆ **415/972-2000.** www.sfgiants.com. Bus: 10, 30, 45, or 47. Metro: N-line.

Major League Baseball

The American League's **Oakland Athletics** (www.athletics.mlb.com) play across the bay in Oakland at the Coliseum, Hegenberger Road exit from I-880. The stadium holds over 50,000 spectators and is accessible through BART's Coliseum station.

Pro Basketball

For now, the **Golden State Warriors** (www.nba.com/warriors) play at the ORACLE Arena, a 19,200-seat facility at 7000 Coliseum Way in Oakland. In 2017, they plan to move to new waterfront digs in the city close to AT&T Park. The season runs November through April, and most games start at 7:30pm.

Pro Football

Beginning in 2014, the **San Francisco 49ers** (www.sf49ers.com) will play at their new Levi's Stadium in Santa Clara—the 2016 Superbowl will be held here. Football season runs August through December. Tickets sell out early in the season but are available at higher prices through ticket agents beforehand and from "scalpers." The 49ers' arch enemies, the **Oakland Raiders** (www.raiders.com), play at the Oakland-Alameda Coliseum, off the I-880 freeway (Nimitz).

DAY TRIPS FROM SAN FRANCISCO

The City by the Bay is, without question, captivating, but don't let it ensnare you to the point of ignoring its environs. The surrounding region offers beautiful natural areas such as Mount Tamalpais, Muir Woods, and Angel Island; scenic waterfront communities such as Carmel, Monterey, Tiburon, and Sausalito; vibrant neighboring cities such as Oakland and Berkeley; and some darn good wine in Napa and Sonoma. In fact, the last is such a draw, we've devoted an entire chapter to wine country (see chapter 11). Whether you use public transportation, rent a car for the day, or take a guided tour, here are a few insider tips for a great day away from the city.

10 BERKELEY

10 miles NE of San Francisco

The "Summer of Love" has long turned to autumn, but it's still fun to visit the iconic University of California at Berkeley and its surrounding town. Never as loopy as portrayed in the media—Berkeley has had 22 Nobel prize winners over the years (eight are active staff)—today, there's still some hippie idealism in the air, but the radicals have aged. The 1960s are present only in tie-dye and paraphernalia shops. The biggest change the town is facing is yuppification; as San Francisco's rent and property prices soar out of the range of the average person's budget, everyone with less than a small fortune is seeking shelter elsewhere, and Berkeley is one of the top picks (although Oakland is quickly becoming a favorite, too). Berkeley is a lively city teeming with all types of people, a beautiful campus, vast parks, great shopping, and some incredible restaurants.

Getting There

The Berkeley **Bay Area Rapid Transit (BART)** station is 2 blocks from the university. The fare from San Francisco is less than $4 one-way. Call ⓒ **511** or visit www.bart.gov for detailed trip information and fares.

If you are coming **by car** from San Francisco, take the Bay Bridge (go during the evening commute, and you'll think Los Angeles traffic is a breeze). Follow I-80 east to the University Avenue exit, and follow University Avenue until you hit the campus. Parking is tight, so either leave your car at the Sather Gate parking lot at Telegraph Avenue and Durant Street, or expect to fight for a spot.

What to See & Do

Your main reason for coming is the free campus tour, which departs Mondays through Saturdays at 10am, and Sundays at 1pm from the **Visitor Services center,** 101 Sproul Hall (*(C)* **510/642-5215;** www.berkeley.edu/visitors), Reservations are required for these tours, so call in advance.

I strongly suggest taking one of these, because they take you into buildings where you otherwise couldn't go without a student I.D. The tours, which are led by trained students, are heavily used by prospective scholars, so in springtime your group may swell to 200 and your guide may dwell rather tediously on the school's rivalry with Stanford, but everyone is welcome, and you'll get heaps of fascinating historical information about the educational institution that fomented some of the strongest protests of the 1960s and 1970s. There are tons of milestones that Cal is responsible for, including the discovery of vitamins B, E, and K, plutonium, uranium 238, and the stumpy London plane tree, a hybrid that you'll only see here and in places in San Francisco.

I consider the grounds, which are handsomely traversed by the quiet Strawberry Creek, as one of America's quintessential college campuses: green, open, and interrupted by inhumanly blocky campus buildings you'd better pray you don't get lost in. You'll see **Le Conte Hall,** where the first atom splitters did their work (keep your eyes peeled for parking signs that read, in total seriousness, "Reserved for NL"—meaning Nobel Laureate. What kind of a car was in that space? I saw a Toyota Prius. You know the parking situation is grim if you need a Nobel Prize to get a space.) The **Doe & Moffitt Library** doesn't allow public access to the 10 million books in its stacks, but its lobby areas, lined with glass cases filled with priceless manuscripts, is open to all. In a reading room upstairs, you'll also find Emanuel Leutze's 1854 *Washington Rallying the Troops at Monmouth,* which was intended to be a companion piece to his *Washington Crossing the Delaware* (now at New York's Met).

Your tour will end with a discussion of the messy student protests for freedom of speech, in 1969, that resulted in the death of a student protester. Although the university is renowned for the radicalism of its students, that label is mostly left over from the 1960s.

UC Berkeley has two noteworthy museums. The first is the **Lawrence Hall of Science ★** (east of campus at 1 Centennial Drive, *(C)* **510/642-5132;** www.lawrencehallofscience.org). Kids can touch and learn at this hands-on museum. Open daily from 10am to 5pm. Admission is $12 for adults; $9 for seniors 62 and over, students, and children 7 to 18; $6 for children 3 to 6; and free for kids 2 and under. The second is the **UC Berkeley Art Museum ★,** 2626 Bancroft Way, between College and Telegraph avenues (*(C)* **510/642-0808;** www.bampfa.berkeley.edu), is open Wednesday through Sunday from 11am to 5pm. Admission is $10 for adults; $7 for seniors, non-UCB students, visitors with disabilities, and children 17 and under; and $6 for UCB students. This museum features paintings, a sculpture garden, a library, and a film study center.

PARKS

Unbeknownst to many travelers, Berkeley has some of the most extensive and beautiful parks around. If you want to wear the kids out or enjoy hiking, swimming, sniffing roses, or just getting a breath of California air, head for **Tilden Park ★,** where you'll find plenty of flora and fauna, hiking trails, an old steam train and merry-go-round, a farm and nature area for kids, and a chilly tree-encircled lake. The East Bay's public transit system, **AC Transit** (*C* **511;** www.actransit.org), runs the air-conditioned no. 67 bus line around the edge of the park on weekdays and all the way to the Tilden Visitors Center on Saturdays and Sundays. Call *C* **888/327-2757** or see www.ebparks.org for further information.

SHOPPING

If you're itching to exercise your credit cards, head to one of two areas: **College Avenue** from Dwight Way to the Oakland border overflows with eclectic boutiques, antiques shops, book stores, and restaurants. The other, more upscale option is **Fourth Street,** in west Berkeley, 2 blocks north of the University Avenue exit. This shopping strip is the perfect place to go on a sunny morning. Grab a cup of java and outstanding pancakes and scones at **Bette's Ocean View Diner,** 1807 Fourth St. (*C* **510/644-3932**). Read the paper at a patio table, and then hit the **Crate & Barrel Outlet,** 1785 Fourth St., between Hearst and Virginia streets (*C* **510/528-5500**). Prices are 30 percent to 70 percent off retail. It's open daily from 10am to 7pm. This area also boasts small, wonderful stores crammed with imported and locally made housewares.

Where to Eat

East Bay dining is a relaxed alternative to San Francisco's gourmet scene. There are plenty of ambitious Berkeley restaurants and, unlike in San Francisco, plenty of parking, provided you're not near the campus. If you want to dine student style, eat on campus Monday through Friday. Buy something at a sidewalk stand or in the building directly behind the Student Union. All the university eateries have both indoor and outdoor seating. Telegraph Avenue has an array of small ethnic restaurants, cafes, and sandwich shops. Follow the students: If the place is crowded, it's good, supercheap, or both.

If you are into organic, it doesn't get much better than **Chez Panisse** ★★★ (1517 Shawtuck Ave.; *C* **510/548-5525** (restaurant), and *C* **510/548-5049** (cafe); www.chezpanisse.com), the original farm-to-table concept of Alice Waters. This restaurant shaped a generation of chefs and is still going strong. Carnivores will love **Café Rouge** (1782 Fourth St., *C* **510/525-1440;** www.caferouge.net), the Mediterranean darling of chef-owner, Marsha McBride, formerly of Zuni Café.

OAKLAND

10 miles E of San Francisco

Although it's less than a dozen miles from San Francisco, Oakland is worlds apart from its sister city across the bay. Originally little more than a cluster of ranches and farms, Oakland exploded in size and stature practically overnight, when the last mile of transcontinental railroad track was laid down. Major shipping ports soon followed and, to this day, Oakland remains one of the busiest industrial ports on the West Coast. The price for economic success, however, is Oakland's lowbrow reputation as a predominantly working-class city; it is forever in the shadow of chic San Francisco. However, as the City by the Bay has become crowded and expensive in the past few years, Oakland has experienced a rush of new residents, businesses, and quality restaurants. As a result, "Oaktown" is in the midst of a renaissance, and its future continues to look brighter. A 2012 *New York Times* ranking of Oakland as the fifth most desirable destination to visit in the *world,* just above Tokyo, raised some eyebrows in San

San Francisco Bay Area

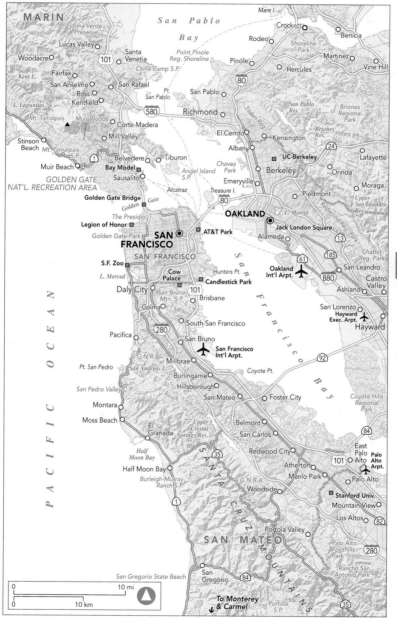

Francisco—but the city's profile is undoubtedly on the rise. Rent a sailboat on Lake Merritt, stroll along the waterfront, see a show at the Paramount Theatre, explore the fantastic Oakland Museum—they're all great reasons to hop the bay and spend a fog-free day exploring one of California's largest and most ethnically diverse cities.

Getting There

BART connects San Francisco and Oakland through one of the longest underwater transit tunnels in the world. Fares range from $3 to $4 one-way, depending on your station of origin; children 4 and under ride free. BART trains operate Monday through Friday from 4am to midnight, Saturday from 6am to midnight, and Sunday from 8am to midnight. Exit at the 12th Street station for downtown Oakland. Call ✆ **511** or visit www.bart.gov for more info.

By car from San Francisco, take I-80 across the San Francisco–Oakland Bay Bridge and follow signs to downtown Oakland. Exit at Grand Avenue South for the Lake Merritt area. *Note:* Make sure you have a map of Oakland or GPS device—you do not want to get lost in Oakland and end up in a bad neighborhood.

For a calendar of events in Oakland, contact the **Oakland Convention and Visitors Bureau,** 463 11th St., Oakland, CA 94607 (✆ **510/839-9000;** www.oaklandcvb.com). The city sponsors eight free-guided tours, including African-American Heritage. Tours are Wednesdays and Saturdays at 10am. Call ✆ **510/238-3234** or visit www2.oakland net.com, and click on "free walking tours" found at the bottom left.

Downtown Oakland lies between Grand Avenue on the north, I-980 on the west, Inner Harbor on the south, and Lake Merritt on the east. Between these landmarks are three BART stations (12th St., 19th St., and Lake Merritt), City Hall, the Oakland Museum, Jack London Square, and several other sights.

What to See & Do

Lake Merritt is one of Oakland's prime tourist attractions, along with Jack London Square (see below). Three and a half miles in circumference, the tidal lagoon was bridged and dammed in the 1860s and is now a wildlife refuge that is home to flocks of migrating ducks, herons, and geese. The 122-acre **Lakeside Park,** a popular place to picnic, feed the ducks, and escape the fog, surrounds the lake on three sides. Visit www2.oaklandnet.com for more info. To get out on the lake, rent a boat from the **Lake Merritt Boating Center** ★ (✆ **510/238-2196**), in Lakeside Park along the north shore. Or, perhaps, take a gondola ride with **Gondola Servizio** (✆ **510/663-6603;** www.gondolaservizio.com). Experienced gondoliers will serenade you, June through October, as you glide across the lake; prices start at $40 for two, depending on the time and gondola style.

Another site worth visiting is Oakland's **Paramount Theatre** ★, 2025 Broadway (✆ **510/893-2300;** www.paramounttheatre.com), an outstanding National Historic Landmark and example of Art Deco architecture and decor. Built in 1931 and authentically restored in 1973, it's the city's main performing-arts center, hosting big-name performers like Smokey Robinson and Alicia Keys. Guided tours of the 3,000-seat theater are given the first and third Saturday morning of each month, excluding holidays. No reservations are necessary; just show up at 10am at the box office entrance on 21st Street at Broadway. The tour lasts 2 hours, cameras are allowed, and admission is $5. Children must be at least 10 years old.

THE USS POTOMAC: FDR's floating white house

It took the Potomac Association's hundreds of volunteers more than 12 years—at a cost of $5 million—to restore the 165-foot presidential yacht *Potomac*, President Franklin D. Roosevelt's beloved "Floating White House." Now a proud and permanent memorial berthed at the Port of Oakland's FDR Pier at Jack London Square, the revitalized *Potomac* is open to the public for dockside tours, as well as historic cruises on the San Francisco Bay. The dockside tours are available Wednesday, Friday, and Sunday from 11am to 3pm mid-January through mid-December. Admission is $10 for ages 13 to 59, $8 for seniors age 60 and over, and free for children age 12 and under. See the website for information about the various historic cruises.

Hours and cruise schedules are subject to change, so be sure to call the Potomac Visitor Center before arriving. Tickets for the Dockside Tour can be purchased at the Visitor Center upon arrival; tickets for the History Cruise can be purchased in advance via **Ticketweb** (*C* **866/468-3399**; www.ticketweb.com) or by calling the **Potomac Visitor Center** (*C* **510/627-1215**; www.uss potomac.org). The Visitor Center is located at 540 Water St., at the corner of Clay and Water streets adjacent to the FDR Pier at the north end of Jack London Square.

The **Oakland Museum of California,** 1000 Oak St. (*C* **510/238-2200;** www. museumca.org) is a favorite with Bay Area fourth grade school children studying the history our fair state. While the Galleries of Art and Natural Science feature the expected paintings and specimens, I particularly like the Gallery of History, which focuses on "Coming to California," with interesting displays of Native American baskets, the Spanish influence, and, of course, the Gold Rush. Upcoming exhibits include "Bay Motion: Capturing San Francisco Bay on Film" (Nov 9, 2013–June 29, 2014); and "Hard Times in the OC" (May 18, 2013–Feb 23, 2014), about the effects of the recession on the Southern California land of those Housewives of Orange County. While the SFMOMA is closed for expansion, important works from the likes of Frida Kahlo, muralist Diego Rivera, and photographer Ansel Adams will be displayed from Sept 20, 2014–Jan 25, 2015. Admission $12 (adults), $9 (seniors and students), $6 (youth), free (8 and under). Open Wed–Sun 11am–5pm (Fri until 9pm).

If you take pleasure in strolling sailboat-filled wharves or are a die-hard fan of Jack London, you'll likely enjoy a visit to **Jack London Square ★** (*C* **510/645-9292;** www.jacklondonsquare.com), the waterfront area where the famous author spent most of his youth. The square fronts the harbor, and is currently undergoing a $400 million revival, which will bring, among other things, new restaurants, entertainment, shops, a farmers' market, and a hotel to the property. In the center of the square is a small model of the Yukon cabin in which Jack London lived while prospecting in the Klondike during the gold rush of 1897. In the middle of Jack London Square is a more authentic memorial, **Heinold's First and Last Chance Saloon** (*C* **510/839-6761;** www. heinoldsfirstandlastchance.com), a funky, friendly little bar and historic landmark. This is where London did some of his writing and most of his drinking. Jack London

Square is at Broadway and Embarcadero. Take I-880 to Broadway, turn south, and drive to the end. Or you can ride BART to the 12th Street station and then walk south along Broadway (about half a mile). Or take bus no. 72R or 72M to the foot of Broadway.

Where to Eat

Living in the shadow of San Francisco has to be tough; it's hard not to compare things like dining, culture, mayors, housing prices, traffic, and crime statistics. Though Oakland has come in a distant second in many categories, the restaurant scene is improving every year—so much so that the powers that be, who hand out the foodie awards and "make" a restaurant by adding it to those elusive "Best of" lists, are starting to wake up and take notice. One such place guaranteed to please is Daniel Patterson's **Plum** ★★ (2214 Broadway; ⒸⒸ 510/444-7586; www.plumoakland.com). It's only been open since 2010, but the simple menus, reasonable prices, and vegetable-heavy, delicious food are all helping put Oakland on the epicurean map. Another favorite is **Yoshi's Jazz Club & Japanese Restaurant** ★ (510 Embarcadero West; ⒸⒸ **510/238-9200;** www.yoshis.com), an off-shoot of the San Francisco club, serving up the unusual combination of jazz and sushi at Jack London Square. Yet another place to nosh is **Bocanova** ★★ (55 Webster St.; ⒸⒸ **510/444-1233;** www.bocanova.com), serving muy delicioso food from North, Central, and South America, again in Jack London Square.

10 ANGEL ISLAND & TIBURON

8 miles N of San Francisco

A California State Park, **Angel Island** is the largest of San Francisco Bay's three islets (the others are Alcatraz and Yerba Buena). The island has been, at various times, a prison, a quarantine station for immigrants, a missile base, and even a favorite site for duels. Nowadays, most visitors are content with picnicking on the large green lawn that fronts the docking area; loaded with the appropriate recreational supplies, they claim a barbecue pit, plop their fannies down on the lush, green grass, and while away an afternoon free of phones, televisions, and traffic. Hiking, mountain biking, and guided tram tours are other popular activities here. Cars are not allowed.

Tiburon, situated on a peninsula of the same name, looks like a cross between a fishing village and a Hollywood Western set—imagine San Francisco reduced to toy dimensions. The seacoast town rambles over a series of green hills and ends up at a spindly, multicolored pier on the waterfront, like a Fisherman's Wharf in miniature. In reality, it's an extremely plush patch of yacht-club suburbia, as you'll see by the marine craft and the homes of their owners. Ramshackle, color-splashed old frame houses line Main Street, sheltering chic boutiques, souvenir stores, antiques shops, art galleries, and dockside restaurants. Other roads are narrow, winding, and hilly and lead up to dramatically situated homes. The view from here of San Francisco's skyline and the islands in the bay is a good enough reason to pay the precious price to live here.

Getting There

Ferries of the **Blue & Gold Fleet** (ⒸⒸ **415/705-5555;** www.blueandgoldfleet.com) from Pier 41 (Fisherman's Wharf) travel to both Angel Island and Tiburon. Boats run on a seasonal schedule; phone or look online for departure information. The round-trip fare to Angel Island is $17 for adults, $9.50 for seniors (65+) and kids (5-12), and free for kids 5 and under when traveling with an adult. The fare includes state park fees. A one-way ticket to Tiburon is $11 for adults, $6.75 for seniors (65+) and kids (5-12), and free for kids 5 and under. Tickets are available at Pier 41 and online. Reservations are not necessary.

By car from San Francisco, take U.S. 101 to the Tiburon/Hwy. 131 exit and then follow Tiburon Boulevard all the way downtown, a 40-minute drive from San Francisco. Good luck finding a parking spot in Tiburon; try the lot behind the **Tiburon Playhouse** movie theater at 40 Main Street. Catch the **Tiburon–Angel Island Ferry** (② **415/435-2131;** www.angelislandferry.com) to Angel Island from the dock at Tiburon Boulevard and Main Street. The 15-minute round-trip costs $14 for adults, $12 for children 6 to 11, $4 for kids 3-5, and $1 for bikes. One child 2 or under is admitted free of charge with each paying adult (after that it's $3.50 each). Boats run on a seasonal schedule, but usually depart hourly from 10am to 5pm on weekends, with a more limited schedule on weekdays. Call ahead or look online for departure information. Tickets can only be purchased when boarding and include state park fees.

What to See & Do on Angel Island

Passengers disembark from the ferry at **Ayala Cove,** a small marina abutting a huge lawn area equipped with tables, benches, barbecue pits, and restrooms. During the summer season, there's also a small store, a gift shop, the Cove Cafe (with surprisingly good grub), and an overpriced mountain-bike rental shop at Ayala Cove.

Angel Island's 12 miles of hiking and bike trails include the **Perimeter Road,** a paved path that circles the island. It winds past disused troop barracks, former gun emplacements, and other military buildings; several turnoffs lead to the top of Mount Livermore, 776 feet above the bay. Sometimes referred to as the "Ellis Island of the West," Angel Island was used as a holding area for detained Chinese immigrants awaiting admission papers from 1910 to 1940. You can still see faded Chinese characters on some of the walls of the barracks where the immigrants were held, sometimes for months.

Besides walking and biking, there are a number of other ways to get around the island, all of which can be booked at www.angelisland.com. Schedules vary depending on the time of year. The 1-hour audio-enhanced open-air **Tram Tour** costs $15 for adults, $14 for seniors, $10 for children 5-11, and is free for children 4 and under. A guided 2½ hour **Segway Tour** costs $65 per person, and is only available for those 16 years and up. Long pants are recommended; closed shoes are mandatory. A guided 2-hour **Electric Scooter Tours** is available for $50, again for those 16 and up. For more information about activities on Angel Island, visit www.angelisland.com.

If you actually want to go "around" the island, guided **sea-kayak tours** ★ are available for all ages. The 2½-hour trips combine the thrill of paddling stable, two-person kayaks with an informative, naturalist-led tour around the island (conditions permitting). All equipment is provided (including a much-needed wet suit), and no experience is necessary. Rates run $75 per person. For more information, contact the Sausalito-based **Sea Trek** at ② **415/488-1000** or www.seatrek.com. *Note:* Tours depart from Ayala Cove on Angel Island, not Sausalito.

What to See & Do in Tiburon

The main thing to do in tiny Tiburon is stroll along the waterfront, pop into the stores, and spend an easy $50 on drinks and appetizers before heading back to the city. With fudge samples, edible Lego bricks, and every imaginable sweet you'd expect to find in Willy Wonka's factory, kids will love **The Candy Store on Main Street** at 7 Main St. (② **415/435-0434;** www.candystoretiburon.com).

Where to Eat in Tiburon

Guaymas ★★★ (5 Main St.; ✆ **415/435-6300;** www.guaymasrestaurant.com) is one of my favorite restaurants anywhere; and I eat out quite regularly. I've been salivating over the fresh-Mex food here since my husband (who grew up down the street) brought me in 22 years ago for guacamole, ceviche, and a sizzling fajita plate. Add on a stunning panoramic view of the city, bobbing sailboats and all, and wicked margaritas; it's a wonder anyone ever leaves. Another favorite is **Sam's Anchor Cafe** ★★ (27 Main St.; ✆ **415/435-4527;** www.samscafe.com), a few doors away. Same stunning view, an even bigger outdoor patio, brunch, and top quality burgers and beer. Want to see for yourself? Check out the **Sam's Cam**—a live webcam—at www.samscafe.com/cam. html.

SAUSALITO

5 miles N of San Francisco

Just off the northeastern end of the Golden Gate Bridge is the picturesque little town of Sausalito, a slightly bohemian adjunct to San Francisco. With fewer than 8,000 residents, Sausalito feels rather like St. Tropez on the French Riviera (minus the beach). Next to the pricey bayside restaurants, antiques shops, and galleries, are hamburger joints, ice-cream shops, and secondhand bookstores. Sausalito's main strip is Bridgeway, which runs along the water; on a clear day the views of San Francisco far across the bay are spectacular. After admiring the view, those in the know make a quick detour to Caledonia Street, 1 block inland; not only is it less congested, but it also has a better selection of cafes and shops. Since the town is all along the waterfront and only stretches a few blocks, it's best explored on foot and easy to find your way around.

Getting There

The **Golden Gate Ferry Service** fleet, Ferry Building (✆ **415/923-2000;** www.golden gate.org), operates between the San Francisco Ferry Building, at the foot of Market Street, and downtown Sausalito. Service is frequent, running at reasonable intervals every day of the year except January 1, Thanksgiving, and December 25. Check the website for an exact schedule. The ride takes a half-hour, and one-way fares are $10.25 for adults; $5 for youth (6-18), seniors (65+), and passengers with disabilities; children 5 and under ride free (limit two children per full-fare adult).

Ferries of the **Blue & Gold Fleet** (✆ **415/705-5555;** www.blueandgoldfleet.com) leave from Pier 41 (Fisherman's Wharf); the one-way cost is $11 for adults, $6.75 for kids 5 to 12, free for 4 and under. Boats run on a seasonal schedule; phone or log onto their website for departure information.

By car from San Francisco, take U.S. 101 N. and then take the first right after the Golden Gate Bridge (Alexander exit). Alexander becomes Bridgeway in Sausalito.

What to See & Do

Above all else, Sausalito has scenery and sunshine, for once you cross the Golden Gate Bridge, you're out of the San Francisco fog patch and under blue California sky (I hope). Houses cover the town's steep hills, overlooking a forest of masts on the waters below. Most of the tourist action, which is almost singularly limited to window-shopping and eating, takes place at sea level on Bridgeway. Sausalito is a mecca for shoppers seeking handmade, original, and offbeat clothes and footwear, as well as arts

A picnic lunch, SAUSALITO-STYLE

If the crowds are too much or the prices too steep at Sausalito's bayside restaurants, grab a bite to go for an impromptu picnic in the park fronting the marina. It's one of the best and most romantic ways to spend a warm, sunny day in Sausalito. The best source for a la carte eats is the Mediterranean-style **Venice Gourmet Delicatessen** at 625 Bridgeway, located right on the waterfront just south of the ferry landing. Since 1964, this venerable deli has offered all the makings for a superb picnic: wines, cheeses, fruits, stuffed vine leaves, salami, lox, prosciutto, salads, quiche, made-to-order sandwiches, and fresh-baked pastries. It's open daily from 9am to 6pm (*C* **415/332-3544;** www. venicegourmet.com).

and crafts. Many of the town's shops are in the alleys, malls, and second-floor boutiques reached by steep, narrow staircases on and off Bridgeway. Caledonia Street, which runs parallel to Bridgeway 1 block inland, is home to more shops. Younger children (up to 8 years old) will love the **Bay Area Discovery Museum,** East Fort Baker, 557 McReynolds Rd. (*C* **415/339-3900;** www.baykidsmuseum.org; admission $11; 9am–5pm daily, except Mondays and major holidays). Set upon 7½ acres at Fort Baker, close to the base of the Golden Gate Bridge, it features a boat to climb on, sand pits, an art studio, and a train room, among other things. After running, jumping and playing, there is a great cafe on-site serving sandwiches, soups, and salads, if the little ones need to recharge.

An unexpected but wholly original sight just off the 101 on the waterfront in Sausalito, the **Bay Model Visitors Center**, 2100 Bridgeway (*C* **415/332-3871;** www.spn. usace.army.mil/missions/recreation/baymodelvisitorcenter.aspx; free admission; typically open Tues–Sun 10am–4pm) is a hangar-like space filled with a working, wet model of the entire Bay Area. Built in 1957 by the U.S. Army Corp of Engineers to help scientists understand the complex patterns of the water currents and the tides, it's capable of duplicating, at a smaller time scale, the way flow works. Buildings aren't represented, but major landmarks such as bridges are identifiable as you walk around the space, which is about the size of two football fields, or 1.5 acres. Water, which is shallow throughout, is studded with some 250,000 copper tabs that help recreate known current patterns.

The facility, the only one of its kind in the world, hasn't been used for research since 2000, leaving it to educate school groups and the odd visitor about Bay conservation. A visit is quite relaxing; many days, you'll be one of the only guests there, and the only sounds in the enormous room will be the faint sound of the water pumps, still working away. The model sits on the site of an important World War II shipbuilding yard, called Marinship ("ma-RINN-ship"), and tucked away to the left of the exit (don't miss it) is a terrific exhibit, full or artifacts and included a video, that chronicles the yard, where an astonishing 93 ships were built in 3½ wartime years.

Where to Eat

I have three personal favorites to recommend in Sausalito. **Poggio ★,** 777 Bridgeway (*C* **415/332-7771;** www.poggiotrattoria.com) is an upscale-casual Italian place, with perfect-for-people-watching outdoor seating in the heart of Sausalito, across the street from the ferry dock. A few blocks away, **Sushi Ran** ★★, 107 Caledonia St. (℃ **415/332-3620;** www.sushiran.com) is by far the best sushi place in Marin County. My other recommendation in Sausalito is **Bar Bocce** ★, 1250 Bridgeway (℃ **415/331-0555;** www.barbocce.com). With outdoor seating featuring cushioned benches wrapped around fire pits, and a tiny sandy beach for the kids a few feet away, this is the perfect place to relax and refresh.

MARIN, MUIR WOODS & MOUNT TAMALPAIS

N of the Golden Gate Bridge

OK, you can take an organized tour to these three spots if you want to, but these day trips are an easy drive. A family of four will save a fortune—and see a lot more—by simply hiring a rental car for about $90 for the day.

Muir Woods

While the rest of Marin County's redwood forests were being devoured to feed San Francisco's turn-of-the-20th-century building spree, Muir Woods, in a remote ravine on the flanks of Mount Tamalpais, escaped destruction in favor of easier pickings.

Although the magnificent California redwoods have been successfully transplanted to five continents, their homeland is a 500-mile strip along the mountainous coast of southwestern Oregon and Northern California. The coast redwood, or *Sequoia sempervirens,* is one of the tallest living things known to man (!); the largest known specimen in the Redwood National Forest towers 368 feet. It has an even larger relative, the *Sequoiadendron giganteum* of the California Sierra Nevada, but the coastal variety is stunning enough. Soaring toward the sky like a wooden cathedral, Muir Woods is unlike any other forest in the world and an experience you won't soon forget.

Teddy Roosevelt himself consecrated this park as a National Monument in 1908. In the 1800s, redwoods were so plentiful here that people thought they'd never run out, and pretty much every single building in San Francisco and beyond was built of the trees, which are the tallest living things on Earth. You could argue that the trees got their revenge on the city, when anything made of them went up in smoke in the fire after the 'quake, and today, Muir Woods is one of the last groves of the trees in the area.

Granted, Muir Woods is tiny compared to the Redwood National Forest farther north, but you can still get a pretty good idea of what it must have been like when these giants dominated the entire coastal region. What is truly amazing is that they exist a mere 6 miles (as the crow flies) from San Francisco—close enough, unfortunately, that tour buses arrive in droves on the weekends. You can avoid the masses by hiking up the **Ocean View Trail,** turning left on **Lost Trail,** and returning on the **Fern Creek Trail.** The moderately challenging hike shows off the woods' best sides and leaves the lazy-butts behind.

To reach Muir Woods from San Francisco, cross the Golden Gate Bridge heading north on Hwy. 101, take the Stinson Beach/Hwy. 1 exit heading west, and follow the signs (and the traffic). The park is open daily from 8am to sunset, and the admission fee is $7 per person 16 and over. Check the website for "fee free" days. There's also a small gift shop, educational displays, and ranger talks. For more information, call the **National Parks Service at Muir Woods** (℃ **415/388-2596**) or visit www.nps.gov/muwo.

Mount Tamalpais

The birthplace of mountain biking, Mount Tam—as the locals call it—is the Bay Area's favorite outdoor playground and the most dominant mountain in the region. Most every local has his or her secret trail and scenic overlook, as well as an opinion on the raging debate between mountain bikers and hikers (a touchy subject). The main trails—mostly fire roads—see a lot of foot and bicycle traffic on weekends, particularly on clear, sunny days when you can see a 100 miles in all directions, from the foothills of the Sierra to the western horizon. It's a great place to escape from the city for a leisurely hike and to soak in breathtaking views of the bay.

To get to Mount Tamalpais by car, cross the Golden Gate Bridge heading north on Hwy. 101, and take the Stinson Beach/Hwy. 1 exit. Follow the signs up the shoreline highway for about 2½ miles, turn onto Pantoll Road, and continue for about a mile to Ridgecrest Boulevard. Ridgecrest winds to a parking lot below East Peak. From there, it's a 15-minute hike up to the top. You'll find a visitor center with a small museum, video, diorama, and store, as well as informative "Mount Tam Hosts" who are more than happy to help you plan a hike, identify plants, and generally share their love of the mountain. Visitor center admission is free; it is open weekends 11am to 4pm. Park hours are 7am to sunset year round. For a list of guided hikes, see www.friendsof mttam.org. You are welcome to hike in the area on your own; it is safe, great for little ones, and the trails are well marked.

Where to Eat

Because my husband grew up in the area, I can recommend a few places only insiders know about. The **Tavern at Lark Creek** ★★, 234 Magnolia Avenue, Larkspur (✆ **415/924-7766;** www.tavernatlarkcreek.com) is one, offering casual dining beside a seasonal creek under the magical redwoods. The deep-fried mac and cheese appetizer is evil-good. Actually, the burgers, salads, and everything else on the menu are great too. After lunch, take a wander, across the street, up Madrone Avenue, and watch local residents zig zag up and down the street between the giant redwoods growing from the middle of the road. Rumor has it the city mayor who suggested removing these beauties, was promptly removed from office. At the corner of Madrone and Magnolia avenues, Dolliver Park, fondly known as "Dark Park," is a shaded playground in a redwood grove, perfect for little ones to run and blow off steam before heading off on your next adventure.

If Italian pastry and a strong latte are what you need for a little refresher, **Emporio Rulli** ★, 464 Magnolia Avenue (✆ **415/924-7478;** www.rulli.com), a couple of blocks from Dark Park, is a fabulous Italian sidewalk cafe, with a good selection of panini sandwiches, light salads, and a lovely wine bar.

No visit to Larkspur is complete without a frozen yogurt at the most popular spot in town, **Mag's Local Yogurt** ★, 467 Magnolia Avenue (✆ **415/891-3012**). The friendly owners are fifth generation Larkspur residents.

High up on the mountain, The **Mountain Home Inn** ★, 810 Panoramic Hwy., Mill Valley (✆ **415/381-9000;** www.mtnhomeinn.com) offers a swell brunch and panoramic views from their outdoor deck.

If you make it over Mount Tam, just past Muir Woods, look for the **Pelican Inn,** 10 Pacific Way, Muir Beach (✆ **415-383-6000;** www.pelicaninn.com). Built in 1979 to resemble a 16th-century English cottage, this is the perfect place to grab a beer at the old-fashioned bar—dartboard and all—and sprawl out on the lawn for lunch after a hike.

THE MONTEREY PENINSULA

112 miles SW to Monterey

The Monterey Peninsula is about an hour and a half south of San Francisco—think of it as a few square miles of land jutting out west of Hwy. 1 as the California Coast winds its way from San Francisco down towards Los Angeles. The peninsula is made up of three main areas—Monterey, Pacific Grove, and Carmel—as well as a number of smaller places like Seaside, Marina, and the golfing mecca of Pebble Beach. Big Sur is a just little farther down scenic Hwy. 1—though not a part of the Monterey Peninsula. I'm adding it here because it's one of those places not to miss if you are in the area with a car.

With a windswept rugged coastline, sugar sand beaches, the Santa Lucia mountain range, waterfalls, streams, cypress forests, and the bountiful Pacific Ocean, driving Hwy. 1 is considered one of the United State's top road trips.

But even before the highway was built, this was a land that attracted settlers in scores.

A Bit of History

For thousands of years, the Oholone and Esselen tribes lived peacefully in the Monterey area, attracted by the plentiful fishing (partially ascribable to the Grand Canyon-sized crevasse, just off the peninsula in the Pacific Ocean). The **Monterey Bay Aquarium** (see below), celebrates, preserves, and teaches about the bountiful sea life the Indians found off the coast.

In 1770, the Spanish missionaries showed up to claim the land for their king— "monte" and "rey" mean "King's Mountain" in Spanish. Franciscan Father, Junipero Serra, was leader of the group that eventually built a chain of 21 missions stretching from San Diego as far north as Sonoma County—all spaced about 1 day's horse ride apart. Indians were rounded up and forced to work in the missions; they were not allowed to speak their native tongue, and, in typical fashion, lost their land and their customs. Many died of diseases brought by the foreigners. The **Mission San Carlos Borromeo de Carmel**—better known as the **Carmel Mission** (see "Things To Do," below) is where Father Serra lived and died; some of the original structure remains.

The Spanish government, worried either pirates or Russia would lay claim to their their colony, built the Presidio at Monterey (as well as three others in San Francisco, San Diego, and Santa Barbara) to protect their turf. The **Royal Presidio Chapel** (see below) has been in continuous use since 1794.

In 1822, Mexico seceded from Spain, keeping the Monterey Peninsula in their control. That rule was short-lived. In 1846, the U.S. declared war on Mexico—and won, meaning that California became a U.S. territory in 1848. And in 1850, conveniently right after gold was discovered in them 'thar hills up north, California became the 31st state.

Now comes the fun part: In the late 1800s, writers and artists began to show up, drawn to the rugged beauty and dramatic vistas of the area. **Cannery Row** (see below) was the setting John Steinbeck used for his classic fictional story about life on the docks at the sardine fisheries in Monterey during the Great Depression. In 1905, an artist colony called the Carmel Arts and Crafts Club was established in Carmel. After that pesky old 1906 earthquake in San Francisco, displaced writers, musicians, poets, and painters flocked to this established artist colony and settled in the area.

Carmel-by-the-Sea became a haven for bohemians. Still a haven for artists, actor Clint Eastwood is a long-term resident, as well as former mayor, of the village.

After being inhabited by a succession of Indians, missionaries, Spanish explorers, Mexicans, U.S. government officials, and displaced artists, finally, the serious money showed up and built a slew of mansions. **17-Mile Drive** (see below) connects Pacific Grove to Carmel-by-the-Sea on a road that curves past $20+ million dollar oceanfront mansions, and world-famous golf courses with names like the Links at Spanish Bay, Spyglass Hill, Cypress Point, Poppy Hills, and the granddaddy of them all—Pebble Beach.

Getting There

To reach the Monterey Peninsula from San Francisco, hop on Hwy. 101 south for a little over an hour. Pass the Gilroy Premium Outlets; about 20 minutes later, follow the signs for Monterey and take Hwy. 156 west for about 15 minutes until you reach Hwy. 1 south. Take Hwy. 1 south for about 10 minutes. Take the Pacific St. exit right into downtown **Monterey.** There are slightly faster routes from Hwy. 1 to downtown Monterey; Pacific Street will take a few more minutes, but you won't get lost. For **Pacific Grove,** continue through Monterey on Lighthouse Avenue. For **Carmel-by-the-Sea,** stay on Hwy. 1 for 4 miles past Monterey. If you have the time, and are so inclined, continue driving past Carmel another half an hour on Hwy. 1 south to **Big Sur.**

Things to Do

THE CITY OF MONTEREY

Though John Steinbeck's "Cannery Row" was a work of fiction, the sardine canneries, the stink of fish, the prostitutes, the dockworkers, and other sorry souls of the story were based upon observations made by the author at a time when the Monterey waterfront supported a rich fishing, processing, and canning business. A stroll down the aptly named **Cannery Row** will let you see a few remaining skeletons of the old cannery buildings.

Another worthy historic sight, established in 1794 and today's oldest continuously operating church in California, as well as the the first stone building erected in the state, the **Royal Presidio Chapel–San Carlos Cathedral** at 500 Church St. (© **831-373-2628;** www.sancarloscathedral.org), is worth a look-see. It continues to hold daily masses that all are welcome to attend.

But let's be real: history is not the primary reason you come here. Visitors from all over the world flock to the extraordinary **Monterey Bay Aquarium** ★★★ at 866 Cannery Row (© **831/648-4800;** www.montereybayaquarium.org). $35 adult, $32 senior (65+) and students (13-17 or college ID), $22 child (3-12yrs), 3 and under free. Hours are roughly daily 9:30am–6pm, except for Christmas. Picture a regular aquarium on steroids—everything here is bigger and better. Highlights include the otter exhibits, the tanks where you touch a sea cucumber, a bat ray, and the giant jellyfish. The aquarium's largest exhibit, The Open Sea, houses sharks, giant blue fin tuna fish, and ancient-looking green sea turtles. You could easily spend a whole day here (and I have).

PACIFIC GROVE

A small residential town just west of Monterey, Pacific Grove is famous for its Victorian B&B's and the thousands of monarch butterflies that migrate down from freezing cold Canada and hang here each year between October and February. Anyone wishing to learn more about these graceful black and orange insects might enjoy a visit to the **Monarch Butterfly Sanctuary** ★ (Ridge Rd between Lighthouse Ave. and Short St.;

831/648-5716; open dawn to dusk). Look, but don't touch; the fine for "molesting" a butterfly is $1,000.

17-Mile Drive ★★: You will pay about $11 for a detailed map of the area and the privilege of driving on a road that will make your jaw ache from hanging open for so long. This curvy drive links together multi-million dollar mansions like pearls on a string—some subtle and classy, others showy and brash. Add in rugged beaches, waves crashing on the rocky shoreline, sea lion covered rocks, and world-class golf courses— and that is one serious necklace. No cruise down 17-Mile Drive is complete without a visit to the **Lone Cypress lookout.** Instead of just looking at the tree—cool as it is— look straight down to see if you can find any sea otters frolicking below you in the surf. This road was originally a path for horse drawn carriages, built in 1881 by, who else, but the "Big Four" (p. 58) who were trying to lure visitors to their Hotel del Monte in Monterey. Bring a picnic or snacks, unless you want to pay a gazillion dollars to eat at one of the golf course restaurants. (If starting on the Carmel side, enter off Ocean Ave., right before the parking lot for Carmel Beach. If starting on the Pacific Grove side, enter off Lighthouse Ave.)

CARMEL-BY-THE-SEA

This quaint town really became a haven for artists after the 1906 San Francisco earthquake displaced a number of San Francisco-based poets, painters, writers, musicians, and other bohemians. They relocated to be part of the already established Carmel Arts and Crafts Club in Carmel-by-the-Sea; many stayed. And even today, the town's small streets are lined with galleries and shops selling paintings, pottery, and other unique items. Cottages that look like they were lifted straight from a fairytale, complete with moss, flower boxes, and thatched roofs, dot the side streets of the village. This architectural style likely was inspired by a small building built by Hugh Comstock in 1924. With $100 worth of materials and no building experience, Comstock and his wife built the "Doll House" using pine needles, plaster, and hand-whittled trim. The resulting uneven look blended so well with the village pines, it became a source of town pride, and something to be copied. At the end of Ocean Avenue, the white sugar sand at **Carmel Beach** is a great place to picnic, read a book, or take a stroll along the shore. The water is usually cold; don't count on swimming.

A final recommended stop in the vicinity: the **Carmel Mission ★** (**831/624-1271;** www.carmelmission.org) at 3080 Rio Road on the outskirts of town. It was built in 1771 by Father Junipero Serra and though most of the original adobe was destroyed over time, some of the early walls remain. Aside from housing a school, the mission serves as a museum for those interested in the lives of early California settlers. The first library in the state of California is here, still intact. The simple cell where Father Serra spent most of his time has been left untouched. His grave is a moving tribute to the man who would help settle California. This mission was the second of what would eventually become a chain of 21 missions. Mission bells are spread sporadically along the highway 101 marking El Camino de Real, or "The Road of Kings," that leads from one mission to the next.

BIG SUR

If you have the time and inclination, Big Sur is another half hour down the coast. There is no town per se, just one gravity-defying bridge after another on a one-lane highway that hugs the cliff high above the crashing surf below. Small hotels, restaurants, and gift shops show up occasionally, but the real reason to take this drive is the view.

Where to Eat

All eateries listed below are in quaint Carmel-by-the-Sea. A couple of blocks off Ocean, **The Village Corner** ★★ at Dolores and Sixth (© **831/624-3588;** www.villagecorner bistro.com) is a romantic Mediterranean bistro featuring a lovely outdoor patio with a fire pit, great food and a casual, California vibe. The **Forge in the Forest** ★ at Junipero and 5th (© **831/624-2233;** www.forgeintheforest.com), is an old blacksmith shop that's been converted into a restaurant, the perfect place to kick back and enjoy a drink in front of one of the many fireplaces. The cheese fondue is served in a sourdough bread bowl; for about $12, this can easily be a meal. The flat iron steak with garlic whipped potatoes is pure perfection. Turophiles will love **The Cheese Shop** ★★★ (© **831/625-2272;** www.thecheeseshopinc.com), found on the lower level of high end Carmel Plaza, a little further up Ocean Avenue. Owner and cheesemonger extraordinaire, Kent Torrey, will happily cut off sample after sample for you, and teach you all about the cheese. He got me hooked on a French triple cream called Domaine du Village—it's like milky, creamy crack. I dare you to walk out of his store without a little wrapped package and giant homemade lavosh crackers. With a huge selection of wine and other international gourmet goodies, Kent's shop is the perfect place to put together a picnic to take to Carmel Beach. For a treat, **Cottage of Sweets** (Ocean Dr. btw. Monte Verde and Lincoln; © **831/624-5170;** www.cottageofsweets. com), is a teeny thatched cottage filled with to-die-for vanilla praline or salty caramel fudge, licorice whips, and Gobstoppers as big as your fist—they claim just breathing the air is 5 calories per sniff.

WINE COUNTRY

The rolling green hills and pocket ponds of this region are so beautiful they could be considered draw enough, but of course, the main reason one comes here is for a love of food and drink. The foodie-ism is contagious. Within 2 or 3 hours of arriving, even someone who knows zip about wine will start to talk about what they're drinking as if they were born experts. It's a transformation that's fun to watch.

Yes, the Wine Country is all about the Good Life, and you may find yourself developing a desire to drop everything and move there to stomp grapes. Use this chapter as a quick primer for a weekend or day trip into grapeland. We'll include a few restaurants, a few hotels, but mostly, this chapter will be about the wineries and sights.

A QUICK LAY OF THE LAND

Picture the whole area as a long uppercase U in which the two top tongs are pinched together around a light mountain range. On the "left," or western tong, of the U is Sonoma County, where the principal north-south road is U.S. 101, which goes straight to the Golden Gate; while in Napa County, the eastern half, it's the more congested 128. In Napa County, the main road is 29, which, especially around rush hour, can be slow going.

At the bottom of the U, the town of Sonoma connects to the town of Napa, 30 minutes east, via 121/12. That's also where the 37 links Napa County to the 101, as well as to Vallejo and I-80; either road can take you back to the city, although the 101 is probably faster.

North from Napa, the principal towns, which gradually grow smaller and quainter, are **Yountville, Oakville, St. Helena** (all adorable), and finally the Main Street town of **Calistoga** (known for hot springs). Not far north from that, 29 turns into 128 and links up with **Geyserville**, at the tippy top of the Sonoma wine region.

From there, heading south through Sonoma County, you hopscotch between populous towns and quiet hamlets. First is **Healdsburg** (a cute weekenders' town square good for strolling), and **Santa Rosa** (bigger and with cheaper motels, but no wineries to speak of within it, though there is an airport here). Route 12, also known as Sonoma Highway, branches off to the east there, taking you through **Kenwood** and the charming town of **Glen Ellen**, and finally **Sonoma,** the county's historic seat. West and southwest of Santa Rosa along 116 are the towns of **Sebastopol** and **Forestville,** and finally, **Guerneville,** where the thick redwood forests begin in what's called the Russian River Valley. The vibe here is more laid-back, and in summer, the big pastimes are canoeing and swimming. Guerneville is also a well-known gay resort town, particularly in summer, although you won't find that it rages often with parties; the visitors tend to be a bit more

Wine Country

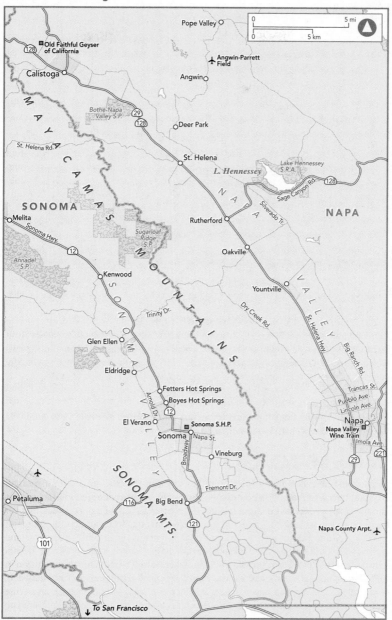

Pope Valley

Old Faithful Geyser
of California

Angwin-Parrett
Field

Calistoga

Angwin

Bothe-Napa
Valley S.P.

Deer Park

St. Helena Rd.

St. Helena

L. Hennessey

Lake Hennessey
S.R.A.

Sage Canyon Rd.

SONOMA

Melita

Sonoma Hwy.

Rutherford

NAPA

Sugarloaf
Ridge
S.P.

Annadel
S.P.

Kenwood

Oakville

Silverado Tr.

Yountville

Trinity Dr.

Dry Creek Rd.

Glen Ellen

Eldridge

Fetters Hot Springs

Boyes Hot Springs

Trancas St.

Pueblo Ave.

Lincoln Ave.

El Verano

Sonoma S.H.P.

Napa

Sonoma

Napa St.

Napa Valley
Wine Train

Vineburg

Imola Ave.

Petaluma

Fremont Dr.

Big Bend

Napa County Arpt.

To San Francisco

207

SHOULD I CHOOSE napa or sonoma?

First of all, it's not a choice. You should visit both. They're right next to each other, after all, and linked by plenty of safe roads. But when it comes to affordability, especially in food, Sonoma wins.

So why does Napa have a great cachet (and higher prices) than Sonoma? Much of it has to do with the rules of appellation. It was a collection of Napa wineries, eager to make a name for Northern California wines, that beat French wines at a blind tasting contest in Paris in 1976. Locals still talk about the so-called "Judgment of Paris," in which Napa wines won against European ones in a blind taste test by French judges, and in 2006, they even re-enacted it on its 30th anniversary. Sonoma was left out of the prestige. That time.

More of a problem is the fact that each county guards its turf jealously, and almost all the maps and brochures you'll find cover either one or the other despite the fact most visitors want to see both. So the counties will tempt you into sticking to one or the other by withholding information from you, but in fact, you can travel between the great sights of both in about 40 or 50 minutes.

Lastly, picnicking is against the law at most, but not all, wineries in Napa (really—blame the restaurant lobby), while in Sonoma, it's more easily done. And since picnicking is one of the essential pleasures of a Wine Country sojourn, why go without it?

middle-aged and settled. For a resource on gay friendly and specific resorts and restaurants, go to www.GayRussianRiver.com.

The character of the two counties varies slightly. While Napa is mostly verdant farmland and some small towns, Sonoma has a few larger communities (Santa Rosa) and its topography is much more varied. There's rolling hills and farms in the east, which gives way to deliciously damp redwood forests in the middle west, to wild and undeveloped seashore. (Remember Hitchcock's *The Birds*? It was shot in Bodega Bay, on the Sonoma Coast. It's still just as rustic now, although it's about 30 minutes' drive through forests from what we consider Wine Country.)

I don't personally think it matters where you start, because loveliness and good wine can be found everywhere in the region.

WHEN TO GO

Because the area is a major draw from the cities in the Bay Area, you'll find that crowds build when people are normally vacationing. **Summers** are ludicrously busy, and the lines of cars and endless traffic on the counties' two-lane roads can truly try the patience then. Still, the land will be simply gorgeous in summer with the grapes sprouting on the vine; it's the season for garden tours, as well. **Fall**, when the grapes are harvested and squeezed, can also be maddening, because so many people want to witness some of the rare action involved in winemaking. I'm a fan of visiting in **winter:** Tourists tend to stay away then so you'll get much more attention and education from the vintners. **Spring** is a close second in terms of seasons, because the area bursts with green. It's never terribly cold—wine country everywhere, by definition, is mostly mild, because that's what makes it good for grape growing.

WINERIES

The fact is that you could tour wineries for months. In Napa alone, there are some 100 wineries to visit.

So don't approach winery circuits the way you might the great museums of Paris or the rides at Disneyland. You can't hit everything, so don't try. The key is to find places that deliver the experience that you want. And that experience may be only partly about the flavor of the wine. Flavor is highly subjective matter, after all, and what I like will not necessarily please even the person standing next to me. That's why, in the pages that follow, I don't spend much time discussing the quality of the wine in each place (though I haven't sent you to any place that's bottling swill). The places I have chosen to highlight possess that extra something that makes them fun or pleasant places to be. Some of them have terrific views, and some have an unusual or rich history, some have excellent art displays, and some provide the better tours in the region. But there are literally hundreds of wineries in the region, so by no means do I consider the following list exhaustive, and by no means should any interested tourist, if they're into visiting wineries, stop with the places that I name here. Like restaurants, wineries are a matter of personal choice, so you should ask everyone you meet which wineries you should go to.

And don't feel pressured! Remember that most casual tourists, particularly ones who fly into the Bay Area and can't carry back lots of luggage, don't go to wineries to purchase wine, necessarily, although plenty of people do buy bottles at the places that strike their fancy. They go for the atmosphere and experience. So don't feel like you have to buy any wine at all. You don't. That said, it's a lot harder to find free tastings than it used to be because of the number of freeloading, vino-guzzling tourists who come and depart without buying a thing.

NAPA VALLEY

Castello di Amorosa Winery ★★ The exuberant, over-the-top European pretensions of some of the area's landlords is on no more immoderate display than at this sublime fake medieval castle—completed 2007—of 107 rooms, 121,000 square feet, a basement dungeon outfitted with antique torture devices, and a 72-foot-long Great Hall with a 22-foot-high coffered ceiling. Its reputation is more for a tourist attraction than for its quality wines, which are only sold here. Entry fees are $19, which includes a tasting, or $9 for those under 21. Combined tours and tastings (1 hr. and 45 min.) go for $34 per person, reservations required. I guess he's gotta pay for his white elephant somehow. It's no Biltmore or Breakers, but there's nothing else like it around, making it at least worth a drive-by. Its owner, Daryl Sattui, also runs the V. Sattui Winery in St. Helena, which is popular with picnickers.

4045 North Saint Helena Highway, Calistoga. ℂ **707/942-8200.** www.castellodiamorosa.com. Open daily Mar–Oct 9:30am–6pm, Nov–Feb 9:30am–5pm.

Chateau Montelena ★ True wine nuts come here. It was a product from the people behind this winery that, in 1976, won a top honor among white wines at the Judgment of Paris. The basic tasting is $20 for four, but this will be credited with a $100 purchase. If you're deeply interested, set aside 45 minutes for its Library Wine Tasting (11:30am and 1:30pm, $50). Reservations are required. This isn't a place well laid out for hordes of casual gawkers, even if the ivy-covered stone castlelike winery building (1882) is pretty and the Chinese garden and 5-acre pond, Jade Lake, make for a lovely place to sit for a few minutes. The people pouring here (they're in the modern ranch-style building) know their wine, and they're still proud of the victory that put Napa on the serious wine drinker's map. In fact, if you've seen the movie *Bottle Shock* (2008), a retelling of the Judgment of Paris, this is the central winery in that story. Look carefully for the easy-to-miss driveway; as you're driving to the winery, if the road you're on starts giving way to hairpins and ever-climbing altitude, you've gone too far, and you're on a mountain pass.

1429 Tubbs Lane, Calistoga. © **707/942-5105.** www.montelena.com. Open daily 9:30am–4pm.

Domaine Charbay Winery & Distillery After you finally reach this mountain-top hideaway, affectionately called "the Still on the Hill," you immediately get the sense that something special is going on here. Owner Miles Karakasevic considers himself more of a perfume maker than a 12th-generation master distiller, and it's easy to see why. The tiny distillery is crammed with bottles of his latest fragrant potions, such as brandy, whole-fruit-flavor-infused vodkas, grappa, and pastis. He's also become known for other elixirs: black walnut liqueur, apple brandy, a line of ports, several cabernet sauvignons, and the charter product—Charbay (pronounced Shar-*bay*)—a brandy liqueur blended with chardonnay.

The low-key tour—which costs $20 per person, is private and exclusive, and includes tastes of premade cocktails—centers on a small, 25-gallon copper alembic still and the distilling process.

4001 Spring Mountain Rd. (5 miles west of Hwy. 29), St. Helena. © **800/634-7845** or 707/963-9327. www.charbay.com. Open daily (except holidays).

The Hess Collection ★★★ A top choice for art lovers, here you'll see an expertly curated set of modern art, collected by Swiss owner Donald Hess (he normally loans his goodies to top museums). He grants his support to twenty living artists, saying he'll reassess when they either die or become "well established." Since he chose both Robert Motherwell (displayed here) and Francis Bacon, I'd say Hess is choosing quite well. The art he has is here arresting, and the way the place mixes winery and the high-end art gallery is satisfying.

4411 Redwood Rd., Napa. © **707/255-1144.** www.hesscollection.com. Visitors center 10am–5:30pm; gallery closes 5pm.

Quixote ★★ Due to zoning laws, this spectacular and truly one-of-a-kind Stags' Leap District winery welcomes up to eight guests per day, all of whom are likely to find themselves as awestruck by the architecture as they are by the powerful petite syrahs and cabernet sauvignons. The hidden, hillside property owned by longtime industry power player Carl Doumani is the only U.S. structure designed by late great European artist Friedensreich Hundertwasser. Whimsical and captivating even to those who know nothing about design, it's a structural fantasy world with undulating lines, a gilded onion dome, and a fearless use of color. During the $25-per-person reservation-only sit-down tasting, visitors can fill their agape mouths with tastes of the winery's current releases.

6126 Silverado Trail, Napa. © **707/944-2659.** www.quixotewinery.com. Tastings by appointment only Tues–Sun.

Robert Mondavi ★★ This swank winery was started by the acknowledged pioneer of modern-day California winemaking who died at 94 in 2008. There's a sign off

The most important tool for a day or week of wine tasting is a **good map.** They're not too hard to find, since they are distributed at restaurants, wineries, and anywhere there are tourists likely to tread. Get one that has all the wineries labeled, because sometimes a place is located off a main road and is only easily locatable with help. Also look for a list of all the county's wineries, because that way you can take stock of the smaller, family-run places that may require you to phone ahead to visit. For Sonoma, my favorite map for its ease of use is *The Official Visitors Map* put out by Sonoma County Tourism Bureau (© 800/576-6662; www.sonomacounty. com). For Napa, there are **download-able maps** at **www.napavalley.org**, the site run by the Napa Valley Conference and Visitors Bureau. If you are unable to download maps before you arrive, don't fret, because they're distributed widely and for free.

Beside that essential winery map, you'll also need **discipline.** It's easy to get pretty drunk during a wine-tasting day, even if you think you're not having much, which would only be your problem if you didn't have to also drive a car. That's why all wineries keep a little spittoon on the bar that's meant for you to use. Don't gulp wine down—taste it in little sips and, if you want, spit it out. (Frankly, you will rarely see anyone use the spittoons—wineries take precautions not to over-serve you instead—but they're there.) If you drink too much, which is unlikely given the small shots of wine each place doles out, call **Vern's Taxi** at © 707/938-5885. There are companies in San Francisco that, for hundreds of dollars, will drive you around the area in a limo, but most of those programs only take you to the most touristy places, although you can pay even more money to customize some tours. It seems to me to be a high price to pay just to be able to drink, especially you can buy any wine you see for home consumption.

the visitor's parking lot directing trucks for "grape delivery"—if your winery needs one of those signs, you're not growing everything yourself on-site, and you're big. The grounds are laid out like a preppy college campus. As you drive up, you're greeted by a handsome bronze-and-glass-mosaic statue of St. Francis by Beniamino Bufano, and from there, the Mission-style buildings open up into a view of the vineyards and the hills beyond. This may be the most theatrical winery that also makes wines that connoisseurs care about. Check into the Visitors Center, to the left, for a highlight history of the winery and to arrange a tour. The Discovery Tour lasts 30 minutes and is offered every weekend in the summer. The cost is $15 for two tastings. Children are welcome. Those 12 and under are free. The year-round 75-minute Signature Tour features a sit-down guided wine tasting (three tastes) and costs $30 per person. You'll stroll the vineyards and the cellars. Children must be 13 years old to attend. After your tour, stroll around the grounds; you'll encounter a collection of more chunky Bufano works; my favorite is the walrus. Benny Bufano was famous for chopping off his trigger finger and mailing it to President Woodrow Wilson rather than fight in World War I. His digital protest didn't seem to affect the power of his art. The tasting rooms generally offer about 10 types that are exclusive to the winery, and the Vineyard Room charges $20 for 4 tastings of Appellation wines. All summer long, the winery hosts outdoor concerts on its grounds, something it's been doing since 1969, 3 years after Mondavi kicked off Napa's post–Prohibition rise.

Highway 29, Oakville. ℂ **888/766-6328.** www.robertmondaviwinery.com. Open daily 10am–5pm; closed holidays.

Schramsberg ★★ This 217-acre sparkling wine estate, a landmark once frequented by Robert Louis Stevenson and the second-oldest property in Napa Valley, is one of the valley's all-time best places to explore. Schramsberg is the label that presidents serve when toasting dignitaries from around the globe, and there's plenty of historical memorabilia in the winery's front room to prove it. But the real mystique begins when you enter the sparkling wine caves, which wind 2 miles (reputedly the longest in North America) and were partly hand-carved by Chinese laborers in the 1800s. The caves have an authentic Tom Sawyer ambience, complete with dangling cobwebs and seemingly endless passageways; you can't help but feel you're on an adventure. The comprehensive, unintimidating tour ends in a charming, cozy tasting room, where you'll sample four surprisingly varied selections of their high-end bubbly. At $50 per person, tasting is mighty pricey, but many feel its money well spent. Note that tastings are offered only to those who take the free tour, and you must make reservations in advance.

1400 Schramsberg Rd. (off Hwy. 29), Calistoga. ℂ **707/942-2414.** www.schramsberg.com. Daily 10am–4pm. Tours and tastings by appointment only. At 10am, 11am, 1pm, and 2:30pm.

Sterling Vineyards ★ Another gimmicky wine visit, but one your camera will love anyway where a $28 aerial tram ($10 for 21 and under) takes you to and through some fantastic views over the area. The main building sits on a hill some 300 feet above the valley floor and the parking lot. Obviously, to visit it completely, you'll need to budget plenty of time and go on a clear day. You've got to pay the fee even if you don't want to ride the tram, but the price also includes a tour (self-guided, not narrated) and a five-wine tasting at your own table. Interesting side note: The bells in the tower used to hang in St. Dunstan's of Fleet Street London, which was destroyed in World War II. There are not a lot of places where kids will be welcomed or engaged in the wine country, but because of the tram, I'd take hard-to-please kids here. Picnicking is allowed.

1111 Dunaweal Lane, Calistoga. ℂ **800/726-6136.** www.sterlingvineyards.com. Open Mon–Fri 10:30am–4:30pm, Sat–Sun 10am–5pm.

SONOMA COUNTY

Armida ★★★ You'll need to bring a few supplies here, meaning a camera for the fab view and some food to eat on its fab patio. People come from miles around—at least, people in the know do—to sit out on its generous wooden deck, which overlooks a man-made reedy pond and an excellent vista beyond. There, you can sit in the sun or in the shade, eat whatever you've brought, and hang out for as long as you like. The winery just asks that you only drink their wine on property. (If you don't, as they explain it, "it upsets our dog.") The tasting center, for its part, is relaxed and nonaggressive, and the winemakers don't take the scene too seriously; one of its wines is called PoiZin (as in "the wine to die for") and the wine club is called Wino. Six specialty wines (usually three red and three white) can be sampled for $10—the fee is waived if you spend $25. It's a warm-hearted place without a slice of pretension, and with very good vino.

2201 Westside Rd., Healdsburg. © **707/433-2222.** www.armida.com. Open daily (except holidays) 11am–5pm.

Benziger Family Winery ★★
Benziger offers one of the better tours: a $20 tram run that concludes with four tastings ($5 for those under 21). This all-organic, sustainable winery is doing things right, and it's fun to see how they go about making good wine without despoiling the land. In winter, sheep wander the property, eating the grass around the vines. (When grapes are going, said our guide, "They can't be trusted.") All organic waste is recycled, and the winery even runs an "insectary" where beneficial bugs are encouraged to breed. The tram tour whisks you about to show the general layout of the property, which occupies a microclimate specific to its valley, and takes you into wine caves that are some 70 feet under the hillside. You'll also hear about the cooperage (barrel making), although you won't see a demonstration. All in all, it's one of the most well-rounded tours on the market, and something about the family-run facility, or maybe its idealism, doesn't make you feel like you're being herded from site to site.

1883 London Ranch Rd., Glen Ellen. © **888/490-2739.** www.benziger.com. Open daily 10am–5pm.

Francis Ford Coppola Winery ★★
When you drive in, you pass through a triumphal arch that says "Francis Ford Coppola presents." Yes, this is the winery owned by the legendary director, and the experience here is as much about his movies as his wine. Here, you'll find a glass case full of his awards, including several Oscars (such as the ones he won for *The Godfather*), two Golden Globes, and two Directors Guild of America awards. You'll also see a giant bamboo cage used as a prop in *Apocalypse Now.* The thrice-daily 45-minute tour (11:30am, 1pm, and 2:30pm) is a good deal; for $20, you see the vineyard, learn about the vintner's grape philosophy, pop into the barrel room where you taste wine right out of barrels, and wind up with a sampling of some reserve wines. Even without the tour, tastings are free (for two pours). This is also one of the few wineries where you'll find picnic tables that are actually in the vineyards rather than in some area by a parking lot or something like that. Add to all this the fact that the staff is more welcoming than at many no-name places. I have to say that Coppola, despite the vanity venture, is one of my favorites wineries to visit, especially when you get to take a look at some movie memorabilia. **Inglenook,** in Napa (another Coppola property), has a longer history and is certainly as pretty as a coffee-table book; tasting tours start at $50 (11am, 2pm, or 3pm for 90 minutes; © 707/968-1161; www.inglenook.com), though there is no charge to walk around the property or visit the museum.

300 Via Archimedes, Geyserville. © **707/857-1400.** www.franciscoppolawinery.com. Open daily 11am–6pm.

Kaz Vineyard & Winery ★★★
It looks like some guy's house because it is: Richard "Kaz" Kasmier makes only 60 barrels a year, but he does it with care and with 10 times fewer sulfites as his competitors. Some say that you really need more sulfites to balance the flavor out, but the many people who are made ill by sulfite-heavy wines will find his efforts useful. His winery is strongly family oriented—the swingset on his

THE wino AWARDS

Of the wineries I write about in this guide, here's how they break down in terms of the experiences they offer.

BEST ALL-AROUND TOUR: Benziger Family Winery (p. 213), an organic, sustainable winery

BEST FOR WINE HISTORY BUFFS: Chateau Montelena (p. 209)

BEST FOR OVER-THE-TOP EXTRAVAGANCE: Castello di Amorosa Winery (p. 209), a 107-room castle with a stocked dungeon

BEST FOR CHAMPAGNE: Korbel (p. 214)

BEST PLACE TO HANG OUT AND ENJOY THE VIEW: Armida (p. 212), where locals meet, relax, and chat on the patio

BEST PLACE FOR MOVIE BUFFS: Rosso & Bianco (p. 213), Francis Ford Coppola's winery

BEST FOR FAMILIES: Sterling Vineyards (p. 212), home of the aerial tram tour

property is for his grandkids, but he encourages any visiting shorty to play on it, and to feed the fish in the koi pond out back. Kaz doesn't take the area's pretentiousness very seriously; when I first called to ask if his winery was open to visitors, I was told, "Yes, but only if you're the *right kind* of visitor." They were kidding, of course, a dry wit made even clearer by the amusing names of his wines: Say "Rah," Red Said Fred, and Moo Vedra among them. Tastings are $5 for five wines or ports. You'll find it a little down the turn-off from Route 12 where you'll also find Landmark Vineyards.

233 Adobe Canyon Rd., Kenwood. ⓒ **877/833-2536.** Tastings $5. www.kazwinery.com. Open Fri–Mon 11am–5pm. Tues–Wed call for an appointment.

Korbel ★★★ One of the best historical tours is at the home of the best-selling premium champagne maker in America that, for reasons that are still not entirely clear to me, claims it is permitted to call itself a champagne maker (usually only wineries in the Champagne region of France may do so). It's been doing it since 1882 here, started by a Czech cigar box maker who got in trouble back home for political unrest. His mom snuck him out of prison by smuggling civilian clothes under her skirts during a visit. That story is interesting enough, but the place is full of stuff like that. For example, the cleared area in front of the work buildings was once the site of the train line to San Francisco, 70 miles south, and 50-minute tours of the property start in the old railway station. Call them whistle-stop tours, then: The old winery is now a history center, with lots of period winemaking implements and photographs, including some fascinating snaps of the property when it was full of redwood stumps. (They called Guerneville "Stumptown" then. There are none left.) Guides keep things witty and fresh; you'll learn a lot about the tools and the process of champagne making wrapped in a mini-history of the area. They run free (includes four tastings) tours daily every hour on the hour from 11am to 3pm in winter, or every 45 minutes in summer, from 11am to 3pm. From mid-April to mid-October, Tues–Sun at 1pm and 3pm, there's also a rose garden tour for more than 250 varieties of roses, many of them antiques planted by the first Czech immigrants. Interestingly, although 1.3 million cases a year are made here, there are only eight people working in the factory, which probably means your tour will outnumber them.

13250 River Rd., Guerneville. ✆ **707/824-7000.** www.korbel.com. Shop/Tasting room open daily 10am–4:30pm.

Robledo Family Winery ★★★   This quiet winery is one of the great personal success stories of the area. The family patriarch came to America from Michuacuan, Mexico, in 1968 and worked as a laborer for the Christian Brothers, respected wine-makers, before working his way up, bit by bit, to finally owning his own spread. There are "live barrels" in the tasting room, which means they're full of aging wine, and the smell throughout the former dairy barn is marvelous. They don't do tours, but because one of Mr. Robledo's kids is usually on duty and there aren't many tourists that come through, you're bound to have a truly interesting and possibly inspiring conversation. Tastings are $5 for six wines, and bottles, which you can't buy anywhere else, start at $22. This winery received a huge honor in early 2008 when Mexican president Felipe Calderón, on the first visit to the region by any Mexican president ever, chose Robledo and no other winery for an appearance. He, too, is from Michuacuan.

21901 Bonness Rd., Sonoma; ✆ **707/939-6903.** www.robledofamilywinery.com. Open daily Mon–Sat 10am–5pm, Sun 11am–4pm.

WHAT TO SEE BEYOND THE WINERIES

Don't bother with the touristy wine train that traverses Napa County; it's a trap on which you're required to eat their food, and you can't get off and on as you wish (and as would actually be useful).

Armstrong Redwoods State Reserve ★★   The 805-acre reserve, 2 miles north of Guerneville, is a place of peace, silence, and very big redwood trees—some of them are more than 300 feet tall and at least 1,400 years old. The moistness of the air means that when the sunlight does manage to break through the density of the ecosystem, it can draw steam off the bark of the mighty trees, creating a seriously beautiful environment. Save the entrance fee by parking at the visitor's center and walking in. There are a few trails, but overall, it's not busy, so it's often pin-drop quiet, putting it ahead of Muir Woods in my book. ✆ **707/869-2015.** www.parks.ca.gov. 8am–1hr. after sunset; $6 per vehicle.

diRosa Preserve ★   Some 2,200 works of art are kept on 900 stunning acres, centering on a 35-acre pond. The works here are delightfully fractured, wild, *avant garde* experiments, many of the kinetic and every one of them by Bay Area hands and minds. There are three tours offering three levels of access to the grounds, which is sort of a ridiculous concept that even the Louvre doesn't try on visitors, but I'd think that the $12 "Introductory" version, a 90 minute overview of the highlights, including the Historic Residence and the core of the collection, will do almost everyone. Pay $3 more, and you can enjoy all of the above as well as extended viewing in the Gatehouse Gallery on a 2-hour tour. Better yet, for a suggested donation of $5 you can enjoy the manageable rotating selection of art in the Gatehouse Gallery without a tour of the

A PAEAN TO Peanuts

Anyone who loves the *Peanuts* comics and TV shows will spend a few hours in happy absorption at the surprisingly lavish **Charles M. Schulz Museum and Research Center** ★★★ (☎ 707/579-4452; www.schulzmuseum.org). Sparky, as he was called, made ungodly amounts of money off the licensing of his creations, and so his estate has the financial wherewithal to burnish his reputation at this two-story facility, which would be worthy of any major artist.

There's lots to see and do at this two-level gallery-cum-library. Of course, there's tons of strips from the entire run of the series—always the original, never copies—and biographical information about Sparky, who died in 2000 (this place opened in 2002). Even more interesting are the many tributes to the strip by other artists, such as a life-sized Snoopy made of Baccarat crystal, Christo's "Wrapped Snoopy House," and a wall mosaic of 3,588 tiles by Yoshitero Otari. The museum preserves Schulz's work room, with its worn drawing board, Higgins ink, and unremarkable book selection. Also fun is the non-stop slate of showings of classic TV specials and movies in a screening room. (Kids will particularly enjoy that as well as the play area outside.)

The museum is located at 2301 Hardies Lane in Santa Rosa. It's open 11am–5pm weekdays, 10am–5pm weekends, and closed on Tuesdays except in the summer. It costs $10 for adults and $5 for youth, seniors, and students.

grounds, pretty as they are. Students of landscaping and architecture won't want to miss it, and nor will fans of eccentric contemporary art. Others may leave scratching their heads. But no one departs without sighing over the greenery at least once. 5200 Carneros Highway/121, Napa. (☎ **707/226-5991.** www.dirosaart.org. Apr–Oct Wed–Sun 10am–6pm (tours from 10am–4pm), Nov–March 10am–4pm (tours from 10am–2pm); closed on holidays. Children 12 and under are free.

Jack London State Historic Park ★ The famous writer's ashes are buried at this historic park, where he spent his final years and his wife stayed on afterward. London's study, in the cottage, contains some artwork from his stories and stuff he picked up on his travels, and elsewhere on the property is a ruin of a magnificent house he tried to build—it burned down before it was done. There's an easy ½-mile trail through the bucolic surroundings. On weekends, docents show up at 11am, 1pm, 2pm and 3pm to give tours. 2400 London Ranch Rd., Glen Ellen. (☎ **707/938-5216.** www.parks.sonoma.net/JLPark.html. Open 9:30am–5pm, cottage noon–4pm on weekends; $6 per vehicle.

Luther Burbank Home & Gardens ★ Horticulturalists will be drawn here. The name doesn't ring a bell for most, but gardeners revere him for developing more than 800 new varieties of plants, particularly roses. His old home is now a national historic landmark. The surrounding acre of land, free and open until sunset, is still tended and contains many of his concoctions. Santa Rosa Avenue at Sonoma Avenue, Santa Rosa. (☎ **707/524-5445.** www.lutherburbank.org.

Sonoma Valley Historical Society ★ Just north of Sonoma Plaza, this often overlooked museum is stuffed with intriguing artifacts, such as painted stage curtain from the long-gone Union Hotel (now a modern bank on the southwest of the square), complete with era ads painted onto it. It was found rolled up in a barn. The women in charge of the place are generous and excited; ask to hear the 1850s Swiss music box and they'll tune it up for you. Not all the exhibits in this museum are labeled so just ask questions—they love telling tales here. 270 First Street West, Sonoma. ✆ **707/938-1762.** www.sonomavalley.com/sonoma-valley-historical-society.L357.html.

Where to Stay in the Napa Valley

Accommodations in Napa Valley run the gamut—from standard motels and floral-and-lace Victorian-style B&Bs to world-class luxury retreats—and all are easily accessible from the main highway that stretches across the valley and leads to its attractions. Most of the romantically pastoral options (think hidden hillside spots with vineyard views or quaint small-town charmers) are found on the outskirts of historic St. Helena, which has the best walking/shopping street, and the equally storied, but more laid-back and affordable than hot-springs-heavy Calistoga, which also boasts some of the region's most affordable options. The few commercial blocks of pastoral Yountville have become a destination in itself thanks to a number of famous restaurants (including world-renowned French Laundry) as well as a handful of high-end hotels and middle-end B&Bs. The most "reasonably priced" (a relative term in this high-priced area) choices are the B&Bs, small hotels, and national chain options in downtown Napa, the closest thing you'll find to a city in these parts. No matter where you stay, you're just a few minutes—or less—away from world-class wineries.

EXPENSIVE

Bardessono ★★★   Green luxury is what's on offer here. Bardssono is one of only 4 LEED-Platinum certified hotels in the U.S. That means that the lovely wood you see throughout the hotel (and it's a woodsy place) is all from salvaged trees, there are solar panels adding their charge and composting going on, and most everything in the hotel—from linens to the food served at the restaurant—has been sourced from within a radius of 100-miles. Of course, most guests aren't staying here to be virtuous. They've chosen the Bardessono for its elegant, proudly-Californian decor (as opposed to the faux French and faux Tuscan styles you see at so many properties); for the high quality of the service; for the hidden pool on the roof of the hotel and the excellent spa; and for the overall comfort of the experience. Plus, since the property is right in the heart of Yountsville, you can head out to some of the best restaurants in the region, enjoy a bottle of wine, and not worry about having to get behind the wheel of a car after the meal (the hotel gives guests a free lift to any Yountsville restaurant that's not in walking distance).

6256 Yount St., Yountsville. ✆**707/204-6000.** www.bardessono.com. $450-$850 double. **Amenities:** On-site restaurant and bar; spa; gym; pool; free rides within Yountsville; bike loans; Wi-Fi (free).

Calistoga Ranch ★★★   Hop onto the golf cart and let the ride take you! Since this is a true ranch, set on an eastern mountainside on 157 pristine hidden-canyon acres, guests spend a lot of time tootling round with staff members to get from their private cabins to the pool or restaurant or car parking area. That's not necessarily a bad thing, as it means that each cabin is unattached from the next, so serenity reigns (tip: those up the hill have the most distance between neighbors). Want to explore wine country? The resort will lend you a Mercedes Benz or a bicycle from their fleet to do so, free of charge. But you may not want to leave the ranch. Why would you when

In the 1800s, the big draw in this region wasn't wine, it was hot mud baths. The Quake of 1906 shifted the location of many of the springs, wiping out most of the wells that then existed in Sonoma County as well, so that today, the best place to participate in a geothermal treatment is Calistoga, in Napa County. Like bungee jumping or hot-air ballooning, it's a once-in-a-lifetime vacation treat that is only available in a special location.

Most places mix the mud and hot springs water (which is a little over 100 degrees) with clay, peat, and volcanic ash from nearby St. Helena volcano, which may stain some swimsuits, so don't wear your best one, or, like most people, don't wear anything at all. These treatments used to be touted as an excellent treatment for arthritis, but modern marketing laws being what they are, they're now meant mostly as stress relievers (supporting scientific studies show that arthritis suffers may, in fact, find some relief).

All of these day spa facilities include mud baths—the most "local" of the treatments. Some of these baths will be thick, others soupy; some will start as mineral water baths before having ash mixed in (to prove it's fresh, I suppose), and others will have a tub pre-mixed before you begin. There's no proven difference between any style. Your place's water should be mineral water, which means drawn hot from the earth. Each maintains a full list of massages, treatments, and other spa procedures from Swedish massage to hydrotherapy, always for a surcharge beyond the mud

bath rate. They list their treatments online.

Dr. Wilkinson's Hot Springs Resort (1507 Lincoln Ave., Calistoga; ℂ **707/942-4102;** www.drwilkinson. com), in a delightfully 1940s motel complex, has been a player in Calistoga for generations and does a range of treatments, but it's basic in the classically medicinal sense that spas once had. The mud bath as described above is $89 and takes a little over an hour.

Golden Haven (1713 Lake St., Calistoga; ℂ **707/942-8000;** www.goldenhaven. com) costs $89 per person (unusually, it has tubs in which couples can fit, making it the honeymooners' choice), but you can score an appointment for $72 per person Monday through Thursday in the winter.

Lavender Hill Spa (1015 Foothill Blvd., Calistoga; ℂ **707/942-4495;** www. lavenderhillspa.com) does everything with Asian flair and additives (a Thai Bath uses milk, the mud bath, kelp), and its mud is thinner than other spas' mud baths. One-hour treatments are $95 per person.

Lincoln Avenue Spa (1339 Lincoln Ave., Calistoga; ℂ **707/942-2950;** www. lincolnavenuespa.com) might be the choice for severe claustrophobes, since they won't have to get into the thick, mucky baths that alarm some people. Instead, they apply mud onto themselves in a private room—with a loved one, if desired—followed by time in a less-constricting steam capsule. That's $79 per person, or $128 for two.

there's so much to do here, from swimming in the natural thermal pool (which, as of the summer of 2013, now has a nearby children's pool), to taking a treatment in their state-of-the-art indoor-outdoor spa, to free classes in yoga or painting? You don't even have to go out for meals: the truly gourmet, lakeside restaurant is open only to guests, so you're guaranteed a place. As for the guest cabins, they're cunningly designed to let nature in. So the shower's outdoors as is much of the living space; and what's inside has a rural-chic feel to it, with wide plank floors, luxurious natural fabrics and the cushiest of beds.

580 Lommel Rd., Calistoga. ℂ **707/254-2800.** www.calistogaranch.com. 46 cottages. $450–$4,000 double. **Amenities:** Restaurant; concierge; gym; Jacuzzi; large heated outdoor pool; room service; spa; Wi-Fi (free).

Meadowood Napa Valley ★★ A true resort experience, Meadowood offers its guests tennis on seven championship courts, hiking trails, a health spa, an expert-level 9-hole golf course, yoga classes, two heated pools, and even international regulation lawns for croquet. The goal, it seems, is to keep guests from straying off the property's 250 pristine, mountainside acres. I'll be frank: they do a good job at making you want to stay put. Especially once you've wandered into your own little enchanted cottage, with its beamed ceilings, private patio, and stone fireplaces. Every guest gets their own free-standing house, some so isolated you need to drive to them and all with deliciously comfortable decor (we'll call it "understated opulence"). Also at Meadowood: an award-winning restaurant.

900 Meadowood Lane, St. Helena. ℂ **800/458-8080** or 707/963-3646. www.meadowood.com. $475–$825 double; $775–$1,250 1-bedroom suite; $1,400–$3,400 2-bedroom suite; $1,875–$4,775 3-bedroom suite; $2,350–$6,150 4-bedroom suite. 2-night minimum stay on weekends. **Amenities:** 2 restaurants; concierge; golf course; health club and full-service spa; Jacuzzi; 2 large heated outdoor pools (adult and family pools); room service; sauna; 7 tennis courts, kitchenettes, Wi-Fi (free).

MODERATE

Cedar Gables Inn ★★ In 1892, Edward S. Churchill commissioned the noted British architect Ernest Coxhead to create this magnificent, 10,000-square-foot Tudor mansion as a wedding present for his engaged son. So it seems appropriate that so many honeymooning couples choose to spend that special vacation here, taking a step into the past among the Inn's rich tapestries and elegant antiques. Rooms are romantic, too, especially the four that have fireplaces (five have whirlpool tubs and all come with a bottle of complimentary port). Guests meet each evening in front of the roaring fireplace in the lower "English tavern" for wine and cheese and at breakfast in the mornings, which is a sumptuous three-course feast. The inn is nonsmoking.

486 Coombs St. (at Oak St.), Napa. ℂ **800/309-7969** or 707/224-7969. www.cedargablesinn.com. 9 units. $189–$329 double. Rates include full breakfast, evening wine and cheese, and port. From Hwy. 29 N., exit onto First St. and follow signs to downtown; turn right onto Jefferson St. and left on Oak St.; house is on the corner. **Amenities:** Free local calls and Wi-Fi.

Chanric Inn ★★★ We've got one big complaint about the Chanric: it's near impossible to get reservations there nowadays, the place has become so beloved. Which shouldn't be surprising considering its art-filled decor (it's an exceptionally lovely place), the lushly planted pool area and the ministrations of the hosts, who make sure their guests' every wishes are fulfilled (even some they might not have known they had). Each morning, hot coffee and biscotti sit outside guestroom doors, which is followed by a gourmet three-course breakfast. Later in the day, guests are treated to hors d'oerves, wine and a champagne nightcap.

1805 Foothill Blvd., Calistoga. ℂ **877/281-3671** or 707/942-4535. www.thechanric.com. 6 units. $299–$429 double. Rates include breakfast. *In room:* Hair dryer, Wi-Fi (free).

INEXPENSIVE

Best Western Plus Elm House Inn ★★★　This may be the nicest Best Western we've ever tried. The rooms are spacious and good-looking, the service gracious, and there are all sorts of extras here one doesn't expect such a good breakfast and freshly-baked cookies in the afternoon, lovely landscaping, a hot tub on the patio and truly expert folks behind the desk (they're helpful in setting up wine tasting itineraries for first timers). In fact, if it weren't called a "Best Western" we'd be tempted to list it as a B&B. The hotel's within walking distance of Napa's downtown center and close to Hwy. 29, the region's thoroughfare.

800 California Blvd., Napa. ✆ **888/849-1997** or 707/255-1831. www.bestwestern.com. 22 units. $119–$279 double. Rates include full breakfast and evening cookies. From Hwy. 29 north, take the First St. exit, take a right onto California Blvd., and the hotel is on the corner of Second St. and California Blvd. **Amenities:** Free phone calls; hot tub; laundry facilities; Wi-Fi (free).

Dr. Wilkinson's Hot Springs Resort ★　An institution among the Calistoga spas, your money here buys you a simple room, but one that's immaculately clean and comfy; some have kitchenettes. Although the buildings are distinctly 1950s motel (standard room sizes, walls made of era brick tile, and the neon sign out front deserves to be in an Americana museum), the resort has gone to extra lengths to renovate the rooms to a more refreshed standard (think: flat screen TV's, iPod docking stations, nice textiles). The patios and outdoor courtyards have been well groomed and are fitting places to unwind before walking out to the shops and food along Lincoln. If you stay here, you can avail yourself of a standard pool plus a pair (indoor and outdoor) of pools fed by mineral water. Then, of course, there's this place's famously medicinal mud bath spa (p. 218). The resort also maintains a few multi-room cottages nearby, which are terrific for families and very well priced.

1507 Lincoln Ave. (Calif. 29, btw. Fairway and Stevenson aves.), Calistoga. ✆ **707/942-4102.** www.drwilkinson.com. 42 units. $149–$299 double; $164–$600 for the Hideaway cottages. **Amenities:** Jacuzzi; 3 pools; spa; Wi-Fi in lobby (free).

Maison Fleurie ★★　Three, ivy-covered houses comprise this charming inn, so the digs vary greatly depending on whether you're in the Provencal-style main house, in the carriage house or the building that once was a bakery. If having a private balcony, patio, or Jacuzzi tub is important to your well being—hey we're not judging—be sure to read the web descriptions carefully. What all rooms have in common is their cozy looks, comfortable beds, and nice private bathrooms. The lovingly tended grounds include a pool and a hot tub. A generous breakfast starts the day; end it in style with afternoon hors d'oeuvres and wine (also complimentary).

6529 Yount St. (btw. Washington St. and Yountville Cross Rd.), Yountville. ✆ **800/788-0369** or 707/944-2056. www.maisonfleurienapa.com. 13 units. $120–$285 double. Rates include full breakfast and afternoon hors d'oeuvres. **Amenities:** Free use of bikes; Jacuzzi; heated outdoor pool; Wi-Fi (free).

Roman Spa Hot Springs Resort ★　It's clean, it's not pricey, and it's well-located (just a block off Calistoga's main street), so why should it matter that there's nothing "Roman," or even remotely chic about this place? Be thankful you're not spending your child's college fund on a room, or on your spa treatments in the mineral pools (three of them, one's an outdoor whirlpool), mud baths, and massage areas here. A good place for families as some units have two bedrooms and full kitchens.

1300 Washington St., Calistoga. ✆ **800/914-8957** or 707/942-4441. www.romanspahotsprings.com. 60 units. $140–$250 double; $230–$450 suite. **Amenities:** 3 mineral pools; sauna; spa.

Where to Eat in Napa Valley

Napa Valley's restaurants draw as much attention to the valley as its award-winning wineries. Nowhere else in the state are kitchens as deft at mixing fresh seasonal, local, organic produce into edible magic, which means that menus change constantly to reflect the best available ingredients. Add that to a great bottle of wine and stunning views, and you have one heck of an eating experience. Here are some picks, from an affordable diner to once-in-a-lifetime culinary experience, and everything in between.

Ad Hoc ★★ INTERNATIONAL For those who'd like to try star chef Thomas Keller's cuisine (see the French Laundry review), but also pay rent this month, Ad Hoc is the solution. Most famous for its fried chicken dinners (served only on Mondays), the restaurant offers a daily changing, prixe fixe menu, which is served family style and ranges across the globe for its inspirations. One day you might get jambalaya and on another day the menu will feature falafel, the one constant being the high quality of both the ingredients and the cooking.

6475 Washington St, Yountville, Napa Valley. ✆ **707/944-2487.** Mon and Thurs–Sat 5–10pm, Sun 10am–1pm and 5–9pm. Prixe fixe $52.

BarBersQ ★ BARBECUE When you just can't stomach another precious salad or truffle-covered something, come here for down-home, genuine Memphis-style BBQ. That means ribs, brisket, beans and ham, fried chicken—yup, it's a carnivores paradise, though this being Napa, anything that once grew in the ground will be locally sourced. Top it all off with addictive chocolate bourbon pecan pie, or Key lime pie—if you can. *One warning:* service can be slow, so takeout is a popular option.

3900 D Bel Aire Plaza, Napa. ✆ **707/224-6600.** www.barbersq.com. Main courses $8–$30. Sun–Thurs 11:30am–8:30pm; Fri–Sat 11:30am–9pm.

Bottega ★★ ITALIAN TV host Michael Chiarello (he's an Emmy winner) was a chef first, and it was this restaurants that rocketed him to fame. As with the many other restos in the area, the ingredients are proudly locavore, but here the cooking is Italian and creative Italian at that. When the weather's chilly, there are few more pleasant places to linger than in front of the fireplace in Bottega's dining room, with a glass of local red in your hand and a perfectly plated pasta under your fork.

6525 Washington St, Yountville, Napa Valley. ✆ **707/945-1050.** www.botteganapavalley.com. Main entrees $15–$25 at lunch, more at dinner. Mon–Fri 11:30am–2:30pm and 5:30–9:30pm, Sat–Sun 11:30am–3pm and 5:30–9:30pm.

The French Laundry ★★★ FRENCH/MOLECULAR GASTRONOMY It's a point of pride that no single ingredient is ever repeated in the nine-dish plus tasting menu at the French Laundry, a menu that changes daily, by the way. But what should also make uber-chef Thomas Keller equally proud is the terrifically kindly service of his staff, who understand that a meal here is supposed to be a special occasion. And so it is, with dishes that often astonish—wait til you taste what he does with tapioca—and always please. This is one place that lives up to its reputation, and its gazillion Michelin stars.

6640 Washington St., Yountville. www.frenchlaundry.com. ✆ **704/944-2380.** Tasting menu $270. Daily lunch Fri–Sun 11am–1pm, dinner 5:30–9:30pm.

Morimoto ★★ JAPANESE Continuing the Napa parade of chefs you watch on TV, this is the offering of Masahiru Morimoto of "Iron Chef." No mere vanity project, Morimoto has called this his flagship, and the food certainly is worthy of that, though it can be hard to decide what to order (the menu could double as a book, it's that thick). Some specials include tofu made fresh at tableside, creative sushi offerings and salads crafted from ingredients that are freshly picked on nearby farms. Along with 200 sakes, Morimoto serves a canny selection of wines from nearby vineyards.

610 Main St., Napa. © **707/252-1600.** www.morimotonapa.com. Main dishes $13-$35. Sun–Thurs 11:30am–2:30pm and 5–midnight, Fri–Sat 11:30am–2:30pm and 5pm–1am.

Terra/Bar Terra ★★ CONTEMPORARY AMERICAN   Casual or dressy dining—you choose at this two-in-one eatery. One side houses a lively bar with terrific (and unusual) eats; the original (Terra) specializes in parts of the critter or critters that many Americans refuse—tripe, trotters, sea urchin, you get the picture—but makes them so delicious, even the most squeamish diners are usually converted by the end of the night. (And for the truly risk averse, there are usually tamer items, such as cod or steak, available as well.) The chef here is Hiro Sone, and I struggled with whether to call the cuisine Asian fusion or contemporary American. Truly this Japanese chef borrows from both traditions and makes them his own. Don't skip the cocktails, which are made from fruits and herbs grown in the owners' garden. Desserts are also primo, so save room!

1345 Railroad Ave. (btw. Adams and Hunt sts.), St. Helena. © **707/963-8931.** www.terrarestaurant. com. Reservations recommended. Bar: Plates $6–$25. Dining room: 3-course $57; 4-course $75; 5-course $90; 6-course $102; chef's menu changes nightly. Wed–Mon 6pm–closing. Closed 2 weeks in early Jan.

Where to Stay in Sonoma County

The biggest choice you need to make when considering where to shack up is whether to stay in downtown Sonoma, which allows for easy access to its walkable shopping and dining square, or anywhere else in the valley, which promises more rural small-town surroundings and guaranteed time in the car to get to any activities. Regardless, you're destined to spend time behind the wheel, as the wineries and attractions are scattered. Keep in mind that during the peak season and on weekends, most B&Bs and hotels require a minimum 2-night stay. Of course, that's assuming you can find a vacancy; make reservations as far in advance as possible. If you are having trouble finding a room, call the **Sonoma Valley Visitors Bureau** (© **866/996-1090** or 707/996-1090; www.sonomavalley.com). The staff will try to refer you to a lodging that has a room to spare, but won't make reservations for you. Another option is the **Bed and Breakfast Association of Sonoma Valley** (© **800/969-4667**), which can refer you to a B&B that belongs to the association. You can also find updated information on their website, **www.sonomabb.com.**

EXPENSIVE

Honor Mansion ★★★   Heading to wine country for your honeymoon? Welcome to the hotel—oh, wait, mansion (it truly is one)—where you'll want to stay. With the exception of the Angel Oak room (which features a schmaltzy, off-putting mural of cherubim), the decor here is to die for, each room different, and featuring such luxe furnishings as sleigh or wrought-iron beds, hand-carved wooden dressers, gazillion thread-count linens, wood burning fireplaces and private patios (some rooms have two!). Every morning, coffee and biscotti arrive at your door at a pre-requested time; that's followed by a sumptuous buffet breakfast in the main house (guest choose from rooms in that house and free standing cottages, including one swank one that's at the bottom of a historic water tower, with an outdoor spa tub on the roof). On-site: a 40-foot lap pool, tennis and basketball courts, a PGA-certified putting green, two competition bocce ball courts, croquet courts and a quarter acre of zinfandel vines. Sorry, to keep the romantic atmosphere intact, kids under 16 are not welcome.

891 Grove St., Healdsburg. ℰ**800-554-4667** or 703/433-4277. www.honormansion.com. $240–$425 double. Rate includes buffet breakfast, evening wine and cheese, free parking.

Kenwood Inn & Spa ★★ You'll feel like you've landed in Italy when you drive up to this Tuscan-inspired resort with it honey-colored villas, its flower-filled flagstone courtyard, and splendid views of vineyard-covered hills. The rooms are just as Italianate, swathed in imported tapestries and velvets, and filled with custom-made furniture, shipped in from across the pond. Plus each gets a fireplace, balcony (except those on the ground floor), and spa tub. What they don't have are TV's, but why would you need one with the on-site, and primo, spa and pool to keep you busy. As for the included breakfast, get ready to skip lunch! You won't need it after the three-course feast that's served here. Alas, this is another hotel that doesn't accept children (those under 17, in this case)

10400 Sonoma Hwy., Kenwood. ℰ **800/353-6966** or 707/833-1293. www.kenwoodinn.com. 29 units. $325-$500 double. Rates include gourmet breakfast. 2-night minimum on weekends. No pets allowed. Children 17 and under not recommended. **Amenities:** Concierge; 2 outdoor hot tubs; heated outdoor pool; indoor soaking tub; full-service spa, free high-speed Internet access.

MacArthur Place ★★★ All the senses are soothed at this gracious inn, a long-time favorite. MacArthur's on-site spa is topnotch, the gardens—lush and filled with lovely sculptures—are exquisite, and who can fault an included (and generous) breakfast buffet that often includes chocolate bread pudding? As for the rooms, they come in a number of varieties: some are set in the 1850s manor house (the property was once a working ranch), while others are scattered around the grounds, in roomy cottages, each unique, luxurious and filled with such niceties as outdoor hot tubs and showers (for the spa suites), wood burning fireplaces, whirlpool tubs and private decks. But what most guests come away raving about here is the service: the staff seem to be picked for their ability to make guests feel, at one and the same time, like they have their privacy, but are being coddled to the nth degree. Final plus: it's within walking distance to a number of terrific cafes and bars.

29 E. MacArthur St., Sonoma. ℰ **800/722-1866** or 707/938-2929. www.macarthurplace.com. 64 units. Sun–Thurs $268–$650 double; Fri–Sat $317–$699 double. Rates include continental breakfast and evening wine and cheese. Free parking. **Amenities:** Steak restaurant and bar; rental bikes; concierge; exercise room; outdoor Jacuzzi; outdoor heated pool; room service; full-service spa; Wi-Fi (free).

MODERATE

Beltane Ranch ★★★ This century-old, plantation style working ranch just about defines the word bucolic. And you can throw "charming" in there for good measure, as well. The rooms are spacious and filled with well-chosen antiques, each with its own sitting area. The 105-acre estate is laced with hiking trails and gardens and it boasts a good tennis court, for those who want to work up a sweat. Breakfast is included and it's superb, the eggs and produce produced right on the ranch. In fact, many guests find it near-impossible to leave the Beltane's expansive wrap-around porch. It's the perfect place to while away the afternoon-into-evening, glass of vino in hand. *Tip:* Request one of the upstairs rooms for the best views.

11775 Sonoma Hwy./Hwy. 12, Glen Ellen. ✆ **707/996-6501.** www.beltaneranch.com. 5 units, 1 cottage. $150–$265 double. Rates include full breakfast. **Amenities:** Outdoor, unlit tennis court; Wi-Fi (free).

Sonoma's Best Guest Cottages ★★ These perfectly adorable little houses, formerly known as Les Petites Maisons, were once grubby workmen's cottages for field hands. But the people who run the Girl and the Fig (see below), waved a magic wand over them, turning them into terrific mini-homes for tourists, candy colored and sweet, with equipped kitchens, living rooms, big bathrooms, wide wood floors, outdoor sitting areas, and a security gate for the parking area. Their location 2 miles east of Sonoma town makes for an ideal home base to explore both counties. And for the reasonable (for the area!) nightly rate, you get enough space for a family of four to six, and the maintenance standards couldn't be higher.

1190 East Napa St., Sonoma. ✆ **800/291-8962** or 707/933-0340. www.sonomasbestcottages.com. $179-$299 per night. 4 units. Amenities: Private gardens; fully-equipped kitchens; bbq grill upon request; Wi-Fi (free).

INEXPENSIVE

Creekside Inn and Resort ★★ I like staying in the Russian River Valley, primarily because I find the thick redwood forests so soothing and at odds with the open farmland I experience all day. The Creekside Inn is a complex of apartments of varying sizes, all built on stilts above the forest floor. There are two options: an individually themed and designed bed and breakfast room (the waffles you'll get are marvelous and the rooms are adorable), and cottages with full kitchens (most have gas fireplaces, and all have private decks and screened in porches). The staff here is genuinely friendly and laid-back, and there's also a pool. The pubs and coffee cafes of downtown Guerneville are a short walk away over a pedestrian bridge.

16180 Neeley Rd., Guerneville. ✆ **707/869-3623.** www.creeksideinn.com. 15 units. $95-$155 double, though many of the pricier cabins (up to $260) will easily house 6 people. **Amenities:** Pool; Wi-Fi (free).

Sonoma Creek Inn ★ An excellent value for the price, the Sonoma Creek Inn is cutely decorated (colorful bedspreads, fun lampshades, the odd tile mosaic in the wall), clean, and friendly. Rooms are a tad more spacious than they are at other converted motels that are a bit older. Another $20 buys you a balcony or a pleasant walled patio with your own fountain, a terrific touch. Its street is a little noisy (well, for Sonoma), and its neighborhood is strictly farm community—meaning it needs some grooming but isn't unsafe—and you'll have to drive a minute or two to get anywhere else in town. Check the website's special offers.

239 Boyes Blvd., Sonoma. ✆ **888/712-1289** or 707/939-9463. www.sonomacreekinn.com. 16 units. Sun–Thurs $99–$159, Fri–Sat $139–$189. Free parking. **Amenities:** Bicycles; concierge services; free phone calls; wine-tasting passes; Wi-Fi (free).

Travelodge Healdsburg ★ I make no promises of beauty for this chain motel—it's in a blah industrial part of town with no bucolic appeal. (Of course, in these parts, bucolic appeal is always just a 2-minute drive away.) But I can vouch for the rates, which are usually among the lowest in the area, and what's more, I can say they've

done an excellent job in renovating and in running this place. It's clean, it's of standard size, and it's an excellent fallback in an expensive area, even if it totally lacks glamour (and does get traffic noise; bring earplugs).

178 Dry Creek Rd., Healdsburg. ℂ **707/433-0101** or 800/499-0103. www.travelodge.com. $76–$150 double. **Amenities:** Free parking; Wi-Fi (free).

Where to Eat in Sonoma County

Barndiva ★★   Over 200, small-batch farmers provide the produce and meats that make a meal at this modern, red barn restaurant so special. You can tell, when you tuck into a dish here, that most of what's on your plate was picked that very morning. If they're on the menu (it changes daily), don't skip the chevre croquettes with tomato jam. And oddly, for a restaurant in wine country, Barndiva is famous for its creative cocktails.

231 Center St., Healdsburg, Sonoma. ℂ **737/431-0100.** www.barndiva.com. Main entrees $17–$32 at lunch, about $10 more at dinner. Wed–Thurs noon–9pm, Fri–Sat noon–10pm, Sun 11am–9pm.

Fremont Diner ★   An adorable, twirly-seated diner that was founded not too long ago, but has the appearance of a classic 1940s diner. The food, too, tastes like it was from that era: real eggs cooked up into fluffy omelettes, serious coffee, brisket hash, excellent fried chicken, and milkshakes so thick they need a spoon. When the weather's nice, people eat outside, though the real character is indoors here.

2660 Fremont Dr., Sonoma. ℂ **707/938-7370.** www.thefremontdiner.com. Main courses $3.25–$12. Mon–Wed 8am–3pm, Thurs–Sun 8am–9pm.

Girl and Fig ★★   Rumor has it that Lady Gaga dined here on her last tour through Sonoma, though she's not the "girl" (or the fig for that matter) in the title of this resto. The "girl" would be considered a woman, now that her restaurant is 16 years old and her name is Sondra Bernstein. The chef/proprietess behind this acclaimed venture, she's become known for both her charcuterie platters and her talent at mixing the cuisine of Provencal with local Sonoma ingredients. It's a delightful place to dine, but if you don't make it here know that you can now buy some of Bernstein's jams and chutneys (and yes, some are made with figs) at stores around the area; they make a great gift.

110 W. Spain St., Sonoma. ℂ **707/938-3634.** www.thegirlandfig.com. Main courses $20–$25. Daily 11:30am–10pm.

Gott's Roadside ★   The original drive-in that spawned the popular outpost in San Francisco's Ferry Building, Gott's does classic comfort food with clean ingredients, served in an old-style counter-service setting. Formerly called Taylor's Refresher, it's been slinging burgers since 1949 and looks like it. Eating here is a nice break from the balsamic vinegar and goat cheese served seemingly everywhere else. Don't skip the milkshakes, served with both spoon and straw, necessary for a drink that's this lusciously thick. Beware if it's cold or rainy, because every seat is outdoors and not every one is sheltered. A third branch, pressed from the same mold, exists at the Oxbow Market in central Napa.

933 Main St., St. Helena, Sonoma County. ℂ **707/963-3486.** www.gotts.com. Main courses $7–$15. Open daily 7am–10pm.

La Bamba ★★   A tourist in the wine region could be forgiven if they are lulled into the belief that everyone in the area is rich, white, and of Italian or Spanish descent. But the locals know better. Many of the people working the land—the ones who prune the vines and make the wine happen—are immigrants (some legal, some not) from Mexico, Colombia, and other Latin countries. And do you think that in the evening, after a hard day spent in the dirt, that they make reservations at places serving fig compote or smoked salmon? Heck. No. For some real local flavor, grab a meal at this beloved taco truck; tacos are just $1.50 each and fillings change daily (though you can usually get the delish *pastor* tacos).

Usually parked at 487 First St. in Sonoma. Daily noon–midnight. No phone or website.

PLANNING YOUR TRIP TO SAN FRANCISCO

A s with any trip, a little preparation is essential before you start your journey. This chapter provides a variety of planning tools, including information on how to get there, how to get around within the city once there, and when to come. And then, in a mainly alphabetical listing, we deal with the dozens of miscellaneous resources and organizations that you can turn to for help.

GETTING THERE

By Plane

The northern Bay Area has two major airports: San Francisco International and Oakland International.

San Francisco International Airport Almost four dozen major scheduled carriers serve **San Francisco International Airport (SFO;** www.flysfo.com), 14 miles directly south of downtown on U.S. 101. Drive time to downtown during commuter rush hour is about 40 minutes; at other times, it's about 20 to 25 minutes. You can also ride BART from the airport to downtown and the East Bay.

Call ℂ **511** or visit www.511.org for up-to-the-minute information about public transportation and traffic.

Oakland International Airport About 5 miles south of downtown Oakland, at the Hegenberger Road exit of Calif. 17 (U.S. 880; if coming from south, take 98th Ave.), **Oakland International Airport (OAK;** www.oaklandairport.com) primarily serves passengers with East Bay destinations. Some San Franciscans prefer this less-crowded, more accessible airport, although it takes about a half-hour to get there from downtown San Francisco (traffic permitting). The airport is also accessible by BART via a shuttle bus.

ARRIVING AT THE AIRPORT

Immigration & Customs Clearance International visitors arriving by air, no matter what the port of entry, should cultivate patience and resignation before setting foot on U.S. soil. U.S. airports have considerably beefed up security clearances in the years since the terrorist attacks of September 11, 2001, and clearing Customs and Immigration can take as long as 2 hours.

GETTING INTO TOWN FROM THE SAN FRANCISCO AIRPORT

One of the fastest and cheapest way to get from SFO to the city is to take **BART** (Bay Area Rapid Transit; © **415/989-2278;** www.bart.gov), which offers numerous stops within downtown San Francisco. This route, which takes about 35 minutes, avoids traffic on the way and costs a heck of a lot less than taxis or shuttles. As of August 2013, a BART ticket is $8.25 ($3.05 youth/senior) for a one-way ride from SFO to the Embarcadero stop. Just jump on the airport's free shuttle bus to the international terminal, enter the BART station there, and you're on your way to San Francisco. Trains leave approximately every 15 minutes.

A **cab** from SFO to Fisherman's Wharf costs about $60, plus tip, and takes around 30 minutes, traffic permitting.

SuperShuttle (© **800/BLUE-VAN** [800/258-3826], or 415/558-8500; www.supershuttle.com) is a private shuttle company that offers door-to-door airport service, in which you share a van with a few other passengers. They will take you anywhere in the city, charging $17 per person to a residence or business. On the return trip, add $10 to $17 for each additional person depending on whether you're traveling from a hotel or a residence. The shuttle stops at least every 20 minutes, sometimes sooner, and picks up passengers from the marked areas outside the terminals' upper levels. Reservations are required for the return trip to the airport only and should be made 1 day before departure. Remember, if it is summertime, or holiday season, you need to be at the airport a good 2 hours before your flight (3 hours for international flights), as TSA security lines can be long. Keep in mind that you could be the first one on and the last one off, so this trip could take a while. For $75, you can either charter the entire van for up to seven people or an ExecuCar private sedan ($85) for up to four people. For more info on the **Execucar,** call © **800/410-4444,** or make a reservation at **www. Execucar.com**.

The San Mateo County Transit system, **SamTrans** (© **800/660-4287** in Northern California, or 650/508-6200; www.samtrans.com), runs two buses between SFO and the Transbay Terminal at First and Mission streets. Bus no. 292 costs $2 and makes the trip in about an hour. The KX Express bus costs $5 and takes just 35 minutes, but permits only one carry-on bag. Both buses run daily.

GETTING INTO TOWN FROM OAKLAND INTERNATIONAL AIRPORT

A **cab** from OAK to Fisherman's Wharf costs about $70, plus tip, and takes around 40 minutes, traffic permitting.

The cheapest way to reach downtown San Francisco is to take the shuttle bus from the Oakland Airport to **BART** (Bay Area Rapid Transit; © **510/464-6000;** www.bart.gov). The AirBART shuttle bus runs about every 10 minutes Mon–Sat from 5am–midnight (Sun 8am–midnight). It makes pickups in between Terminals 1 and 2 near the ground transportation sign. Tickets must be purchased at the Oakland Airport's vending machines prior to boarding. The cost is $3 ($1 children/seniors) for the 10-minute ride to BART's Coliseum station in Oakland. BART fares vary, depending on your destination; the trip to the Embarcadero costs $3.85 ($1.40 children/seniors) and takes 15 minutes once you're on board. The entire excursion should take around 45 minutes.

By Car

San Francisco is easily accessible by major highways: **I-5,** from the north, and **U.S. 101,** which cuts south-north through the peninsula from San Jose and across the Golden Gate Bridge to points north. If you drive from Los Angeles, you can take the longer coastal route (437 miles and 11 hr.) or the inland route (389 miles and 8 hr.). From Mendocino, it's 156 miles and 4 hours; from Sacramento, 88 miles and 1½ hours; from Yosemite, 210 miles and 4 hours.

If you are driving and aren't already a member, it's worth joining the **American Automobile Association** (AAA; ℂ 800/922-8228; www.csaa.com). Memberships start as low as $57 per year, and provide roadside and other services, including massive hotel discounts, to motorists. **Amoco Motor Club** (ℂ 800/334-3300; www.bpmotor club.com) is another recommended choice.

By Train

Traveling by train takes a long time and usually costs as much as, or more than, flying. Still, if you want to take a leisurely ride across America, rail may be a good option.

San Francisco–bound **Amtrak** (ℂ 800/872-7245; www.amtrak.com) trains leave from New York and cross the country via Chicago. The journey takes about 3½ days, and seats sell quickly. When checking in August 2013, the lowest one-way fare costs $411 from New York and $246 from Chicago. Round-trip tickets from Los Angeles start at $89 and involve two buses and a train. All trains arrive in Emeryville, just north of Oakland, and connect with regularly scheduled buses to San Francisco's Ferry Building and the Caltrain station in downtown San Francisco.

Caltrain (ℂ 800/660-4287; www.caltrain.com) operates train service between San Francisco and the towns of the peninsula. The city depot is at 700 Fourth St., at Townsend Street.

GETTING AROUND

For a map of San Francisco's public transportation options, see the inside back cover of this guide. You can call ℂ **511** for current transportation and traffic information. The best way to figure out how to get around San Francisco is www.511.org. Input your current and desired addresses, and the site will give you all your transportation options, including fares, what type of transportation, and when the next bus, for example, will be at your stop. For more "Getting Around" advice, see p. 23.

Hint: The **historic F-Line** streetcar runs from the Castro to Fisherman's Wharf, with stops a block or two from the Mission District, Civic Center, Union Square, SoMa, Ferry Building, Exploratorium, Coit Tower, North Beach, and Pier 39—in other words, most of the places you want to visit.

By Public Transportation

The **San Francisco Municipal Transportation Agency,** 1 S. Van Ness Ave., better known as "Muni" (ℂ 415/673-6864; www.sfmta.com), operates the city's cable cars, buses, and streetcars. Together, these three services crisscross the entire city. Fares for buses and streetcars are $2 for adults, 75¢ for seniors 65 and over, children 5 to 17, and riders with disabilities. Cable cars, which run from 6:30am to 12:50am, cost a whopping $6 for all people 6 and over ($3 for seniors and riders with disabilities before 7am or after 9pm). Needless to say, they're packed primarily with tourists. Exact change is

Muni Discounts

Muni discount passes, called **Passports** (www.sfmta.com), entitle holders to unlimited rides on buses, streetcars, and cable cars. A Passport costs $14 for 1 day, $22 for 3 days, and $28 for 7 consecutive days. There is no discount for children or seniors. Passports are sold at a number of locations throughout the city listed on the website. Another option is buying a **CityPASS** (www.city pass.com; $84 adults, $59 kids 5–11), which entitles you to unlimited Muni rides for 7 days, plus admission to four (or five, depending on which you choose) attractions for 9 days. These passes are sold online, or at any of the CityPASS attractions.

required on all vehicles except cable cars. Fares are subject to change. If you're standing waiting for Muni and have wireless Web access (or from any computer), check www.nextmuni.com to get up-to-the-minute information about when the next bus or streetcar is coming. Muni's NextBus uses satellite technology and advanced computer modeling to track vehicles on their routes. Each vehicle is fitted with a satellite tracking system, so the information is constantly updated.

For detailed route information, click "Muni Route Maps" on the website at www. sfmta.com/maps. Each route has its own map, and when you click on the map, you will see live-time details of where the buses are at that moment¾you can even watch them slowly crawl across your computer screen as the move. For a big picture look at all Muni routes, click on "Muni System Maps".

CABLE CAR   San Francisco's cable cars might not be the most practical means of transport, but the rolling historic landmarks are a fun ride. The three lines are concentrated in the downtown area. The most scenic, and exciting, is the **Powell–Hyde line,** which follows a zigzag route from the corner of Powell and Market streets, over both Nob Hill and Russian Hill, to a turntable at gas-lit Victorian Square in front of Aquatic Park. The **Powell–Mason line** starts at the same intersection and climbs Nob Hill before descending to Bay Street, just 3 blocks from Fisherman's Wharf. The least scenic is the **California Street line,** which begins at the foot of Market Street and runs a straight course through Chinatown and over Nob Hill to Van Ness Avenue. All riders must exit at the last stop and wait in line for the return trip. The cable car system operates from approximately 6:30am to midnight, and each ride costs $6.

BUS   Buses reach almost every corner of San Francisco and beyond—they even travel over the bridges to Marin County and Oakland. Overhead electric cables power some buses; others use conventional gas engines. All are numbered and display their destinations on the front. Signs, curb markings, and yellow bands on adjacent utility poles designate stops, and most bus shelters exhibit Muni's transportation map and schedule. Many buses travel along Market Street or pass near Union Square and run from about 6am to midnight. After midnight, there is infrequent all-night "Owl" service. For safety, avoid taking buses late at night.

Popular tourist routes include bus number 71, which run to Golden Gate Park; 41 and 45, which travel along Union Street; and 30, which runs between Union Square, Chinatown, Ghirardelli Square, and the Marina District. A bus ride costs $2 for adults and 75¢ for seniors 66 and over, children 5 to 17, and riders with disabilities.

STREETCAR Six of Muni's seven streetcar lines, designated J, K, L, M, N, and T, run underground downtown and on the streets in the outer neighborhoods. The sleek rail cars make the same stops as BART (see below) along Market Street, including Embarcadero Station (in the Financial District), Montgomery and Powell streets (both near Union Square), and the Civic Center (near City Hall). Past the Civic Center, the routes branch off: The J line takes you to Mission Dolores; the K, L, and M lines run to Castro Street; and the N line parallels Golden Gate Park and extends all the way to the Embarcadero and AT&T Park. The newest one (called T-Third Street, opened in 2007) runs to AT&T Park and the San Francisco Caltrain station and then continues south along Third Street, ending near Monster (Candlestick) Park.

Streetcars run about every 15 minutes, more frequently during rush hours. They operate Monday through Friday from 5am to 12:15am, Saturday from 6am to approximately 12:15am, and Sunday from approximately 8am to 12:20am. The L and N lines operate 24 hours a day, 7 days a week, but late at night, regular buses trace the L and N routes, which are normally underground, from atop the city streets. Because the operation is part of Muni, the fares are the same as for buses, and passes are accepted.

The most recent line to this system is not a newcomer at all, but is, in fact, an encore performance of rejuvenated 1930s streetcars from all over the world. The beautiful, retro multicolored F-Market and Wharves streetcar runs from 17th and Castro streets to the Embarcadero; every other streetcar continues to Jones and Beach streets in Fisherman's Wharf. This is a quick, charming, and tourist-friendly way to get up- and downtown without any hassle.

BART BART, an acronym for **Bay Area Rapid Transit** (© **415/989-2278;** www. bart.gov), is a futuristic-looking, high-speed rail network that connects San Francisco (starting just south of the airport) with the East Bay—Oakland, Richmond, Concord, Pittsburg, and Fremont. Four stations are on Market Street (see "Streetcar," above). One-way fares range from $1.75 to $11, depending on how far you go. Machines in the stations dispense tickets that are magnetically encoded with a dollar amount. Computerized exits automatically deduct the correct fare. Children 4 and under ride free. Trains run every 15 to 20 minutes, Monday through Friday from 4am to midnight, Saturday from 6am to midnight, and Sunday from 8am to midnight. In keeping with its futuristic look, BART now offers online trip planners that you can download to your smartphone or tablet.

The 33-mile BART extension, which extends all the way to San Francisco International Airport, opened in June 2003. See above for information on getting into town from the airport.

By Taxi

This isn't New York, so don't expect a taxi to appear whenever you need one—if at all. If you're downtown during rush hour or leaving a major hotel, it won't be hard to hail a cab; just look for the lighted sign on the roof that indicates the vehicle is free. Otherwise, it's a good idea to call one of the following companies to arrange a ride; even then, there's been more than one time when the cab never came for us. What to do? Call back if your cab is late and insist on attention, but don't expect prompt results on weekends, no matter how nicely you ask. The companies are **Nation and Veteran's Cab** (© **415/552-1300**), **Luxor Cabs** (© **415/282-4141**), **De Soto Cab** (© **415/970-1300**), **Green Cab** (© **415/626-4733**), **Metro Cab** (© **415/920-0700**, and **Yellow Cab** (© **415/626-2345**). For an estimate of fares, including an allowance for traffic, visit www.taxifarefinder.com.

By Car

You don't need a car to explore downtown San Francisco. In fact, with the city becoming more crowded by the minute, a car can be your worst nightmare—you're likely to end up stuck in traffic with lots of aggressive and frustrated drivers, pay upwards of $50 a day to park (plus a whopping new 14% parking lot tax), and spend a good portion of your vacation looking for a parking space. Don't bother. However, if you want to venture outside the city, driving is the best way to go. If you want to take a daytrip to Napa or Muir Woods, picking up a car in the city early in the morning, and returning it that evening, will save a fortune for a family of four.

Before heading outside the city, especially in winter, call ✆ **800/427-ROAD (7623)** for California **road conditions.** You can also call ✆ **511** for current traffic information.

CAR RENTALS   All the major rental companies operate in the city and have desks at the airports. When we checked (August 2013), you could get a compact car at the airport for a week starting at $335, including all taxes and other charges, but prices change dramatically on a daily basis and depend on which company you rent from. A 1 day rental from Fisherman's Wharf was $90, all in.

Some of the national car-rental companies operating in San Francisco include **Alamo** (✆ 800/327-9633; www.alamo.com), **Avis** (✆ 800/331-1212; www.avis.com), **Budget** (✆ 800/527-0700; www.budget.com), **Dollar** (✆ 800/800-4000; www.dollar.com), **Enterprise** (✆ 800/325-8007; www.enterprise.com), **Hertz** (✆ 800/654-3131; www.hertz.com), **National** (✆ 800/227-7368; www.nationalcar.com), and **Thrifty** (✆ 800/367-2277; www.thrifty.com).

Car-rental rates vary even more than airline fares. Prices depend on the size of the car, where and when you pick it up and drop it off, the length of the rental period, where and how far you drive it, whether you buy insurance, and a host of other factors. A few key questions can save you hundreds of dollars, but you have to ask—reservations agents don't often volunteer money-saving information:

○ Are weekend rates lower than weekday rates? Ask if the rate is the same for pickup Friday morning, for instance, as it is for Thursday night. Reservations agents won't volunteer this information, so don't be shy about asking.

○ Does the agency assess a drop-off charge if you don't return the car to the same location where you picked it up?

○ Are special promotional rates available? If you see an advertised price in your local newspaper, be sure to ask for that specific rate; otherwise, you could be charged the standard rate. Terms change constantly.

○ Are discounts available for members of AARP, AAA, frequent-flier programs, or trade unions? If you belong to any of these organizations, you may be entitled to discounts of up to 30%.

○ How much tax will be added to the rental bill? Will there be local tax and state tax?

○ How much does the rental company charge to refill your gas tank if you return with the tank less than full? Most rental companies claim their prices are "competitive," but fuel is almost always cheaper in town, so you should try to allow enough time to refuel the car before returning it.

Some companies offer "refueling packages," in which you pay for an entire tank of gas upfront. The cost is usually fairly competitive with local prices, but you don't get credit for any gas remaining in the tank. If a stop at a gas station on the way to the airport will make you miss your plane, then by all means take advantage of the fuel purchase option. Otherwise, skip it.

Keep in mind the following handy driving tips:

- California law requires that drivers and passengers all wear seat belts.
- You can turn right at a red light (unless otherwise indicated), after yielding to traffic and pedestrians, and after coming to a complete stop.
- Cable cars always have the right of way, as do pedestrians at intersections and crosswalks.
- Pay attention to signs and arrows on the streets and roadways, or you might suddenly find yourself in a lane that requires exiting or turning when you want to go straight. What's more, San Francisco's many one-way streets can drive you in circles, but most road maps of the city indicate which way traffic flows.

Most agencies enforce a minimum-age requirement—usually 25. Some also have a maximum-age limit. If you're concerned that these limits might affect you, ask about rental requirements at the time of booking to avoid problems later.

Make sure you're insured. Hasty assumptions about your personal auto insurance or a rental agency's additional coverage could end up costing you tens of thousands of dollars, even if you are involved in an accident that is clearly the fault of another driver.

If you already have your own car insurance, you are most likely covered in the United States for loss of or damage to a rental car and liability in case of injury to any other party involved in an accident. Be sure to check your policy before you spend extra money (around $10 or more per day) on the **collision damage waiver (CDW)** offered by all agencies.

Most major credit cards (especially gold and platinum cards) provide some degree of coverage as well—if they were used to pay for the rental. Terms vary widely, however, so be sure to call your credit card company directly before you rent and rely on the card for coverage. If you are uninsured, your credit card may provide primary coverage as long as you decline the rental agency's insurance. If you already have insurance, your credit card may provide secondary coverage, which basically covers your deductible. However, note that *credit cards will not cover liability,* which is the cost of injury to an outside party and/or damage to an outside party's vehicle. If you do not hold an insurance policy, you should seriously consider buying additional liability insurance from your rental company, even if you decline the CDW.

International visitors should note that insurance and taxes are almost never included in quoted rental car rates in the U.S. Be sure to ask your rental agency about additional fees for these. They can add a significant cost to your rental car.

If you're visiting from abroad and plan to rent a car in the United States, keep in mind that foreign driver's licenses are usually recognized in the U.S., but you may want to consider obtaining an international driver's license.

PARKING   If you want to have a relaxing vacation, don't even attempt to find street parking on Nob Hill, in North Beach, in Chinatown, by Fisherman's Wharf, or on Telegraph Hill. Park in a garage or take a cab or a bus. If you do find street parking, pay attention to street signs that explain when you can park and for how long. Be especially careful not to park in zones that are tow areas during rush hours. And be forewarned, San Francisco has instituted a 14% parking tax, so don't be surprised by that garage fee!

Curb colors also indicate parking regulations. *Red* means no stopping or parking, *blue* is reserved for drivers with disabilities who have a disabled plate or placard, *white* means there's a 5-minute limit and the driver must stay in the vehicle, *green* indicates a 10-minute limit, and *yellow* and *yellow-and-black* curbs are for stopping to load or unload passengers or luggage only. Also, don't park at a bus stop or in front of a fire hydrant, and watch out for street-cleaning signs. If you violate the law, you might get a hefty ticket or your car might be towed; to get your car back, you'll have to get a release from the nearest district police department and then go to the towing company to pick up the vehicle.

When parking on a hill, apply the hand brake, put the car in gear, and *curb your wheels*—toward the curb when facing downhill, away from the curb when facing uphill. Curbing your wheels not only prevents a possible "runaway" but also keeps you from getting a ticket—an expensive fine that is aggressively enforced.

In a high tech city like San Francisco, it only follows there would be a way to use your computer or smartphone when parking a car. Launched in 2010, **www.sfpark.org** is an award-winning website (a phone app is available too) that collects and displays real-time information about available parking in the city, in an effort to stop people from driving in circles, polluting our city, while hunting for a spot. You can look at a map of the city parking garages, get addresses, directions, hourly prices, and even see how many spots are available inside each garage. If you hit the green "pricing" key, it will show dark green for more expensive garages and light green for the less expensive places. For metered street parking, the map will show red in areas of limited street parking, navy for some availability, and light turquoise for good availability. For both garage and metered parking, prices are regularly adjusted up or down monthly, depending on demand.

By Ferry

TO/FROM SAUSALITO OR LARKSPUR The **Golden Gate Ferry Service** fleet (*©* **415/455-2000;** www.goldengateferry.org) shuttles passengers daily between the San Francisco Ferry Building, at the foot of Market Street, and downtown Sausalito and Larkspur. Service is frequent, departing at reasonable intervals every day of the year except January 1, Thanksgiving Day, and December 25. Phone or check the website for an exact schedule. The ride to Sausalito or Larkspur takes about half an hour. One-way fares to Sausalito are $10.25 for adults, $5 for seniors (65+), passengers with disabilities, and youth (6–18). One-way fares to Larkspur are $9.50 for adults, $4.75 for seniors (65+), passengers with disabilities, and youth (6–18). Children 5 and under travel free when accompanied by a full-fare paying adult (limit two children per adult).

Ferries of the **Blue & Gold Fleet** (*©* **415/773-1188** for recorded info; for tickets and schedules, visit www.blueandgoldfleet.com) provide round-trip service to downtown Sausalito, Tiburon, and Angel Island. For Sausalito and Tiburon, the one-way fare is $11 for adults, $6.75 for kids (5–11) and seniors (65+). The Angel Island one-way fare is $8.50 for adults, $4.75 for children (6–12) and seniors (65+). Boats run on a seasonal schedule, so check the website for details. Boats leave from Pier 41, and tickets can be purchased at the pier.

[FastFACTS] SAN FRANCISCO

Area Codes The area code for San Francisco is **415;** for Oakland, Berkeley, and much of the East Bay, **510;** for the peninsula, generally **650.** Napa and Sonoma are **707.** Most phone numbers in this book are in San Francisco's 415 area code, but there's no need to dial it if you're within the city limits.

ATMs In the land of shopping malls and immediate gratification, there's an ATM on almost every block—often droves of them. In fact, finding a place to withdraw cash is one of the easiest tasks you'll partake in while visiting San Francisco.

Nationwide, the easiest and best way to get cash away from home is from an ATM (automated teller machine), sometimes referred to as a "cash machine" or "cashpoint." The **Cirrus** (ⓒ **800/424-7787;** www.mastercard.com) and **PLUS** (ⓒ **800/847-2911;** www.visa.com) networks span the country; you can find them even in remote regions. Go to your bank card's website to find ATM locations at your destination. Be sure you know your daily withdrawal limit before you depart.

Note: Many banks impose a fee every time you use a card at another bank's ATM, and that fee is often higher for international transactions (up to $5

or more) than for domestic ones (where they're rarely more than $3). In addition, the bank from which you withdraw cash may charge its own fee. To compare banks' ATM fees within the U.S., use www.bankrate.com. Visitors from outside the U.S. should also find out whether their bank assesses a 1% to 3% fee on charges incurred abroad.

Tip: One way around these fees is to ask for cash back at grocery, drug, and convenience stores that accept ATM cards and don't charge usage fees (be sure to ask). Of course, you'll have to purchase something first.

Business Hours Most banks are open Monday through Friday from 9am to 5pm as well as Saturday mornings. Many banks also have ATMs for 24-hour banking. (See "ATMs," above.) Most stores are open Monday through Saturday from 10 or 11am to at least 6pm, with shorter hours on Sunday. But there are exceptions: Stores in Chinatown, Ghirardelli Square, and Pier 39 stay open much later during the tourist season, and large department stores, including Macy's and Nordstrom, keep late hours. Most restaurants serve lunch from about 11:30am to 2:30pm and dinner from about 5:30 to 10pm. They sometimes serve later on weekends.

Nightclubs and bars are usually open daily until 2am, when they are legally bound to stop serving alcohol.

Car Rental See "By Car," under "Getting Around," above.

Cellphones See "Mobile Phones," later in this section.

Crime See "Safety," later in this section.

Disabled Travelers Most disabilities shouldn't stop anyone from traveling. There are more options and resources out there than ever before.

Most of San Francisco's major museums and tourist attractions have wheelchair ramps. Many hotels offer special accommodations and services for wheelchair users and other visitors with disabilities. As well as the ramps, they include extra-large bathrooms and telecommunication devices for hearing-impaired travelers. The Visitors Information Center (p. 245) should have the most up-to-date information.

Travelers in wheelchairs can request special ramped taxis by calling **Yellow Cab** (ⓒ **415/626-2345**), which charges regular rates for the service. Travelers with disabilities can also get a free copy of the *Muni Access Guide,* published by the San Francisco Municipal Transportation

Agency, Accessible Services Program, One South Van Ness, 3rd floor (📞 **415/ 923-6142**), which is staffed weekdays from 8am to 5pm. Many of the major car-rental companies offer hand-controlled cars for drivers with disabilities. **Alamo** (📞 **800/651-1223**), **Avis** (📞 **800/331-1212,** ext. 7305), and **Budget** (📞 **800/314-3932**) have special hotlines that help provide such a vehicle at any of their U.S. locations with 48 hours' advance notice; **Hertz** (📞 **800/654- 3131**) requires between 24 and 72 hours' advance notice at most locations.

Organizations that offer a vast range of resources and assistance to travelers with disabilities include **MossRehab** (📞 **800/CALL- MOSS** [2255-6677]; www. mossresourcenet.org), the **American Foundation for the Blind** (**AFB**; 📞 **800/232-5463;** www. afb.org), and **SATH** (Society for Accessible Travel & Hospitality; 📞 **212/447- 7284;** www.sath.org). **AirAmbulanceCard.com** is now partnered with SATH and allows you to preselect top-notch hospitals in case of an emergency.

Access-Able Travel Source (📞 **303/232-2979;** www.access-able.com) offers a comprehensive database on travel agents from around the world with experience in accessible travel, destination-specific access information, and links to such resources as

service animals, equipment rentals, and access guides.

Many travel agencies offer customized tours and itineraries for travelers with disabilities. Among them are **Flying Wheels Travel** (📞 **507/451-5005;** www. flyingwheelstravel.com) and **Accessible Journeys** (**610/521-0339;** www. disabilitytravel.com).

Flying with Disability (**www.flying-with- disability.org**) is a comprehensive information source on airplane travel. **Avis Rent A Car** (📞 **800/962- 1434**) has an "Avis Access" program that offers services for customers with special travel needs. These include specially outfitted vehicles with swivel seats, spinner knobs, and hand controls; mobility scooter rentals; and accessible bus service. Be sure to reserve well in advance.

Also check out the quarterly magazine *Emerging Horizons* (**www.emerging horizons.com**), available by subscription ($17 a year U.S.; $22 outside U.S.).

The "Accessible Travel" link at **Mobility-Advisor. com** (**www.mobility-advi- sor.com**) offers a variety of travel resources to persons with disabilities.

British travelers should contact **Holiday Care** (📞 **0845-124-9971** in U.K. only; www.holidaycare.org. uk) to access a wide range of travel information and resources for seniors and those with disabilities.

Discounts For local discounts on attractions and restaurants, sign up for regular emails from www. groupon.com and www. dailydeals.sfgate.com. To be a "deal" on these websites, a merchant has to give a huge discount. I have received offers for Aquarium of the Bay tickets for $11 (regular price is $22), $70 worth of drinks and appetizers for $29 at restaurants listed in Chapter 5, $28 for a Blue and Gold Bay Cruise for Two (a $56 value), and many more great offers. You purchase the deal for future use; make sure to read the fine print. It is free to sign up for these deals; go online and make San Francisco your "home."

Doctors See "Hospitals" below.

Drinking Laws The legal age for purchase and consumption of alcoholic beverages is 21; proof of age is required and often requested at bars, nightclubs, and restaurants, so it's always a good idea to bring ID when you go out. Supermarkets and convenience stores in California sell beer, wine, and liquor. Most restaurants serve alcohol, but some serve only beer and wine. By law, all bars, clubs, restaurants, and stores cannot sell or serve alcohol after 2am, and "last call" tends to start at 1:30am. Do not carry open containers of alcohol in your car or any public area that isn't zoned for alcohol consumption. The police can fine you on the spot. And nothing will ruin your trip faster than getting a citation for DUI (driving under the influence).

Driving Rules See "Getting Around," earlier in this chapter.

Earthquakes In the rare event of an earthquake, *don't panic*. If you're in a tall building, don't run outside; instead, move away from windows and toward the building's center. Crouch under a desk or table, or stand against a wall or under a doorway. If you're in bed, get under the bed, stand in a doorway, or crouch under a sturdy piece of furniture. When exiting the building, use stairwells, *not* elevators. If you're in your car, pull over to the side of the road and stop, but wait until you're away from bridges or overpasses, as well as telephone or power poles and lines. Stay in your car. If you're outside, stay away from trees, power lines, and the sides of buildings.

Electricity Like Canada, the United States uses 110 to 120 volts AC (60 cycles), compared to 220 to 240 volts AC (50 cycles) in most of Europe, Australia, and New Zealand. Downward converters that change 220–240 volts to 110–120 volts are difficult to find in the United States, so bring one with you.

Embassies & Consulates All embassies are in the nation's capital, Washington, D.C. Some consulates are in major U.S. cities, and most nations have a mission to the United Nations in New York City. If your country isn't listed below, call for directory information in Washington, D.C. (② **202/555-1212**), or check www.embassy.org/embassies.

The embassy of **Australia** is at 1601 Massachusetts Ave. NW, Washington, DC 20036 (② **202/797-3000;** www.usa.embassy.gov.au). Consulates are in New York, Honolulu, Houston, Los Angeles, and San Francisco.

The embassy of **Canada** is at 501 Pennsylvania Ave. NW, Washington, DC 20001 (② **202/682-1740;** www.canadianembassy.org). Canadian consulates are in Buffalo (New York), Detroit, Los Angeles, New York, and Seattle.

The embassy of **Ireland** is at 2234 Massachusetts Ave. NW, Washington, DC 20008 (② **202/462-3939;** www.embassyofireland.org). Irish consulates are in Boston, Chicago, New York, San Francisco, and other cities. See the website for a complete listing.

The embassy of **New Zealand** is at 37 Observatory Circle NW, Washington, DC 20008 (② **202/328-4800;** www.nzembassy.com/usa). New Zealand consulates are in Los Angeles, Salt Lake City, San Francisco, and Seattle.

The embassy of the **United Kingdom** is at 3100 Massachusetts Ave. NW, Washington, DC 20008 (② **202/588-6500;** http://ukinusa.fco.gov.uk/en). British consulates are in Atlanta, Boston, Chicago, Cleveland, Houston, Los Angeles, New York, San Francisco, and Seattle.

Emergencies Call ② **911** to report a fire, call the police, or get an ambulance anywhere in the United States. This is a toll-free call. (No coins are required at public telephones.)

Family Travel If you have enough trouble getting your kids out of the house in the morning, dragging them thousands of miles away may seem like an insurmountable challenge. But family travel can be immensely rewarding, giving you new ways of seeing the world through smaller pairs of eyes.

To make things easier for families vacationing in San Francisco, we include two family-friendly lists that highlight the best hotels (p. 64) and attractions (p. 135) for parents and kids.

Recommended family travel websites include **Family Travel Forum** (www.familytravelforum.com), a comprehensive site that offers customized trip planning; **Family Travel Network** (www.familytravelnetwork.com), an online magazine providing travel tips; and **TravelWith YourKids.com** (www.travelwithyourkids.com), a comprehensive site written by parents for parents offering sound advice for long-distance and international travel with children.

Health If you worry about getting sick away from home, you may want to consider **medical travel insurance.** (See www.frommers.com "tips and tools," then "insurance" for detailed information.) In most cases, however, your existing health plan will provide all the coverage you need, but be sure to carry your identification card in your wallet.

If you suffer from a chronic illness, consult your doctor before your departure. Pack **prescription medications** in your carry-on luggage, and carry them in their original containers, with pharmacy labels—otherwise they won't make it through airport security. Visitors from outside the U.S. should carry generic names of prescription drugs. For U.S. travelers, most reliable healthcare plans provide coverage if you get sick away from home. Foreign visitors may have to pay all medical costs upfront and be reimbursed later.

Hospitals **Saint Francis Memorial Hospital,** 900 Hyde St., between Bush and Pine streets on Nob Hill (✆ **866/240-2087** or 415/353-6000; www.saintfrancismemorial.org), provides emergency service 24 hours a day; no

appointment is necessary. The hospital also operates a **physician-referral service** (✆ **800/333-1355** or 415/353-6566).

Insurance For information on traveler's insurance, trip cancellation insurance, and medical insurance while traveling, please visit www.frommers.com "tips and tools," then "insurance" for detailed information.

Internet & Wi-Fi You'll find that many cafes have wireless access, as do most hotels. Check www.wififreespot.com for a huge list of free Wi-Fi hotspots—including every Starbucks and Peet's coffee shop, Barnes and Noble, Fed Ex office, and McDonald's. You can also log onto www.cybercafe.com. The Metreon Entertainment Center in SoMa is completely wired, as are City Hall (p. 121) and San Francisco International Airport. In July 2013, Google gave the city a $600,000 gift to cover the cost of free Wi-Fi in 31 parks for at least 2 years. San Francisco has a goal to have city-wide internet access as soon as possible.

When all else fails, ask a friendly local where you can get Wi-Fi nearby. Most will know a good spot.

Legal Aid While driving, if you are pulled over for a minor infraction (such as speeding), never attempt to pay the fine

directly to a police officer; this could be construed as attempted bribery, a much more serious crime. Pay fines by mail, or directly into the hands of the clerk of the court. If accused of a more serious offense, say and do nothing before consulting a lawyer. In the U.S., the burden is on the state to prove a person's guilt beyond a reasonable doubt, and everyone has the right to remain silent, whether he or she is suspected of a crime or actually arrested. Once arrested, a person can make one telephone call to a party of his or her choice. The international visitor should call his or her embassy or consulate.

LGBT Travelers Since the 1970s, the Castro has acted as the city's center of gay life and nightlife in the city—though with society's changing norms, gay life has become less centralized (some might say less ghettoized) over the years. For some gay travelers, this is still the Place to Be, especially on a festival weekend, when the streets are filled with out and proud revelry; for other gays, the neighborhood is a quaint relic of the past to be visited occasionally (while shielding their children's eyes from the sex toys in the shop windows). For other San Franciscans and many travelers, it's a fun area with some wonderful shops.

Gays and lesbians make up a good portion of San Francisco's population, so it's no surprise that clubs and bars all over town cater to them. Although lesbian interests are concentrated primarily in the East Bay (especially Oakland), a significant community resides in the Mission District, around 16th and Valencia streets and in Hayes Valley.

Several local publications concentrate on in-depth coverage of news, information, and listings of goings-on around town for gays and lesbians. The *Bay Area Reporter* (www.ebar. com) has the most comprehensive listings, including a weekly calendar of events. Distributed free on Thursday, it can be found stacked at the corner of 18th and Castro streets and at Ninth and Harrison streets, as well as in bars, bookshops, and stores around town. It may also be available in gay and lesbian bookstores elsewhere in the country.

The **International Gay and Lesbian Travel Association (IGLTA; ⓒ 954/630-1637;** www.iglta.org) is the trade association for the gay and lesbian travel industry, and offers an online directory of gay- and lesbian-friendly travel businesses and tour operators. **Purple Roofs** (www.purple-roofs.com) lists gay friendly hotels, B&B's, travel agents, and tour operators. **San Francisco Travel** (www. sanfrancisco.travel/lgbt) has put together LGBT

itineraries, and can help you plan your wedding in the city. **Gay.com Travel** (www.gay.com) owns **Out Traveler** (www.outtraveler. com). Both provide regularly updated information about gay-owned, gay-oriented, and gay-friendly lodging, dining, sightseeing, nightlife, and shopping establishments in every popular destination worldwide, including, of course, San Francisco. Many agencies offer tours and travel itineraries specifically for gay and lesbian travelers. San Francisco–based **Now. Voyager** (www.now voyager.com) has been making travel arrangements for the LGBT community for 28 years. **Olivia** (ⓒ **800/631-6277;** www. olivia.com) offers lesbian cruises and resort vacations, as well as airline discounts. The Canadian website **GayTraveler** (www. gaytraveler.com) offers ideas and advice for gay travel all over the world. For travel guides, try *Spartacus International Gay Guide* (Bruno Gmünder Verlag; www. spartacusworld.com/ gayguide), or the **Damron** guides (www.damron.com), both with separate, annual books for gay men and lesbians. **San Francisco Pride** (www.sfpride.org/travel) is another good resource for LGBT friendly travel in the city. For more gay and lesbian travel resources, visit frommers.com.

Mail At press time, domestic postage rates

were 33¢ for a regular postcard, 46¢ for a large postcard and 46¢ for a regular letter. Always include zip codes when mailing items in the U.S. If you don't know your zip code, visit www.usps.com/zip4. For international mail, a postcard costs $1.10. Look at www.usps.com to determine the price to send a letter.

If you aren't sure what your address will be in the United States, mail can be sent to you, in your name, c/o General Delivery at the main post office of the city or region where you expect to be. The addressee must pick up mail in person and must produce proof of identity (driver's license, passport). Most post offices will hold mail for up to 1 month, and are open Monday to Friday from 8am to 6pm, and Saturday from 9am to 3pm.

Medical Requirements Unless you're arriving from an area known to be suffering from an epidemic (particularly cholera or yellow fever), inoculations or vaccinations are not required for entry into the United States.

Mobile Phones Just because your cellphone works at home doesn't mean it'll work everywhere in the U.S. (thanks to our nation's fragmented cellphone system). It's a good bet that your phone will work in major cities, but take a look at your wireless company's coverage map on its website before heading out; T-Mobile, Sprint, and Nextel are particularly weak in rural areas. If you need to stay in touch at a destination where you know your phone won't work, **rent** a phone that does from **InTouch USA** (𝓒 **800/872-7626;** www. intouchglobal.com), but be aware that airtime is pricey.

If you're not from the U.S., you'll be appalled at the poor reach of our **GSM** (Global System for Mobile Communications) **wireless network,** which is used by much of the rest of the world. Your phone will probably work in most major U.S. cities; it definitely won't work in many rural areas. To see where GSM phones work in the U.S., check out www.t-mobile.com/coverage/national_popup.asp. And you may or may not be able to send SMS (text messaging) home.

Money & Costs

Frommer's lists exact prices in the local currency. The currency conversions quoted were correct at press time. Since rates fluctuate, before departing it is a good idea to consult a currency exchange website such as www.xe.com to check up-to-the-minute rates.

It's always advisable to bring money in a variety of forms on a vacation: a mix of cash, credit cards, and ATM cards. You should also have enough petty cash upon arrival to cover airport incidentals, tipping, and transportation to your hotel before you leave home. You can always withdraw money upon arrival at an airport ATM, but you'll still need to make smaller change for tipping.

The most common bills in the U.S. are the $1 (a "buck"), $5, $10, and $20 denominations. There are also $2 bills (seldom encountered), $50 bills, and $100 bills. (The last two are usually not welcome as payment for small purchases.)

Coins come in seven denominations: 1¢ (1 cent, or a penny); 5¢ (5 cents, or a nickel); 10¢ (10 cents, or a dime); 25¢ (25 cents, or a quarter); 50¢ (50 cents, or a half dollar); the gold-colored Sacagawea coin, worth $1; and the rare silver dollar.

Credit cards are the most widely used form of payment in San Francisco: **Visa** (Barclaycard in Britain), **MasterCard** (Eurocard in Europe, Access in Britain, Chargex in Canada), **American Express, Diners Club,** and **Discover.** They also provide a convenient record of all your expenses

and offer relatively good exchange rates. You can withdraw cash advances from your credit cards at banks or ATMs, but high fees make credit card cash advances a pricey way to get cash.

It's highly recommended that you travel with at least one major credit card. You must have a credit card to rent a car, and hotels and airlines usually require a credit card imprint as a deposit against expenses.

ATM cards with major credit card backing, known as **"debit cards,"** are now a commonly acceptable form of payment in most stores and restaurants. Debit cards draw money directly from your checking account. Some stores enable you to receive cash back on your debit-card purchases as well. The same is true at most U.S. post offices. Make sure your rental car company accepts debit cards; some require you to have a very large dollar amount available for them to "hold" until you return the vehicle in perfect shape. Other rental car companies do not accept debit cards.

Beware of hidden credit card fees while traveling. Check with your credit or debit card issuer to see what fees, if any, will be

THE VALUE OF THE U.S. DOLLAR VS. OTHER POPULAR CURRENCIES (AS OF AUGUST 2013)

US$	Can$	UK£	Euro (€)	Aus$	NZ$
1	1.028	0.66	0.75	1.12	1.25

WHAT THINGS COST IN SAN FRANCISCO	US$
Taxi from SFO to downtown	$60
Inexpensive hotel room, double occupancy	$120–$150
Moderate hotel room, double occupancy	$150–$200
Cup of small coffee (Peet's or Starbucks)	$2
1 gallon of regular gas	$4
Admission to museums	$10–$35
Glass of Napa Valley red wine	$10–$15
Bus or streetcar fare for adults	$2
Cable car fare	$6

charged for overseas transactions. Recent reform legislation in the U.S., for example, has curbed some exploitative lending practices. But many banks have responded by increasing fees in other areas, including fees for customers who use credit and debit cards while out of the country—even if those charges were made in U.S. dollars. Fees can amount to 3% or more of the purchase price. Check with your bank before departing to avoid any surprise charges on your statement.

The important advice is to check with your bank before you travel, to find out about any fees and let them know you're going (so you don't find yourself turned away as a fraud at the ATM).

Newspapers & Magazines   The city's main daily is the *San Francisco Chronicle* (www.sfgate.com), which is distributed throughout the city. Check out the *Chronicle's* Sunday edition, which includes a pink "Datebook" section—a preview of the week's upcoming events. The free *San Francisco Examiner* (www.sfexaminer.com) is published Monday through Friday with a weekend edition. The free weekly *San Francisco Bay Guardian* (www.sfbg.com) and *San Francisco Weekly* (www.sfweekly.com), tabloids of news and listings, are indispensable for nightlife information; they're widely distributed through street-corner kiosks and at city cafes and restaurants.

Of the many free tourist-oriented publications, the most widely read are *San Francisco Guide* (www.sfguide.com), a handbook-size weekly containing maps and information on current events, and *Where San Francisco* (www.wheremagazine.com), a glossy regular format monthly magazine. You can find them in most hotels, shops, and restaurants in the major tourist areas.

Packing   Dress warm, even in the summer. As the saying goes in San Francisco, if you don't like the weather, wait 5 minutes. Because of offshore breezes, microclimates, and the prevalence of fog in the summer, the temperature changes constantly in San Francisco, particularly if you're on the move. Even if it's sunny and warm at noon, bring a sweater or light jacket just in case—when the fog rolls in its gets chilly fast. For more helpful information on packing for your trip, head to Frommers.com and click on the Tools section, which contains a number of packing tips and information.

Passports   Virtually every air traveler entering the U.S. is required to show a passport. All persons, including U.S. citizens, traveling by air between the United States and Canada, Mexico, Central and South America, the Caribbean, and Bermuda are required to present a valid passport. *Note:* U.S. and Canadian citizens entering the U. S. at land and sea ports of entry from within the western hemisphere must now also present a passport or other documents compliant with the Western Hemisphere Travel Initiative (WHTI; see www.getyouhome.gov for details).

Australia Australian Passport Information Service (✆ **131-232;** www.passports.gov.au).

Canada Passport Office, Department of Foreign Affairs and International Trade, Ottawa, ON K1A 0G3 (✆ **800/567-6868;** www.ppt.gc.ca).

Ireland Passport Office, Frederick Buildings, Molesworth Street, Dublin 2 (✆ **+353 1 671 1633;** www.foreignaffairs.gov.ie).

New Zealand Passports Office, Department of Internal Affairs, Level 3, 109 Featherston St., Wellington, 6040 (✆ **0800 22 50 50** in New Zealand or +64 (4) 463 9360; www.passports.govt.nz).

United Kingdom Visit your nearest passport office, major post office, or travel agency or contact the **HM Passport Office,** 4th Floor, Peel Building, 2 Marsham St., London, SW1P 4DF (✆ **0300/222-0000;** www.ips.gov.uk).

United States To find your regional passport office, check the U.S. State Department website (www.travel.state.gov/passport) or call the **National Passport Information Center** (✆ **877/487-2778**) for automated information.

Police In an emergency, dial ✆ **911.** For nonemergency police matters, call ✆ **415/553-0123.**

Safety For a big city, San Francisco is relatively safe and requires only that you use common sense (for example, don't leave your new video camera on the seat of your parked car). However, in neighborhoods such as Lower Haight, the Mission, the Tenderloin (a few blocks west of Union Square), and Fisherman's Wharf (at night especially), it's a good idea to pay attention to yourself and your surroundings.

Avoid carrying valuables with you on the street, and don't display expensive cameras or electronic equipment. Hold on to your pocketbook, and place your billfold in an inside pocket. In theaters, restaurants, and other public places, keep your possessions in sight.

Remember also that hotels are open to the public, and in a large hotel, security may not be able to screen everyone entering. Always lock your room door—don't assume that inside your hotel you are automatically safe.

Driving safety is important, too. Ask your rental agency about personal safety, and ask for a traveler-safety brochure when you pick up your car. Ask for written directions to your destination or a map with the route clearly marked. (Many agencies offer the option of renting a cellphone for the duration of your car rental;

check with the rental agent when you pick up the car.) Try to arrive and depart during daylight hours.

Recently, more crime has involved cars and drivers. If you drive off a highway into a doubtful neighborhood, leave the area as quickly as possible. If you have an accident, even on the highway, stay in your car with the doors locked until you assess the situation or until the police arrive. If you're bumped from behind on the street or are involved in a minor accident with no injuries, and the situation appears to be suspicious, motion to the other driver to follow you. Never get out of your car in such situations. Go directly to the nearest police precinct, well-lit service station, or 24-hour store.

Always try to park in well-lit and well-traveled areas. Never leave any packages or valuables in sight. If someone attempts to rob you or steal your car, don't try to resist the thief or carjacker. Report the incident to the police department immediately by calling ✆ **911.** This is a free call, even from pay phones.

Senior Travel Nearly every attraction in San Francisco offers a senior discount; age requirements vary, and specific prices are listed in Chapter 6. Public transportation and movie theaters also have reduced rates. Don't be shy about asking for discounts, but always carry some kind of identification, such as a driver's license, that shows your date of birth.

Members of **AARP,** 601 E St. NW, Washington, DC 20049 (📞 **888/687-2277;** www.aarp.org), get discounts on hotels, airfares, and car rentals. AARP offers members a wide range of benefits, including *AARP The Magazine* and a monthly newsletter. Anyone 50 and over can join.

Recommended publications offering travel resources and discounts for seniors include the quarterly magazine *Travel 50 & Beyond* (www.travel50and beyond.com) and the bestselling paperback *Unbelievably Good Deals and Great Adventures That You Absolutely Can't Get Unless You're Over 50 2009–2010 Edition* (McGraw-Hill), by Joann Rattner Heilman.

Smoking If San Francisco is California's most European city in looks and style, the comparison stops when it comes to smoking in public. Each year, smoking laws in the city become stricter. Ergo, heavy smokers are in for a tough time in San Francisco. Smoking is illegal inside most buildings, at entryways, bus stops, public parks, beaches, and at any outdoor public events. Hotels are also increasingly going nonsmoking, though some still offer smoking rooms. You can't even smoke in California bars unless drinks are served solely by the owner (though you will find

that a few neighborhood bars turn a blind eye and pass you an ashtray). San Francisco International Airport no longer has hazy, indoor smoking rooms; there are a few designated areas outside, pre-security.

Student Travel A valid student ID will often qualify students for discounts on airfare, accommodations, entry to museums, cultural events, movies, and more in San Francisco. Check out the **International Student Travel Confederation** (**ISTC;** www.istc.org) website for comprehensive travel services information and details on how to get an **International Student Identity Card (ISIC),** which qualifies students for substantial savings on rail passes, plane tickets, entrance fees, and more. It also provides students with basic health and life insurance and a 24-hour help line. The card is valid for a maximum of 18 months. You can apply for the card online or in person at **STA Travel** (📞 **800/781-4040** in North America, 134 782 in Australia, or 0333/321-0099 in the U.K.; www.statravel. com), the biggest student travel agency in the world; check out the website to locate STA Travel offices worldwide. If you're no longer a student but are still under 26, you can get an **International Youth Travel Card (IYTC)** from the same people, which entitles you to some discounts. **Travel CUTS** (📞 **800/667-2887;**

www.travelcuts.com) offers similar services for both Canadians and U.S. residents. Irish students may prefer to turn to **USIT** (📞 **01/602-1906;** www.usit. ie), an Ireland-based specialist in student, youth, and independent travel.

Taxes The United States has no value-added tax (VAT) or other indirect tax at the national level. Every state, county, and city may levy its own local tax on all purchases, including hotel and restaurant checks and airline tickets. These taxes will not appear on price tags. Sales tax in San Francisco is 8.75%. Hotel tax is charged on the room tariff only (which is not subject to sales tax) and is set by the city, ranging from 12% to 17% around Northern California.

Telephones Many convenience groceries and packaging services sell **prepaid calling cards** in denominations up to $50. Many public pay phones at airports now accept American Express, MasterCard, and Visa. **Local calls** made from a pay phones cost 50¢¾that is, if you can find one. They are a dying breed; there are only about 200 left in the city. Most long-distance and international calls can be dialed directly from any phone. **To make calls within the United States and to Canada,** dial 1 followed by the area code and the seven-digit number. **For other international calls,** dial

011 followed by the country code, city code, and the number you are calling.

Calls to area codes **800, 888, 877,** and **866** are toll-free. However, calls to area codes **700** and **900** (chat lines, bulletin boards, "dating" services, and so on) can be expensive—charges of 95¢ to $3 or more per minute. Some numbers have minimum charges that can run $15 or more.

For **reversed-charge or collect calls,** and for person-to-person calls, dial the number 0 then the area code and number; an operator will come on the line, and you should specify whether you are calling collect, person-to-person, or both. If your operator-assisted call is international, ask for the overseas operator.

For **directory assistance** ("Information"), dial ✆ 411 for local numbers and national numbers in the U.S. and Canada. For dedicated long-distance information, dial 1, then the appropriate area code plus 555-1212.

Time The continental United States is divided into **four time zones:** Eastern Standard Time (EST), Central Standard Time (CST), Mountain Standard Time (MST), and Pacific Standard Time (PST). Alaska and Hawaii have their own zones. For example, when it's 9am in San Francisco (PST), it's 10am in Denver (MST), 11am in Chicago (CST), noon in New York City (EST), 5pm in London (GMT), and 2am the next day in Sydney.

Daylight saving time is in effect from 1am on the second Sunday in March to 1am on the first Sunday in November, except in Arizona, Hawaii, the U.S. Virgin Islands, and Puerto Rico. Daylight saving time moves the clock 1 hour ahead of standard time.

For help with time translations, and more, download our convenient Travel Tools app for your mobile device. Go to www.frommers.com/go/mobile and tap on the Travel Tools icon.

Tipping In hotels, tip **bellhops** at least $1 per bag ($2–$3 if you have a lot of luggage) and tip the **chamber staff** $1 to $2 per day (more if you've left a big mess for him or her to clean up). Tip the **doorman** or **concierge** only if he or she has provided you with some specific service (for example, calling a cab for you or obtaining difficult-to-get theater tickets). Tip the **valet-parking attendant** $1 every time you get your car.

In restaurants, bars, and nightclubs, tip **service staff** and **bartenders** 15% to 20% of the check, tip **checkroom attendants** $1 per garment, and tip **valet-parking attendants** $1 per vehicle.

As for other service personnel, tip **cabdrivers** 15% of the fare, tip **skycaps** at airports at least $1 per bag ($2–$3 if you have a lot of luggage), and tip **hairdressers** and **barbers** 15% to 20%.

The important thing is not to stiff those who depend on tips. Waiters are taxed based on the assumption you've given a tip, whether or not you actually have.

Toilets Those weird, oval-shaped, olive-green kiosks on the sidewalks throughout San Francisco are high-tech self-cleaning public toilets. They've been placed on high-volume streets to provide relief for pedestrians. French potty-maker JCDecaux gave them to the city for free—advertising covers the cost. It costs 25¢ to enter, with no time limit, but we don't recommend using the ones in the sketchier neighborhoods such as the Mission because they're mostly used by crackheads and prostitutes. Toilets can also be found in hotel lobbies, bars, restaurants, museums, department stores, railway and bus stations, and service stations. Large hotels and fast-food restaurants are often the best bet for clean facilities. Restaurants and bars in resorts or heavily visited areas may reserve their restrooms for patrons. For a list of "bathrooms for everyone," check out www.safe2pee.org.

VAT See "Taxes," above.

Visas The U.S. State Department has a **Visa Waiver Program (VWP)** allowing citizens of the following countries to enter the United States without a visa for stays of up to 90 days: Andorra, Australia, Austria, Belgium, Brunei, Czech Republic, Denmark, Estonia, Finland, France, Germany, Greece, Hungary, Iceland, Ireland, Italy, Japan, Republic of Korea, Latvia, Liechtenstein, Lithuania, Luxembourg, Malta, Monaco, the Netherlands, New Zealand, Norway, Portugal, San Marino, Singapore, Slovakia, Slovenia, Spain, Sweden, Switzerland, and the United Kingdom. (**Note:** This list was accurate at press time; for the most up-to-date list of countries in the VWP, consult http://travel.state.gov/visa.) Even though a visa isn't necessary, in an effort to help U.S. officials check travelers against terror watch lists before they arrive at U.S. borders, visitors from VWP countries must register online through the Electronic System for Travel Authorization (ESTA) before boarding a plane or a boat to the U.S. Travelers must complete an electronic application providing basic personal and travel eligibility information. The Department of Homeland Security recommends filling out the form at least 3 days before traveling. Authorizations will be valid for up to 2 years or until the traveler's passport expires, whichever comes first. Currently, there is one US$14 fee for the online application. Existing ESTA registrations remain valid through their expiration dates. **Note:** Any passport issued on or after October 26, 2006, by a VWP country must be an **e-Passport** for VWP travelers to be eligible to enter the U.S. without a visa. Citizens of these nations also need to present a round-trip air or cruise ticket upon arrival. E-Passports contain computer chips capable of storing biometric information, such as the required digital photograph of the holder. If your passport doesn't have this feature, you can still travel without a visa if the valid passport was issued before October 26, 2005, and includes a machine-readable zone; or if the valid passport was issued between October 26, 2005, and October 25, 2006, and includes a digital photograph. For more information, go to http://travel.state.gov/visa. Canadian citizens may enter the United States without visas, but will need to show passports and proof of residence.

Citizens of all other countries must have (1) a valid passport that expires at least 6 months later than the scheduled end of their visit to the U.S.; and (2) a tourist visa.

For information about **U.S. visas,** go to http://travel.state.gov and click on "Visas." Or go to one of the following websites:

Australian citizens can obtain up-to-date visa information from the **U.S. Embassy Canberra,** Moonah Place, Yarralumla, ACT 2600 (📞 **02/6214-5600**), or by checking the U.S. Diplomatic Mission's website at http://canberra.usembassy.gov/visas.html.

British subjects can obtain visa information by calling the **U.S. Embassy Visa Information Line** (📞 **020 3608 6998** from within the U.K. or 📞 **703/439-2367** from within the U.S. or by visiting the "Visas" section of the American Embassy London's website at http://london.usembassy.gov/visas.html.

Irish citizens can obtain up-to-date visa information through the **U.S. Embassy Dublin,** 42 Elgin Rd., Ballsbridge, Dublin 4 (📞 **353 1 668 8777** from within the Republic of Ireland; http://dublin.usembassy.gov).

Citizens of **New Zealand** can obtain up-to-date visa information by contacting the **U.S. Embassy New Zealand,** 29 Fitzherbert Terrace, Thorndon, Wellington (📞 **644/462-6000;** http://newzealand.usembassy.gov).

Visitor Information The **San Francisco Visitor Information Center,** on the lower level of Hallidie

Plaza, 900 Market St., at Powell Street (© **415/391-2000;** www.sanfrancisco travel.com), is the best source of specialized information about the city. Even if you don't have a specific question, you might want to request the free *Visitors Planning Guide* and the *San Francisco Visitors* kit, which includes a 6-month

calendar of events; a city history;shopping and dining information; several good, clear maps; plus lodging information.

To view or download a free state guide and travel planner, log onto the **California Tourism** website at www.visitcalifornia.com. U.S. and Canadian residents can receive free

travel planning information by mail by calling © **800/CALIFORNIA** (225-4367). Most cities and towns also have a tourist bureau or chamber of commerce that distributes information on the area.

Wi-Fi See "Internet & Wi-Fi," earlier in this section.

Index